African Americans
in Science

African Americans in Science

An Encyclopedia
of People and Progress

CHARLES W. CAREY JR.

VOLUME ONE

A B C · C L I O

Santa Barbara, California   Denver, Colorado   Oxford, England

Library of Congress Cataloging-in-Publication Data

Carey, Charles W.
African Americans in science : an encyclopedia of people and progress / Charles W. Carey, Jr.
    p. cm.
Includes bibliographical references and index.
ISBN 978-1-85109-998-6 (hard copy : alk. paper)
ISBN 978-1-85109-999-3 (ebook)
1. African American scientists. 2. Scientists—United States. I. Title.
Q141.C2138 2008
500.896'073—dc22
2008024609

12 11 10 9 8   1 2 3 4 5 6 7 8 9 10

Editorial Manager: James P. Sherman
Submission Editors: Alex Mikaberidze and Kim Kennedy White
Production Editor: Christian Green
Production Manager: Don Schmidt
Media Editor: Ellen Rasmussen
Media Resources Manager: Caroline Price
File Management Coordinator: Paula Gerard

This book is also available on the World Wide Web as an eBook.
Visit www.abc-clio.com for details.

ABC-CLIO, Inc.
130 Cremona Drive, P.O. Box 1911
Santa Barbara, California 93116–1911

This book is printed on acid-free paper ∞
Manufactured in the United States of America

Contents

List of Entries

Preface

Several years ago, I was invited by the good folks at Facts On File to write a book about Americans who had won the Nobel prize in either medicine or physiology, chemistry or physics. By the time it was published, *American Scientists* (2005) had morphed into a book about American scientists who had made contributions in every scientific discipline, including astronomy and astrophysics, botany, biology, and geology and geophysics, fields that do not have a Nobel prize of their own. One of the questions that arose during the process of bringing *American Scientists* to press was, "Why aren't there more African Americans in this book?" My first answer, of course, was that no African American scientist has ever won a Nobel Prize, and approximately two-thirds of the scientists featured in *American Scientists* are Nobel laureates. However, the question piqued my interest in black scientists, even though I had included a dozen or so in *American Scientists*. So when ABC-CLIO approached me about writing a book about African Americans in science, I accepted the challenge.

I say "challenge" because black scientists seem to be undervalued by American society in general and by the African American community in particular. Pick up any volume that features biographical sketches of American blacks; two examples that come to mind readily are *Contemporary Black Biography* (1991–2009) and *Who's Who Among African Americans* (1996–2008), but there are others. It is much easier to find in their pages biographical information about basketball players and rappers than about scientists. Indeed, one might come to the conclusion that the African American community is not very proud of its scientists, because they receive little publicity from the black press. So another reason that makes it difficult to write about African American scientists is that the raw biographical data, such as when one was born or who one's parents are, is often impossible to locate. For this reason, a number of African American scientists whose work should be recognized in a volume such as this could not be included.

Nevertheless, it is still possible to write a rather hefty volume about African Americans in science, even if black scientists as individuals often fly under the radar. Two types of institutions that have long sustained the practice of science by black Americans are the historically black colleges and universities (HBCUs) and the historically black professional scientific organizations. Frankly, I was amazed to discover the breadth and depth of cutting-edge scientific research that is being conducted at HBCUs, and, if this book could impart only one message to the world, that it is what it would be. I was also impressed by the strenuous efforts being made by the faculties and administrations at HBCUs, as well as by the leadership and rank and file of black scientific associations to recruit, train, retain, and promote promising young black students into careers related to science. By the time this work came to its finish, I was somewhat surprised to notice that the section on black scientific institutions is considerably longer than the section on black scientists themselves. This fact reflects how critically important institutions such as HBCUs and black scientific associations are to perpetuating African Americans in science.

This work is divided into four parts. The first addresses the accomplishments of individual black scientists who have made a number of important contributions to science. The second addresses some of the issues that are of critical importance to the African American scientific community, such as science education and careers for blacks and the whole range of topics related to health disparities. The third addresses scientific fields, and it outlines in more general terms the contributions made by the scientists featured in the first part. The fourth addresses the scientific research and training that, for the most part, are being conducted now or have been in the recent past.

Several people at ABC-CLIO made it possible for me to bring this work to the attention of the public. Steven Danver conceived of the idea, recruited me to write the book, and encouraged me throughout the writing process. Alex Mikaberidze provided many helpful comments as I was writing the book, and Kim Kennedy-White did the same thing after I had completed the first draft. Each of them helped me make this a better book, and I thank them for their help.

Charles W. Carey Jr.

REFERENCES AND FURTHER READING

Carey, Charles W. Jr. *American Scientists*. New York: Facts on File, 2005.

Henderson, Ashyia N., ed. *Contemporary Black Biography: Profiles from the International Black Community*, vol. 31. Detroit, MI: Gale Cengage, 2001.

Who's Who Among African Americans, 21st ed. Detroit, MI: Gale Group, 1996–2008.

Introduction

Charles W. Carey Jr.

Prior to the Civil Rights Movement of the 1960s, African Americans who wanted to pursue careers in the sciences faced a number of obstacles. These obstacles included restricted access to educational programs as well as to teaching and research positions that would have allowed them to blossom as scientists. Nevertheless, black scientists have made a number of important contributions to every branch of science, especially anthropology, astronomy and astrophysics, biochemistry, biology, chemistry, computer science, microbiology, and physics. Despite the easing of admissions restrictions on blacks who wanted to attend historically white research universities, where the vast majority of American scientists receive their training, most of today's African American scientists have received at least part of their education and training at one or more of the nation's historically black colleges and universities (HBCUs). These schools have received enough funding from a variety of sources that they are now able to conduct an impressive array of cutting-edge scientific research. The United States has yet to produce a black Nobel laureate in an area of science but, because of developments stemming from the Civil Rights Movement, the day that an African American receives a Nobel Prize in Physiology or Medicine, Physics, or Chemistry is rapidly approaching. Granted, a number of obstacles remain in the way of the African American who wishes to pursue a career in science. Nevertheless, a great many institutions, organizations, and public and private agencies are working to remove those obstacles, which will greatly improve the ability of the United States to conduct cutting-edge scientific research.

Scientists

African American scientists first made their mark in the field of astronomy, in the person of the first known African American scientist, the astronomer Benjamin Banneker (1731–1806). Banneker taught himself astronomy by reading books. Evidently, he was an excellent teacher, because before long he had trained himself to calculate some of the most precise ephemerides (tables listing the future positions of planets and major stars) developed in the United States during the 18th century.

The next famous African American scientist, chronologically speaking, was the botanist George Washington Carver (ca. 1860–1943). Carver is best known for developing more than 100 uses for peanuts, but, as a scientist, his interests and accomplishments ranged far beyond the peanut. Carver's primary research interest was horticulture, and his most important contribution in this area was to develop a cotton plant, called Carver's Hybrid, that is highly resistant to insect infestation. He also demonstrated that sweet potatoes, black-eyed peas, and soybeans restore nitrogen to the soil, which eventually led to the restoration of the vitality and profitability of agriculture in the southern United States.

Prior to the Civil Rights Movement, racial prejudice denied most African Americans the opportunity to obtain a science-based education or to earn a living as a scientist. To the degree that blacks were encouraged or even permitted to practice science, their opportunities came mostly in the area of medical research, but even here the opportunities were limited. Nevertheless, more than a dozen black scientists who were born in the 19th century made important scientific contributions during the first six decades of the 20th century. Biologist Charles H. Turner (1867–1923) discovered that ants, bees, and cockroaches can see, hear, and smell, and he described Turner's circling, the ambulatory process by which ants find their way back to their nest. Zoologists Ernest E. Just (1883–1941) and Roger Arliner Young (1899–1964) studied fertilization and growth in animal eggs. Their work demonstrated the existence of fertilizin, the sticky substance that enables sperm to stick to eggs, and the effects of radiation on the growth and development of marine eggs. In chemistry, St. Elmo Brady (1884–1966) conducted groundbreaking research concerning alkaloids and the chemical composition of certain seeds and beans. His work inspired the research of Percy L. Julian (1899–1975), who developed a score of products from soybean oil and a useful method for synthesizing progesterone, the female hormone from which birth control pills are made. The industrial chemist Lloyd A. Hall (1894–1971) developed some of the first artificial flavors, discovered why fatty and oily foods become rancid, and developed methods for preserving meats. In physics, Elmer S. Imes (1883–1941) developed methods for learning more about the various elements and compounds by studying the infrared light emitted by atoms and molecules. He also made the first accurate measurement of the distance between atoms in a molecule.

The majority of early black scientists were not biologists, chemists, or physicists, but rather surgeons or physicians who conducted medical research.

Daniel H. Williams (1856–1931) performed one of the first successful surgical operations involving the human heart. Charles V. Roman (1864–1934) and W. Harry Barnes (1887–1945) contributed to a better understanding of the medical conditions that affect the eyes, ears, nose, and throat and developed surgical techniques for treating several of these conditions. Solomon C. Fuller (1872–1953) shed light on the physiological causes of schizophrenia, Alzheimer's disease, and bipolar disorder. William A. Hinton (1883–1959) showed how syphilis works in the human body, and he developed two tests for diagnosing the disease. Arnold H. Maloney (1888–1955) discovered a drug for treating victims of barbiturate poisoning, and Louis T. Wright (1891–1952) conducted some of the earliest research concerning cancer chemotherapy drugs; Wright's work was continued by his daughter, Jane C. Wright (1919–). Julian H. Lewis (1891–1989) wrote *The Biology of the Negro* (Chicago: Chicago University Press, 1942), the first known textbook on comparative racial pathology, which compared the biological and physiological traits of the Negroid and Caucasian races and how differences in these traits affect the ability of each race to cope with and be susceptible to certain diseases and medical conditions.

The generation of black scientists born between 1900 and 1930 also experienced racial barriers to their desire to pursue scientific careers, but not to the same degree as the generations that had come before them. After World War I, some of the strictures of Jim Crow (legal segregation) laws were eased, and many more were lessened as a result of World War II. Six black chemists and one black physicist are known to have worked during World War II on the development of the United States' most secret weapon, the atomic bomb; their involvement in such a project would have been unthinkable just a few decades earlier.

Thus, opportunities for this generation of black scientists were opening up in all fields of scientific endeavor, not just medical research. In physics, Warren E. Henry (1909–2001) showed how extremely low temperatures affect the magnetic properties of iron, gold, chromium, uranium, plutonium, and the rare earth elements. Charles E. Anderson (1919–1994) developed a computerized system for forecasting tornadoes and hailstorms. Walter S. McAfee (1914–1995) calculated the speed of the moon and developed a method for detecting the radio echo of a laser beam bounced off the moon. Randolph W. Bromery (1926–) developed methods for finding major deposits of crude oil and other valuable minerals by using magnetic detection and radiometrics, the measurement of radioactive material. Meredith C. Gourdine (1929–1998) shed much light on the physical principles underlying electrogasdynamics (EGD), the flow of electrically charged particles suspended in a gas through an electric field, and magnetohydrodynamics (MHD), which substitutes a magnetic field for the electric field; he also developed inexpensive methods for using

EGD and MHD to generate high-voltage electricity. The astrophysicist Carl A. Rouse (1926–) developed one of the first computer models of the sun. J. Ernest Wilkins (1923–) helped develop the atomic bomb; he also devised many of the mathematical formulas used to develop nuclear power for peaceful purposes and helped design some of the first nuclear power plants.

In biology, Samuel M. Nabrit (1905–2003) demonstrated the process by which fish replace lost tailfins. James H. M. Henderson (1917–) proved the existence of the plant growth hormones known as auxins. Welton I. Taylor (1919–) developed tests to identify the presence in processed food of the bacteria that cause botulism, salmonellosis, and shigellosis. Emmett W. Chappelle (1925–) used laser-induced fluorescence, the optical emission from molecules that have been excited to higher-than-normal energy levels by absorbing the electromagnetic radiation generated by a laser, and the firefly bioluminescence reaction, the biochemical process by which fireflies produce light, to develop methods for detecting the presence of bacteria in outer space, among crops and aquatic plant life, and in biological fluids, drinking water, and foods. The zoologist Margaret S. Collins (1922–1996) discovered *Neotermes luykxi*, also known as the Florida dampwood termite.

In chemistry, Lloyd M. Cooke (1916–2001) made major contributions to the processes by which cellulose and viscose are manufactured into paper products and synthetic fibers. W. Lincoln Hawkins (1911–1992) helped explain why plastics behave as they do. Henry A. Hill (1915–1979) developed several of the chemical processes by which plastics are constructed from polymers. Lloyd A. Quarterman (1918–1982) helped develop the atomic bomb; he also proved that the so-called inert gases are actually capable of taking part in chemical reactions by developing three different compounds that include the inert gas xenon.

Despite these advancements, Jim Crow laws still held considerable influence over American society and therefore over the American scientific community. But the logic of Jim Crow demanded that blacks be allowed to serve as surgeons and physicians, even if only to their own race, and so medical research continued to be the most promising field of scientific endeavor for African American scientists. Leonidas H. Berry (1902–1995) developed surgical techniques and instruments for examining the interiors of the abdominal cavity and the intestines and for removing diseased tissue from the stomach. Charles W. Buggs (1906–1991) developed methods for killing *E. coli, Staphylococcus*, and other strains of bacteria harmful to humans. W. Montague Cobb (1904–1990) demonstrated that the bone structures of whites and blacks are virtually identical, thus helping to eliminate the pseudoscientific theories that blacks were inferior to whites physiologically. Charles R. Drew (1904–1950) developed procedures for collecting, storing, and transporting large quantities of blood. Flemmie P. Kittrell (1904–1980) demonstrated that people who eat enough food to not feel hungry can still suffer from malnourishment if the nutritional quality of the food is poor. Frederick D. Stubbs (1906–1947) developed a procedure for removing diseased tissue from the lungs of patients suffering from pulmonary tuberculosis. Harold D. West (1904–1974) shed light on the chemical composition of certain amino acids and helped develop the earliest procedures for synthesizing the amino acid threonine. Herman R. Branson (1914–1995) played a major role in the discovery that polypeptides, the molecules that serve as the building blocks for proteins, take the shape of a helix; this discovery led to the discovery that strands of DNA are arranged in double helical form. Daniel A. Collins (1916–) shed much light on the role played by hormones in the growth and development of teeth. Lloyd N. Ferguson (1918–) elucidated the biochemical processes by which the taste buds tell the brain how something tastes. Samuel P. Massie (1919–2005) helped develop pharmaceutical drugs for treating malaria, meningitis, gonorrhea, and herpes. Henry C. McBay (1914–1995) developed a process for synthesizing a protein that is an effective treatment for prostate cancer. Vivien T. Thomas (1910–1985) helped cure blue baby syndrome by participating in the development of a surgical procedure for that condition. Eugene W. Adams (1920–) shed much light on how cancer grows and spreads in humans by showing how cancer develops in dogs. Jewel Plummer Cobb (1924–) demonstrated that melanoma (skin cancer) can be caused by overexposure to the sun's ultraviolet rays. Marie Maynard Daly (1921–2003) shed much light on the biochemical aspects of hypertension (high blood pressure), arteriosclerosis (hardening of the arteries), and other medical conditions related to the cardiovascular system. Cecile Hoover Edwards (1926–) showed that vegetarians can obtain all of the essential amino acids their bodies need from a properly planned and maintained vegetarian diet. Angella D. Ferguson (1925–) developed some of the earliest data on and treatments for sickle cell disease. Carroll M. Leevy (1920–) developed procedures and techniques for diagnosing and treating hepatitis, gallstones, liver cirrhosis, various metabolic and genetic disorders, and hepatocellular cancer. The psychiatrist Chester M. Pierce (1927–) showed how humans are affected by stressful environments such as outer space and the ghetto.

The major event that opened more doors to blacks who wished to pursue careers as scientists was *Brown v. Board of Education* [347 U.S. 483 (1954)], the U.S. Supreme Court decision that outlawed segregated schools and that served as the tool by which segregation in general would be dismantled. Two black scientists, Mamie Phipps Clark (1917–1983) and Margaret Morgan Lawrence (1914–), played a critical role in helping the Court to arrive at its decision. Clark, a psychologist, and Lawrence, a pediatric psychiatrist, demonstrated that the state-sanctioned manifestation of racism as expressed by the existence of segregated schools contributed in a major way to the negative image most black children had of themselves. When Clark and Lawrence's expert testimony was presented to the Court, the result was a 9–0 decision against segregated schools. In time, this ruling was used to eliminate overt segregation in every aspect of American society, including American science. As a result, the generation of African Americans born after 1929 had opportunities to pursue scientific careers well beyond those their predecessors had to choose from.

The end of legal segregation did nothing to diminish the importance of medicine and physiology as an arena in which black scientists could gain renown, and a number of black scientists who were born after 1929 chose medical research as their field of practice. Samuel L. Kountz (1930–1981) developed many of the procedures and apparatus used today in kidney transplantations. LaSalle D. Leffall (1930–) developed surgical techniques for extracting cancerous tumors without disturbing the surrounding healthy tissue. John C. Norman (1930–) helped develop one of the first successful partial artificial hearts. Patricia S. Cowings (1948–) developed a biofeedback exercise for astronauts to use when they feel the onset of space sickness. Joseph C. Dunbar (1944–) demonstrated the connection between diabetes and a variety of medical conditions that affect the cardiovascular system. Renty B. Franklin (1945–) demonstrated that zinc plays an important role in controlling the growth of tumors in the prostate gland. John K. Haynes (1943–) discovered why blood cells affected by sickle cell disease take on their distinctive sickle-like shape. Benjamin S. Carson (1951–) served as principal surgeon during the first two successful procedures to separate Siamese twins who were joined at the head, and he perfected the hemispherectomy into a safe and effective procedure for treating children who suffer from severe seizures. A. Oveta Fuller (1955–) demonstrated how the herpes simplex virus enters a cell.

Nevertheless, the end of legal segregation offered increased opportunities to blacks who wished to pursue scientific careers in areas not related to medicine and physiology. In biology, Joan Murrell Owens (1933–) discovered one new genus and three new species of button corals. Carolyn Branch Brooks (1946–) demonstrated the nature of the symbiotic relationship between some legumes and soil bacteria. Herman E. Eure (1947–) helped explain the phenomenon known as seasonal abundances, whereby parasites increase and decrease their populations during certain seasons of the year. Ambrose Jearld (1944–) helped develop many of the techniques used to manage commercial fishing ecosystems. George M. Langford (1944–) discovered the existence of an intracellular network that is used mostly to transfer biomaterial over relatively short distances.

In chemistry, Gloria M. Anderson (1938–) explained the process of epoxidation (the linking of two organic compounds by one atom of oxygen).

Linneaus C. Dorman (1935–) developed more than two dozen synthetic peptides, chains of proteins that do not exist in nature, and then found dozens of industrial and medical applications for them. James A. Harris (1932–) played a major role in developing transuranium elements 104 and 105. James King (1933–) described the bond that links atoms of carbon and fluorine in chlorofluorocarbons, which have been linked to the depletion of the Earth's ozone layer, and Joseph S. Francisco (1955–) studied the potential replacements for chlorofluorocarbons to see how they would affect the ozone layer. John W. Macklin (1939–) developed techniques for identifying unknown chemical compounds as small as a billionth of a billionth of a gram. Fitzgerald B. Bramwell (1945–) shed light on the nature of the artificial chemical compounds known as organotins (which include one or more bonds between an atom of carbon and an atom of tin). Slayton A. Evans (1943–2001) developed a method for facilitating the production of alpha-amino phosphonic acids (human-made compounds from which a number of pharmaceutical drugs are manufactured).

In physics, George R. Carruthers (1939–) developed the process and apparatus for learning more about the astrophysical properties of the stars by examining the ultraviolet radiation they emit, and George E. Alcorn (1940–) developed a similar process using X-rays. Wade M. Kornegay (1934–) helped develop the wideband radar systems used by the U.S. military to track incoming Soviet intercontinental ballistic missiles. Arthur B. C. Walker (1936–2001) developed X-ray telescopes and spectroscopes for obtaining high-resolution images of the atmospheres of the sun and other stars, the remnants of supernovas, and the distribution of elements throughout interstellar space. Wesley L. Harris (1941–) shed light on the aeroacoustical principles underlying the flight of helicopters and developed methods to make them fly more quietly. Sylvester J. Gates (1950–) developed the leading theory for explaining how gravity is transmitted. Neil deGrasse Tyson (1958–) has written a number of books and articles that explain some of the most esoteric principles of astronomy and astrophysics in terms that the general educated public can understand and appreciate.

In the earth sciences, Mack Gipson (1931–1995) helped develop the technique known as sequence stratigraphy, which investigates deep layers of sedimentary rock and the mineral deposits they contain by reading the seismic lines caused by shock waves directed deep into the Earth. Warren M. Washington (1936–) developed some of the first computer programs and networks for forecasting global weather. Evan B. Forde (1952–) shed much light on the formation, evolution, and sedimentary processes of the submarine canyons in the western Atlantic Ocean. He also helped develop methods for mapping hydrothermal plumes and for forecasting and tracking hurricanes. In computer science, Philip Emeagwali (1954–) demonstrated that thousands of small computers working together on the same task are actually more powerful than a supercomputer. He also developed a computerized weather forecasting network that inspired the development of the World Wide Web, the global network that links millions of computers.

The end of legal segregation also opened up two new careers to black scientists born after 1929: astronaut and science administrator. Guion S. Bluford (1942–), Ronald E. McNair (1950–1986), Bernard A. Harris (1956–), Mae C. Jemison (1956–), and Michael P. Anderson (1959–2003) conducted scientific research as mission specialists aboard flights to outer space. In terms of science administration, the pediatric endocrinologist Joycelyn Elders (1933–) and the biologist David Satcher (1941–) became U.S. surgeon general. Walter E. Massey (1938–) is a physicist who became president of the American Association for the Advancement of Science and director of the National Science Foundation. Kenneth Olden (1938–) is a cell biologist who became director of the National Institute of Environmental Health Sciences and the National Toxicology Program. Margaret Mayo Tolbert (1943–) is a biochemist who became director of the U.S. Department of Energy's New Brunswick Laboratory. Shirley A. Jackson (1946–) is a physicist who became chair of the Nuclear Regulatory Commission and the president of Rensselaer Polytechnic Institute, a major scientific research university. Shirley M. Malcolm (1946–) is a biologist who became a high-level administrator with the National Science Foundation and the American Association for the Advancement of Science.

Institutions

Black scientists never would have made their contributions to science had it not been for the help of institutions. These institutions include historically black colleges and universities (HBCUs), historically black hospitals, historically black professional organizations, professional scientific associations, advocacy groups, and agencies of the federal government. Each type of institution has supported the rise of the black scientist, sometimes by providing education and training, sometimes by furnishing financial assistance, sometimes by giving employment, and sometimes by doing all three.

HBCUs conduct scientific research of all kinds, partly as a means of increasing the body of scientific knowledge and partly as a means of training the black scientists of the future. It has been estimated that HBCUs, though they teach only approximately 20 percent of the black students enrolled in college, have produced between 50 and 90 percent of the black scientists educated in the United States, by educating them at either the undergraduate or graduate level. Although just about all of the HBCUs conduct scientific research of some sort, the ones whose efforts are most noteworthy are Alabama A&M

University, Alabama State University, Central State University, Clark Atlanta University, Delaware State University, Fisk University, Florida A&M University, Fort Valley State University, Hampton University, Howard University College of Medicine, Jackson State University, Kentucky State University, Langston University, Lincoln University of Missouri, Morgan State University, Norfolk State University, North Carolina A&T State University, North Carolina Central University, Prairie View A&M University, South Carolina State University, Southern University, Spelman College, Tennessee State University, Texas Southern University, Tougaloo College, Tuskegee University, the University of Arkansas at Pine Bluff, the University of the District of Columbia, the University of Maryland Eastern Shore, the University of the Virgin Islands, Virginia State University, West Virginia State University, Winston-Salem State University, Xavier University of Louisiana, as well as the Charles R. Drew University of Medicine and Science, the Howard University College of Medicine, Meharry Medical College, the Morehouse School of Medicine, and the Tuskegee School of Veterinary Medicine. As of 2008, these HBCUs were conducting cutting-edge research in fields such as microelectronics, photonics, surface chemistry, theoretical physics, high-performance computing, high-performance polymers and composites, electro-optical materials, cancer research, infrared spectroscopy, pharmaceutical sciences, neuroscience, terrestrial and extraterrestrial atmospheres, nanomaterials, energy research, aerospace science, health disparities, biotechnology, agriculture and aquaculture, among others.

Historically black hospitals were established for two reasons. One was to provide African Americans with the best possible health care, something they could scarcely hope to receive from a white-majority hospital that segregated its black patients and often provided them with minimal care. The other was to provide black physicians, surgeons, and nurses with a venue to learn and practice medicine. The most important of these hospitals were Freedmen's Hospital in Washington, D.C., Harlem Hospital in New York City, Homer G. Phillips Hospital in St. Louis, Mercy-Douglass Hospital in Philadelphia, and Provident Hospital and Training School in Chicago. These hospitals, as well as the other historically black hospitals in communities across the nation, provided a great many of the early black physicians and surgeons with their earliest training. Also serving as laboratories for those blacks who wished to conduct medical research, these hospitals were the sites of a great many of the medical contributions made by black medical researchers.

Despite the many accomplishments of black scientists, the number of black Americans who take up careers in science is surprisingly low. The percentage of black American scientists is remarkably lower than the percentage of black Americans. For example, blacks account for approximately 3 percent of the nation's medical researchers, and they account for less than 0.25 percent of the nation's computer scientists. To remedy this situation, many organizations and agencies in the public and private sectors are working diligently to recruit more young African Americans to careers in science. The leaders of these organizations and agencies know that America's future is only as bright as the minds of its scientists and that to deny anyone who is capable of conducting scientific endeavors the opportunity to do so is to deny the nation at large the fruits of those labors.

One vehicle for promoting careers in science for African Americans is the community of historically black professional organizations. These organizations include the Association of Black Anthropologists, the Association of Black Cardiologists, the Association of Black Psychologists, the Black Entomologists, the Black Psychiatrists of America, the National Association of Black Geologists and Geophysicists, the National Association of Minority Medical Educators, the National Dental Association, the National Medical Association, the National Organization for the Professional Advancement of Black Chemists and Chemical Engineers, the National Society of Black Physicists, the Network of Minority Research Investigators, the NIH Black Scientists Association, the Society of Black Academic Surgeons, and the Student National Medical Association. These groups offer academic scholarships to promising black undergraduate and graduate students who wish to pursue careers in science, but they also work to heighten the awareness of black K–12 students to the possibility that they too can become scientists. Surveys have shown that black children are just as interested in becoming scientists as any other children but that they don't pursue careers in science because they believe such careers are not open to them. To counter this false impression, most black professional scientific organizations have developed so-called ambassador programs, whereby black scientists visit schools to talk about science and simply to act as visible proof that black people can work in scientific fields too.

Mirroring the efforts of the black professional organizations are other, nonminority professional scientific associations that conduct similar programs. These organizations include the American Association for the Advancement of Science, the American Association for Cancer Research, the American Chemical Society, the American College of Veterinary Pathology, the American Dental Education Association, the American Geological Institute, the American Institute of Biological Sciences, the American Medical Association, the American Medical Student Association, the American Physical Society, the American Psychological Association, the American Society for Cell Biology, the American Society for Microbiology, the Association of American Medical Colleges, the Biophysical Society, the Endocrine Society, the Federation of American Societies for Experimental Biology, and the Society for Neuroscience. These organizations offer scholarships to promising black students, but they also work to encourage more blacks to consider careers in science and to recruit more black scientists to join their organizations.

Recruiting and training African Americans into careers in science is also the focus, at least in part, of a number of advocacy groups. These groups include the Alfred P. Sloan Foundation; Building Engineering and Science Talent; the Camille and Henry Dreyfus Foundation; Delta Sigma Theta; the Dental Pipeline; the Development Fund for Black Students in Science and Technology; the Diversity Institute; the Environmental Careers Organization; the Ford Foundation Diversity Fellowships program; the Gates Millennium Scholars program; the Health Professionals for Diversity Coalition; the Historically Black College and University/Minority Institution Environmental Technology Consortium; the Leadership Alliance; MESA (Mathematics Engineering Science Achievement) USA; the Meyerhoff Scholars Program; Minorities in Agriculture, Natural Resources and Related Sciences; the Minority Environmental Leadership Development Initiative; the National Association for Equal Opportunity in Higher Education; the National Coalition of Underrepresented Racial and Ethnic Groups in Engineering and Science; the National Consortium for Graduate Degrees for Minorities in Engineering and Science; the Partnership for Minority Advancement in the Biomolecular Sciences; the Pfizer Medical Humanities Initiative; the Quality Education for Minorities Network; Significant Opportunities in Atmospheric Research and Science; the Southern Regional Education Board; the Star Schools Program; the Thurgood Marshall College Fund; the United Negro College Fund Special Programs Corporation; and the Ventures Scholars Program. Each of these groups takes its own approach, but to a considerable degree each is interested in increasing the number of black scientists.

The federal government also devotes a considerable amount of its resources to recruiting more African Americans into careers in science. The federal agencies most involved in this effort are the Department of Energy, the National Aeronautics and Space Administration, the National Institutes of Health, and the National Science Foundation. Each of these agencies supports several initiatives that provide financial assistance to black students who have demonstrated the potential to become scientists, but they also fund a number of projects designed to improve or enhance the ability of HBCUs to continue producing the lion's share of black scientists. Most important, these agencies offer jobs to black scientists and then help them advance their careers by providing them with additional training and increased responsibilities.

Issues

To be sure, the story of African Americans in science has not always been a pretty one. For centuries, black Americans were denied opportunities to obtain the sort of education that is required for a career in science. Those who

somehow managed to obtain such an education were often denied the opportunity to pursue their careers. On rare occasions, African Americans were used
as guinea pigs to test medical theories or to find out more about how a certain disease progresses if left untreated. The most shameful incident of this
type was the Tuskegee Syphilis Experiment, whereby the federal government
allowed hundreds of syphilitic black men to suffer from their disease for
decades without being treated, even though treatment existed. Even worse,
these men were allowed to infect their unsuspecting spouses and children
with syphilis. This grisly experiment goes a long way toward explaining why
many African Americans do not trust the medical establishment to this day,
particularly in terms of seeking medical care and donating organs. It might
also help explain why black students are not more inclined to pursue careers
in science.

Issues with greater currency for the 21st century include medical education
and careers for blacks, science education and careers for blacks, and health
disparities. Despite the best efforts of the institutions and agencies mentioned,
medical education continues to be a prohibitively expensive proposition for
many African Americans who would otherwise become physicians and surgeons. Although American universities, hospitals, and other medical research
institutions have eliminated institutional racism, covert racism among individuals remains an obstacle to the hiring and promotion of black medical
researchers. Meanwhile, schools that seek to recruit more blacks for careers
as scientists are confounded by the attitude, which is widespread among black
communities, that science is not something that black people can or should
do. And, although most American corporations and scientific entities have
also purged themselves of overt racism, racial prejudice continues to play a
restrictive role in the hiring and promotion of black scientists. Much progress
has been achieved in the more than 50 years since *Brown v. Board of Education* outlawed racial segregation, but much work remains to be done to
eliminate racial prejudice from the entities in the United States that are devoted
to scientific research.

Health disparities and inequalities in the quality of health and health care
also plague the African American community. The medical conditions that
contribute the most to health disparities among African Americans are asthma,
cardiovascular disease, cancer, diabetes, HIV/AIDS, obesity, and sickle cell
disease. No one knows for sure what causes health disparities in these areas.
In some cases, it seems clear that the disparity is a manifestation of cultural,
socioeconomic, and environmental inequalities. In other cases, it most likely
arises from racial and ethnic prejudice that prevents minorities in general from
receiving first-class health care. But to a certain degree, such as with sickle cell
disease, the disparity probably has a cause rooted in genetics. Whatever the

cause or causes, health disparities are real and the American medical community continues to deal with them.

Despite the present-day obstacles and past history, by the early 21st century African Americans are perfectly positioned to play a leading role in the scientific affairs of the United States. Centuries of discrimination against black scientists are giving way to tolerance and acceptance, and the United States has become aware that it must mobilize all of its creative energy to maintain its scientific position in the world. Although much progress remains to be made, much has already been achieved, such that the future for the African American in science has never been brighter.

Chronology

1792   Benjamin Banneker publishes his first almanac.

1847   David J. Peck becomes the first African American to receive an MD from an American college.

1862   Freedmen's Hospital in Washington, D.C., is established.

1867   Howard Medical College (today's Howard University College of Medicine) is established.

1876   Edward A. Bouchet becomes the first African American to receive a PhD in physics.
Meharry Medical College is established.

1889   Alfred O. Coffin becomes the first African American to receive a PhD in biology.

1891   Provident Hospital and Training School is established in Chicago, Illinois.

1892   *The Medical and Surgical Observer,* the first medical journal devoted exclusively to the professional needs of African American physicians and surgeons, is published.

1893   Daniel Hale Williams performs one of the first successful surgical operations involving the human heart.

1895   The National Medical Association is established.

1903   George Washington Carver demonstrates that peanuts restore nitrogen to the soil.

1907   Charles H. Turner becomes the first African American to receive a PhD in zoology.

1909   Solomon C. Fuller undertakes research that eventually demonstrates that atherosclerosis plays no role in the development of Alzheimer's disease.

1910   The Flexner Report on Medical Education, which led to the closing of many black medical schools, is published.

1915   Julian H. Lewis becomes the first African American to receive a PhD in physiology.

1916   St. Elmo Brady becomes the first African American to receive a PhD in chemistry.

1918   The John A. Andrew Clinical Society is established.

1920   Elmer S. Imes offers experimental support for the quantum theory, contributing to its development into the branch of physics known as quantum mechanics.

Francis C. Sumner becomes the first African American to receive a PhD in psychology.

1921   Lincoln University of Missouri opens its doors.

1923   Beta Kappa Chi is begun as a science honor society for African Americans.

The Tuskegee Veterans Administration Hospital is opened.

1924   Roger Arliner Young describes the excretory apparatus of *Paramecium*.

1925   Xavier University of Louisiana is established.

1927   Harry Barnes becomes the first African American surgeon to be certified by an American medical board of certification.

William Hinton develops the Hinton test for diagnosing syphilis.

1931   Roscoe L. McKinney becomes the first African American to receive a PhD in anatomy.

Ruth E. Moore becomes the first African American to receive a PhD in bacteriology.

1932   Robert S. Jason becomes the first African American to receive a PhD in pathology.

Lloyd A. Hall develops a method for using salt imbedded with nitrates to preserve meat.

Samuel M. Nabrit demonstrates a correlation between the size of the bones in a fish's fin and the rate at which the fin is able to regenerate.

The National Dental Association is established.

The Tuskegee Syphilis Experiment is implemented.

1934   Paul B. Cornely becomes the first African American to receive a PhD in public health.

1935   Jessie Mark becomes the first African American to receive a PhD in botany.

1936   W. Montague Cobb demonstrates that the differences in bone structures of African Americans and whites are virtually indistinguishable.

1937   Homer G. Phillips Hospital is established in St. Louis.

1938   Frederick D. Stubbs undertakes research that eventually results in the development of surgical techniques for treating pulmonary tuberculosis.

Harold D. West synthesizes the essential amino acid threonine.

1939 Ernest E. Just publishes *Basic Methods for Experiments on Eggs of Marine Animals* (Philadelphia, PA: P. Blakiston's Son & Co.).

1940 Charles R. Drew develops the methods and procedures necessary for establishing the world's first blood bank.

The Carver Research Foundation is founded.

1941 Leonidas H. Berry demonstrates that alcoholism does not cause chronic gastritis.

Langston University is established.

1942 Julian Lewis publishes *The Biology of the Negro* (Chicago: University of Chicago Press).

Marguerite T. Williams becomes the first African American to receive a PhD in geology.

1944 The Tuskegee School of Veterinary Medicine is established.

Vivien T. Thomas plays a major role in the first successful performance of the Blalock-Taussig procedure.

1945 James H. M. Henderson undertakes research that eventually demonstrates how plant growth hormones affect the development of the sweet potato.

Prairie View A&M University is established.

1946 Mamie Phipps Clark demonstrates that racial segregation results in a negative self-image among African American children; in 1954 this evidence helps compel the U.S. Supreme Court to outlaw segregated schools in its landmark decision, *Brown v. Board of Education* [347 U.S. 483 (1954)].

Flemmie P. Kittrell undertakes research that eventually discovers what she calls hidden hunger (malnourishment on a full stomach).

Walter S. McAfee calculates the speed of the moon.

1947 Charles W. Buggs demonstrates that bacteria are capable of building a resistance to antibacterial drugs.

Roy C. Darlington becomes the first African American to receive a PhD in pharmacy.

1948 Herman R. Branson contributes to a better understanding of the physical nature of the hemoglobin molecule.

Louis T. Wright establishes the Cancer Research Foundation at Harlem Hospital and begins conducting some of the earliest research on cancer and chemotherapeutic drugs.

Mercy-Douglass Hospital is established in Philadelphia.

1949 Percy L. Julian develops a method for synthesizing cortisone from soybean oil.

1950 The Minority Institutions Science Improvement Program (MISIP) is initiated.

1951   Texas Southern University is established.

1953   Florida A&M University is founded.

1954   Jewel Plummer Cobb undertakes research eventually showing that melanoma can be caused by overexposure to the sun's ultraviolet rays.

Samuel P. Massie publishes "The Chemistry of Phenothiazine."

1957   Carroll M. Leevy publishes *Practical Diagnosis and Treatment of Liver Disease* (New York: Hoeber-Harper, 1957).

1958   Tennessee State University opens its doors.

1960   Charles E. Anderson becomes the first African American to receive a PhD in meteorology.

1961   Harvey W. Banks becomes the first African American to receive a PhD in astronomy.

Edward J. Dwight Jr. becomes the first African American chosen for the astronaut program.

Linneaus Dorman undertakes research that eventually results in the development of a synthetic peptide from which artificial bone replacement material is made.

Henry A. Hill begins developing chemical intermediates for use in the manufacture of synthetic fibers.

Samuel L. Kountz helps perform the first successful kidney transplant between two people who are not twins.

1963   Chester M. Pierce undertakes research that eventually shows how extreme exotic environments affect humans.

1964   Meredith C. Gourdine undertakes research concerning electrogasdynamics that eventually results in the development of methods for removing smoke from burning buildings, fog from airport runways, pollution from the air, and salt from seawater.

Warren Washington begins developing the first computer model for forecasting the weather.

The Student National Medical Association (SNMA) is established.

1965   Welton I. Taylor develops methods for detecting the presence of harmful bacteria in processed foods.

Central State University is established.

1968   Daniel Collins publishes *Your Teeth: A Handbook of Dental Care for the Whole Family* (Garden City, NY: Doubleday).

The Association of African American Psychologists is established.

1969   The African American Psychiatrists of America is established.

George R. Carruthers invents an image converter for detecting ultraviolet (UV) radiation.

Lloyd M. Cooke publishes *Cleaning Our Environment—The Chemical Basis for Action* (Washington, DC: American Chemical Society).

Clarence Ellis becomes the first African American to receive a PhD in computer science.

James A. Harris helps develop transuranium element 104, also known as rutherfordium.

Earl D. Shaw undertakes research that eventually results in the development of the spin-flip Raman tunable laser.

Alabama A&M University, Alabama State University, North Carolina Central University, and Winston-Salem State University are established.

Clarence A. Ellis becomes the first African American to receive a PhD in computer science.

1970 Slayton A. Evans undertakes research that eventually results in the development of an asymmetric synthesis method for synthesizing alpha-amino phosphonic acids.

MESA (Mathematics Engineering Science Achievement) USA is initiated to help African Americans improve academically in science.

The University of Maryland Eastern Shore is established.

1971 Wesley L. Harris demonstrates the structure of normal shock waves generated by aircraft.

The Sickle Cell Disease Association of America (SCDAA) is established.

1972 John C. Norman publishes *Cardiac Surgery* (New York: Appleton-Century-Crofts).

Lloyd A. Quarterman develops a method for studying various chemical compounds by first dissolving them in hydrogen fluoride.

Fisk University is founded.

North Carolina A&T State University is established.

The Roman-Barnes Society, a professional organization of African American ophthalmologists and otolaryngologists, is started up.

W. Lincoln Hawkins is named director of Bell Telephone Laboratories' department of applied research.

The American Geological Institute establishes the Minority Participation Program.

The American Physical Society establishes the Committee on Minorities in Physics.

The Association of Research Directors, 1890 Land Grant Universities is founded.

Kentucky State University and the University of Arkansas at Pine Bluff are established.

1973 Lloyd Ferguson publishes *Highlights of Alicyclic Chemistry* (Danbury, CT: Franklin Books).

The National Organization for the Professional Advancement of Black Chemists and Chemical Engineers is established.

1974   The Association of Black Cardiologists is founded.

Jackson State University is established.

The Southern University and A&M College System is established.

1975   Margaret Morgan Lawrence publishes *Young Inner City Families: Development of Ego Strength Under Stress* (New York: Behavioral Publications).

The Association of Black Anthropologists is founded.

Morgan State University is established.

The National Association of Minority Medical Educators is founded.

1976   The National Consortium for Graduate Degrees for Minorities in Engineering and Science (the National GEM Consortium) is inaugurated.

1977   The National Society of Black Physicists is established.

Patricia S. Cowings begins developing biofeedback techniques and psychophysiological methods that allow astronauts to overcome space sickness without using drugs.

The National Agricultural Research, Extension and Teaching Policy Act (Evans-Allen Act) provides increased federal funding for agricultural research at state-supported historically African American colleges and universities.

The University of the District of Columbia is established.

1978   George E. Alcorn begins developing a spectrometer that can study stars by examining the X-rays they emit.

The Morehouse School of Medicine is established.

1979   The American Psychological Association establishes the Office of Ethnic Minority Affairs.

Virginia State University and Norfolk State University are established.

1980   Renty B. Franklin undertakes research that eventually shows how imbalances in hormone and mineral levels contribute to the development of tumors in the prostate gland.

1981   Carolyn Branch Brooks undertakes research that eventually sheds light on the symbiotic relationship between soil bacteria and crops.

The National Association of Black Geologists and Geophysicists is established.

1983   Guion S. Bluford, the first African American astronaut to fly in space, conducts scientific experiments aboard the space shuttle *Challenger*.

Sylvester Gates publishes *Superspace or 1001 Lessons in Supersymmetry* (San Francisco: Benjamin/Cummings Publishing).

The Development Fund for African American Students in Science and Technology (DFBSST) is established.

1984   The Department of Energy establishes the Historically Black Colleges and Universities and Other Minority Institutions Program.

Hampton University is established.

1985   Emmett W. Chappelle identifies the laser-induced fluorescence (LIF) signatures of five major plant types.

Tuskegee University is established.

The American Society for Cell Biology establishes the Minority Affairs Committee.

1986   Dale Brown Emeagwali demonstrates that low-level organisms contain isozymes of kynurenine formamidase.

Joseph Francisco undertakes research that eventually shows that fluorinated ethers in the Earth's upper atmosphere produce greenhouse gases in a way that contributes to global warming.

Ronald E. McNair conducts scientific experiments aboard the space shuttle *Challenger*.

The International Society on Hypertension in Blacks is established.

The University of the Virgin Islands is established.

Joan Murrell Owens discovers the genus of button corals known as *Rhombopsammia*.

1987   Benjamin S. Carson serves as principal surgeon for the team that performed the first successful separation of Siamese twins joined at the head.

Philip Emeagwali develops a program that allows more than 65,000 computers in various locations to work together to solve the same problem.

The Thurgood Marshall College Fund is founded.

Charles E. Anderson begins developing a computer system to identify potential tornadoes by using geosynchronous satellite imagery.

The Charles R. Drew University of Medicine and Science is established.

Arthur B. C. Walker obtains the first high-resolution images of the Sun's corona.

1988   The Department of Education establishes the Star Schools Program, a distance learning program intended to improve the science instruction received by African American K–12 students.

Walter E. Massey becomes president of the American Association for the Advancement of Science.

Minorities in Agriculture, Natural Resources and Related Sciences is founded.

Clark Atlanta University is established.

1989   The Society of Black Academic Surgeons is organized.

The Meyerhoff Scholars Program is organized to support African Americans working toward doctoral degrees in the sciences or engineering at the University of Maryland Baltimore County.

1989   The Partnership for Minority Advancement in the Biomolecular Sci-
(cont.)   ences is established.
1990   The Environmental Careers Organization organizes its Diversity Initiative to attract more African Americans to careers in the environmental sciences.

The Historically Black College and University/Minority Institution
Environmental Technology Consortium is established.

The Minority University–Space Interdisciplinary Network is founded.

The National Center on Minority Health and Health Disparities is
begun.

The Quality Education for Minorities Network (QEM) is established.

The Minorities in Medicine Program is established.

1991   Kenneth Olden is named director of the National Institute of Environmental Health Sciences.

Cecile Hoover Edwards coauthors *Human Ecology: Interactions of
Man with His Environment; an Introduction to the Academic Discipline of Human Ecology* (Dubuque, IA: Kendall/Hunt).

1992   Mae C. Jemison conducts scientific experiments aboard the space
shuttle *Endeavor*.

George M. Langford discovers an alternative network for intracellular
motility in the endoplasmic reticulum.

The American Medical Association establishes the Minority Affairs
Consortium.

The Leadership Alliance is established to recruit more African Americans into careers as professors and administrators in biology, chemistry, and physics.

South Carolina State University is established.

1993   Joycelyn Elders is named U.S. Surgeon General.

The Camille and Henry Dreyfus Foundation establishes the American
Chemical Society Award for Encouraging Disadvantaged Students into
Careers in the chemical sciences.

Bernard A. Harris conducts scientific experiments aboard the space
shuttle *Columbia*.

The American Dental Education Association establishes the Center for
Equity and Diversity.

Delaware State University is established.

The Southern Regional Education Board State Doctoral Scholars Program for increasing the number of minority students who earn doctoral degrees in science and related disciplines is founded.

1994   The American Chemical Society establishes the ACS Scholars Program
for minority students.

John W. Macklin offers experimental support for the theory that complex organic molecules reached Earth from outer space.

Joseph C. Dunbar undertakes research that eventually shows how insulin and leptin affect the pressure and flow of blood.

1995 Shirley A. Jackson is named chair of the Nuclear Regulatory Commission.

Gibor Basri proves the existence of brown dwarfs, small stars that emit very little visible light.

1996 The Endocrine Society begins sponsoring "Shortcourses in Endocrinology" at historically African American colleges and universities.

The National Institute of General Medical Sciences establishes the Minority Biomedical Research Support initiative.

Fort Valley State University is founded.

The Savannah River Environmental Sciences Field Station, the first field station in the United States devoted entirely to minority graduate and undergraduate research in the biological sciences, is established.

1998 David Satcher is named U.S. surgeon general.

Evan B. Forde begins developing methods for using the QuikSCAT satellite as a tool for identifying potential hurricanes.

1999 The Gates Millennium Scholars program begins awarding scholarships to African American students pursuing graduate degrees in science and related fields.

2000 The American Association for Cancer Research establishes the Minorities in Cancer Research program.

Black Entomologists is organized.

2001 Building Engineering and Science Talent (BEST), Inc., is established to implement the recommendations of the Commission on the Advancement of Women and Minorities in Science, Engineering and Technology Development.

The Robert Wood Johnson Foundation establishes the Dental Pipeline as a means of making dental education for African Americans more affordable.

The Institute of Medicine publishes *The Right Thing to Do, the Smart Thing to Do: Enhancing Diversity in Health Professions* (Washington, DC: National Academies Press).

2002 The Council for Chemical Research Diversity Award is established.

Delta Sigma Theta Sorority establishes the Science and Everyday Experiences Initiative for African American children in grades K–8.

The National Aeronautics and Space Administration Minority Institution Research Support program is established.

2002 The National Coalition of Underrepresented Racial and Ethnic Groups
(cont.) in Engineering and Science is established.

The Network of Minority Research Investigators is founded.

2003 The Minority Environmental Leadership Development Initiative is established.

The American Medical Student Association establishes the Achieving Diversity in Dentistry and Medicine Program.

The Wayne State University Center for Urban and African American Health is established.

Michael Anderson oversees scientific experiments conducted on board the space shuttle *Columbia*.

2004 Neil deGrasse Tyson publishes *Origins: Fourteen Billion Years of Cosmic Evolution* (New York: W. W. Norton).

The American Association for the Advancement of Science establishes the Minority Writers Internship.

The Diversity Institute is established as a professional development program for faculty and graduate students in science, technology, engineering, and mathematics.

West Virginia State University is founded.

The Institute of Medicine publishes *In the Nation's Compelling Interest: Ensuring Diversity in the Health Care Workforce* (Washington, DC: National Academies Press).

The Sullivan Commission on Diversity in the Healthcare Workforce publishes *Missing Persons: Minorities in the Health Professions* (http://www.aacn.nche.edu/Media/pdf/SullivanReport.pdf) (Durham, NC: Sullivan Commission, 2004).

2005 The Daniel Hale Williams Preparatory School of Medicine is established.

A. Oveta Fuller demonstrates how the herpes simplex virus gains entry into a cell.

Joseph Graves publishes *The Race Myth: Why We Pretend Race Exists in America* (New York: Plume Books).

2008 Leland Melvin flies aboard the Space shuttle *Atlantis*.

Note: Dates listed for many of the historically black colleges and universities (HBCUs) are the year the school became a university, not when the school was founded.

Biographies

African Americans have made a number of important contributions to every branch of science, especially astronomy and astrophysics, biology, microbiology, biochemistry, chemistry, computer science, physics, and anthropology. Prior to the 1960s, the majority of black scientists were physicians or surgeons engaged in medical research, mostly because the reality of legal segregation dictated that blacks were permitted to practice medicine and conduct experiments related to medicine and physiology, even if only among their race. After the 1960s, however, every field of science was thrown open to African Americans who sought to pursue careers in scientific research.

Black astronomers and astrophysicists made some of the first calculations of the positions of the planets and stars as seen from North America. They figured out how to bounce a radio signal off the moon and how to determine the elements that make up a star and our sun in particular. They developed theories and methods for arriving at a better understanding of the behavior of black holes. They proved the existence of brown dwarfs (stars that emit very little light), and they helped explain how hydrocarbons were formed in the early days of the universe.

Black biologists developed hybrid plants and other techniques for increasing the yields of a variety of crops. They proved the existence of growth hormones in plants, and they showed how certain plants produce toxins to drive away harmful insects and bacteria. They helped explain how a sperm cell fertilizes an egg cell, and they contributed to a better understanding of the behavior of protozoans. They discovered new species of insects and sea corals and explained how ants and bees find their way back to their nests. They helped demonstrate that melanoma (skin cancer) can be caused by overexposure to the sun. They shed important light on intracellular motility (the process by which biochemical compounds are transported within a cell). They demonstrated some of the harmful side effects that pesticides have on animals, and they showed how certain species of birds can learn to sing new songs by imitating humans.

Black microbiologists developed methods for checking processed foods for the presence of the bacteria that cause botulism, tetanus, gangrene, dysentery, and other kinds of food poisoning. They showed how certain viruses, such as the herpes simplex virus and adeno-associated virus, insinuate themselves into a cell. They made important discoveries regarding the symbiotic relationships between legumes and soil bacteria, and they helped explain the phenomenon known as seasonal abundances, whereby the parasites that infest animals increase or decrease their populations during certain seasons of the year.

Black biochemists developed methods for detecting the presence of life in outer space and for counting the bacteria in urine, blood, spinal fluids, drinking water, and foods. They demonstrated the biochemical aspects of certain medical conditions related to cardiovascular disease, and they explained how the shape and structure of certain biomolecules affect the way they react chemically with other biomolecules. They explained how detoxification enzymes inhibit the ability of chemotherapeutic drugs to destroy cancerous cells, and they helped explain how the production of glucose is regulated in liver cells. They contributed to a better understanding of the chemical composition of amino acids, and they participated in the first successful attempt to synthesize the amino acid threonine.

Black chemists demonstrated that the inert gases are not so inert by getting one of then, xenon, to react with fluorine. They shed light on the nature of the chemical bonds that link chlorine and fluorine in chlorofluorocarbons (CFCs), the chemical compound most responsible for depleting the Earth's ozone layer, and they tested the replacements for CFCs to make sure they would not also harm the atmosphere. They developed hundreds of industrial and commercial products from peanuts and soybeans, and they developed synthetic materials as well as many applications for them. They developed methods for preserving food and discovered why fatty and oily foods become rancid. They helped explain the behavior of organotins and organophosphates, two chemical compounds that do not exist in nature, and they played a major role in the discovery of two transuranium elements. They developed processes for making therapeutic drugs from dangerous, unstable compounds, and they participated in the development of the first atomic bomb.

Black computer scientists wrote the program for linking tens of thousands of computers to solve one problem, thus contributing in a major way to the development of the World Wide Web. They helped develop the world's most powerful supercomputers, as well as the software that enables people to use computers to work together on the same problem, even when they are in different places. They developed computer systems that are accessible by people with disabilities, including blind programmers.

Black physicists figured out how to use magnetic and radiation detection methods to find large deposits of crude oil and other minerals, as well as how to use radar to detect incoming intercontinental ballistic missiles. They developed methods for using electrogasdynamics and magnetohydrodynamics to generate large amounts of high-voltage electricity inexpensively. They broadened our understating of a wide range of physical phenomena from plasma to polarons, from superconductivity to superfluidity. They showed that proteins are arranged in a helix, thus contributing to the discovery that DNA is shaped like a double helix. They made the first accurate measurement of the distance between atoms in a molecule, and they helped prove the validity of Albert Einstein's quantum theory. They developed many of the mathematical formulas for deploying spacecraft in outer space and then bringing them back safely, and they helped develop the methods and equipment for using lasers to study biological systems.

Black medical researchers developed procedures and instruments for removing diseased tissue from the stomach and lungs and for examining the abdominal cavity and the intestines. They developed surgical procedures for removing tumors, separating Siamese twins, and restoring the flow of blood to the lungs of children. They developed the procedures and equipment for transplanting kidneys. They performed one of the first surgical procedures on the heart, and they played a major role in developing the procedures and equipment for transplanting hearts. They discovered most of what is known about sickle cell disease, including what causes it and how best to treat it. They shed light on the nutritional value of a vegetarian diet and discovered hidden hunger, which results from filling the stomach with food that has little nutritional value. They developed the procedures for handling and preserving blood in blood banks, and they explained some of the biochemical causes of mental illness. They developed the first procedures for testing chemotherapeutic drugs, and they showed how syphilis progresses in humans.

Black anthropologists demonstrated that, in terms of bone structure, virtually no differences exist between African Americans and European Americans. They shed important light on the secret working of voodoo societies in the Caribbean and on the heredity of complexion. They developed new ways to study so-called primitive people that do away with preconceived notions about primitiveness and cultural superiority.

Even when legal segregation made it difficult for blacks to become scientists, those who yearned to conduct scientific research often found ways to do so. In the process, they made a number of important contributions to every field of science. Now that legal segregation has ended and public and private institutions have determined to help rather than hinder the progress of black scientists, the scientific contributions made by African Americans in the future promise to be significant indeed.

Adams, Eugene W.
(1920–) Veterinary Pathologist

Eugene Adams conducted important research on the pathology (growth and development) of various cancers in dogs. His research contributed to a better understanding of how cancer grows and spreads in humans. He also played a major role in improving the quality of veterinary science in several developing nations.

Adams was born on January 12, 1920, in Guthrie, Oklahoma, to Clarence and Lucille Adams. As a boy he dreamed of becoming a dentist, but he changed his mind after moving with his family to Wichita, Kansas. There he met Thomas G. Perry, a black veterinarian who in the 1920s opened one of the first animal hospitals in the Midwest. After completing his first two years at Kansas State University (KSU), Adams transferred into KSU's school of veterinary medicine and received a DVM in 1944.

For the next seven years, he worked as a meat inspector for the Department of Agriculture in St. Louis, inspecting the organs of thousands of animals each day for diseases that would make them unfit for human consumption. In 1951, he became an instructor of pathology and parasitology at Tuskegee Institute (today Tuskegee University) School of Veterinary Medicine; except for several leaves of absence, he remained at Tuskegee for the rest of his career. During two leave periods, he studied comparative pathology at Cornell University, receiving an MS and a PhD in 1957 and 1962, respectively. In 1956, he married Myrtle Adams, with whom he had three children.

Adams's primary research interest involved cancer in dogs. He was particularly interested in transmissible tumors—cancerous growths that can be transferred from a tumorous organism to a healthy organism with the result that the tumor begins growing in the healthy organism too. During the course of his investigations, he discovered that a dog that had survived the growth and surgical removal of a tumor was immune to new growths, even when injected with new growths of the same type of tumor from other dogs. He also discovered that an implanted tumor causes the healthy dog's blood to develop certain types of proteins that are normally produced in reaction to a viral infection. Together with the work of other cancer researchers, Adams's findings lent further support to the theory that some cancers, perhaps even a great many, are caused by viruses.

In 1970, Adams was recruited by KSU to establish a school of veterinary medicine at Nigeria's Ahmadu Bello University as part of a U.S. federal aid program. As part of that initiative, he helped identify the diseases that plague domestic animals in Nigeria. He also helped establish a center where animals could be tested for those diseases, as well as a mobile clinic that could examine animals in the remote countryside. In addition, he developed disease prevention and treatment programs, in addition to a slaughterhouse inspection program.

Upon returning to Tuskegee in 1972, Adams was made a dean and given responsibility for developing veterinary medicine programs for students from the Caribbean and Africa. These responsibilities included identifying the diseases endemic to the various countries and developing programs to teach students how to handle those diseases upon their return. In 1983, he was named the vice provost for international programs, and in this capacity he oversaw the development of foreign assistance programs in agricultural science, animal health care, and health education in Caribbean and African nations.

In 1989, Adams retired to his home in Tuskegee, although he maintained an active interest in the school's affairs for some years thereafter. During his retirement he played an active role in the Henry A. Wallace Institute for Alternative Agriculture (today the Henry A. Wallace Center for Agricultural and Environmental Policy), an organization that seeks to shape U.S. agricultural and food policy by analyzing, researching, and evaluating innovative agriculture and food systems to ensure that they are socially equitable and environmentally sustainable.

See also: Tuskegee School of Veterinary Medicine; Tuskegee University

REFERENCES AND FURTHER READING

Hayden, Robert C. *Eleven African American Doctors*, rev. ed. New York: Twenty-First Century Books, 1992: 138–153.

Alcorn, George E., Jr.
(1940–) Physicist

George Alcorn made important contributions to physics as a researcher and as an administrator. His work with plasma physics and X-ray spectrometry resulted in the development of more than 25 patentable devices or processes, several of which were used in the space program. As a high-level manager, he oversaw the development of sophisticated technologies for the National Aeronautics and Space Administration (NASA) and then worked to ensure that those technologies were made available to the private business sector.

Alcorn was born on March 22, 1940. His father, George Sr., was an automobile mechanic, and his mother, Arletta, was a homemaker. He majored in physics at Occidental College (California), and after receiving a BA in 1962, he entered Howard University, where he received an MS in nuclear physics in 1963 and a PhD in atomic and molecular physics in 1967. He spent the next 11 years in the private sector, and in 1969 he married Marie DaVillier, with whom he has one child.

Between 1967 and 1978, Alcorn worked as a senior scientist at Philco Ford, as a senior physicist at PerkinElmer, and as an advisory engineer at IBM. In each of these positions, his research focused on developing new methods for the production of high-performance semiconductor devices, and his work contributed to the development of two advanced manufacturing technologies, plasma etching and sputtering. The operative force in plasma etching is plasma, in physics the soupy mixture of ions and electrons that results when a solid is vaporized by intense heat so that it resembles neither a solid, liquid, nor gas. Alcorn's plasma etching process increases the bond strength of the various elements that compose the semiconductor material while removing contaminating materials and residue from the device's surface. His sputtering technique offered a sophisticated method for applying very thin layers of filmy coating to a semiconductor device to give it special capabilities.

While in graduate school, Alcorn had become involved with the space program. During his summers, he worked for North American Rockwell's space division, which at the time was primarily involved with supporting NASA's mission to put a man on the moon, and his doctoral dissertation on the formation of negative ions was financed in part by a NASA grant. In 1978, Alcorn went to work for NASA, where he spent the rest of his career.

From 1978 to 1984, Alcorn worked to develop a new type of imaging X-ray spectrometer. X-ray spectrometry is used to study stars and other remote objects in space by examining the electromagnetic waves those bodies emit that fall within the X-ray spectrum. The method is particularly useful for determining the elements the bodies are composed of, because each element emits its own unique spectral signature. During this period, he also developed a chemical ionization mass spectrometer that can detect on other planets the presence of amino acids, which are essential for life on Earth.

In 1984, NASA named Alcorn a deputy project manager for the International Space Station (ISS) mission, and for the next six years he oversaw the development of advanced technologies for use on the ISS. In 1990, he was named manager for advanced programs at NASA's Goddard Space Flight Center in Greenbelt, Maryland, and two years later he became chief of Goddard's office of commercial programs. This office is charged with overseeing the declassification and adaptation of advanced technologies developed by NASA for use in nonspace-related commercial and industrial applications. In addition to his duties as chief, he served as project manager for the development and commercialization of the Airborne LIDAR Topographic Mapping System (ALTMS). ALTMS gathers elevation data for the production of topographic maps, and it is particularly useful for mapping remote areas that are covered with dense vegetation. The system makes use of the Global Positioning System (GPS), an inertial reference system, and an advanced laser technology known as LIDAR (Light Detection and Ranging), also known as laser radar. NASA became interested in LIDAR as a way to determine the elevation of various landforms on the planets and moons in the solar system, because LIDAR can "see" through soft but thick layers of material such as dust; LIDAR can also be used to measure chemical concentrations, such as ozone, water vapor, and pollutants, in the atmosphere.

In 2005, Alcorn was named assistant director for standards and excellence in NASA's Applied Engineering and Technology Directorate. In addition to his duties at NASA, he has devoted himself to the education of potential black scientists. He taught physics and engineering at Howard University and the University of the District of Columbia for a number of years, and he founded a program called Saturday Academy. Funded in part by the Meyerhoff Foundation, Saturday Academy encourages middle school students in Baltimore's inner city to become scientists or engineers.

See also: Howard University; National Aeronautics and Space Administration; University of the District of Columbia

REFERENCES AND FURTHER READING

Krapp, Kristine, ed. *Notable Black American Scientists.* Detroit, MI: Gale Research, 1999: 2–3.

Physicists of the African Diaspora. "George Edward Alcorn." [Online article or information; retrieved August 22, 2007.] http://www.math.buffalo.edu/mad/physics/alcorn_georgeE.html.

Spangenburg, Ray, and Kit Moser. *African Americans in Science, Math, and Invention.* New York: Facts On File, 2003: 1–2.

Anderson, Charles E.
(1919–1994) Meteorologist

One of the most exciting developments in the recent history of meteorology is the use of data collected by satellites as a tool for forecasting the weather. Charles E. Anderson's contribution in this regard was to develop a computerized forecasting system to predict severe storms such as tornadoes and hailstorms.

Anderson was born on August 13, 1919, on a farm near Clayton, Missouri. At age 10, he and his parents left their farm and moved to nearby St. Louis. After completing his secondary education in the local schools, he entered Lincoln University of Missouri in Jefferson City, where he majored in chemistry. In 1941, he received a BS and joined the U.S. Army Air Corps (today the U.S. Air Force), which sent him to the University of Chicago to study meteorology. After receiving an MS in meteorology in 1943, he was assigned as a weather officer to the Tuskegee Airmen, a group of African American fighter pilots who escorted bombing missions over Germany during World War II. That same year he married Marjorie Anderson, with whom he had two children.

When the war ended, the army sent Anderson to the Polytechnic Institute of Brooklyn (New York), and in 1948 he received an MS in chemistry. He spent the next year as a research and development officer at the Watson Laboratories in New Jersey before being named chief of the cloud physics branch of the Air Force's Geophysics Research Laboratory in Boston. His primary duty in this position was to study the physical processes governing the formation and function of cumulus clouds, the fluffy clouds that occupy the Earth's atmosphere between 3,000 and 20,000 feet. To this end, he developed a method for studying the bands of ultraviolet light that cumulus clouds emit under vacuum conditions at high altitudes. He was also charged with developing a method for making rain by seeding clouds with various chemicals. One offshoot of this project was his development of a way to make the vapor trails of jet aircraft invisible. Meanwhile, he continued to further his education at the Massachusetts Institute of Technology, and in 1960 he received a PhD in meteorology. Shortly thereafter, he resigned from the military to become head of the atmospheric analysis group of the Douglass Aircraft Missiles and Space Systems Division in Los Angeles.

Anderson's primary responsibility with Douglass was to develop a method for forecasting the cloud structure of the atmosphere so that the National Aeronautics and Space Administration (NASA) and the military could launch their rockets under the best possible atmospheric conditions. To this end, he co-developed with Joanne Simpson the first computer model of a cloud filled with moisture. In 1965, he was named director of the Environmental Science Service Administration's Office of Federal Coordination in Meteorology in Washington, D.C. His primary responsibility was to coordinate U.S. involvement in World Weather Watch, the World Meteorological Organization's program for the nearly instantaneous exchange of weather information between any two points on the planet.

In 1966, Anderson left government service to become assistant director of the Space Science and Engineering Center at the University of Wisconsin. In this position, he began developing computer models that utilized satellite data to study severe storms, especially hailstorms and tornadoes. In 1984, a complex system of severe thunderstorms created seven Force 5 tornadoes in Barneveld, Wisconsin, known collectively as the Barneveld Tornado. Anderson used a computer to analyze the debris trail left by the Barneveld Tornado to identify it as a spiral mesolow, a previously unknown type of tornado.

In 1987, Anderson left Wisconsin for North Carolina State University. By this time, oceanographers had begun using remote sensing via satellite to study the oceans; Anderson adapted their methods to use remote sensing to study severe storms and tornadoes. By making use of geosynchronous satellite imagery, he developed a computer-based system that analyzes how storm centers spin in such a way that a tornado can be predicted up to one hour before it actually strikes. He later modified this system so that it could forecast hail-producing thunderstorms as well. Anderson's ability to predict tornadoes made it possible to implement an early-warning system in the Midwest's so-called Tornado Alley, thus helping to save hundreds of lives.

Anderson was elected to membership in the American Association for the Advancement of Science. He conducted weather-related research until his death on October 21, 1994, in Durham, North Carolina. In 1999, the National Center for Atmospheric Research established the Charles Anderson Award in his honor.

See also: American Association for the Advancement of Science; Lincoln University of Missouri; National Aeronautics and Space Administration

REFERENCES AND FURTHER READING

Carey, Charles W. Jr. *American Scientists.* New York: Facts On File, 2005: 5–6.

Sammons, Vivian Ovelton. *Blacks in Science and Medicine.* New York: Hemisphere Publishing, 1990: 11.

Stamatel, Janet P. "Charles Edward Anderson." *Contemporary Black Biography*, vol. 37. Detroit, MI: Gale Cengage, 2003: 4–7.

Anderson, Gloria L.
(1938–) Physical Chemist

Gloria Anderson is one of the first organic chemists to experiment with fluorine as a way to better understand what happens during certain chemical reactions. She also developed new processes for synthesizing several organic compounds.

Anderson was born Gloria Long on November 5, 1938, in Altheimer, Arkansas. Her parents, Charley and Elsie, were sharecroppers. After graduating from high school at age 16, she entered the Arkansas Agricultural, Mechanical and Normal College (today the University of Arkansas at Pine Bluff) and received a BS in chemistry in 1958. She taught seventh grade science for a few months before entering the graduate program at Atlanta (today Clark Atlanta) University, where she received an MS in chemistry in 1961. Over the next three years, she taught chemistry at South Carolina State University and Morehouse College in Atlanta, and then she enrolled at the University of Chicago, receiving a PhD in organic chemistry in 1968. That same year, she was named chair of the chemistry department at Morris Brown College in Atlanta. In 1960, she married Leonard Anderson; they had one child before divorcing in 1977.

As a physical chemist, Anderson strove to understand why certain chemical reactions take place the way they do. Early in her career, she studied chemical reactions via spectroscopy, the study of the spectral lines of electromagnetic radiation that every substance emits. These lines identify each element and compound in much the same way that a barcode identifies a product. For example, one of her first research projects analyzed a new process for synthesizing butadiene (a type of synthetic rubber) by studying the shifts in the infrared emissions that the various intermediate products emitted. Later, she used nuclear magnetic resonance (NMR), a method that identifies atoms by measuring their magnetic moment, a function of their magnetic strength.

In graduate school, Anderson undertook a study of the various properties of a rare isotope of fluorine known as fluorine–19. Fluorine is the most reactive of the elements (to date, it is the only element that is known to be able to react with one of the noble, or inert, gases); so it makes a perfect tool for studying chemical reactions. Once she had come to understand how fluorine–19 behaves, she substituted it for various chemical groups in a molecule and then used NMR to see how the molecule's electron density changed, thus shedding light on how chemicals react at the molecular level. This method was particularly effective at illuminating the mechanism of epoxidation, whereby two organic compounds are linked together by means of an oxygen atom. She also developed new methods for synthesizing a number of organic compounds, including solid-fuel rocket propellants and analogs of amantadine, an antiviral drug that is also used to treat Parkinson's disease.

Anderson remained at Morris Brown for the rest of her career. In addition to her teaching duties, she served as acting vice president for academic affairs, as dean of science and technology, and as interim president for two terms. She also served on several advisory committees for the U.S. Food and Drug Administration.

See also: Chemistry; Clark Atlanta University; South Carolina State University; University of Arkansas at Pine Bluff

References and Further Reading
Warren, Wini. *Black Women Scientists in the United States*. Bloomington: Indiana University Press, 1999: 1–12.

Anderson, Michael P.
(1959–2003) Astronaut

Despite its tragic loss, STS-107, the last flight of the space shuttle *Columbia*, managed to return some valuable scientific data to Earth. The experiments that collected this data were overseen by Michael Anderson, the mission's payload commander. Most of the mission's 80-plus experiments, which ran the gamut from physics to biochemistry, were completed successfully, and slightly more than half of the data these experiments collected was returned to Earth for further evaluation.

Anderson was born on Christmas Day, 1959, in Plattsburgh, New York. His father, Bobby, served in the U.S. Air Force, and his mother, Barbara, was a homemaker. As a youngster, Anderson moved with his family to his father's various assignments, settling at last at Fairchild Air Force Base near Spokane, Washington, where he grew up. After graduating from high school in nearby Cheney, he entered the University of Washington, where he studied physics and astronomy and joined the Air Force Reserve Officers Training Corps. In 1981, he received a BS and a commission as a second lieutenant, and for the next five years he served as a communication maintenance and computer systems maintenance officer at bases in Mississippi and Texas. In 1986, he completed his pilot training and was assigned to the Strategic Air Command's headquarters near Omaha, Nebraska, as a pilot of an airborne command post. While stationed in Omaha, he attended Creighton University and received an MS in physics in 1990. His last air force assignment saw him return to Plattsburgh, with the rank of lieutenant colonel, as an instructor pilot and tactics officer with an air refueling wing stationed at Plattsburgh Air Force Base. At some point, he married Sandy Hawkins, with whom he had two children.

In 1994, Anderson was selected by the National Aeronautics and Space Administration (NASA) to be an astronaut. He spent the next four years training to be a mission specialist at the Johnson Space Center in Houston. In 1998, he flew aboard the space shuttle *Endeavour* on an eight-day mission to deliver scientific equipment and supplies to the Russian space station, *Mir*. In 2003, he was chosen to return to space as part of the crew of the space shuttle *Columbia* for a 16-day science and research mission. Anderson served as the mission's payload commander, which made him responsible for the successful completion of the more than 80 scientific experiments that were to be carried out onboard. He also served as a mission specialist on the Blue Team, one of two teams that conducted experiments in 12-hour shifts; so he personally took part in about half of the experiments.

As payload commander, Anderson achieved an admirable success record. Many of the results of the experiments pertaining to the physical sciences were returned via telemetry to Earth as soon as they were gathered; so the data these experiments acquired was not completely lost when *Columbia*'s mission was interrupted prematurely. These experiments included Mechanics of Granular Materials, which tested sand columns under conditions of microgravity as a means of better understanding how earthquakes disturb sand and soil; Critical Viscosity of Xenon, a National Institute of Standards and Technology experiment designed to shed light on the behavior of

As payload commander of STS-107, the last flight of the space shuttle Columbia*, astronaut Michael Anderson oversaw all scientific experiments conducted during the mission.* (National Aeronautics and Space Administration)

complex fluids like paint and whipped cream that must flow freely while being applied but then firm up afterward; STARNAV, a star tracker navigation system developed by Texas A&M University that can determine the altitude of a spacecraft without any previous knowledge of its position; STARS, a collection of student experiments that explored how low gravity affects the behavior and development of ants, bees, silkworms, and fish eggs, the random crystal growth of cobalt and calcium, and the web spinning ability of spiders; the Solar Constant Experiment, a project by the Royal Meteorological Institute of Belgium to measure the solar constant (the average rate at which radiant energy from the sun is received by the Earth) and to identify variations in its value during a solar cycle; the Low Power Transceiver Experiment, a test of a spacecraft's ability to operate its communication and navigation equipment simultaneously; and the Mediterranean Israeli Dust Experiment, which captured a photographic image of a gray, smoky haze that hangs over the Amazon rainforest, thus contributing to a better understanding of how smoke from automobiles, factories, and fires can influence weather and climate. Unfortunately, data and samples from experiments pertaining to the life sciences, such as the European Space Administration's Advanced Respiratory Monitoring System (ARMS), which investigated how the heart and lungs respond to the microgravity conditions of space flight, and the Physiology and Biochemistry Team group of experiments were lost when *Columbia* failed to return.

Anderson died on February 1, 2003, somewhere over the southern United States as *Columbia* was returning from space. In recognition of his contributions and sacrifice, he was posthumously awarded the Congressional Space

Medal of Honor, the NASA Distinguished Service Medal, and the Defense Distinguished Service Medal.

See also: Astronomy and Astrophysics; Biochemistry; National Aeronautics and Space Administration; Physics

REFERENCES AND FURTHER READING
National Aeronautics and Space Administration. "Astronaut Bio: Michael P. Anderson." [Online article or information; retrieved August 26, 2005.] http://www.jsc.nasa.gov/Bios/htmlbios/anderson.html.

Banneker, Benjamin
(1731–1806) Astronomer

To determine latitude and longitude in the 18th and 19th centuries, navigators and surveyors used ephemerides, which were tables giving the calculated positions of the planets and major stars on a number of future dates in a regular sequence. Benjamin Banneker helped both navigators and surveyors get the job done by calculating the most accurate ephemerides of the day for the Mid-Atlantic states. He also played an important role on the surveying team that laid out Washington, D.C.

Banneker was born on November 9, 1731, in Oella, Maryland. His parents, Robert and Mary, were farmers. Except for a few lessons in a rural schoolhouse, where he learned to read, write, and make simple arithmetical computations, he received no formal education. But once he learned to read, he was able to teach himself about virtually any subject that caught his interest. For example, in the 1750s he built a mechanical chiming clock despite having never seen one except in a book. Legend has it that he learned about a clock's inner workings by taking apart a pocket watch and studying its various components. Lacking the funds with which to purchase expensive metal castings, he carved most of the gears and other parts from hardwood, and he made his own calculations about how many teeth each gear should have in order for the clock to keep precise time. The clock worked so well that it kept nearly perfect time until long after his death.

In 1771, Banneker met George Ellicott, who had moved from Philadelphia to Oella to grow and mill wheat. Ellicott was a trained surveyor and an amateur astronomer, and he taught Banneker how to use a telescope. In time, Ellicott became so impressed with Banneker's latent scientific capabilities that he loaned him a telescope and some books on astronomy. By 1789, Banneker had taught himself enough about astronomy to calculate an ephemeris (the singular of ephemerides), and in 1790, he produced ephemerides for inclusion in an almanac for the year 1791.

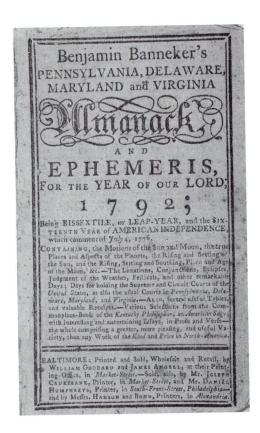

Benjamin Banneker's almanacs contained the most precise calculations of the future positions of planets and stars of any almanac published in 18th-century America. (Library of Congress)

In 1791, Banneker went to work for Andrew Ellicott, the surveyor who had been put in charge of laying out the streets of the nation's capital. Ellicott had asked his cousin George to help him, but George was so busy with his farm and mill that he sent Banneker in his place. For three months in early 1791, Banneker supervised Ellicott's astronomy tent, making sure that the astronomical clock kept accurate time and generally seeing to it that the surveying team had the best possible astronomical data at its disposal.

Upon being relieved by George Ellicott, Banneker returned to his farm. Having prepared ephemerides for someone else's almanac, he now began to prepare them for an almanac of his own. At the time, farmers relied heavily on almanacs to determine the best time for planting and harvesting crops, and many of these determinations were made by consulting the ephemerides in an almanac. Banneker's first almanac was published in 1792 under the title *Benjamin Banneker's Pennsylvania, Delaware, Maryland and Virginia Almanack and Ephemeris, for the Year of Our Lord 1792....* The first issue sold moderately well, but once Mid-Atlantic farmers discovered that Banneker's charts were more accurate than those in other almanacs, the demand for a second almanac was considerable. Banneker published five more almanacs, stopping in 1797 for reasons that are not altogether clear. Nevertheless, he continued to calculate astronomical tables for his own amusement until just before his death.

Banneker's almanac attracted much attention in Europe. He had given a manuscript copy to Thomas Jefferson, an amateur astronomer who at the time was the U.S. secretary of state. Jefferson was so impressed with Banneker's ephemerides that he purchased a number of copies of the almanac and distributed them to his friends and diplomatic contacts in Europe. The quality of Banneker's ephemerides were compared with a number of the ones that had been computed by trained European astronomers, and Banneker's were found to be at least as accurate, if not more so.

Banneker lived his entire life on the family farm in Oella. He never married, but instead cared for his aging parents until their deaths in the 1770s. He died at his farm on October 19, 1806.

See also: Astronomy and Astrophysics

REFERENCES AND FURTHER READING

Bedini, Silvio A. *The Life of Benjamin Banneker: The First African American Man of Science*, 2nd ed. Baltimore: Maryland Historical Society, 1999.

Carey, Charles W. Jr. *American Scientists*. New York: Facts On File, 2005: 16–17.

Cerami, Charles A. *Benjamin Banneker: Surveyor, Astronomer, Publisher, Patriot*. New York: Wiley, 2002.

Spangenburg, Ray, and Kit Moser. *African Americans in Science, Math, and Invention*. New York: Facts On File, 2003: 8–10.

Barnes, W. Harry
(1887–1945) Surgeon

Harry Barnes was the first black surgeon to be certified by an American board of certification, in his case the American Board of Otolaryngology. He was one of the country's foremost experts in otolaryngology, the study of the anatomy, function, and diseases of the ear, nose, and throat, and in bronchoesophagology, a related field that deals with the bronchial tubes and esophagus.

Barnes was born on April 4, 1887, in Philadelphia. As a boy, he decided to become a doctor, and he spent the summer after graduating from high school preparing for the University of Pennsylvania Medical School scholarship exam. He placed first and won the scholarship, becoming the first black to do so, and in 1912, he received an MD. That same year, he married Mattie Thomas, with whom he had five children. While interning at Frederick Douglass and Mercy hospitals (which were later combined to form Mercy-Douglass Hospital) in Philadelphia, he became interested in otolaryngology. In

1913, he was named assistant otolaryngologist at Douglass, and eight years later he was promoted to chief otolaryngologist.

In 1924, Barnes took a leave of absence from his various positions to study otolaryngology at the universities of Paris and Bordeaux in France. Upon returning to the United States, he became a student of Chevalier Jackson, a Philadelphia surgeon and the nation's foremost authority in bronchoesophagology. In 1927, he was certified by the American Board of Otolaryngology, and in 1931, he was named professor of bronchoesophagology at Howard Medical School (today Howard University College of Medicine) in Washington, D.C. He taught at Howard for the next 12 years while continuing to practice otolaryngology in Philadelphia. He also organized and headed a department of bronchoesophagology at Mercy Hospital, taught at Philadelphia's Jefferson Medical School, operated as a surgeon for the U.S. Public Health Service, and practiced as a resident at the University of Pennsylvania Hospital.

A surgical innovator, Barnes developed a number of new surgical techniques for treating conditions of the ears, nose, and throat. He was one of the first promoters of the prophylactic tonsillectomy (the removal of the tonsils before they become infected) and of the administration of anesthesia to a patient about to undergo a tonsillectomy. He developed simplified procedures for removing nasopharyngeal fibromas (tumors found in the nose and throat). He provided more thorough descriptions of tuberculous laryngitis, acute mastoiditis (inflammation of the mastoid process, a nipple-like outgrowth of the temporal bone behind the ear), otomastoiditis (an acute bacterial infection of the middle ear), and abscesses in the cerebellum as a result of otitis media (inflammation of the middle ear).

Although virtually his entire career was devoted to otolaryngology and bronchoesophagology, Barnes made an important contribution to neurosurgery as well. In 1910, the eminent American neurosurgeon Harvey W. Cushing developed a surgical procedure for operating on the pituitary gland, which lies on the underside of the brain, by cutting through the sphenoidal sinus, the sinus cavity behind the eye. The procedure was made difficult by the fact that a surgeon cannot make direct visual contact with the pituitary gland from the sphenoidal sinus, and so a hypophyscope, a device for seeing through the sphenoidal sinus to the pituitary gland, was developed. Unfortunately, this device did not work very well until the late 1920s, when Barnes made some basic improvements to it. Barnes's hypophyscope has long since been replaced by operating microscopes and fiber optic devices, but at the time it provided neurosurgeons with an important tool.

Barnes served as president of the National Medical Association and the Philadelphia Academy of Medicine and Allied Science, and he cofounded the Society for the Promotion of Negro Specialists in Medicine. In 1943, he suffered a stroke that forced him to retire, and he died on January 15, 1945, in

Philadelphia. In 1968, a group of black otolaryngologists and ophthalmologists who were excluded from the American Academy of Ophthalmologists and Otolaryngologists because of their race founded a national association of their own; they named it the Roman-Barnes Society in honor of Victor Roman, a noted ophthalmologist, and Barnes.

See also: Howard University College of Medicine; Mercy-Douglass Hospital; National Medical Association; Roman-Barnes Society

REFERENCES AND FURTHER READING

McMurray, Emily, ed. *Notable Twentieth-Century Scientists.* Detroit, MI: Gale Research, 1995: 114–115.

Spangenburg, Ray, and Kit Moser. *African Americans in Science, Math, and Invention.* New York: Facts On File, 2003: 11–12.

Basri, Gibor B.
(1951–) Astrophysicist

Gibor Basri proved the existence of brown dwarfs (small stars that emit very little visible light). His research has contributed to a better understanding of the magnetic activity of stars, and as of 2007, he was participating in a project to discover Earth-like planets throughout the universe.

Basri was born on May 3, 1951, in New York City. His father, Saul, was a physics professor, and his mother, Phyllis, was a dance teacher. As a young boy he moved with his family to Fort Collins, Colorado, where his father had joined the faculty at Colorado State University. He received a BS in physics from Stanford University in 1973 and a PhD in astrophysics from the University of Colorado at Boulder in 1979. After conducting postdoctoral research at the University of California at Berkeley (Cal-Berkeley) for three years, he joined the faculty at Cal-Berkeley as a professor of astronomy, a position he held for more than 25 years. He and his wife, Jessica, have one child.

Basri's early research was concerned with star formation and the T Tauri stars, a class of stars that are younger than the sun and whose core temperatures are too low to sustain hydrogen fusion. In the 1990s, he became one of the first astrophysicists to take up the study of brown dwarfs, also known as failed stars because of their low luminescence. The existence of brown dwarfs was first theorized in the early 1960s, but, because they emit hardly any visible light, it was not until 1995 that a research team, headed by Basri, discovered a young brown dwarf.

Basri's other major research interest involves the magnetic activity of stars. To this end, he has developed many of the theories and methods for the measurement of stellar magnetic fields and for understanding the relation between a star's magnetic activity and its rate of rotation. In 2001, he became a co-investigator on the National Aeronautics and Space Administration's Kepler Mission, which seeks to discover true Earth analogs (planets that have a mass equal to Earth's and that transit a sun-like star in one year). The project will utilize a spaceborne telescope that will watch 100,000 stars continuously for four years. His role in the mission is to determine how stellar activity affects the brightness of stars in such a way that masks our ability to identify the transit of a terrestrial planet.

In 2007, Basri took on the additional duties of vice chancellor for equity and inclusion. One of his duties in this regard is to recruit and retain more minorities to faculty positions and into Cal-Berkeley's graduate programs in science, technology, engineering, and mathematics.

See also: National Aeronautics and Space Administration

REFERENCES AND FURTHER READING
Astronomy Department, the University of California at Berkeley. "Gibor Basri, Professor of Astronomy." [Online article or information; retrieved October 25, 2007.] http://astro.berkeley.edu/~basri/.

Berry, Leonidas H.
(1902–1995) Gastroenterologist

Leonidas Berry was an internationally recognized authority on gastroenterology (the study of the structure and diseases of the digestive organs) and endoscopy (the examination of the body's interior cavities and organs). His important contributions to medical science include the development of the Eder-Berry gastrobiopsyscope and the Berry endoscope.

Berry was born on July 20, 1902, in Woodsdale, North Carolina. His father, Llewellyn, was an African Methodist Episcopal minister, and his mother, Beulah, was a homemaker. As a young boy, he moved with his family to various communities in North Carolina and Virginia, where his father was assigned until 1914, when the family settled in Norfolk, Virginia. After receiving a BS from Wilberforce College (Ohio) in 1924, he entered the University of Chicago's Rush Medical College, earning a second BS in 1925 and an MD in 1930. He interned at Freedmen's Hospital in Washington, D.C., and then returned to Chicago to complete his education by receiving an MS in pathology from the University of Illinois Medical School in 1933. In 1934, he became a junior attending physician at Provident Hospital, Chicago's preeminent medical facility for blacks.

As a young physician, Berry became interested in internal medicine, especially gastroenterology. At the time, however, little was known about how a living digestive tract worked, because very few doctors had seen the insides of one. To solve this problem, in 1932, the German physician Rudolph Schindler developed the first gastroscope. This device consisted of rubberized, semiflexible tubing that contained lenses and a tiny electric light; by sliding it into the stomach via the mouth, an examining physician could observe a living stomach. Berry learned how to operate a gastroscope from Schindler himself, who came to Chicago to teach in 1935. Berry began using the gastroscope to examine the lining of the stomachs of alcoholics to see what sort of damage excessive drinking did to the digestive organs. To his surprise, he found chronic gastritis (the inflammation of the stomach's mucous membrane) in only about one-third of the 100 alcoholics he examined. This finding contradicted the conventional wisdom about alcoholism as a cause of chronic gastritis, and in 1941, he presented his findings in a paper before the American Medical Association. He thus became the first African American to present a paper to that organization, which at the time denied membership to black physicians.

In 1946, Berry became the first black physician on the staff at Michael Reese Hospital as well as the first black internist at Cook County Hospital, both in Chicago; meanwhile, he continued to treat patients and conduct research at Provident. He developed the Eder-Berry gastrobiopsyscope, the first direct vision suction instrument for removing diseased tissue from the stomach for microscopic examination; Berry's version of this device is now on display at the Smithsonian Institution in Washington, D.C. In addition to performing gastroscopic studies of the stomach, he branched out into endoscopy. To this end, he developed the Berry endoscope, essentially a more slender, flexible version of the Schindler gastroscope, which he used to examine the interiors of the abdominal cavity and of the small and large intestines. Berry's two medical inventions contributed to the development by others of such devices as the fiberoptic gastrocamera, a very small camera that can be inserted through the anus or other body cavity in medical examinations; although Berry did not develop this device, he was the first gastroenterologist to use it. He performed many groundbreaking studies concerning the esophagus, bulbar and postbulbar duodenum, proctosigmoid, colon, and peritoneum, and he published much of this work in *Gastrointestinal Pan-Endoscopy* (Springfield, IL: Charles C. Thomas, 1974) and *The Clinical Significance of Gastrointestinal Endoscopy* (1976). He also made a training film for medical students, *The Technic of Gastroscopy*, during the 1960s.

Berry served as president or chief of a number of medical associations. As president of the Cook County Hospital Physicians' Association, he developed a citywide plan for treating young narcotics addicts. Known as the Berry Plan, it called for the establishment of medical counseling clinics for the prevention and follow-up care of young drug users. It was implemented and operated by the Illinois State Department of Health for eight years, with Berry as its coordinator. As head of the African Methodist Episcopal Church's Health Commission, he organized a group of Chicago's African American physicians, nurses, and technicians, known as the Flying Black Medics, to administer to the health needs of the African American community in Cairo, a small community in southern Illinois. As president of the National Medical Association, the national organization of black physicians, from 1965 to 1966, he worked to integrate the nation's medical organizations and institutions such as the American Medical Association and the American Gastroenterological Association.

By 1975, when he retired from the medical profession, Berry had become the chief of endoscopy service and senior attending physician at Cook, as well as the senior attending physician at Reese and Provident. He was married twice, in 1937 to Ophelia Harrison, with whom he had one child and in 1959 to Emma Willis. He died on December 4, 1995, in Chicago. The Leonidas Berry Society on Digestive Diseases and the Leonidas Berry Society for Afro-American Gastroenterologists were named in his honor.

See also: American Medical Association; Freedmen's Hospital; National Medical Association; Provident Hospital and Training School

REFERENCES AND FURTHER READING

Berry, Leonidas H. *I Wouldn't Take Nothin' for My Journey: Two Centuries of an Afro-American Minister's Family.* Chicago: Johnson Publishing, 1981.
National Library of Medicine. "Finding Aid to the Leonidas H. Berry Papers, 1907–1982." [Online article or information; retrieved August 22, 2007.] http://www.nlm.nih.gov/hmd/manuscripts/ead/berry.html.

Bluford, Guion S., Jr.
(1942–) Astronaut

Guion Bluford was the first African American to fly in space. As a mission specialist on two flights and payload commander on two others, he participated in hundreds of scientific experiments in outer space. After retiring from the National Aeronautics and Space Administration (NASA), he became an executive with an aerospace engineering firm, and in this position he oversaw the development of a number of systems and apparatus for NASA.

Bluford was born on November 22, 1942, in Philadelphia. His father, Guion, was a mechanical engineer and his mother, Lolita, was a teacher. As a boy, he developed an interest in flying and science, and so he set out to become an aerospace engineer. After finishing high school, he entered Pennsylvania State University, where he studied aerospace engineering and joined the Air Force Reserve Officer Training Corps, and in 1964, he received a BS and a commission as a second lieutenant. Two years later, he completed his flight training and was sent to Vietnam, where he flew 144 combat missions. Upon returning to the United States, he served as a flight instructor before being sent to the Air Force Institute of Technology at Wright-Patterson Air Force Base in Ohio, where he received an MS and a PhD in aerospace engineering in 1974 and 1978, respectively. While in graduate school, he was also assigned to the USAF Flight Dynamics Laboratory at Wright-Patterson as a staff development engineer specializing in fluid dynamics, and by the time he had received his doctorate, he had become chief of the laboratory's aerodynamics and airframe branch. In 1964, he married Linda Tull, with whom he has two children.

In 1978, Bluford was accepted into NASA's astronaut program, becoming a member of the first class of space shuttle astronauts. He spent the next three and a half years undergoing training as a mission specialist, receiving specialized training in astronomy, aerodynamics, geology, meteorology, computer science, guidance and navigation, and flight medicine. In 1982, he was chosen for the crew of the space shuttle *Challenger*, which was scheduled to fly the following year. The mission, called STS-8 by NASA, lasted from August 30 to September 5, 1983, and as a mission specialist Bluford helped conduct a number of experiments in space. These experiments included the collection of medical information from crew members relative to the biophysiological effects of space flight and the operation of the continuous flow electrophoresis system (CFES). CFES is an advanced technology for separating biomolecules (the biochemical molecules in living things) and detecting the chemical compounds contained in them, thus making it useful as a tool for cancer research and other applications related to molecular biology.

Bluford next flew as a mission specialist in October and November 1985 aboard the *Challenger* (STS-61A), the German D-1 Spacelab mission. This mission was the first shuttle mission dedicated to Spacelab, a compact manned space laboratory, and it was conducted under the direction of the German Aerospace Research Establishment. During the mission, he participated in about half of the 75 experiments performed in Spacelab in such fields as fluid physics, materials processing, life sciences, and navigation.

Bluford's next flight came in April–May 1991 aboard the space shuttle *Discovery* (STS-39), and as payload commander, he oversaw the operation of the AFP-675 payload. This group of experiments obtained far-ultraviolet (FUV) light measurements of Earth's upper atmosphere, the stars of 12 star fields, and *Discovery*'s FUV glow. It also obtained simultaneous spectral and spatial measurements of atmospheric emissions such as the aurora borealis, X-ray data from a number of astronomical targets, and measurements concerning the positive ion and neutral gas composition of the atmospheres of Saturn and its largest moon, Titan. Bluford also oversaw the infrared background

Astronaut Guion Bluford exercises on a treadmill aboard the space shuttle Challenger *in September 1983.* (National Aeronautics and Space Administration)

signature survey experiment, which tested state-of-the-art infrared sensor technology by using infrared sensors to observe from a distance the firing of *Discovery*'s engines. His last flight was in December 1992 aboard the *Discovery* (STS-53). This mission, for which he also served as payload commander, mostly performed classified experiments for the Department of Defense and NASA.

In 1993, Bluford retired from the air force and NASA and went to work as a vice president and general manager of NYMA, Inc.'s engineering services division in Greenbelt, Maryland, which provided support for NASA operations at the Goddard Space Flight Center in Greenbelt. Over the next 10 years, this division became part of other, larger companies, and in 2002, Bluford was working for Northrop Grumman as vice president of the microgravity research and development/operations division of its subsidiary, Logicon. In this capacity, he served as Logicon's program manager for the Microgravity Research, Development and Operations Contract at the NASA Glenn Research Center in Cleveland. Under this contract, Logicon designs, develops, integrates, and provides operational support for the NASA Fluids and Combustion Facility, as well as associated space flight experiment hardware for the International Space Station, where conditions of microgravity prevail.

In addition to his other duties, Bluford has served as a board member of the American Institute of Aeronautics and Astronautics and a member of the National Research Council's Aeronautics and Space Engineering board. His many honors include induction into the International Space Hall of Fame and having a school, Guion Bluford Elementary School in Philadelphia, named after him.

See also: Astronomy and Astrophysics; Cancer; Computer Science; National Aeronautics and Space Administration

REFERENCES AND FURTHER READING

National Aeronautics and Space Administration. "Astronaut Bio: Guion S. Bluford, Jr." [Online article or information; retrieved August 28, 2005.] http://www.jsc.nasa.gov/Bios/htmlbios/bluford-gs.html.

Spangenburg, Ray, and Kit Moser. *African Americans in Science, Math, and Invention.* New York: Facts On File, 2003: 16–18.

Brady, St. Elmo
(1884–1966) Chemist

St. Elmo Brady was the first African American to earn a PhD in chemistry. He conducted groundbreaking research concerning acids and alkaloids, and he contributed to the development of the infrared spectroscopy program at Fisk University.

Brady was born on December 22, 1884, in Louisville, Kentucky. In 1908, he received a BS in chemistry from Fisk University in Nashville, Tennessee, and joined the faculty at Tuskegee Institute (today Tuskegee University). Four years later, he was offered a scholarship to attend the University of Illinois, which he accepted, receiving an MS and a PhD in chemistry in 1914 and 1916, respectively. He then returned to Tuskegee, but left in 1920 to accept a position at Howard University. In 1927, he returned to Fisk to chair the chemistry department, a position he held for the rest of his career.

Brady's early research concerned the relationship between an organic acid's structure (how its atoms and molecules are linked) and its strength. In a related project, he investigated the use of hydrochloric acid as a means of determining the properties of certain alkaloids (naturally occurring compounds produced by plants that have a pharmacological effect on humans, such as caffeine, nicotine, and morphine). At Fisk, he conducted research related to the chemical composition of magnolia seeds and castor beans. This research later helped inspire Percy L. Julian, who conducted extensive research with soybeans, to become a chemist.

As chair of the chemistry department, Brady established the first graduate program in chemistry at a historically black college or university. The curriculum included lectures by famous chemists whom Brady invited to come to Fisk to discuss their latest research. With the assistance of his former professors at Illinois, he instituted a summer program in infrared spectroscopy (the study of atoms and molecules by examining the bands of infrared light they emit). Eventually, this program was taken over by his colleagues in the physics department and developed into the Fisk Infrared Spectroscopy Research Laboratory and the Fisk Infrared Institute, one of the most highly regarded laboratories dedicated to infrared spectroscopy in the world.

In 1952, Brady retired from Fisk to his home in Nashville. He died there in 1966.

See also: Chemistry; Fisk University; Historically Black Colleges and Universities; Howard University; Julian, Percy L.; Tuskegee University

REFERENCES AND FURTHER READING

JustGarciaHill.org. "Brady, St. Elmo, Ph.D., (1884–1966)." [Online article or information; retrieved August 27, 2007.] http://justgarciahill.org/jghdocs/webbiographydtl.asp.

The Faces of Science: African Americans in the Sciences. "St. Elmo Brady." [Online article or information; retrieved August 27, 2007.] https://webfiles.uci.edu/mcbrown/display/brady.html.

Bramwell, Fitzgerald B.
(1945–) Chemist

Fitzgerald Bramwell conducted research concerning some of the more unusual carbon-based molecules. In addition to providing a better understanding of the behavior of such molecules, he helped develop new compounds that have important commercial and industrial applications.

Bramwell was born on May 16, 1945, in Brooklyn, New York. His father, Fitzgerald, was a chemical engineer, and his mother, Lula, was a high school principal. After finishing at Phillips Academy, a well-known college preparatory school in Andover, Massachusetts, he entered Columbia University and received a BS in chemistry in 1966. He completed his graduate studies in chemistry at the University of Michigan, receiving an MS and a PhD in 1967 and 1970, respectively. He worked for a year as a research engineer for the ESSO Research and Engineering Corp. in Linden, New Jersey, before joining the faculty at Brooklyn College, where he remained for the next 24 years. At an unknown date, he married Charlott [sic] Burns, with whom he had four children.

Bramwell's early research focused on aromatic hydrocarbons (molecules consisting of carbon and hydrogen atoms whereby the carbon atoms are arranged in a ring); they are called aromatic because they give off an agreeable odor. As a graduate student, he was particularly interested in corranulene ($C_{20}H_{10}$), a bowl-shaped molecule that was first synthesized at the University of Michigan the year before he arrived, and paracyclophane ($C_{16}H_{16}$), a polymer that becomes highly reactive in the presence of visible light. Later researchers built on his work by discovering a relatively inexpensive way to use corranulene to make buckyballs, spherical carbon molecules that possess tremendous strength and flexibility. His work with ESSO examined the electrical properties of the more mundane hydrocarbons from which petroleum products are manufactured. While at Brooklyn College, he became involved in some of the aromatic hydrocarbon research being conducted at Bell Telephone Laboratories (BTL) in nearby Murray Hill, New Jersey, and he consulted on a BTL project to develop a carbon-based superconductor, a material that conducts electricity with no resistance at extremely low temperatures. Previously, all superconductors had been made from metals; so it was hoped that a superconductor made from organic material would combine the flexibility of a polymer with the electrical conductivity of a metal while also being inexpensive to produce.

Bramwell's later research focused on the synthesis and characterization of organotins (chemical compounds not found in nature that feature at least one bond between an atom of carbon and an atom of tin). The nontoxic organotins are used as stabilizers and catalysts in chemical reactions and as glass coatings, whereas the toxic organotins are used as pesticides and fungicides.

Toward the end of his time at Brooklyn College, Bramwell became more involved in administration, becoming acting dean for research and graduate studies in 1989 and dean of the college in 1990. Five years later, he was named vice president of research and graduate studies at the University of Kentucky (UK). In this position, he focused on patenting much of the research performed at the university, thus making it easier to bring the UK researchers' technology to market. He also assisted more than 20 small, high-tech companies in Kentucky with their start-up plans and forged a research partnership with the U.S. Department of Energy's Argonne National Laboratory, one of the nation's leading facilities for nuclear research. In 2001, he stepped down as vice president to return to teaching. His publications include *Investigations in General Chemistry: Quantitative Techniques and Basic Principles* (1977) and *Basic Laboratory Principles in General Chemistry: with Quantitative Techniques* (1990).

See also: Department of Energy

REFERENCES AND FURTHER READING

Kessler, James H., J. S. Kidd, Renee A. Kidd, and Katherine A. Morin, eds. *Distinguished African American Scientists of the 20th Century*. Phoenix, AZ: Oryx Press, 1996: 16–19.

Krapp, Kristine M., ed. *Notable Black American Scientists*. Detroit, MI: Gale Research, 1999: 41–42.

Spangenburg, Ray, and Kit Moser. *African Americans in Science, Math, and Invention*. New York: Facts On File, 2003: 25–27.

Branson, Herman R.
(1914–1995) Biophysicist

Herman Branson's work spanned the spectrum of physics, chemistry, and biology, but he is best known for his work as a biophysicist. He helped discover that polypeptides (the molecules from which proteins are built) are arranged in helical form, and he contributed to the discovery that sickle cell disease results from a genetic defect.

Branson was born on August 14, 1914, in Pocahontas, Virginia. His father, Harry, was a coal miner, and his mother, Gertrude, was a homemaker. As a boy, he moved with his family to Washington, D.C., where he grew up. He attended the University of Pittsburgh for two years before transferring to Virginia State University, where he received a BS in physics in 1936. He then entered the graduate program at the University of Cincinnati and received a PhD in physics in 1939. After teaching mathematics and physics at Dillard University in New Orleans for two years, in 1941, he joined the faculty at Howard University in Washington, D.C., as a professor of physics and chemistry. That same year, he was named chair of the physics department, a position he held for 27 years. In this capacity, he directed the various physical research projects undertaken at Howard by the Office of Naval Research, the Atomic Energy Commission, and the Research Corporation. At an unknown date, he married Corolynne Gray, with whom he had two children.

In 1948, Branson received a research grant from the National Research Council to work with the eminent chemist Linus C. Pauling at the California Institute of Technology (Caltech). Like Branson, Pauling's early research focused on structural chemistry (the study of how a molecule's bonds affect its operation), but by 1948, he had become more interested in biochemistry (the study of the chemical functions that take place in living organisms). When Branson joined him, Pauling was studying proteins (the complex molecules that are necessary for all biochemical processes) and specifically hemoglobin (the protein-coloring matter in red blood corpuscles that carries oxygen to the tissues). For the next year, Branson and Pauling studied the structural chemistry of hemoglobin, among other proteins. Although Branson returned to his regular duties at Howard in 1949, his year at Caltech helped Pauling develop a deeper understanding of the hemoglobin molecule, and in 1950, shortly after Branson's departure from Caltech, Pauling showed that a genetic deformity in the hemoglobin molecule that hampers its ability to bond with oxygen is the cause of sickle cell disease, a medical condition that is hereditary among African Americans and other people of African descent. The deformity causes the red corpuscles in hemoglobin to assume a sickle-like shape; hence the name of the condition. This discovery, in which Branson played a major supporting role, was the first time that a hereditary disease was explained in terms of a molecule's structural chemistry. It was also one of the reasons why Pauling was awarded the 1954 Nobel Prize in Chemistry.

While at Caltech, Branson also contributed indirectly to the discovery that deoxyribonucleic acid (DNA) molecules take the shape of a double helix. In the course of studying proteins, he, Pauling, and Robert Corey demonstrated that polypeptides (the molecules from which proteins are built) are constructed in the form of an alpha, or single, helix. Based on this discovery, in 1952, Pauling proposed that DNA molecules are shaped like triple helixes. This theory was quickly shown to be wrong, but it nevertheless inspired James D. Watson and Francis Crick to develop, in 1953, the double-helix model of DNA.

Branson's research following his Caltech days mostly involved biophysics, particularly the connections between mathematics, which is the language of physics, and biology. To this end, he developed an integral equation of biological systems while introducing information theory (which is concerned with the content and transmission of communications and the storage and retrieval of information in computers) to the study of biological molecules. He also did some work concerning the use of radioactive and stable isotopes in transport studies in biology.

In 1968, Branson accepted the presidency of Central State University in Wilberforce, Ohio. He left after two years to assume the presidency of Lincoln University, near Philadelphia, and he held this position until his retirement in 1985. From 1975 to 1985, he served as a member of the National Research Council. He spent his retirement in Washington, D.C., where he died on June 7, 1995. In 2004, the National Society of Black Physicists began sponsoring the Herman R. Branson Summer Mini-Course in Biophysics at Hampton University (Virginia). Named in Branson's honor, the course aims to encourage minority students to consider careers in biophysics, and it targets junior and senior undergraduate students in the quantitative sciences, mathematics, and biology.

See also: Biology; Central State University; Chemistry; Howard University; physics; Virginia State University

REFERENCES AND FURTHER READING

Physicists of the African Diaspora. "Herman Branson." [Online article or information; retrieved September 3, 2005.] http://www.math.buffalo.edu/mad/physics/branson_herman.html.

Spangenburg, Ray, and Kit Moser. *African Americans in Science, Math, and Invention*. New York: Facts On File, 2003: 27.

Bromery, Randolph W.
(1926–) Geophysicist

Randolph Bromery was a leading expert in using magnetic detection and radiometrics to identify possible sites of valuable mineral deposits. He also served for a number of years as a college administrator.

Bromery was born on January 18, 1926, in Cumberland, Maryland. His father, Lawrence, was a dining room supervisor, and his mother, Edith, ran a catering service. After finishing high school in 1942, he moved to Detroit and went to work as a tool and die maker in an automobile factory. Shortly thereafter he enlisted in the U.S. Army and served during World War II in the Army Air Corps' Tuskegee Airmen. In 1946, he entered the University of Michigan, transferring a year later to Howard University, where he majored in mathematics. A dispute involving four credits in physical education prevented him from receiving his BS degree in 1948, the year after he married Cecile Trescott, with whom he had five children. Nevertheless, because of his mathematical background and flying experience, he was able to land a job as an exploration geophysicist with the U.S. Geological Survey's (USGS) newly established Airborne Geophysics Group.

During his early days with USGS, Bromery helped develop more than 140 aeromagnetic maps of the Eastern United States from Maine to Virginia. The data for these maps was collected from airplanes carrying sophisticated magnetic detection equipment. Later, in the laboratory, researchers could identify the types of rocks underlying the soil by quantifying the differences in their magnetic material. Once the rocks were so identified, a researcher could study an aeromagnetic map and make educated guesses about where and how large deposits of previously unknown minerals might be. In the 1950s, he began using radiometrics, the measurement of radioactive material, as a means of identifying previously unknown deposits of uranium and other fissionable material in the western United States. In the 1960s, he performed a geologic sketch of northwestern Oregon and an airborne magnetometer survey of Southern California, and he traveled to Africa under the auspices of the U.S. Agency for International Development to make airborne geophysical surveys of Liberia and Nigeria.

Meanwhile, Bromery was able to work out the dispute with Howard concerning his BS degree in mathematics, which he received in 1956. He also enrolled in graduate school, receiving an MS in geology from American University in 1962 and a PhD in geology from Johns Hopkins University in 1968. His doctoral dissertation studied the possible routes for a high-speed rail line between Boston and Washington, and his recommendations informed the decision-making process used by Amtrak officials to construct their main line in the Northeast Corridor.

In 1967, Bromery left USGS to join the faculty at the University of Massachusetts (U. Mass.) as a professor of geology; he was named department chair two years later. In addition to his teaching duties, he cofounded the Weston Geophysical Corporation, a consulting firm that specializes in seismic nuclear test monitoring, and Geoscience Engineering Corporation, today part of ENSR International, a global environmental consulting and engineering firm, and he worked as a mineral location consultant to Exxon and Kennecott Copper.

In 1988, Bromery left teaching and consulting to become a full-time college administrator. In fact, he had gotten involved in this area at U. Mass., where he held a number of administrative posts, including chancellor, but at this point, he took the post of acting president of Westfield State College (Massachusetts). Two years later, he was named chancellor of the Massachusetts State Board of Regents of Higher Education, and in 1992, he was named president of Springfield College (Massachusetts). He stepped down in 1998 but later took over as president of Roxbury Community College. Bromery's many honors include election to a term as president of the Geological Society of America. In 2003, he retired to his home in Amherst, Massachusetts.

See also: Howard University

REFERENCES AND FURTHER READING

Kessler, James H., J. S. Kidd, Renee A. Kidd, and Katherine A. Morin, eds. *Distinguished African American Scientists of the 20th Century.* Pheonix, AZ: Oryx Press, 1996: 22–27.

Krapp, Kristine M., ed. *Notable Black American Scientists.* Detroit, MI: Gale Research, 1999: 43–45.

Spangenburg, Ray, and Kit Moser. *African Americans in Science, Math, and Invention.* New York: Facts On File, 2003: 28.

Brooks, Carolyn B.
(1946–) Microbiologist

Carolyn Brooks conducted innovative research on how certain bacteria contribute to plant growth. She also experimented with ways to make plants more resistant to insects by exposing them to bacterial infections.

Brooks was born Carolyn Branch on July 8, 1946, in Richmond, Virginia. Her father, Charles, was a truck driver, and her mother, Shirley, was a store clerk. She became interested in microbiology after meeting a microbiologist during a summer science program for black students at Richmond's Virginia Union University. After receiving a BS and an MS in biology in 1968 and 1971, respectively, she entered the graduate program at Ohio State University and received a PhD in microbiology in 1977. She spent the next four years teaching at Kentucky State University (KSU) before joining the faculty at the University of Maryland Eastern Shore (UMES), where she eventually became program coordinator of the plant and soil science group, codirector of the Center for Plant and Microbial Biotechnology, and dean of the school of agriculture and natural sciences. In 1966, she married Henry Brooks, with whom she had three children.

Brooks focused her early research on the microbiology of mammals. As a graduate student, she studied the T-cells (the white blood cells that attack and kill foreign antigens), which the body employs against *plasmodium*, the protozoans that cause malaria. She identified the specific chemical coding on the cell walls of plasmodium to which antimalarial T-cells are attracted, as well as the chemicals that the T-cells use to kill plasmodium by dissolving its cell wall. At KSU, she investigated whether the levels of certain essential minerals, such as iron and potassium, found in a strand of hair were indicative of the levels of these minerals throughout the rest of the organism.

At UMES, Brooks shifted the focus of her research to the relationship between microbiology and agriculture. She was particularly interested in the symbiotic relationship between specific types of soil bacteria and specific types of legumes (the plant family that includes peas and beans). In such a relationship, the bacteria form colonies in the outer layer of the roots of the legume, causing the roots to swell and form small blisters. The bacteria in these blisters absorb nitrogen from the air; as they process the nitrogen into other biochemical compounds, the legume ends up absorbing additional nitrogen, thus increasing its ability to manufacture the amino acids it needs to grow. After coming to understand how this relationship works for a specific legume, a species of African groundnut, she then sought ways to enhance the ability of nonlegumes, such as corn and wheat, to attract nitrogen-fixing bacteria. Meanwhile, she traveled extensively to the African nations of Togo, Senegal, and Cameroon, where her groundnut thrives, to help local agronomists and agricultural specialists increase the beneficial activity of nitrogen-fixing soil bacteria in the groundnut and other legumes.

Another interesting project undertaken by Brooks involves increasing the resistance of crops to insects. Since a plant species' resistance to insects is governed by genetics, the usual way to achieve such resistance is through genetic engineering (the process by which a specific gene is separated from one organism and implanted into another). Brooks, however, began investigating whether enhanced insect resistance could be imparted to a plant through the colonization of certain bacteria, which would then infect the host plant in such a way as to make it unattractive to certain insects.

In addition to her other activities, Brooks participated in an initiative by the U.S. Agency for International Development and the Department of Agriculture to strengthen research ties between U.S. and African universities.

See also: Kentucky State University; Microbiology; University of Maryland Eastern Shore

REFERENCES AND FURTHER READING

Kessler, James H., J. S. Kidd, Renee A. Kidd, and Katherine A. Morin, eds. *Distinguished African American Scientists of the 20th Century.* Phoenix, AZ: Oryx Press, 1996: 27–31.

Krapp, Kristine M., ed. *Notable Black American Scientists.* Detroit, MI: Gale Research, 1999: 45.

Spangenburg, Ray, and Kit Moser. *African Americans in Science, Math, and Invention.* New York: Facts On File, 2003: 28–30.

Buggs, Charles W.
(1906–1991) Microbiologist

Charles Buggs made some of the earliest studies regarding the ability of bacteria to develop resistance to antibiotic drugs. He also played a leading role in the development of medical education programs at the Charles R. Drew University of Medicine and Science, where he is known today as the Father of Allied Health.

Buggs was born on August 6, 1906, in Brunswick, Georgia, to John and Leonora Buggs. In 1928, he received a BS in zoology from Morehouse College in Atlanta. After teaching biology at Dover State College (Delaware) for a year, he entered the graduate program at the University of Chicago but was forced to leave almost immediately for financial reasons. He taught for another year, this time at a high school in Key West, Florida, before entering the University of Minnesota, where he received an MS and a PhD in zoology in 1931 and 1934, respectively. He then taught chemistry for a year at Bishop College in Mobile, Alabama, before joining the faculty at Dillard University in New Orleans, Louisiana, as a professor of biology and chair of the natural sciences division. In 1943, he took a teaching position at Wayne State University School of Medicine in Detroit, but he returned to Dillard six years later. In 1956, he left Dillard again, this time for Howard University in Washington, D.C., where he taught microbiology for the next 15 years. At an unknown date he married Maggie Bennett, with whom he had one child.

As a graduate student, Buggs became interested in bacteriology. One of his earliest studies concerned the efficacy of electrophoresis (a process whereby particles are suspended in a fluid that is subjected to the influence of an electric field) as a means of killing or retarding the growth of two common strains of bacteria, *Escherichia coli* and *Staphylococcus aureus*. This study led naturally to an interest in antibiotic drugs (pharmaceutical drugs that can kill or retard the growth of bacteria and other microbes). In 1940, Selman A. Waksman developed one of the first antibiotics, actinomycin, from the secretions of a strain of bacteria found in soil. Actinomycin proved to be too strong to administer to humans, however; so three years later Waksman developed another antibiotic, streptomycin, from another strain of soil bacteria. Streptomycin proved to be an effective treatment for a number of bacterial infections, but Buggs soon discovered that certain types of bacteria built up resistance to streptomycin so that it is no longer an effective treatment for the infections they cause. He published his work on this subject in a 1947 article in the *Journal of the National Medical Association*. This article made the medical community aware of the limitations of the earliest antibiotics and led to the development of new antibiotics for killing highly resistant bacteria. He also demonstrated that penicillin, an antibiotic developed in 1928, had an effect on the ability of a skin graft to take, and he studied the value of using pharmaceutical drugs to speed up the setting of bone fractures.

Buggs also made two important contributions to science education, particularly the improvement of medical education for blacks. Concerned that the nation was not producing enough black physicians and other medical specialists at a time when most African Americans relied on black physicians to treat them, in the late 1940s, he surveyed the state of premedical education at the leading black colleges and made a number of recommendations concerning ways to improve their premedical programs. These findings and recommendations were published in his book, *Premedical Education for Negroes: Interpretations and Recommendations Based Upon a Survey in Fifteen Selected Negro Colleges* (1949), which eventually led to increased federal funding for black premedical education. In 1969, while still teaching at Howard, he became a project director for the Charles R. Drew Postgraduate Medical School at the University of California at Los Angeles (today the Charles R. Drew University of Medicine and Science), a medical school located in inner-city Los Angeles so that it could better serve the medical education needs of minorities. In 1971, he left Howard to be the dean of Drew's College of Allied Health. In this capacity, he pioneered the development of Drew's allied health programs, which today provide training for such fields as health information technology, nuclear medicine technology, urban public health, pharmacy technology, physicians' assistant, radiography, and substance abuse counseling. While at Drew, he also taught microbiology at the California State University at Long Beach.

Buggs retired in 1981. He died on September 13, 1991.

See also: Charles R. Drew University of Medicine and Science; Howard University; Medical Education for Blacks; Microbiology

REFERENCES AND FURTHER READING

Salzman, Jack, David Lionel Smith, and Cornel West, eds. *Encyclopedia of African American Culture and History*. New York: MacMillan, 1996: 467.

Spangenburg, Ray, and Kit Moser. *African Americans in Science, Math, and Invention*. New York: Facts On File, 2003: 32–33.

Carruthers, George R.
(1939–) Astrophysicist

George Carruthers is a pioneer in the study of ultraviolet (UV) radiation as a means of learning more about the Earth's outer atmosphere and heavenly bodies in deep space. His most important contribution in this regard was the invention of the far-ultraviolet camera/spectrograph, which permitted astrophysicists to see farther into deep space than they had ever seen before.

Carruthers was born on October 1, 1939, in Cincinnati. His father, George, was a civil engineer, and his mother, Sophia, was a homemaker. As a boy, he developed a strong interest in astronomy, and at age 10, he built his own telescope from cardboard tubing and lenses he had ordered through the mail. His father died when he was 12, after which he moved with his mother to Chicago, where he grew up. He studied physics at the University of Illinois at Champaign-Urbana and received a BS in aeronautical engineering in 1961, an MS in nuclear engineering in 1962, and a PhD in aeronautical and astronautical engineering in 1964. In 1964, he went to work as a research physicist for the Space Science Division of the Naval Research Laboratory (NRL) in Washington, D.C., where he has spent the rest of his career. In 1973, he married Sarah Redhead.

Carruthers's research at NRL focuses on ultraviolet (UV) astronomy. Astronomers are able to see deep into outer space by examining the various frequencies of electromagnetic radiation that all heavenly bodies emit, and Carruthers chose to concentrate on examining UV radiation. On the spectrum of electromagnetic radiation, the UV band lies between the visible light and the X-ray bands. Studying UV emissions is the best way to study very hot heavenly bodies, such as stars that burn much hotter than the sun. Although the human eye cannot detect UV radiation, special devices known as spectroscopes, spectrometers, and spectrographs can, and the data they collect can be translated into a form that can be studied and interpreted by an astronomer.

To facilitate the collection of such data, in 1969, Carruthers invented an image converter for detecting UV radiation. This device employed a windowless tube with a solid photocathode and an internal mirror for converting UV radiation to visible light. This device revolutionized how scientists studied UV emissions, and for inventing it, Carruthers received a patent and a number of prestigious awards, including election to the National Inventors Hall of Fame.

The problem with studying UV emissions from Earth is that the Earth's atmosphere absorbs most of the UV emissions that reach it. Carruthers overcame this problem, however, by conceiving of the far-ultraviolet camera/spectrograph and then leading the research team that designed it, built it, and

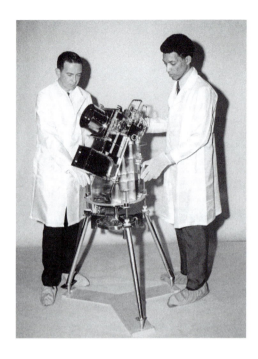

Dr. George Carruthers, right, and William Conway, project manager at the Naval Research Institute, examine the lunar surface far-ultraviolet camera spectrograph. (U.S. Naval Research Laboratory)

developed the procedures for deploying and operating it on the moon. In effect, the far-ultraviolet camera/spectrograph turned the moon into a deep space observatory that is not affected by the distortions created by the Earth's atmosphere. The device, a gold-plated apparatus weighing 50 pounds, was placed on the moon by the crew of *Apollo 16* in 1972. By the end of the mission it had transmitted back to Earth hundreds of images of the Earth's atmosphere and geocorona (the set of concentric circles of light that surround the planet), along with images of newly discovered stars and nebulas in the Milky Way and deep space.

Because of the success of the far-ultraviolet camera/spectrograph, Carruthers was able to design and implement other far-UV experiments, at first as an experiment's principal investigator and, beginning in 1982, as the head of the Space Science Division's Ultraviolet Measurements Group. These experiments were carried aloft by a variety of manned and unmanned spacecraft, including several space shuttle missions and *Skylab 4* in 1974. They provided the first global images of Earth's ionosphere, the outermost layer of the atmosphere, and of the UV glow that is emitted by that portion of Earth that is turned away from the Sun. They also collected huge amounts of data concerning stars, nebulas, comets, and other heavenly bodies. Much of this data was collected by electronic telescopes that transform UV radiation into electrical signals that are relayed to Earth and televised.

One of the most exciting discoveries made by Carruthers's experiments involved the detection and measurement of a number of common elements such as hydrogen, oxygen, nitrogen, and carbon in their cool, unexcited states in deep space. The discovery of these elements allowed astrophysicists to obtain more accurate information concerning the chemical composition of interstellar gases and planetary atmospheres and to measure the energy output of very hot stars. The study of UV radiation also gave scientists a new tool for examining certain expanses of the Earth's atmosphere for concentrated pollutants.

In addition to his duties at NRL, Carruthers has served on a number of advisory panels and boards for the National Aeronautics and Space Administration (NASA). He has also played an active role in the National Technical Association (NTA). NTA is a professional association of scientists and engineers committed to ensuring that minorities, women, and youth have the skills needed for a scientific or technological career, and Carruthers served as editor of the *Journal of the National Technical Association* and *NTA Newsletter*. In this same vein, he was the technical editor for *Careers in Science and Technology* (1993), a publication issued jointly by NTA, NASA, and the Department of Energy.

See also: Astronomy and Astrophysics; Department of Energy; National Aeronautics and Space Administration

REFERENCES AND FURTHER READING

Sammons, Vivian Ovelton. *Blacks in Science and Medicine.* New York: Hemisphere Publishing, 1990: 49.

Spangenburg, Ray, and Kit Moser. *African Americans in Science, Math, and Invention.* New York: Facts On File, 2003: 37–38.

Carson, Benjamin S.
(1951–) Pediatric Neurosurgeon

Ben Carson served as the principal surgeon for two of the most remarkable operations in the history of Siamese twins. In the process, he developed several groundbreaking surgical techniques and helped perfect state-of-the-art surgical technology.

Carson was born on September 8, 1951, in Detroit. His father, Robert, abandoned the family when Ben was 8 years old, and his mother, Sonya, supported the family by working at several jobs. As a boy, he decided to become a physician, and after winning a scholarship, he received a BS in psychology from Yale University in 1973 and then entered the University of Michigan Medical School with the intention of becoming a psychiatrist. While a medical student, however, he developed a strong interest in neurosurgery, and, after receiving an MD in 1977, he completed his internship and residency in neurosurgery at Johns Hopkins Hospital in Baltimore. After working for a year as the senior neurosurgical resident at the Sir Charles Gardiner Hospital in Perth, Australia, in 1984, he returned to Johns Hopkins as director of pediatric neurosurgery, thus becoming the youngest person in the nation to hold such a position. In addition to his duties as director, he teaches neurosurgery, oncology, plastic surgery, and pediatrics at Johns Hopkins. In 1975, he married Candy Rustin, with whom he has three children.

Carson's first major contribution was to revive the hemispherectomy as a viable procedure for children who suffer from conditions such as Rasmussen's encephalitis, which cause severe seizures. A hemispherectomy involves removing one hemisphere, or half, of the brain, a procedure that normally would be fatal for an adult. A child, however, can recover from the operation without any deleterious side effects, because its brain is still developing and so the remaining hemisphere can easily take on the duties of the removed hemisphere. The performance of hemispherectomies had been abandoned due to the unacceptably high mortality rate, but Carson developed techniques that made the procedure safe and effective. He performed his first hemispherectomy in 1985 on a 4-year-old girl named Maranda Francisco, who had been having up to 100 severe seizures per day since she was 18 months old. Carson also developed a number of radical techniques for performing craniofacial reconstruction following brain surgery and pediatric neuro-oncology (the removal of brain tumors from children).

Carson achieved international fame in 1987, when he served as the principal surgeon for the procedure that separated Patrick and Benjamin Binder, two 7-month-old Siamese twins from Germany. This operation was complicated by the fact that the Binders were occipital craniopagus twins, meaning they were born joined at the back of the head. Further complicating the issue was the fact that the Binders also shared the sagittal superior sinus, the major blood drainage system of the brain. Prior to Carson's efforts, every operation to separate occipital craniopagus twins had failed, because one or both twins had died. Nevertheless, Carson put together a surgical team of 70 specialists and assistants, which tried to ensure success by developing a number of groundbreaking procedures such as circulatory bypass, induced hypothermia, and deliberate cardiac arrest to preserve brain function during the 22-hour-long operation. Although the twins suffered severe neurological damage, the operation enabled each Binder twin to survive on his own.

In 1997, Carson built on this success by leading the South African Zambian team that separated two 11-month-old Zambian boys, Luka and Joseph Banda, at South Africa's Ga-Rankuwa Hospital. The Bandas were type–2 vertical craniopagus twins, meaning they were joined together at the top of the head but facing opposite directions. As with the Binders, such an operation had never been performed successfully, but Carson oversaw its successful completion, and this time without any apparent neurological damage to either twin. He prepared for the operation by using a three-dimensional computerized model of the twins' brains to conduct mock surgeries. Although the boys shared no gray matter, they did share a number of blood vessels, so Carson's toughest problem involved what to do with these blood vessels. Fortunately, the model allowed him to sever and reconnect the blood vessels in several ways, thus optimizing his ability to predict which reconnection would work best for each twin.

Following the success of the Banda operation, which lasted 28 hours, Carson felt compelled to take some time off from neurosurgery and travel the country instead. He spent much of his time talking to children from underprivileged backgrounds, like his own, in an effort to help such youngsters achieve the sort of success he had achieved. To this end, he also wrote two books, *Think Big: Unleashing Your Potential for Excellence* (Grand Rapids, MI: Zondervan, 1992) and *The Big Picture: Getting Perspective on What's Really Important in Life* (Grand Rapids, MI: Zondervan, 1999), in addition to an autobiography, *Gifted Hands* (Grand Rapids, MI: Zondervan, 1990).

REFERENCES AND FURTHER READING

Carson, Ben. "Mini-Biography." [Online article or information; retrieved September 9, 2005.] http://www.drbencarson.com/snapshot.html.

Carson, Ben, and Cecil B. Murphey. *Gifted Hands: The Ben Carson Story*. Grand Rapids, MI: Zondervan, 1990.

Johns Hopkins Medicine. "Hopkins Neurosurgeon Separates Zambian Siamese Twins, Practiced with 3-D 'Workbench.'" [Online article or information; retrieved October 30, 2007.] http://www.hopkinsmedicine.org/press/1998/JANUARY/980115.HTM.

Carver, George Washington
(ca. 1860–1943) Botanist

In the late 19th and early 20th centuries, many Southern farmers lived lives of quiet desperation. By focusing their farming activities on the production of cotton, they did not grow enough food to eat; so when their crops failed or the market for cotton was glutted, they often went hungry. George Washington Carver concentrated his scientific research on helping Southern farmers become economically self-sufficient by showing them how to grow inexpensive vegetables that could be prepared into nourishing meals. He is best known for his work with the peanut, but his work with other legumes is equally impressive.

Carver was born into slavery sometime around 1860 on a farm in Diamond, Missouri. For the first five years of his life, his legal name was simply George. His mother, Mary, was a slave owned by Moses and Susan Carver. The identity of his father remains unknown, but he was probably a slave on a nearby farm who may have died shortly before George was born. The Carver farm was raided during the Civil War, and George and his mother were kidnapped and taken to Arkansas. The Carvers were unable to get his mother back, but they did pay a ransom for George. From that point on, the Carvers raised George as if he were their own son, and, when he was freed after the war, he took the last name Carver as a sign of his gratitude.

In 1877, Carver moved to Neosho, Missouri, where there was a public school for blacks. After learning as much there as he could, in 1879, he moved to Kansas, earning a living as a laundryman and cook while attending school in several Kansas towns such as Minneapolis, which allowed blacks to attend the local high school. At some point, he met another black man named George Carver; so to keep from being confused with that man he took the middle name "Washington." In 1884, he graduated from high school and was accepted into Highland College (Kansas), but, when he showed up to enroll, he was turned away because of his race. So, instead of going to college, he spent the next six years drifting across Kansas, working variously as a wheat farmer and laundryman.

In 1890, Carver learned that Simpson College in Indianola, Iowa, accepted black students; he applied and was admitted. Two years later, he transferred from Simpson to Iowa State College, where he studied horticulture and botany, subjects that had fascinated him ever since he was a little boy. He received a BS and an MS in 1894 and 1896, respectively; while a graduate student, he also taught freshman horticulture and managed the school's greenhouse, where he began experimenting with the development of hybrid plants.

In 1896, Carver was recruited by Booker T. Washington to be the head of the agriculture department at Washington's college for blacks, the Tuskegee Institute in Tuskegee, Alabama (today Tuskegee University). Almost immediately, Carver became aware of the desperate situation of many of Alabama's farmers, white and black. Their biggest problem was that they relied almost exclusively on growing cotton. Unfortunately, cotton had been grown on the same fields for so long that it had leached most of the nutrients, especially nitrogen, from the soil. To make matters worse, most farms were too small to grow lots of cotton as well as enough food for a farm family to eat. Farmers counted on producing a bumper crop of cotton each year, but, since they could not afford fertilizer, the crop was normally poor. Add to this the effect of the boll weevil, an insect that destroyed millions of pounds of cotton each year by infesting the cotton bolls before they were ready to be picked, and it is easy to see why many Southern farm families went hungry.

Confronted with this serious situation, Carver began looking for ways to help Southern farmers farm scientifically and thus improve their lives. First, he encouraged farmers to grow more food, especially crops that were nutritious and cheap to grow. By 1900, he was showing farmers how to raise a con-

Botanist George Washington Carver developed better methods for growing sweet potatoes, black-eyed peas, and peanuts, as well as hundreds of ways to use them. (Library of Congress)

siderable amount of sweet potatoes on a small plot of marginal soil, as well as how to prepare sweet potatoes into staples such as flour, sugar, and bread. He also showed farmers how to raise more pork on less money by feeding their hogs acorns, which grew wild in Southern forests, rather than expensive cornmeal. To educate farmers about these and other developments, Carver distributed pamphlets and established a traveling demonstration school. Staffed by his Tuskegee students, the wagon toured the South showing farmers how to raise more while spending less.

Carver's next step was to help Southern farmers reclaim land that had been impoverished by the overproduction of cotton. In 1902, he discovered that rotating a field between cotton one year and black-eyed peas the next completely restored the nitrogen that cotton leached from the soil, thus eliminating the need for expensive fertilizer. Then he developed more than 40 recipes for converting black-eyed peas into inexpensive food items such as pancakes, pudding, and croquettes.

Of course, Carver is best known for his work with peanuts, a wild legume that most Southern farmers simply ignored. Around 1903, Carver realized that peanuts, which are related to black-eyed peas, could also restore nitrogen to the soil, and he urged farmers to grow them in addition to black-eyed peas. Before long, Southern farmers were producing bumper crops of peanuts; so Carver set out to develop new uses for them. He quickly discovered that peanuts are full of vegetable oil, and that the oil is easily extracted and made into a variety of products. By 1916, he had developed more than 100 different products from peanut oil, including cheese, facial creams, printer's ink, medicine, shampoo, soap, vinegar, and wood stain. Further investigation showed that roasted peanuts could be ground into a smooth, creamy butter that contains more protein than butter made from corn oil and that lasts longer than dairy butter. By the 1920s, people across the United States had discovered that peanut butter spread on a slice of bread was a delicious, nutritious, and inexpensive snack.

Lastly, Carver decided to do something about the boll weevil. While at Iowa State, he had developed a number of successful hybrid plants, and so he set out to produce a strain of cotton that was resistant to the boll weevil. In 1915, he developed a hybrid cotton plant that matures quicker than other cotton plants so that its bolls, or cotton pods, can be harvested before the boll weevil has time to infest them. This plant, known today as Carver's Hybrid, did not rid the South of the boll weevil problem, but it did reduce it significantly.

Carver spent his entire professional career at Tuskegee. He died there, having never married, on January 5, 1943. He left his small savings to the school to fund research in agricultural chemistry. One offshoot of Carver's gift is the George Washington Carver Research Foundation (Carver Research Foundation), an important source of money for scientific research by African Americans.

See also: Carver Research Foundation; Tuskegee University

REFERENCES AND FURTHER READING

Carey, Charles W. Jr. *American Scientists*. New York: Facts On File, 2005: 53–55.

Gates, Henry L., and Cornel West. *The African-American Century: How Black Americans Have Shaped Our Country*. New York: Free Press, 2000.

McMurry, Linda O. *George Washington Carver: Scientist and Symbol*. Norwalk, CT: Easton Press, 1994.

Spangenburg, Ray, and Kit Moser. *African Americans in Science, Math, and Invention*. New York: Facts On File, 2003: 38–40.

Tiner, John H. *100 Scientists Who Shaped World History*. San Mateo, CA: Bluewood Books, 2000.

Chappelle, Emmett W.
(1925–) Biochemist

Emmett Chappelle's career is a perfect example of how research originally conducted for purposes of space exploration can ultimately have an even more important impact on Earth. Chappelle originally focused his research on detecting life in outer space, but he also adapted his work so that it had a number of important applications for everyday life.

Chappelle was born on October 24, 1925, in Phoenix. His parents were cotton and dairy farmers. In 1942, he graduated from high school and joined the U.S. Army; assigned to the infantry, he fought in Italy during World War II. In 1946, he returned to the United States and enrolled in Phoenix College,

Biochemist Emmett Chappelle developed methods for detecting life in outer space. (National Aeronautics and Space Administration)

receiving an AA in electrical engineering two years later. He then entered the University of California at Berkeley and received a BS in biochemistry in 1950. After teaching biochemistry at Meharry Medical College in Nashville, Tennessee, for two years, he decided to complete his education, receiving an MS in biochemistry from the University of Washington in 1954 and a PhD in biochemistry from Stanford University in 1958. He then went to work as a staff scientist for the Martin Marietta Corporation's Research Institute for Advanced Studies in Baltimore, leaving after five years to become a senior biochemist at Hazelton Laboratories in Falls Church, Virginia. In 1966, he joined the research staff at the National Aeronautics and Space Administration's (NASA) Goddard Space Flight Center in Greenbelt, Maryland, where he spent the rest of his career.

Chappelle's early NASA research involved exobiology (the search for possible life-forms on other planets). To this end, he became interested in astrochemistry, specifically the detection of adenosine triphosphate (ATP), the chemical compound that fuels all cellular activity, as a possible indicator of extraterrestrial life. Having designed and fabricated an instrument for detecting ATP, he began thinking of ways to use it to identify the presence of extraterrestrial bacteria, one of the simplest and hardiest forms of life. Meanwhile, in the late 1960s, he began experimenting with the firefly bioluminescence reaction as a way to detect and count bacteria rapidly. Fireflies produce light by means of a chemical reaction consisting of a chemical compound known as luciferin, the enzyme luciferase, ATP, and oxygen. When these four components are combined, light is produced. One offshoot of this project was the development, in 1975, by Chappelle and Grace Picciolo, of techniques that are still widely used on Earth to detect the bacteria in urine, blood, spinal fluids, drinking water, and foods.

The success of his research with firefly bioluminescence led Chappelle to study other forms of luminescence (chemically produced light) as ways to detect life. In the late 1970s, his efforts were devoted to developing methods for detecting various forms of living vegetative matter in outer space by measuring, from space-borne sensing devices, laser-induced fluorescence (LIF, the optical emission from molecules that have been excited to higher energy levels by absorbing the electromagnetic radiation generated by a laser). Compared to other methods of studying a substance's electronic structure, fluorescence detection is more sensitive because the fluorescence signal has a very low background, thus greatly reducing signal interference or even avoiding it altogether.

By 1985, Chappelle had begun to adapt the techniques of LIF so that they could be used for terrestrial and oceanographic applications. Specifically, he collaborated with scientists at the Beltsville (Maryland) Agricultural Research Center to adapt the techniques of LIF so that it could gauge via airborne monitoring devices the growth of healthy crops while measuring the stress they experience. In 1985, he published his findings concerning the LIF frequency signatures of five major plant types. Six years later, he identified the pigment responsible for the blue fluorescence band in the LIF frequencies of green plants and began exploring the potential for using this band to estimate remotely their various rates of photosynthesis. In 1999, he collaborated with the U.S. Geological Survey on a project to use LIF to monitor how changes in global climatic patterns affect submerged aquatic vegetation along the Gulf Coast from Brownsville, Texas, to St. Petersburg, Florida.

In 2001, Chappelle retired to his home in Baltimore.

See also: Meharry Medical College; National Aeronautics and Space Administration

REFERENCES AND FURTHER READING

Kessler, James H., J. S. Kidd, Renee A. Kidd, and Katherine A. Morin, eds. *Distinguished African American Scientists of the 20th Century*. Phoenix, AZ: Oryx Press, 1996: 46–49.

Spangenburg, Ray, and Kit Moser. *African Americans in Science, Math, and Invention*. New York: Facts On File, 2003: 42–43.

Clark, Mamie P.
(1917–1983) Psychologist

Mamie Clark is best remembered for her work on the negative self-image of black children as a result of segregation and racism. Her research in this regard was presented before the U.S. Supreme Court as expert testimony during the landmark case *Brown v. Board of Education* [347 U.S. 483 (1954)], which marked the beginning of the end of segregated public schools.

Clark was born Mamie Phipps on October 18, 1917, in Hot Springs, Arkansas. Her father, Harold, was a physician, and her mother, Katie, was a homemaker. At age 17, she entered Howard University with the intention of becoming a mathematician, but she soon changed her major to psychology, receiving a BS in 1938 and an MS in 1939.

Clark began her groundbreaking research while a graduate student at Howard. She had come in contact with Ruth and Gene Horowitz (they later changed their last name to Hartley), two Columbia researchers who were studying self-identification with preschool children. With their assistance and encouragement, she established a similar study in an all-black nursery school in Washington, D.C. Using a coloring test and a doll test of her own device, she determined that black children become aware of their racial identity around three years of age and that awareness initiates a perception of inferiority in the child. She presented her findings to the academic community in her master's thesis, "The Development of Consciousness of Self in Negro Pre-School Children."

At this point, Clark's husband, Kenneth, whom she had married in 1937, and with whom she would have two children, became interested in her work, and together they pursued her line of inquiry further. By 1946, they had compiled irrefutable evidence that the racial self-identification of black children and the negative self-image that it engenders were caused by society's negative views toward blacks, which were manifested in the form of segregation. These findings were presented by Kenneth Clark before the various state courts in the proceedings leading up to *Brown v. Board* and again before the Supreme Court in 1954. These findings influenced the Court profoundly, which eventually ruled unanimously that segregated public schools were inherently unequal to black students and therefore unconstitutional.

Meanwhile, Clark had continued her studies in developmental psychology at Columbia University, receiving a PhD in 1944. She spent the next two years working as a research psychologist for the American Public Health Institute and the U.S. Armed Forces Institute, and in 1946, she became the psychologist at the Riverdale Home for Children, in essence an orphanage for black girls. That same year, she cofounded the Northside Testing and Consultation Center (later

Psychologist Mamie Phipps Clark and her husband, Kenneth, influenced the Supreme Court's decision in Brown v. Board *by showing that segregated schools cause African American children to develop negative self-images.* (Library of Congress)

the Northside Center for Child Development), a child guidance center in Harlem, and served as its executive director for the next 33 years.

Northside had originally been established as a means of providing psychiatric and psychological services to poor black youths who were being underserved by the state and local governments. But in the course of delivering these services, Clark realized that a high degree of educational retardation existed in the black community that was not being addressed by the public school system. To remedy this defect, she began offering remedial classes in reading and arithmetic to students who had been placed erroneously in tracks for students who were mentally retarded. In many cases, the extra tutoring that Northside provided completely erased all signs of what had been interpreted as mental retardation.

Clark retired in 1979, although she continued to remain active in a variety of community affairs. She died on August 11, 1983.

See also: Howard University

REFERENCES AND FURTHER READING
Warren, Wini. *Black Women Scientists in the United States*. Bloomington: Indiana University Press, 1999: 29–37.

Cobb, Jewel Plummer
(1924–) Cell Biologist

Jewel Plummer Cobb was one of the first researchers to investigate the effectiveness of potential cancer chemotherapy drugs. She also developed a number of cutting-edge methods for cultivating and experimenting with cancer cells in a laboratory environment.

Cobb was born Jewel Isadora Plummer on January 17, 1924, in Chicago. Her father, Frank, was a physician, and her mother, Carriebel, was a teacher. Having decided to become a biologist while still in high school, Cobb majored in biology at the University of Michigan and Talladega College (Alabama), receiving a BS from the latter in 1944. She then entered the graduate program at New York University to study cell physiology and received an MS and a PhD in 1947 and 1950, respectively.

Cobb's doctoral research investigated how the enzyme tyrosinase governs the synthesis of melanin, the dark pigment found in skin, hair, feathers, scales, eyes, and certain internal membranes. Produced in the appropriate amounts, melanin protects the skin from harmful ultraviolet rays and absorbs heat from sunlight, the mechanism by which cold-blooded animals stay warm. The production of too much melanin, however, can result in melanoma, a dark-colored tumor derived from melanin-pigmented skin cells.

Cobb continued her research on melanin as a postdoctoral researcher at the Cancer Research Foundation at Harlem Hospital, one of the first cancer research laboratories in the country. Working in collaboration with Louis T. Wright and Jane C. Wright, she investigated the factors influencing the growth and life cycle of normal and cancerous pigment cells. She also studied the changes produced in cancerous cells by a number of different chemical compounds. These compounds included triethylene melamine (a hydrogen mustard compound that was originally developed for use in chemical warfare), aureomycin (one of the first antibiotics), and derivatives of folic acid, which is essential to cell growth. To this end, Cobb developed new ways to grow cancerous cells in an artificial environment such as a test tube or petri dish, using specimens acquired from autopsies and from patients undergoing surgery. In this way, her research complemented that of Jane Wright, who studied the growth and life cycle of tumors in living organisms.

In 1952, the National Cancer Institute awarded Cobb a two-year fellowship to conduct cancer research at the University of Illinois Medical School. At Illinois, she established a state-of-the-art tissue culture research laboratory and continued her study of normal and cancerous pigment cells, but she also expanded her research to include cancerous cell growth in the human bladder. In 1954, the same year she married Roy Cobb, with whom she had one child, she returned to the Cancer Research Foundation, which moved the following year from Harlem Hospital to New York University.

During her second stint at the foundation, Cobb studied the ability of melanin to protect melanoma patients from radiation and X-ray treatments, thus nullifying the effectiveness of such treatments. Her research concerning melanin also produced the first evidence that melanoma can be caused by overexposure to the sun's ultraviolet rays. She also studied the chemotherapeutic effects of actinomycin D (another antibiotic), A-methopterin (also known as methotrexate, which interferes with the ability of folic acid to enhance cell growth), and Thio-Tepa (a nitrogen mustard derivative). Although her research with these compounds failed to discover an effective chemotherapy agent, it did provide later researchers with the protocols for investigating other potential chemotherapy drugs.

In 1960, Cobb joined the faculty at Sarah Lawrence College (New York) as a professor of biology. By then her cancer research had shifted to studying the anticancer effects of hormones, specifically the female hormone 17B estradiol and the male hormone testosterone. In 1969, she was named dean of Connecticut College, and from that point she began to spend less time on research and more on administration, although she did help establish a state-of-the-art tissue culture research laboratory, as she had at Illinois and Sarah Lawrence. In 1976, she became the dean of Douglass College, the women's division of Rutgers University, and in 1981, she was named president of California State University at Fullerton, a position she held until her retirement in 1990.

See also: Biology; Cancer; Harlem Hospital; National Cancer Institute; Wright, Jane C.; Wright, Louis T.

REFERENCES AND FURTHER READING

Kessler, James H., J. S. Kidd, Renee A. Kidd, and Katherine A. Morin, eds. *Distinguished African American Scientists of the 20th Century*. Phoenix, AZ: Oryx Press, 1996: 49–53.

Spangenburg, Ray, and Kit Moser. *African Americans in Science, Math, and Invention*. New York: Facts On File, 2003: 43–44.

Warren, Wini. *Black Women Scientists in the United States*. Bloomington: Indiana University Press, 1999: 40–49.

Cobb, W. Montague
(1904–1990) Physical Anthropologist

Perhaps the most unfortunate misuse of science has been the claim by several anthropologists that Africans and their descendants are different physiologically from other humans. This claim has been made to justify such odious practices as Jim Crow laws in the United States and apartheid in South Africa, and it has helped to perpetuate a number of racial myths. W. Montague Cobb helped refute this claim by demonstrating that racial differences between African Americans and other humans are virtually nil in terms of their bone structures. In the process of accomplishing this, he compiled one of the largest skeleton collections in the United States, and he made his collection available to other anatomical researchers.

Cobb was born on October 12, 1904, in Washington, D.C. His father, William, was a printer, and his mother, Alexzine, was a homemaker. In 1925, he received a BA in science from Amherst College (Massachusetts) and then spent the summer at the Woods Hole Marine Biology Laboratory on Cape Cod. The noted biologist Ernest Everett Just was conducting research at Woods Hole that summer, and he persuaded Cobb to enroll in the Howard University Medical School (today the Howard University College of Medicine). After receiving an MD in 1929, Cobb entered Western Reserve University (today Case Western University) in Cleveland. At Western Reserve, Cobb studied under T. Wingate Todd, who had assembled the country's largest privately owned collection of skeletons, which was an invaluable tool for studying human anatomy. In 1932, Cobb received a PhD in physical anthropology and returned to Howard to teach anatomy, and he remained there for the rest of his career. At an unknown date, he married Hilda Smith, with whom he had two children.

Shortly after joining the Howard faculty, Cobb decided to put together a skeleton collection like Todd's at Howard. He obtained more than 700 skeletons by removing them from cadavers, and he was able to document fully the features of another 300 skeletons. In time, it became known as the Cobb Collection, and it was the third-largest skeleton collection in the nation. Because these skeletons came from both genders and from many racial and ethnic backgrounds, they provided Howard's medical students with a unique training tool. They also served as an important research tool for studying the growth and development of human bones, especially those that form part of the skull.

Cobb focused his early research on the bones that make up the cranium, and he showed that the cranium develops quickly and remains stable after birth. He further demonstrated that the closure of the cranial suture (the line of junction between two of the cranial bones) does not indicate how old the skeleton is, despite the beliefs of a number of anatomists. He also showed that the facial bones, unlike the cranial bones, develop very slowly, and so they are susceptible to modification by diet and other environmental considerations.

In the 1930s, Cobb undertook a thorough study of the differences between the bones of African Americans and European Americans. At the time, it was believed that the bone structures of the two races were significantly dissimilar, and this belief was employed to explain why African Americans athletes

Physical anthropologist W. Montague Cobb dispelled the myth that African American athletes are better than other athletes because their bones are shaped differently. (National Library of Medicine)

tended to outperform European American athletes. Cobb showed this belief to be a myth by demonstrating that the bone structures of the two races are virtually indistinguishable. He published his findings concerning bone structure and athleticism in "Race and Runners," *Journal of Health and Physical Education* [3, 56 (1936)].

Cobb served as president of the National Medical Association (NMA), the organization formed by black physicians who were denied admission to the all-white American Medical Association, and he edited the NMA's journal for 28 years. He also worked to obtain better hospital care for blacks who were denied admission to all-white hospitals, and in 1957, he founded the Imhotep National Conference on Hospital Integration (Imhotep was the Egyptian demigod of medicine). He also served a term as president of the American Association of Physical Anthropologists and as vice president of the American Association for the Advancement of Science, and he played a major role in establishing the Student National Medical Association. He retired from Howard in 1973, although he continued to do research and publish for another 14 years. He died on November 20, 1990, in Washington, D.C.

See also: American Association for the Advancement of Science; American Medical Association; Howard University College of Medicine; Just, Ernest E.; National Medical Association; Student National Medical Association

REFERENCES AND FURTHER READING
Carey, Charles W. Jr. *American Scientists.* New York: Facts On File, 2005.
Hayden, Robert C. *Eleven African American Doctors*, rev. ed. New York: Twenty-First Century Books, 1992: 72–87.
Spangenburg, Ray, and Kit Moser. *African Americans in Science, Math, and Invention.* New York: Facts On File, 2003: 44–46.

Collins, Daniel A.
(1916–) Dentist

Daniel Collins focused his research on the role played by hormones in the growth and development of teeth. He also made important contributions to a better understanding of the causes of facial pain, as well as the deleterious effects on the human body of ingesting too much Vitamin D.

Collins was born on January 11, 1916, in Darlington, South Carolina. His father, Andrew, owned a heavy equipment company, and his mother, Lucy, taught school and managed a small grocery store. After receiving a BS in chemistry from Paine College in Augusta, Georgia, in 1936, he worked for his father for a few years before entering the dentistry program at Meharry Medical College in Nashville, Tennessee. He received a DDS in 1941, and then spent the next year conducting research concerning tooth decay in children at the Guggenheim Dental Clinic in New York City. He then entered the University of California at San Francisco (UCSF) College of Dentistry, receiving an MS in dentistry in 1944. That same year, he was named an instructor at UCSF. At some point, he married DeReath James, with whom he had four children.

Collins's early research focused on the role played by hormones and vitamins in the growth and development of dental tissue and teeth. He was particularly interested in how growth hormone affects the development of dental tissues such as the temporomandibular joint (the joint that connects the jawbone to the skull). When this joint becomes aged, injured, or diseased, the teeth grind against each other, producing pain and damaged teeth. By experimenting with rats whose pituitary gland (the gland that produces growth hormone) had been removed and comparing the development of their temporomandibular joints with those of normal rats, he was able to demonstrate that a lack of growth hormone caused the joint to age prematurely. By the same token, he also demonstrated that injections of growth hormone caused the prematurely aged joints to be restored to a healthy, youthful state.

Having demonstrated that the pituitary gland plays an important role in the development of dental tissue, Collins next set out to determine what, if any, role it plays in the development of teeth. He quickly discovered that a lack of growth hormone causes the structure of the tooth to break down. Specifically, holes appear in the outer enamel layer, the tooth becomes misshapen, and the pulp (the inner core that contains the blood vessels) shrinks.

In the late 1940s, Vitamin D was seen as a cure-all for virtually every medical condition, so Collins began experimenting on dogs to discover what effect, if any, massive amounts of Vitamin D had on the development of teeth. He discovered that, when ingested in large amounts, Vitamin D leeches calcium from the bones into the bloodstream. Eventually, enough calcium builds up to block the blood vessels in pulp, thus causing the teeth to become distorted and weak. Coupled with the findings of other researchers, who had discovered that calcium leeched from bones also clogs the blood vessels in the body's major organs, Collins's findings led the U.S. Food and Drug Administration to regulate the amount of Vitamin D that could be put into milk and that could be sold without a prescription.

While an instructor at UCSF, Collins cofounded the Consultative Oral and Facial Pain Service for purposes of investigating the nature of facial pain as it relates to dental tissue. He soon discovered that the majority of facial pain results either from inflammation of the teeth and jawbone or from the malfunctioning of blood vessels or muscles. He continued to investigate facial pain after being drafted into the U.S. Army in 1956 and assigned to the Dental Division of the Armed Forces Institute of Pathology at Walter Reed Hospital in Washington, D.C. Part of his research involved phantom pain (the pain felt in a limb that has been amputated), and he discovered that this phenomenon is triggered by a neuroma (a tiny swelling on the cut end of a nerve). While in the army, he also investigated the effect that a new technique for grinding teeth, known as high-speed instrumentation, had upon the nerves within the tooth, as well as the various cancers that affect dental health.

In 1958, Collins left the army and returned to UCSF, but he left teaching two years later to establish a private practice in San Francisco and to serve as codirector of the Comprehensive Dental Health Care Project at San Francisco's Mount Zion Hospital. Shortly thereafter, he was named to the California State Board of Public Education, and over the following years, he became more involved in writing and publishing and less involved in dentistry. In 1968, he wrote *Your Teeth: A Handbook of Dental Care for the Whole Family* (Garden City, NY: Doubleday). Most of his publishing-related work, however, involved the production of grade school textbooks, and from 1972 to 1976, he worked part-time for Harcourt Brace Jovanovich's Division of Urban Education. In 1976, he closed his dental practice to become president of the division, a position he held until he retired in 1981. He spent his retirement doing community work, including serving as chairman of the board of trustees of his alma mater, Paine College.

See also: Meharry Medical College

REFERENCES AND FURTHER READING

Hayden, Robert C. *Eleven African American Doctors*, rev. ed. New York: Twenty-First Century Books, 1992: 102–123.

Medical Makers. "Dr. Daniel Collins." [Online article or information; retrieved October 25, 2005.] http://www.thehistorymakers.com/biography/biography.asp?bioindex=1080&category=medicalMakers.

Collins, Margaret S.
(1922–1996) Zoologist

Margaret Collins was one of the world's foremost authorities on termites. During her career, which included fieldwork throughout North and South America, she discovered *Neotermes luykxi*, more commonly known as the Florida dampwood termite.

Collins was born Margaret James in 1922 in Institute, West Virginia. Her father, Rollins, was a professor at West Virginia State College (today West Virginia State University), and her mother, Luella, was a homemaker. As a young girl, she loved nothing better than to roam the woods near her home looking for unusual insects and other small creatures. At age 14, she entered West Virginia State, where she majored in biology and received a BS in 1943. She spent the next seven years studying zoology at the University of Chicago and teaching biology at Howard University. Upon receiving a PhD in 1950, she taught for an additional year at Howard before accepting a faculty position at Florida Agricultural and Mechanical College (today Florida A&M University). She returned to Howard in 1964, where she remained for the rest of her teaching career.

Collins's mentor at the University of Chicago was Alfred Emerson, a termite expert who maintained a field station in Kartabo, British Guiana (today Guyana). She soon caught his love of studying termites, and she wrote her doctoral dissertation on the differences in toleration of drying between species of termites. Her research at Florida A&M focused on the termites of Florida, because she conducted extensive fieldwork in the Everglades and Highlands State Park. In the early 1960s, she expanded her research to include the termites of northern North America by conducting fieldwork at the Minnesota Agricultural Experimental Station. During the late 1960s, she conducted fieldwork in the Sonoran Desert of Arizona and western Mexico. Meanwhile, she made plans to travel to Guyana, and in 1979, she reopened Emerson's field station in Kartabo. From 1979 to 1984, she spent her summers at Kartabo, in the process discovering a number of new species of termites, as well as beetles, butterflies, and birds. She also served as a consultant to the Guyanese Army, providing information such as how to build so as to minimize termite damage and how to utilize termite waste products to strengthen concrete and other building materials. Meanwhile, her research at Howard during the school year focused on the chemical defense mechanisms termites use to defend themselves against predators.

Collins retired from Howard in 1983, but shortly thereafter she became a research associate at the Smithsonian Institution's National Museum of Natural History. In this capacity, she reorganized the museum's holding on termites, adding to it the specimens she had collected during her trips throughout the Americas; today this part of the museum's holdings is known as the Collins Collection. She returned to fieldwork in 1994, making one last trip to Guyana before becoming affiliated with the National Trust for the Cayman Islands' Visiting Scientists Programme. While cataloguing the termite species on Little Cayman Island, she uncovered the presence of a damaging termite, *Coptotermes havilandi,* which is a foreign species clearly introduced by accident. Unlike other native termites, *C. havilandi* is able to attack the ironwood posts of traditional buildings while also causing extensive damage in newer houses. After making the discovery, she worked with researchers at the University of Florida's Fort Lauderdale *Coptotermes* laboratory to develop an experimental, nontoxic control program.

Collins was married twice, in 1942 to Bernard Strickland, and in 1951 to Herbert Collins, with whom she had two children; both marriages ended in divorce. In addition to her other duties, she served a term as president of the Entomological Society of America. She died in April 1996 while doing fieldwork in the Cayman Islands.

See also: Florida A&M University; Howard University; West Virginia State University

REFERENCES AND FURTHER READING
Warren, Wini. *Black Women Scientists in the United States.* Bloomington: Indiana University Press, 1999: 52–66.

Cooke, Lloyd M.
(1916–2001) Chemist

Lloyd Cooke was an industrial chemist who specialized in the chemical processes by which cellulose is manufactured into paper, paper products, synthetic fibers, and other industrial and commercial products. He also

Chemist Lloyd Cooke wrote one of the first textbooks used in college courses on environmental studies. (Bettmann/Corbis)

authored a handbook that became one of the earliest texts used in college courses on environmental studies.

Cooke was born on June 7, 1916, in La Salle, Illinois. His father, William, was an engineer and architect, and his mother, Anna, was a homemaker. As a youngster, he became interested in science, and so he majored in chemistry at the University of Wisconsin, receiving a BS in 1937. Four years later, he completed his education by receiving a PhD in organic chemistry from McGill University in Montreal. After graduation, he went to work as a research chemist for the Corn Products Refining Company (CPC) in Chicago, and in 1946, he took a similar position with Visking Corporation. Eight years later, he was named assistant manager of one of Visking's research divisions. In 1957, when Visking was acquired by Union Carbide, he was named assistant director of research. That same year, he married Vera Schlegel, with whom he had two children.

In graduate school, Cooke had become interested in the chemistry of cellulose, the basic structural component of plant cell walls. Cellulose comprises about one-third of all vegetable matter, and it is the most abundant of all naturally occurring organic compounds. He had focused his early research for CPC, Visking, and Union Carbide on cellulose and starch (a granular organic compound that is produced by all green plants). Specifically, he was looking to develop new processes for converting the derivatives of cellulose and starch into such commodities as paper products, plastics, photographic film, tape, and synthetic fibers such as rayon. In the process, he became an expert on the chemistry of viscose (a solution of cellulose treated with caustic alkali and carbon disulfide that is used in the manufacture of rayon and synthetic films). He later became interested in polymers (long chains of carbohydrates that closely resemble the complex structure of cellulose).

In 1965, Cooke left the laboratory to become Union Carbide's manager of market research, and two years later he was named manager of planning. In this latter capacity, he authored *Cleaning Our Environment–The Chemical Basis for Action* (Washington, DC: American Chemical Society, 1969). This work was originally intended to serve as a handbook for environmentalists and legislators, but it was quickly discovered by college professors who used it as a textbook in their chemistry and environmental studies courses.

In 1970, Cooke became Union Carbide's director of urban affairs, and in this capacity he worked to promote the study of mathematics and science in the public schools of the nation's largest cities. His many honors include election to the National Academy of Sciences. After retiring from Union Carbide, he established Lloyd M. Cooke Associates, a consulting firm. He died in 2001.

REFERENCES AND FURTHER READING

Krapp, Kristine, ed. *Notable Black American Scientists*. Detroit, MI: Gale Research, 1999: 78–79.

Spangenburg, Ray, and Kit Moser. *African Americans in Science, Math, and Invention*. New York: Facts On File, 2003: 47–48.

Cowings, Patricia S.
(1948–) Psychophysiologist

A major problem for the early astronauts was space sickness, a condition similar to seasickness or motion sickness. While seasickness and motion sickness can be treated with pharmaceutical drugs, space sickness cannot, because the drugs impair the astronaut's ability to perform tasks. Patricia Cowings addressed this problem by developing the Autogenic Feedback Training Exercise (AFTE), by which astronauts use biofeedback techniques to cope with space sickness.

AFTE was later adapted for use by airplane pilots to help them cope with motion sickness and by cancer patients trying to cope with chemotherapy treatment.

Cowings was born on December 15, 1948, in New York City. Her father, Albert, owned a grocery store, and her mother, Sadie, was a teacher. She studied psychology in college, receiving a BA from the State University of New York in 1970 and an MA and a PhD from the University of California at Davis in 1973. She then won a National Research Council grant to conduct research at the National Aeronautics and Space Administration's (NASA) Ames Research Center at Moffett Field in California. In 1975, she joined the San Jose State University Foundation as a research specialist, but she returned to Ames two years later to be a research psychologist in the psychophysiological research laboratory. Cowings was the first U.S. woman ever to undergo astronaut training, and she served as a backup payload specialist for one of the first science-oriented space shuttle missions. But rather than going into space herself, she opted to participate in NASA missions as a researcher, and she was eventually named director of her laboratory. In 1980, she married William Toscano, a fellow NASA researcher, with whom she has one child.

Cowings focused her primary research on developing treatments for zero-gravity sickness syndrome, better known as space sickness. The more time astronauts spend in outer space during a NASA mission or on a space station, the more susceptible they become to space sickness. In the 1970s, Cowings began working to develop a program for combating space sickness that employed biofeedback techniques and psychophysiological methods rather than the use of drugs. The result is AFTE, a program consisting of a dozen 30-minute sessions in which astronauts are taught biofeedback techniques. During these sessions, astronauts are trained to recognize the symptoms of space sickness and then condition their physiological responses accordingly. Specifically, AFTE teaches astronauts how to control their heartbeat and blood pressure, overcome feelings of nausea and fainting, and relax certain muscles that are particularly susceptible to space sickness. She also developed a physiological monitoring system that can be worn by astronauts that sends feedback to a computer terminal, thus providing astronauts with real-time displays of changes in various categories such as cardiac output and blood pressure. Almost two-thirds of the program's graduates are able to deal with space sickness so that it does not affect them at all, and an additional one-fifth are able to cope with space sickness well enough to keep it from affecting their job performance. AFTE was tested extensively during the 1980s and was first implemented during the eight-day Spacelab-J mission in 1992. Cowings published her findings regarding space sickness and AFTE in a number of articles, some of them coauthored by her husband, and as an essay in "Motion and Space Sickness" [in George H. Crampton, *Motion and Space Sickness* (Boca Raton, FL: CRC Publishing, 1990: 354–372)].

Psychophysiologist Patricia Cowings assisted astronauts by developing the Autogenic Feedback Training Exercise, biofeedback techniques that help them cope with space sickness. (National Aeronautics and Space Administration)

AFTE proved to have several applications other than in space medicine. It has been adapted by other researchers for use in treating hypertension, chemotherapy-related nausea, air and sea sickness, and various disorders of the autonomic nervous system. It promises to be of use in treating such neuropathological conditions as epilepsy, attention deficit disorder, and mild head trauma, as well as fatigue, jet lag, insomnia, and high work-induced stress.

Following the successful implementation of AFTE, Cowings devoted her research to developing exercise programs for astronauts. These programs are designed to allow astronauts to maintain muscle strength and tone during long-term missions under the zero-gravity conditions of space flight and the microgravity conditions that prevail on a space station. She also taught psychiatry on an adjunct basis at the University of California at Los Angeles. Her many awards include membership in the American Association for the Advancement of Science.

See also: American Association for the Advancement of Science; National Aeronautics and Space Administration

REFERENCES AND FURTHER READING
Carey, Charles W. Jr. *American Scientists*. New York: Facts On File, 2005: 75–77.

Spangenburg, Ray, and Kit Moser. *African Americans in Science, Math, and Invention*. New York: Facts On File, 2003: 48–49.

Warren, Wini. *Black Women Scientists in the United States*. Bloomington: Indiana University Press, 1999: 67–71.

Daly, Marie M.
(1921–2003) Biochemist

Marie Daly was the first African American woman to earn a PhD in chemistry. She also did pioneering work on the effects of high blood pressure and arterial blockage on the ability of the arteries to perform their duties.

Daly was born on April 16, 1921, in Queens, New York City. Her father, Ivan, was a postal clerk, and her mother, Helen, was a homemaker. Her father had studied chemistry at Cornell University, and as a youngster, Daly developed an interest in science from him. After graduating from Hunter College High School, an all-girl school that encouraged young women to pursue professional goals, she studied chemistry in college and received three degrees: a BS from Queens College in 1942, an MS from New York University in 1943, and a PhD from Columbia University in 1948. She taught physical science at Howard University in Washington, D.C., for two years before returning to New York City to conduct postgraduate research at the Rockefeller Institute for Medical Research (today Rockefeller University) on a one-year fellowship from the American Cancer Society. When the fellowship ended in 1951, she was retained by Rockefeller as an assistant investigator for another four years.

At Rockefeller, Daly collaborated with senior biochemist Alfred E. Mirsky, who, in 1948, had discovered ribonucleic acid (RNA) in human chromosomes. With Mirsky, she studied how proteins such as enzymes affect cell metabolism. She focused her earliest work with Mirsky on the purines and pyrimidines. These are two of the chemical building blocks from which nucleic acids are constructed; in turn, nucleic acids make up DNA (deoxyribonucleic acid) and RNA (ribonucleic acid). Next, she studied histones (a class of protein substances that possess specific basic properties) in terms of their properties and amino acid composition (amino acids are the basic building blocks of all proteins). She was particularly interested in histones with a high content of lysine, a biochemical compound that is synthesized from glycine, the simplest of the amino acids. This project was followed by a study of the uptake of glycine by certain components of cell nuclei as well as liver proteins. Other studies included the formation of protein in the pancreas and the protein metabolism in the chromosomes of nondividing cells.

In 1955, Daly returned to Columbia to teach biochemistry at the College of Physicians and Surgeons. At Columbia, Daly shifted the focus of her research to the biochemical aspects of heart conditions such as hypertension (high blood pressure) and atherosclerosis (arterial blockage). After studying how blood pressure and the cholesterol content of blood serum and tissues affect atherogenesis (the growth and development of arteries), she began studying the effects of cholesterol and certain enzymes on the aorta, the body's chief artery, specifically in terms of their ability to induce hypertension.

In 1960, Daly left Columbia to teach and conduct research at the Albert Einstein College of Medicine at Yeshiva University, where she remained for the next 26 years. She continued to study the aorta, particularly the effect of hypertension on the composition of lipids (one of the chief components of living cells) in the aorta's intima-media (middle layer), the effects of age and hypertension on the ability of the aorta's smooth muscles to utilize glucose (the biochemical compound that fuels the muscles), and the effect of hypertension and atherosclerosis on the digestive organelles of arterial cells. Meanwhile, her biochemical research was branching out, as she studied the uptake, synthesis, and distribution of creatine (an amino acid found particularly in muscles, cell cultures, and tissues). She also branched into fields unrelated to biochemistry; for example, she investigated such issues as the structural abnormalities of the foot and ankle, how therapeutic progress can be measured in part by tactile contact, and the effects of cigarette smoking on the functions of a dog's heart.

In 1961, Daly married Vincent Clark. In 1986, she retired to her summer home in East Hampton, New York, although she continued to conduct research at Einstein Medical College. By then her attention had turned to bacteriology, particularly the ability of some bacteria to resist certain antibiotic drugs. In 1988, she established a scholarship for African American chemistry and physics majors at Queens College in memory of her father. She died on October 28, 2003.

See also: Chemistry; Howard University

REFERENCES AND FURTHER READING

McMurray, Emily J., ed. *Notable Twentieth-Century Scientists*. Detroit, MI: Gale Research, 1995: 448–449.

Spangenburg, Ray, and Kit Moser. *African Americans in Science, Math, and Invention*. New York: Facts On File, 2003: 55–56.

Warren, Wini. *Black Women Scientists in the United States*. Bloomington: Indiana University Press, 1999: 71–73.

Dorman, Linneaus C.
(1935–) Chemist

Linneaus Dorman was a leading expert in the field of synthetic peptides, the production of chains of proteins that do not exist in nature. Of the more than two dozen synthetic peptides he developed, he is best remembered for two: one helps safeguard the environment from chemical fertilizers, and the other serves as a useful replacement for bone.

Dorman was born on June 28, 1935, in Orangeburg, South Carolina. His parents, John and Georgia, were teachers. He became interested in chemistry as a young boy playing with a chemistry set; so his parents sent him to high school at the South Carolina State College (today University) laboratory school in Orangeburg, where the curriculum focused on the basic sciences. After receiving a BS in chemistry from Bradley University (Illinois) in 1956, he obtained a fellowship from the Dow Chemical Company to work on his doctorate at the University of Illinois, where he received a PhD in 1961. In 1957, he married Phae Hubble, with whom he had two children.

As a graduate student, Dorman spent his summers at the U.S. Department of Agriculture's Northern Regional Research Laboratory in Peoria. Here he experimented with methods for making chemical fertilizers that would not harm the environment and that would be harder for living organisms to ingest. He continued with these experiments after going to work in 1961 as a research chemist at the Dow Chemical Research Center in Midland, Michigan, and eventually he developed a plastic binder for use with chemical fertilizers. In essence, the binder is a thin plastic shell that encases the fertilizer; since the shell degrades slowly over time, the chemicals in the fertilizer are released into the plant over a longer period of time so that the plant can utilize them more fully. The binder has a sticky outer surface that makes the chemicals more likely to stick to the plant they are supposed to fertilize rather than running off into a stream. Thus, in addition to protecting the environment, Dorman's binder also supports an increase in crop yield.

Dorman's other major contribution involved the development of an artificial bone replacement material. Natural bone is composed of various peptides and calcium salts; so he set out to duplicate this arrangement as much as possible. First, he developed a totally new peptide, polymethyl glutamate, by altering the molecular structure of one of the amino acids (the building blocks from which all proteins are made). Next, he imbedded the polymethyl glutamate molecules with tiny granules of calcium phosphate (a hard substance that occurs naturally in certain rocks). The polymethyl glutamate gave the artificial bone material flexibility, and the calcium phosphate gave it strength. Last, to give the bone material even greater strength and flexibility, he cross-linked all of the molecules with each other, in essence rearranging their chemical bonding patterns so that the many molecules were rearranged into gigantic molecules that are big enough to see with the naked eye.

Dorman made a number of other synthetic peptides for use in medical applications. One, derived naturally from the protein fibrinogen, was used to prevent blood clotting, one of the major causes of heart attacks. Others had potential applications as treatments for various mental illnesses. His many nonmedical peptides included one for breaking down synthetic rubber so that it could be recycled, thus helping to get rid of some of the millions of used tires that might otherwise clog up landfills.

Although Dorman never taught, he took an interest in the affairs of Saginaw Valley State College (Michigan), serving on its board of directors for more than 10 years. In 1994, he retired from Dow to his home in Midland, but he remained active in community affairs for a number of years thereafter. His many honors include Dow Chemical's Inventor of the Year award and the National Organization for the Professional Advancement of Black Chemists and Chemical Engineers' Percy Lavon Julian Award.

See also: Chemistry; Julian, Percy L.; National Organization for the Professional Advancement of Black Chemists and Chemical Engineers; South Carolina State University

REFERENCES AND FURTHER READING

Kessler, James H., J. S. Kidd, Renee A. Kidd, and Katherine A. Morin, eds. *Distinguished African American Scientists of the 20th Century.* Phoenix, AZ: Oryx Press, 1996: 67–71.

Krapp, Kristine M., ed. *Notable Black American Scientists.* Detroit, MI: Gale Research, 1999: 95–96.

Spangenburg, Ray, and Kit Moser. *African Americans in Science, Math, and Invention.* New York: Facts On File, 2003: 61–63.

Drew, Charles R.
(1904–1950) Blood Plasma Scientist

The discovery of the various blood types in the early 20th century meant that a surgeon could administer blood to patients during an operation without killing them. But before this could happen, the problems associated with the collection, typing, storage, and transportation of blood had to be worked out. Charles Drew addressed these problems by establishing the first large-scale blood bank program in the United States. The methods and procedures he developed for handling and preserving blood in large quantities made it possible for organizations such as the American Red Cross to establish national blood collection programs throughout the world.

Drew was born on June 3, 1904, in Washington, D.C. His father, Richard, was a carpet layer, and his mother, Nora, was a teacher. An honor student in high school, he became interested in science while attending Amherst College (Massachusetts). In 1926, he received a BA and joined the faculty at Morgan College (today Morgan State University) in Baltimore, where he taught biology and chemistry. Two years later, he entered McGill University Medical School in Montreal, and in 1933, he received an MD and a CM (master of surgery). After

Blood plasma scientist Charles Drew established the first large-scale blood bank program in the United States. (National Library of Medicine)

completing his internship and residency in Montreal, in 1935, he was named a professor of pathology at Howard University Medical School (today Howard University College of Medicine) in Washington, D.C.

In 1938, Drew took a leave of absence from Howard to obtain a doctor of science in medicine degree from Columbia University Medical School in New York City. Drew had done some research concerning blood transfusions while at McGill, and at Columbia, he became interested in blood banking. Working in conjunction with New York surgeons John Scudder and E. H. L. Corwin, in 1938, Drew established a blood bank at Presbyterian Hospital, which was affiliated with Columbia. He wrote his doctoral dissertation on the preservation of banked blood, and after receiving his degree in 1940, he returned to Howard to teach surgery. That same year, he married Minnie Robbins, with whom he had four children.

Shortly after returning to Howard, Drew was contacted by the British government to see whether he would help establish a blood bank for British troops who were being wounded in World War II. He quickly agreed, and in 1940, he was named medical director of the Blood for Britain Project. Working from New York City, Drew directed the preparation of liquid plasma from whole blood and then oversaw its shipment from the United States to Great Britain. Because of the distance involved and the urgency of the need, Drew developed methods and procedures for collecting, preserving, and shipping large amounts of liquid plasma swiftly and effectively.

Drew's operation was so successful that in early 1941 he was recruited by the American Red Cross (ARC) to be the medical director of the blood program it was organizing in case the United States was drawn into the war. After getting the ARC blood bank up and running, he returned to Howard to be head of the surgery department. He remained interested in the ARC's programs, however, and when the ARC decided to reject blood from African American donors, he protested on the grounds that there was no scientific evidence to justify such a rejection.

Drew spent the rest of his career at Howard. In 1946, he took on the additional duties of medical director at Freedmen's Hospital in Washington, D.C. He died on April 1, 1950, as the result of an automobile accident near Burlington, North Carolina, while traveling to a medical convention in Tuskegee, Alabama. Allegedly, he died because Burlington's all-white hospital refused to admit him. In fact, he was treated in the hospital's segregated emergency room by the top-flight black physicians and surgeons he was traveling with.

He received a number of posthumous awards, but two in particular are worth mentioning. In 1966, the Charles R. Drew Postgraduate Medical School of the University of California at Los Angeles (today the Charles R. Drew University of Medicine and Science) was named in his honor, and in 1981, the U.S. Post Office issued a Charles R. Drew commemorative postage stamp.

See also: Biology; Charles R. Drew University of Medicine and Science; chemistry; Freedmen's Hospital; Howard University College of Medicine; Morgan State University

References and Further Reading
Carey, Charles W. Jr. *American Scientists*. New York: Facts On File, 2005: 91–92.

Hayden, Robert C. *Eleven African American Doctors,* rev. ed. New York: Twenty-First Century Books, 1992: 170–185.

Love, Spencie. *One Blood: The Death and Resurrection of Charles R. Drew*. Chapel Hill: University of North Carolina Press, 1996.

Spangenburg, Ray, and Kit Moser. *African Americans in Science, Math, and Invention*. New York: Facts On File, 2003: 63–64.

Wynes, Charles E. *Charles Richard Drew: The Man and the Myth*. Urbana: University of Illinois Press, 1988.

Dunbar, Joseph C., Jr.
(1944–) Physiologist

Joseph Dunbar was one of the nation's leading experts on diabetes. His research demonstrated the connection between diabetes and other seemingly unrelated medical conditions affecting the cardiovascular system.

Dunbar was born on August 27, 1944, in Vicksburg, Mississippi, but he grew up in nearby Port Gibson. His father, Joseph Sr., was a county agent for

Ferguson, Lloyd N.
(1918–) Biochemist

Lloyd Ferguson's research led to a better understanding of the biochemistry of taste as well as the biochemistry of cancer chemotherapy.

Ferguson was born on February 9, 1918, in Oakland, California. His father, Noel, was an insurance clerk, and his mother, Gwendolyn, was an elevator operator. As a young boy, he became interested in chemistry, and by the time he entered high school, he had already developed his own formula for moth repellant, spot remover, silver polish, and lemonade mix, all of which he sold to his neighbors. After finishing high school, he worked for the Works Progress Administration and the Southern Pacific Railroad before entering the University of California at Berkeley, where he received a BS in chemistry in 1940 and a PhD in biochemistry in 1943.

As a graduate student, Ferguson studied under Melvin Calvin, winner of the 1961 Nobel Prize in Chemistry. Calvin won the Nobel for tracing the chemical pathway that carbon dioxide undergoes in plants to be converted into sugars, from which their cells derive energy, but the work Ferguson did with Calvin involved a national defense project. Specifically, the military was looking for a reversible source of oxygen for high-altitude aviation and submarines. Together, Ferguson and Calvin developed a crystalline substance that absorbs oxygen from the air and releases it when needed. Eventually, this compound was developed by the Monsanto Company to produce oxygen for industrial purposes.

In 1944, Ferguson accepted a teaching position at the North Carolina Agricultural and Technical College (today North Carolina A&T State University) and married Charlotte Welch, with whom he had three children. A year later, he left to join the faculty at Howard University in Washington, D.C., as a professor of chemistry. In 1958, he took over as head of the chemistry department, and in this capacity he instituted the first doctoral program in chemistry at a historically black university. In 1965, he left Howard to teach and to chair the chemistry department at California State University at Los Angeles (Cal State), where he remained for the rest of his career.

Ferguson's research at Howard and Cal State focused on the structure of biomolecules (the organic, or carbon-bearing, molecules found in living creatures). He was particularly interested in how a biomolecule's ability to interact with other molecules, both organic and inorganic, is affected by its physical structure, particularly the number of electrons that two bonding atoms share and the angles at which the atoms bond. Much of his attention in this regard was devoted to studying the alicyclic compounds (compounds in which three or more carbon atoms are linked together in a ring). Alicyclic compounds featuring three or four carbon atoms tend to be relatively unstable, because their covalent bonds (a chemical bond formed by the sharing of two electrons) occur at angles that are relatively small. He published much of his work with alicyclic compounds in a two-volume textbook, *Highlights of Alicyclic Chemistry* (Palisade, NJ: Franklin, 1973, 1977), which he coauthored with Donald R. Paulson, one of his Cal State colleagues. Meanwhile, he authored five more chemistry textbooks about the behavior of organic molecules and biomolecules: *Electron Structures of Organic Molecules* (Upper Saddle River, NJ: Prentice Hall, 1952), *Textbook of Organic Chemistry* (1st ed, out of print 1958; 2nd ed, New York: Van Nostrand, 1965), *The Modern Structural Theory of Organic Chemistry* (Upper Saddle River, NJ: Prentice Hall, 1963), *Organic Chemistry: A Science and an Art* (Bel Air, CA: Willard Grant Press, 1972), and *Organic Molecular Structure: A Gateway to Advanced Organic Chemistry* (Bel Air, CA: Willard Grant Press, 1975).

Ferguson also devoted a considerable amount of effort to understanding the mechanics of the human sense of taste. Not surprisingly, given his background as a structural chemist, he tried to understand taste in terms of the differences between the molecular structures of substances that taste sour, those that taste sweet, and those that have no taste at all. Specifically, he was interested in gustatory chemoreceptors (specialized cells in the taste buds that identify specific chemical combinations and then generate the appropriate nerve impulse, which then signals the brain what is being tasted. He also examined a number of cancer chemotherapy drugs in an effort to describe the processes by which such drugs work, so that more effective ones could be developed.

Ferguson retired in 1986, although he continued to conduct research at Cal State as a professor emeritus until 1991, when he relocated to Fair Oaks, California. He was a founding member of the National Association for the Professional Advancement of Black Chemists and Chemical Engineers, which later honored him by naming its Lloyd N. Ferguson Young Scientist Award in his honor. The award is presented annually to recipients who have shown early promise and accomplishments in their field (with up to 10 years of professional experience) and have demonstrated the potential to sustain a productive scientific career.

See also: Biochemistry; Cancer; Chemistry; Howard University; National Organization for the Professional Advancement of Black Chemists and Chemical Engineers; North Carolina A&T State University

REFERENCES AND FURTHER READING

Ferguson, Lloyd N., with Gabrielle S. Morris. *Increasing Opportunities in Chemistry, 1936–1986.* Berkeley, CA: Regional Oral History Office, The Bancroft Library, University of California, 1992.

McMurray, Emily J., ed. *Notable Twentieth-Century Scientists.* Detroit, MI: Gale Research, 1995: 622–623.

Spangenburg, Ray, and Kit Moser. *African Americans in Science, Math, and Invention*. New York: Facts On File, 2003: 79–82.

Forde, Evan B.
(1952–) Oceanographer

Evan Forde is a recognized authority on the formation, evolution, and sedimentary processes of the submarine canyons off the United States' Atlantic coastline. His research has contributed to a better understanding of such phenomena as gravity-induced mass sediment movements on continental slopes, three-dimensional mapping of hydrothermal plumes, the study of the ocean-atmosphere exchange of anthropogenic carbon dioxide, and the forecasting and tracking of hurricanes.

Forde was born on May 11, 1952, in Miami. He became interested in becoming a marine scientist at an early age for two reasons: His parents were science teachers, and one of his favorite television programs was *The Undersea World of Jacques Cousteau*. As a geology major at Columbia University in New York City, he specialized in oceanography and received a BS in 1974 and an MS in marine geology and geophysics in 1976. While at Columbia, he began working part time for the National Oceanic and Atmospheric Administration (NOAA), and, upon completing his education, he became a full-time researcher for NOAA, where he spent the rest of his career.

Forde's early research for NOAA was conducted at the Atlantic Oceanographic and Meteorological Laboratory's marine geology and geophysics laboratory in Miami, and it consisted of compiling and studying basic data about the Atlantic Ocean. He studied the behavior of waves and tides and the chemical composition and age of seawater. He monitored the level of pollutants and carbon dioxide in the ocean atmosphere; researched the forces that create underwater landslides, mudslides, and avalanches; used sound to map the ocean floor and subsurface sediment layers; and used optical devices to scan the deep ocean layers for evidence of underwater volcanoes. In the process, he also took thousands of samples of deep sea sediments and rocks. His atmospheric studies included tropical meteorology, and in this regard he contributed significantly to a better understanding of how hurricanes form, grow, operate, and dissipate.

While studying the sedimentary composition and geological processes affecting the submarine canyons and slides off the North American coastline, Forde participated in a number of dives aboard research submersibles (one- or two-person vessels that can submerge and operate deep under water). In 1980, while exploring the Norfolk Submarine Canyon off the coast of New Jersey, Forde's submersible, Alvin, was trapped for 12 minutes by a small, underwater landslide. Nevertheless, he continued to dive, and on one research trip he discovered massive sediment slumping that led the Department of Interior to cancel the rights for billions of dollars of offshore drilling sites off the coast of Cape May, New Jersey. In addition to gathering basic data, Forde also developed some important theories about how the Atlantic's submarine canyons formed, and these theories are still accepted today as being the most likely explanation for their formation.

In 1982, Forde transferred to the Ocean Chemistry Division, where he took up the study of the various aspects of hydrothermal plumes (mixtures of seawater and partially molten volcanic material that are caused by underwater volcanic activity). In 1998, he was named research oceanographer of the Satellite Remote Sensing Group. In this capacity, he helped develop methods for using the QuikSCAT satellite as a tool for identifying potential hurricanes as they form in the Atlantic off the African coast, as well as to pinpoint where they will make landfall in North America.

REFERENCES AND FURTHER READING

Krapp, Kristine, ed. *Notable Black American Scientists*. Detroit, MI: Gale Research, 1999: 119.

Spangenburg, Ray, and Kit Moser. *African Americans in Science, Math, and Invention*. New York: Facts On File, 2003: 82–83.

Francisco, Joseph S., Jr.
(1955–) Physical Chemist

Joseph Francisco was a leading expert in the field of atmospheric chemistry, the study of the chemical reactions that take place in Earth's upper atmosphere. His most important contribution demonstrated the likely effect that the potential replacements of chlorofluorocarbons would have on the ozone layer.

Francisco was born on March 26, 1955, in New Orleans to Joseph and Lucinda Francisco. As a young boy, he went to live with his mother's parents, Melvin and Sarah Walker, in Beaumont, Texas, where he grew up. During his adolescence, he developed an interest in chemistry by working part time in a local pharmacy. After receiving a BS in chemistry from the University of Texas in 1977, he worked for a year as a research chemist for the Monsanto Chemical Company in Texas City. He then entered the graduate program at the Massachusetts Institute of Technology (MIT) and received a PhD in chemistry in 1983. He spent the next three years conducting postdoctoral research at Cambridge University in England and MIT before joining the faculty at Wayne State University in Detroit. In 1995, he was named a professor of chemistry and of earth and atmosphere sciences at Purdue University, where he has remained for the rest of his career.

Francisco's research focused on the physical processes that govern chemical reactions, and he sought to arrive at a better understanding of why and how chemical bonds are made and broken. To this end, he became adept at the use of spectroscopy (the study of the electromagnetic radiation emitted by atoms and molecules) as a means of studying the dynamics of chemical reactions. He was particularly interested in femtochemistry (the use of fast laser techniques to record the actual events that take place during the transition state in a chemical reaction). In essence, a laser flash of several millionths of a billionth of a second initiates a chemical reaction, and subsequent flashes illuminate the changes taking place in the various chemical bonds as the reaction takes place.

Francisco's primary research studied the potential replacements for chlorofluorocarbons (CFCs, the chief ingredients in refrigerants and aerosols) and how they would affect the upper atmosphere. The Nobel Prize winner Mario Molina had shown in the late 1970s that CFCs deplete the ozone layer of the atmosphere when they decompose, thus leaving chlorine atoms free to react with ozone. Since the ozone layer protects life on Earth from most of the harmful effects of sunlight, Molina's revelation led several industrial countries to ban CFCs. However, no one knew exactly how the potential replacements for CFCs might react once they found their way into the upper atmosphere; so Francisco devoted much of his research to providing answers to this question.

At Wayne State and Purdue, Francisco established laboratories in which he could simulate the chemical environment of Earth's upper atmosphere. Then, using sophisticated computer modeling programs, femtochemistry, and other spectroscopic techniques, he examined a number of potential replacements for CFCs. Because many of these compounds break down in less than 60 microseconds in upper-atmospheric conditions, he used femtochemistry to record the changes these compounds undergo. Most of his work involved hydrofluorocarbons (HFCs) and fluorinated ethers. Because HFCs replace chlorine with hydrogen, which occurs in abundance in the upper atmosphere, he was able to determine that HFCs pose little if any threat to the ozone layer. And while he was able to demonstrate that fluorinated ethers are just as safe as HFCs in terms of their effect on the ozone layer, he also showed that they absorb infrared light from the sun in such a way that produces greenhouse gases, thus contributing in a major way to global warming.

Francisco's research has been published in more than 300 articles in such prestigious journals as *Journal of Chemical Physics*, *Journal of the American Chemical Society*, and *Proceedings of the National Academy of Sciences*. His publications include a textbook, *Chemical Kinetics and Dynamics* (New York: Dover Publications, 1989, 2nd ed.). His many honors include election to fellowship in the American Association for the Advancement of Science and to a term as president of the National Organization for the Professional Advancement of Black Chemists and Chemical Engineers.

See also: American Association for the Advancement of Science; Chemistry; National Organization for the Professional Advancement of Black Chemists and Chemical Engineers; Wayne State University

REFERENCES AND FURTHER READING

Kessler, James H., J. S. Kidd, Renee A. Kidd, and Katherine A. Morin, eds. *Distinguished African American Scientists of the 20th Century.* Phoenix, AZ: Oryx Press, 1996: 103–106.

Krapp, Kristine M., ed. *Notable Black American Scientists.* Detroit, MI: Gale Research, 1999: 120.

Spangenburg, Ray, and Kit Moser. *African Americans in Science, Math, and Invention.* New York: Facts On File, 2003: 83–84.

Franklin, Renty B.
(1945–) Physiologist

Renty Franklin was a leading expert on the biology of the prostate gland and prostate cancer. His major contribution was to show that zinc plays a central but mysterious role in controlling the growth of tumors in the prostate gland.

Franklin was born on September 2, 1945, in Birmingham, Alabama. His parents, George and Pinkie, owned and operated a grocery store. At age 16, he entered Morehouse College in Atlanta, receiving a BS in biology in 1966 and an MS in biology from Atlanta (today Clark Atlanta) University the following year. He taught biology for two years at St. Augustine's College in Raleigh, North Carolina, and then enrolled in Howard University, where he received a PhD in physiology in 1972. He taught physiology at the Howard University College of Medicine for the next eight years, and in 1980, he was named a professor of physiology at the University of Maryland Dental School's department of biomedical sciences in Baltimore. At an unknown date, he married Therese Langston, with whom he had two children.

Franklin's early research focused on the ability of certain hormones and minerals to regulate the activities of specific organs and tissues. In graduate school, he demonstrated how a hormone secreted by the parathyroid gland controls the process by which the kidneys remove citric acid from the bloodstream and expel it from the body in urine. In the mid-1970s, he studied the effect of minerals on bodily functions, particularly how a high level of a certain mineral in the bloodstream often precedes the onset of a specific disease or medical condition.

In the 1980s, Franklin set out to obtain a better understanding of how imbalances in hormone and mineral levels contribute to the development of tumors in the prostate gland. The prostate gland normally secretes an extraordinarily high level of citric acid (citrate), while accumulating large amounts of zinc. At the time, it was known that citrate production and zinc accumulation are regulated by two hormones, testosterone and prolactin, but little was known about how they do it. Since prostate cancer eliminates the prostate gland's ability to produce citrate and accumulate zinc, Franklin set out to learn more about the molecular mechanisms by which testosterone and prolactin regulate citrate production and zinc accumulation. Eventually, he discovered that prolactin activates the enzyme protein kinase C (PKC), which activates a biochemical compound known as transcription factor AP1, which triggers certain genes that play a major role in regulating the metabolism to express themselves.

Meanwhile, Franklin had discovered that citrate production and zinc accumulation are interrelated. Specifically, high levels of zinc in the prostate inhibit the enzyme aconitase from transforming citrate into other biochemical compounds. Thus, when the prostate stops accumulating zinc, it also stops producing citrate. Having made this discovery, he began investigating the possibility that prostate cancer could be cured or controlled by the uptake of zinc to prostate cells. Eventually, he was able to demonstrate that, when normal prostate cells are exposed to zinc, they accumulate high zinc levels and their growth is controlled, but when malignant prostate cells lose their ability to accumulate zinc, they begin multiplying uncontrollably. He further demonstrated that high levels of zinc act as a brake on runaway prostate cell growth by increasing apoptosis (the process by which defective cells destroy themselves). Specifically, treating prostate cells with zinc triggered apoptosis by forcing the cells to release a chemical called cytochrome c, which in turn activates destructive enzymes called caspases, which cut the activating cells to shreds. Although much work remains to be done in this area, Franklin's research suggests that, if zinc accumulation can block apoptosis in prostate cells, then restoring the ability to retain zinc in malignant cells could halt their spread or even perhaps stop prostate cancer cells from getting started.

Franklin remained at Maryland for the rest of his career. He was eventually named director of the dental school's molecular and cell biology program, and he played an important role in establishing its hormone-controlled cancer program.

See also: Biology; Cancer; Clark Atlanta University; Howard University; Howard University College of Medicine

REFERENCES AND FURTHER READING

Kessler, James H., J. S. Kidd, Renee A. Kidd, and Katherine A. Morin, eds. *Distinguished African American Scientists of the 20th Century*. Phoenix, AZ: Oryx Press, 1996: 324–328.

Krapp, Kristine M., ed. *Notable Black American Scientists*. Detroit, MI: Gale Research, 1999: 1130–1131.

Spangenburg, Ray, and Kit Moser. *African Americans in Science, Math, and Invention*. New York: Facts On File, 2003: 139–142.

Fuller, A. Oveta
(1955–) Microbiologist

Almyra Oveta Fuller was one of the world's foremost experts on herpes simplex virus, a leading cause of sexually transmitted diseases, as well as a fatal form of viral encephalitis. Her research showed how herpes simplex virus enters a cell, a promising first step toward finding a cure for the various forms of herpes.

Fuller was born on August 31, 1955, in Mebane, North Carolina. Her father, Herbert, was a farmer, and her mother, Deborah, was a teacher. She completed her college education at the University of North Carolina at Chapel Hill, receiving a BA in biology in 1977 and a PhD in microbiology in 1983. She spent the next five years conducting postgraduate research at the University of Chicago, and in 1988, she joined the faculty at the University of Michigan Medical School's department of microbiology and immunology. In 1984, she married Jerry Caldwell, with whom she had one child.

As a graduate student, Fuller became interested in virology (the study of viruses and how they attack and infect other living organisms). She focused her postdoctoral research on the herpes viruses, which cause a number of diseases such as cold sores, genital herpes, mononucleosis, shingles, and chicken pox. She was particularly interested in learning more about how the herpes viruses penetrate the walls of the cells they infect. Although these viruses can infect virtually any type of cell, they tend to attack soft tissue, such as the linings of certain parts of the body; so she explored the possibility that the cell walls of soft tissue are constructed in a different manner or of different material than the cell walls of other types of tissue. This line of inquiry demonstrated that each strain of herpes virus requires the presence of specific amino acids in the potential host cell's wall before it can attach itself to the cell. Although this discovery did not lead to an immediate cure for herpes, it provided researchers with a valuable clue as to why certain individuals and species are susceptible to a certain virus while others are immune.

At Michigan, Fuller's research focused on the two strains of the herpes simplex virus: HSV-1, which causes oral herpes, and HSV-2, which causes genital herpes. As of 2005, it was estimated that 45 million people suffered from genital herpes and that millions more suffered from oral herpes. Although pharmaceutical drugs existed to treat outbreaks of oral and genital herpes, none existed that could eliminate the infections; so people infected by either strain remained so for life. Although Fuller was unable to develop a cure, by 2005, the research team she led at Michigan had discovered the means by which HSV gains entry into a cell.

Fuller and her associates discovered a previously unknown receptor, a position on the cell membrane that acts like a door through which only one specific biochemical compound may gain entry into the cell. Known as B5, this receptor is found on the cell wall of virtually every human cell. Its purpose remains unknown, but Fuller and her team discovered that HSV attaches itself to the cell wall at B5 and then triggers the receptor to let it enter the cell. The triggering mechanism is probably related to the peculiar coiled shape of the B5 receptor, because this shape causes the B5 receptor to mate perfectly with the structure of the proteins HSV uses to attach itself to a cell. The research team also located the gene that controls production of the B5 receptor and detailed some of its structure.

Fuller's team also developed a method that might lead to the development of a way to safeguard humans from HSV infection and that led to the development of a system to test new herpes-fighting drugs. First, they spliced the DNA sequence that encodes B5 into the genetic material of HSV-resistant pig cells, thus making the pig cells susceptible to HSV. Next, they added to the HSV-susceptible cells a synthetic peptide (a protein chain) that mimics the structure of a small region of the B5 receptor. When HSV tries to infect the cells by entering through the B5 receptor, it tries instead to engage with the synthetic peptide and thus is prevented from infecting its intended target.

See also: Biology; Microbiology

REFERENCES AND FURTHER READING

Kessler, James H., J. S. Kidd, Renee A. Kidd, and Katherine A. Morin, eds. *Distinguished African American Scientists of the 20th Century*. Phoenix, AZ: Oryx Press, 1996: 112–116.

Krapp, Kristine M., ed. *Notable Black American Scientists*. Detroit, MI: Gale Research, 1999: 121–122.

Spangenburg, Ray, and Kit Moser. *African Americans in Science, Math, and Invention*. New York: Facts On File, 2003: 86–87.

Fuller, Solomon C.
(1872–1953) Neurologist

Solomon Fuller was one of the first neuropsychiatrists (medical researchers who explore the biochemical causes of mental illness). His research shed much light on the nature of mental illness in general, and he also did some important groundbreaking work with Alzheimer's disease.

Fuller was born on August 11, 1872, in Monrovia, Liberia. His father, Solomon, owned a coffee plantation, and his mother, Anna, was a missionary and teacher. In 1889, he came to the United States to attend Livingstone College in Salisbury, North Carolina. After graduating, he studied to be a physician at Long Island College Hospital in Brooklyn, New York, and Boston University School of Medicine (BUSM), receiving an MD from the latter in

1897. Upon completion of a two-year internship at Westborough State Hospital, during which he studied pathology (the origin, nature, and progress of disease in general), he was named a pathologist there and an instructor of pathology at BUSM, where he remained for the rest of his career.

At Westborough, Fuller became interested in the pathology and psychology of mental illness. He was particularly interested to know whether a connection existed between patients' behavior and the state of their brain cells. To this end, he began examining the brains of dead people who had suffered from mental illness. By using an instrument that could cut slices of brain tissue so thin that light could pass through them, he was able to take pictures (photomicrographs) of the tissue samples and then study the photomicrographs for abnormalities in the cells. Meanwhile, he began studying psychiatry and neurology at the Carnegie Laboratory in New York City and the University of Munich in Germany; at the latter, he was a graduate research assistant to Alois Alzheimer, who in 1906 would identify the mental condition among senior citizens that bears his name. In 1909, the same year he married Meta Warrick, with whom he had three children, Fuller began teaching neurology at BUSM, and for the rest of his career he focused on the causes of mental illness. From 1913 to 1937, he edited the *Westborough State Hospital Papers*, a medical journal that focused on the psychiatric, pathological, and neurological aspects of mental illness. Many of the articles in the *Papers* reported Fuller's groundbreaking work with schizophrenia, Alzheimer's disease, and manic-depressive psychosis, also known as bipolar disorder.

Early in Fuller's career, most psychiatrists believed that mental conditions resulted from purely psychological factors, not chemical imbalances; so Fuller's work was given little credence. However, as time progressed, Fuller's views came more into vogue, and today the psychochemical relationship is clearly understood and accepted by virtually all psychiatrists, psychologists, and neurologists. One important aspect of Fuller's work concerning Alzheimer's disease concerned the connection between Alzheimer's and arteriosclerosis (hardening of the arteries). Most physicians believed that such a connection existed, but Fuller insisted that it did not. Unfortunately, he could neither prove nor disprove the connection, but his insistence led other researchers to look for alternative causes. Although the cause of Alzheimer's remains to be discovered, by the 1950s, it had been demonstrated conclusively that arteriosclerosis had nothing to do with the disease.

Fuller retired from teaching in 1937, having attained the position of head of BUSM's department of neurology five years earlier, but he continued to conduct research as a staff neuropathologist for several Boston-area hospitals until his death. He died on January 16, 1953, at his home in Framingham, Massachusetts. His many honors include the naming in his honor of the Solomon Carter Fuller Institute, a joint project of the Black Psychiatrists of America and the American Psychiatric Association; BUSM's Dr. Solomon Carter Fuller Mental Health Center; and Fuller Middle School in Framingham.

See also: Black Psychiatrists of America

REFERENCES AND FURTHER READING

Hayden, Robert C. *Eleven African American Doctors*, rev. ed. New York: Twenty-First Century Books, 1992: 18–35.

Spangenburg, Ray, and Kit Moser. *African Americans in Science, Math, and Invention*. New York: Facts On File, 2003: 87–89.

Gates, Sylvester J., Jr.
(1950–) Theoretical Physicist

As a theoretical physicist, Sylvester Gates created abstract mathematical models to explain what happens to matter at incredibly small dimensions. His principal contribution to theoretical physics was a theory concerning the nature of the graviton, a theory that contributed to a better understanding of how all the forces of the universe relate to one another.

Gates was born on December 15, 1950, in Tampa. His father, Sylvester, was a sergeant in the U.S. Army, and his mother, Charlie, was a homemaker. As a boy, he moved with his family to Orlando, where he grew up. After finishing high school, he entered the Massachusetts Institute of Technology (MIT), receiving a BS in physics and a BS in mathematics in 1973 and a PhD in physics in 1977. He spent the next five years conducting postgraduate research at Harvard University and the California Institute of Technology. In 1982, he returned to MIT to teach applied mathematics, but he left two years later to teach physics at the University of Maryland at College Park. With the exception of a leave of absence from 1991 to 1993, during which he taught physics and chaired the physics department at Howard University, he spent the rest of his career at Maryland. In 1984, he married Dianna Abney, with whom he has two children.

Gates's early research involved two related areas of study, elementary particle physics and quantum field theory. Elementary particle physics involves the study of the subatomic particles that make up larger subatomic particles but that are not themselves constructed from smaller particles. The two best-known elementary particles are quarks and leptons. Quarks are the basic building blocks that comprise the particles found in an atomic nucleus such as protons and neutrons, and leptons are the subatomic particles found outside the nucleus such as the electron. Quantum field theory attempts to explain how and why the various subatomic particles, elementary and otherwise, interact with one another.

Like many theoretical physicists who studied quantum field theory in the 1980s, Gates became intrigued with developing a grand unified theory (GUT) for linking the four elementary forces of physics: electromagnetism, gravity, the strong nuclear force (which binds together quarks), and the weak nuclear force (which is responsible for certain types of radioactivity). Much work in this area had already been done; for example, the British physicist James Clerk Maxwell had shown that electricity and magnetism are both manifestations of electromagnetism; Richard P. Feynman, Julian S. Schwinger, and Shinichiro Tomonaga had developed quantum electrodynamics, which explains the strong nuclear force in terms of electromagnetism; and Steven Weinberg, Sheldon L. Glashow, and Abdus Salam developed the electroweak unification theory, which links the seemingly unrelated physical forces of electromagnetism and the weak nuclear force. The problem with developing a successful GUT is incorporating gravity into the theory, because gravity is the only force that is not known to be transmitted via a particle. Many theoretical physicists, including Gates, have postulated the existence of a gravity-carrying particle called the graviton, but its existence has yet to be demonstrated. Even Albert Einstein, the greatest theoretical physicist of all time, could not overcome this stumbling block, as he sought without success to develop a GUT by developing the same sort of mathematical relationship between electromagnetism and gravity that he had established for energy and matter ($E = mc^2$).

The problem with most failed GUTs is that they consider subatomic particles to be points. While the particle-as-point perspective explains many aspects of particle behavior, it leaves many others unexplained. This deficiency led to the development of string theory, which considers particles to be strings rather than points; next to a point, a line or string is the least complicated geometrical form.

The first string theory was advanced in the 1970s by Yoichiro Nambu, but it contained a number of inconsistencies. These inconsistencies were eliminated later in the decade by Joël Scherk and his colleagues, who introduced the concept of supersymmetry into string theory. Supersymmetry provides a mathematical means of linking quarks and leptons in such a way that is consistent with string theory; as a result, the combination of string theory and supersymmetry is known as superstring theory.

Gates's major contribution to superstring theory involved a more complete development of the idea of the heterotic string (a particular type of closed string). According to superstring theory, a string can be either open or closed; an open string resembles a sheet of paper, and a closed string resembles a tube. Open and closed strings vary in terms of their angular momentum (spin), a measurement of the force that keeps an object, such as a gyroscope or a spinning top, rotating about a fixed point. An open string can have a spin no greater than 1, but a closed string can have a spin as great as 2. A heterotic

Theoretical physicist Sylvester Gates has offered the best explanation to date concerning the nature of the graviton, the hypothetical subatomic particle that transmits gravity. (Courtesy Sylvester J. Gates)

string is a closed string in which the vibrations related to spin travel counterclockwise in a way that is totally different from the way they travel clockwise. Because the theorized behavior of the heterotic string corresponds more or less with the theorized behavior of the elusive graviton, Gates postulated that the graviton is actually a heterotic string. Since then, his postulation has been supported by the work of several other theoretical physicists, thus potentially bringing the physical community one step closer to the development of a grand unified theory.

During his brief sojourn at Howard in the 1990s, Gates established the Center for the Study of Terrestrial and Extraterrestrial Atmospheres. He was a charter fellow of the National Society of Black Physicists, and he later served a term as its president. His publications include *Superspace or 1001 Lessons in Supersymmetry* (Reading, MA: Benjamin/Cummings Publishing, 1983) and "Taking the Particle Out of Particle Physics" [*Quotient* 12, 4 (1986)]. His awards include the American Association for the Advancement of Science's 2006 Public Understanding of Science and Technology Award.

See also: American Association for the Advancement of Science; Howard University; National Society of Black Physicists; Physics

REFERENCES AND FURTHER READING

McMurray, Emily J., ed. *Notable Twentieth-Century Scientists*. Detroit, MI: Gale Research, 1995: 734–735.

Physicists of the African Diaspora. "Sylvester James Gates." [Online article or information; retrieved September 23, 2005.] http://www.math.buffalo.edu/mad/physics/gates_sylvester.html.

University of Maryland, Department of Physics. "Sylvester J. Gates Jr." [Online article or information; retrieved September 22, 2005.] http://www.physics.umd.edu/people/faculty/gates.html.

Gipson, Mack Jr.
(1931–1995) Geologist

Mack Gipson helped popularize the technique of sequence stratigraphy as a method for locating valuable deposits of petroleum. He also helped establish the National Association of Black Geologists and Geophysicists, the first professional organization dedicated to advancing the careers of black geoscientists.

Gipson was born on September 15, 1931, in Trenton, South Carolina. His parents, Mack and Artie, were farmers. As a young man, he moved with his grandmother to Augusta, Georgia, so that he could attend high school, and, after graduating, he entered Augusta's Paine College, receiving a BS in science and mathematics in 1953. He taught high school science in Augusta for a year before being drafted into the U.S. Army. Although he had originally planned to teach high school science for the rest of his career, during his time in the army he became interested in a career as a geologist. Upon being discharged in 1956, he married Alma Gadison, with whom he had four children, and entered the graduate program at the University of Chicago, receiving an MS and a PhD in geology in 1961 and 1963, respectively.

While in graduate school, Gipson supported himself and his family by working as a geologist for the Walter H. Flood Company. In this capacity, he conducted much of the geological work necessary for locating the runways at Chicago's O'Hare International Airport. He continued to work for Flood until 1964, when he joined the faculty at Virginia State University (VSU).

Gipson's primary research involved the depth and composition of shales (sedimentary rocks consisting of silt-like and clay-like particles), formed during the Pennsylvanian period, a geologic period that occurred approximately 300 million years ago. Pennsylvanian shales are particularly important economically, because they contain most of the known U.S. coal, oil, and natural gas deposits. By the mid-1970s, he became one of the first geologists to locate oil fields among Pennsylvanian shales by using sequence stratigraphy, known at the time as seismic stratigraphy. This technique involves directing strong shock waves deep into the earth and then interpreting the seismic lines thus generated to determine the nature and location of deep layers of sedimentary rock and the deposits that those layers are likely to contain. In 1975, he left VSU to work full time for the Exxon Company, one of the world's leading refiners of petroleum products, and over the next 11 years, he prospected for oil for Exxon and other companies in Alaska, Florida, Mexico, Czechoslovakia, and Pakistan. He published many of his findings concerning the scientific aspects of his prospecting efforts in the *Journal of Sedimentary Research* and the *Journal of Petroleum Geology*.

Gipson was also interested in geologic formations that had no economic importance. In the 1960s, he participated in a University of Chicago project to gain a better understanding of how the ocean floors were formed and evolved. In the 1970s, he served as a consultant to the National Aeronautics and Space Administration (NASA) by explaining that certain pyramid-like formations on the surface of the planet Mars were probably extinct volcanoes that had been carved into their present shape by sandstorms.

As one of the first African American geoscientists, Gipson felt a need to help other blacks enjoy careers in geology and geophysics. Consequently, when a group of black geologists in the Houston area contacted him about forming a professional advocacy group, he agreed to host an organizational meeting in his Houston home. He also provided sage advice for setting up the organization, known today as the National Association of Black Geologists and Geophysicists (NABGG), and today he is recognized by the NABGG as its founding advisor.

In 1986, Gipson joined the faculty at the University of South Carolina, where he remained for the rest of his career. He died on March 10, 1995, in Columbia, South Carolina. Following his death, the NABGG named the Mack Gipson Award in his honor.

See also: National Aeronautics and Space Administration; National Association of Black Geologists and Geophysicists; Virginia State University

REFERENCES AND FURTHER READING
Kessler, James H., J. S. Kidd, Renee A. Kidd, and Katherine A. Morin, eds. *Distinguished African American Scientists of the 20th Century*. Phoenix, AZ: Oryx Press, 1996: 120–123.
Krapp, Kristine M., ed. *Notable Black American Scientists*. Detroit, MI: Gale Research, 1999: 130–131.
Spangenburg, Ray, and Kit Moser. *African Americans in Science, Math, and Invention*. New York: Facts On File, 2003: 93–94.

Gourdine, Meredith C.
(1929–1998) Physicist

Two interesting methods for generating high-voltage electricity are electrogasdynamics (EGD) and magnetohydrodynamics (MHD). In EGD, forces are produced by electrically charged particles suspended in a gas that is flowing through an electric field. MHD is similar to EGD except that it substitutes a magnetic field for the electric field and its forces can be produced by a liquid as well as a gas. Although EGD and MHD were discovered in the 18th century, they remained poorly understood as recently as the late 1950s. Meredith Gourdine demonstrated how and why EGD and MHD work, and he developed dozens of processes that employ either one or the other.

Gourdine was born on September 26, 1929, in Newark, New Jersey. His father was a painting contractor, and his mother was a teletype operator. At age six, he moved with his family to New York City, where he grew up. He studied engineering physics at Cornell University, and in 1953, he received a BS. He spent the next two years as an officer in the U.S. Navy, and then he enrolled in the California Institute of Technology (Caltech), receiving a PhD in engineering physics in 1960. While completing his graduate studies, he also worked as a technical staffer for the Ramo-Woolridge Corporation and as a senior research scientist at the Jet Propulsion Laboratory (JPL), which Caltech administered for the National Aeronautics and Space Administration (NASA).

Gourdine became interested in EGD after learning about it in graduate school. It seemed to him that EGD had the potential to generate enormous amounts of high-voltage electricity inexpensively, and, while he was at JPL, he began to investigate EGD more thoroughly. By 1960, he had devised solutions to most of the obstacles that had prevented EGD from being used on a wide scale. Neither Caltech nor NASA showed any interest in Gourdine's work, however; so in 1960, he left to become the laboratory director at Plasmodyne Corporation.

At Plasmodyne, Gourdine began studying MHD, which had recently been used by other researchers to develop a high-voltage generator, albeit a rather small one. Before long, he had developed a method for using plasma (in physics, the electrically charged particles produced when atoms in an extremely hot gas become ionized) as a source for generating power via MHD. Plasmodyne, however, showed no more interest in MHD than JPL or NASA had in EGD; so in 1962, he left to become chief scientist for the Curtiss-Wright Corporation's Aero Division. Curtiss-Wright demonstrated the same ho-hum attitude toward EGD and MHD as his previous employers had; so in 1964, Gourdine relocated to Livingston, New Jersey, where he founded his own company, Gourdine Systems. In fact, the only organization that showed any interest in EGD or MHD at this time was the White House; in 1964, President Lyndon B. Johnson appointed Gourdine to serve on the President's Panel on Energy.

The focus of Gourdine Systems was on ways to use EGD to solve everyday problems, as well as to generate electricity. Over the next nine years, Gourdine showed that EGD offers an inexpensive but effective way to remove smoke from burning buildings, fog from airport runways, pollution from the air, and salt from seawater. He also used EGD to design improvements to circuit breakers, acoustic imaging, air monitors, and spray paint systems. In 1973, he moved to Houston, where he founded Energy Innovations, which focused on using EGD and MHD to develop direct energy-conversion devices, such as generators that convert natural gas and low-grade coal into electricity.

In 1953, Gourdine married June Cave, with whom he had three children. They later divorced, and he married Carolina Bailing, with whom he had one child. He was elected to the National Academy of Engineering, and he received more than 70 patents for applications and devices related to EGD and MHD. He died on November 20, 1998, in Houston.

See also: National Aeronautics and Space Administration; Physics

REFERENCES AND FURTHER READING
Carey, Charles W. Jr. *American Scientists.* New York: Facts On File, 2005: 148–149.
McMurray, Emily J., ed. *Notable Twentieth-Century Scientists.* Detroit, MI: Gale Research, 1995: 805–807.
Spangenburg, Ray, and Kit Moser. *African Americans in Science, Math, and Invention.* New York: Facts On File, 2003: 94–96.

Graves, Joseph L., Jr.
(1955–) Biologist

Joseph Graves made significant contributions to the scientific understanding of aging. He has also written much about the social construction of race and the lack of scientific evidence to support the notion that race is rooted in biology.

Graves was born on April 27, 1955, in Westfield, New Jersey. His father, Joseph, worked for a lumber company, and his mother, Helen, was a housekeeper. After finishing high school, he studied ecology and evolutionary biology at Oberlin College (Ohio), receiving an AB in 1977. He spent the next 11 years studying biology, tropical diseases, ecology, and evolutionary biology at the University of Lowell (Massachusetts), the University of Michigan, and Wayne State University (Detroit). After receiving a PhD in environmental, evolutionary, and systematic biology from Wayne State in 1988, he completed two years of postdoctoral research at the University of California at Irvine (Cal-Irvine). In 1990, he joined the faculty at Cal-Irvine as a professor of biology, leaving in 1994 to become a professor of evolutionary biology at Arizona State University-West. From 2004 to 2005, he was university core director and professor of biology at Fairleigh Dickinson University (Teaneck, New Jersey), and in 2005, he was named dean of university studies and professor of biology at North Carolina A&T State University. In 1984, he married Suekyung Joe, with whom he has two children.

Graves's first major research interest involved the role played by genetics in aging. He was particularly interested in exploring a theory of aging, first suggested by the evolutionary biologist George C. Williams and later corroborated mathematically by William D. Hamilton, that certain genes confer increased fitness early in life but cause decreased fitness later in life. His work in this regard focused on *Drosophila melanogaster* (the common fruit fly), the subject of choice for genetic researchers since fruit flies were used by Thomas Hunt Morgan, winner of the 1933 Nobel Prize in Medicine or Physiology, to demonstrate the validity of Gregor Mendel's theories about heredity. After participating in research that attempted to localize the genes that postpone aging in *Drosophila*, Graves compared the flight duration, wingbeat frequency, resistance to desiccation, and ability to produce and metabolize glycogen in fruit flies that were genetically selected for either long life or short life. Later studies examined the effects of population density on longevity. By 1994, he and his collaborators had demonstrated that the Williams–Hamilton theory of aging was essentially correct. Since then, other researchers have begun investigating the possibility that Graves's findings can help explain why and how humans age.

While he was experimenting with the genetic components of aging, Graves was also doing research related to the social construction of race. Like many scientists, Graves believes that there is no biological justification for the notion that races exist among modern humans but that popular notions about race and racism in Western society remain strong because race has become a powerful social construction. His published work in this regard includes *The Race Myth: Why We Pretend Race Exists in America* (New York: Plume Books, 2005) and *The Emperor's New Clothes: Biological Theories of Race at the Millennium* (New Brunswick, NJ: Rutgers University Press, 2001).

While teaching in California and Arizona, Graves implemented several programs to attract more minority students to the study of science. He also worked to protect the teaching of evolutionary science in the Arizona public schools. His honors include election to fellowship in the American Association for the Advancement of Science.

See also: North Carolina A&T State University; Wayne State University

REFERENCES AND FURTHER READING

University Studies at North Carolina A&T University. "Joseph L. Graves, Jr., Ph.D." [Online article or information; retrieved October 27, 2007.] http://www.ncat.edu/~univstud/faculty.html.

Hall, Lloyd A.
(1894–1971) Chemist

The preservation of food, especially meat, without altering its taste has been one of the biggest problems that industrial chemists have been called upon to solve. One solution that was used for years, the treatment of meat with crystals containing sodium chloride and various nitrates, was developed by Lloyd Hall. Hall also contributed to food science by developing a method for sterilizing spices and other products, discovering why fatty and oily foods become rancid, and developing some of the first artificial flavors.

Hall was born on June 20, 1894, in Elgin, Illinois. His father, Augustus, was a minister, and his mother, Isabel, was a homemaker. He developed an interest in chemistry while in high school, and in 1916, he received a BS in pharmaceutical chemistry from Northwestern University. He spent the next year as a research chemist for the Chicago Department of Health while taking graduate courses in chemistry at the University of Chicago. During World War I, he inspected gunpowder and explosives for the U.S. Army Ordnance Department. In 1919, he became chief chemist at John Morrell & Company, a meat-packing company in Ottumwa, Iowa. He returned to Chicago in 1921 to work as the chief chemist of Boyer Chemical Laboratory, and in 1922, he founded Chemical Products Corporation, a food science consulting firm. Three years later, he joined Griffith Laboratories as chief chemist and director of research, a position he held for the rest of his career.

Hall's first contribution to food science involved the development of an improved method for using salt to preserve meat. At the time, meat processors used ordinary table salt to cure, or preserve, meat, while treating the meat with sodium nitrate and potassium nitrate to preserve its flavor and color. All too often, however, the nitrates worked faster than the table salt, so that sometimes the meat spoiled and sometimes it just developed a peculiar taste. In 1932, Hall solved the problem by combining table salt and the nitrates into one crystal. To a strong solution of saltwater, he added small amounts of nitrates. This solution was then evaporated by being passed over heated metal rollers. This step caused the nitrates to become imbedded in the salt crystals, so that, when the crystals were injected into the meat, the nitrates could not go to work until after the salt had dissolved. One problem with this method was that the modified salt crystals often caked, making them difficult to apply; so Hall developed an anticaking additive from glycerine and alkali metal tartrate. Not only did the additive prevent caking, but it also caused the salt crystals to be distributed more evenly, thus doing a better job of preserving the meat. This method worked so well that it soon became the standard method for preserving processed meat products, and it remained the standard for decades.

Hall's second contribution to food science involved improving the methods by which meat is preserved by spices. It was generally believed that spices preserve meat as well as its flavor, but Hall discovered that untreated spices contain so many molds, yeasts, and bacteria that they actually cause meat to spoil faster. To solve this problem, he developed a process for removing the contaminants from spices. After a number of failed experiments, he discovered that small amounts of pesticides and insecticides decontaminate spices without rendering them inedible. Eventually, he discovered that putting the spices in a vacuum and then treating them with ethylene oxide gas completely killed all the microscopic pests. This method became known as the ethylene oxide Vacugas treatment or the Vacugas sterilization treatment. It worked so well that it became standard procedure not only for food manufacturers, but also for manufacturers of pharmaceuticals, hospital supplies, and cosmetics.

Hall's third contribution involved the use of antioxidants to prevent fatty and oily foods from becoming rancid. He discovered that rancidity occurs because certain ingredients in the fats or oils become oxidized but that unrefined vegetable oils containing antioxidants, known as tocopherols, do not become rancid. After identifying a number of chemical compounds that contain a high percentage of antioxidants, such as lecithin, propyl gallate, ascorbyl palmitate, citric acid, propylene glycol, and sodium chloride, he developed methods for using these compounds to treat foods, particularly bakery products, that are highly susceptible to oxidation.

Hall's last contribution was the development of some of the first artificial flavors. He created a group of flavoring materials known as protein hydrolysates simply by removing the water from plant proteins. This development proved to be a boon to the processed food industry, which was looking for ways to preserve and enhance the flavor of ready-to-eat foods. It also proved to be a boon to Griffith Laboratories as well, which profited tremendously from the manufacture and sale of artificial flavors.

Hall cofounded the Institute of Food Technologists, the first professional organization for chemists involved in food processing and preservation. He also served as a commissioner of the Illinois State Food Commission, a director of the American Institute of Chemists, a director of the Science Advisory Board on Food Research, a member of the American Food for Peace Council, and a consultant to the United Nations' Food and Agricultural Organization.

In 1919, Hall married Myrrhene Newsome, with whom he had two children. He retired from Griffith Laboratories in 1959 and moved to Pasadena, California. He died on January 2, 1971, in Altadena, California.

See also: Chemistry

REFERENCES AND FURTHER READING

Carey, Charles W. Jr. *American Scientists.* New York: Facts On File, 2005: 156–157.

Smith, Caroline B. D. "Lloyd A. Hall." *Contemporary Black Biography*, vol. 8. Detroit, MI: Gale Cengage, 1994: 99–102.

Spangenburg, Ray, and Kit Moser. *African Americans in Science, Math, and Invention.* New York: Facts On File, 2003: 102–103.

Harris, Bernard A., Jr.
(1956–) Astronaut

As a physician who specialized in internal medicine, Bernard Harris devoted much of his scientific career to space medicine; specifically, he was interested in learning more about how living in space affects humans. He pursued this interest both as an astronaut and as an earthbound scientist.

Harris was born on June 26, 1956, in Temple, Texas, to Bernard and Gussie Harris. His parents' marriage ended when he was young, and he moved with his mother to San Antonio, where he grew up. After receiving a BS in biology from the University of Houston in 1978, he entered the Texas Technological University School of Medicine and received an MD in 1982. He spent the next three years as a resident in internal medicine at the Mayo Clinic in Rochester, Minnesota, and then received a fellowship from the National Aeronautics and Space Administration (NASA) to conduct research at its Ames Research Center in Mountain View, California. In 1988, he received training as a flight surgeon at the Aerospace School of Medicine in San Antonio, and in 1990, he was chosen to enter the astronaut program. At an unknown date, he married Sandra Lewis, with whom he has one child.

Harris's research at Ames involved studying the effects of space travel on the musculoskeletal system (muscles and bones) of the human body. He was particularly interested in disuse osteoporosis, a decrease in the calcified mass of the bones that is caused by a marked reduction in physical activity such as occurs during a space mission of 7 to 10 days' duration. Upon entering the astronaut program, he transferred to the Johnson Space Center in Houston, where he participated in the Exercise Countermeasure Project. This project conducted clinical investigations into space adaptation and developed a series of exercises that astronauts could do while in space to avoid medical conditions such as disuse osteoporosis.

As a mission specialist, Harris conducted scientific experiments during two space shuttle missions. The first, STS-55, took place in April–May 1993 aboard the shuttle *Columbia*. Harris conducted experiments involving the life sciences and physics aboard the Spacelab D-2 module, an international effort led

Astronaut Bernard Harris specialized in space medicine, the study of how living in space affects the human body. (National Aeronautics and Space Administration)

by the German Aerospace Research Establishment but in which NASA, the European Space Administration, and agencies in France and Japan also participated. The D-2 mission, as it was also known, conducted 88 experiments in the areas of fluid physics, materials sciences, life sciences, biological sciences, technology, Earth observations, atmospheric physics, and astronomy. Many of the experiments advanced the research of the D-1 mission, which was conducted in 1985, by conducting similar tests, using upgraded processing hardware or by implementing methods that took full advantage of the technical advancements since then. The D-2 mission also contained several new experiments that were not previously flown on the D-1 mission. Since the mission specialists worked in 12-hour shifts and the experiments were conducted around the clock, Harris participated in about half of them.

Harris's second mission, STS-63, took place in February 1995 aboard the shuttle *Discovery*. This mission was the first mission of the joint Russian–American Space Program, and its primary objective was to perform a rendezvous and flyby of the Russian space station *Mir*. To this end, the mission sought to verify flight techniques, communications, and navigation aid sensor interfaces, as well as engineering analyses associated with *Discovery/Mir* proximity operations in preparation for a future docking mission. A secondary objective was to conduct the 20 experiments that comprised the SPACEHAB-3 payload, and Harris, as the mission's payload manager, was responsible for ensuring that these experiments were carried out correctly and successfully. These experiments included 11 biotechnology experiments, three advanced materials development experiments, four technology demonstrations, and two pieces of supporting hardware measuring on-orbit accelerations. Perhaps the two most interesting experiments were Astroculture and Immune. The purpose of Astroculture was to validate the performance of plant growth technologies, such as energy-efficient lighting and removal of pollutants from indoor air, in microgravity, as a step toward providing a life support system for plants in space. Immune made use of the known tendency of spaceflight to suppress the body's immune system to test the ability of certain substances to prevent or reduce this suppression, and its purpose was to identify possible pharmacological treatments for autoimmune diseases such as AIDS.

During the mission, Harris also participated in a two-man space walk (extravehicular activity [EVA] in NASA parlance). The purpose of the EVA was to test out the methods and procedures for handling large objects, working with tools, guiding objects into position, and securing them into place that would be used later to build the International Space Station under the conditions of microgravity that prevail in space.

In 1996, Harris resigned from NASA and went to work for Spacehab, Inc., a Houston firm that provides various products and services in support of manned and unmanned space missions, as their chief scientist and vice president of science and health services. That same year, he received an MS in biomedical science from the University of Texas Medical Branch in Galveston, and he began teaching internal medicine on a part-time basis at several Texas universities. In 2000, he was named vice president of business development for Space Media, Inc., and in this capacity he oversaw the development of an international space education program for students. He is the founder and president of the Harris Foundation, which supports math and science education and crime prevention programs for American youth.

See also: Astronomy and Astrophysics; Biology; National Aeronautics and Space Administration; Physics

REFERENCES AND FURTHER READING
National Aeronautics and Space Administration. "Biographical Data: Bernard A. Harris, Jr. (M.D.)." [Online article or information; retrieved October 30, 2007.] http://www.jsc.nasa.gov/Bios/htmlbios/harris.html.
Spangenburg, Ray, and Kit Moser. *African Americans in Science, Math, and Invention.* New York: Facts On File, 2003: 103–104.

Harris, James A.
(1932–) Nuclear Chemist

James Harris played a major role in the discovery of the transuranium elements 104 and 105. He also developed techniques for detecting secret nuclear testing.

Harris was born on March 26, 1932, in Waco, Texas. His father, Frank, was a farmer, and his mother, Martha, was a cook. At age 12, he moved in with an aunt in Oakland, California, where he grew up. After receiving a BS in chemistry from Huston-Tillotson College (Texas, now Huston-Tillotson University) in 1953, he served two years in the U.S. Air Force before going to work as a chemist for Tracerlab, Inc., in Richmond, California. In this capacity, he tested the radioactive fallout from secret tests of nuclear bombs conducted by the Soviet Union to determine the exact nature of the bomb's fissionable material. In 1960, he joined the scientific staff at the nuclear chemistry division of the Lawrence Radiation Laboratory (Rad Lab) at the University of California at Berkeley, and for the next four years he helped develop highly sensitive devices for detecting trace (extremely small) amounts of elements. In 1957, he married Helen Harris, with whom he had five children.

When Harris went to work at the Rad Lab, it was the world's foremost research institution in terms of the discovery of human-made elements, particularly the transuranium elements. Prior to Harris's arrival, Rad Lab researchers had discovered 10 transuranium elements: neptunium (element 93), plutonium (94), americium (95), curium (96), berkelium (97), californium (98), einsteinium (99), fermium (100), mendelevium (101), and nobelium (102), and shortly after his arrival, they discovered lawrencium (103); the element number indicates the number of neutrons contained in the nucleus of one atom. Harris's original role in this ongoing project was to develop innovative ways to detect whatever new element Rad Lab researchers had developed, because most transuranium elements are so unstable that they exist for no more than a few seconds.

In 1964, Harris began preparing the atomic samples from which the next previously undiscovered transuranium elements would be produced. In essence, transuranium elements are produced by bombarding a group of target atoms with relatively slow moving neutrons from other elements, such as carbon or nitrogen. If one of the target atoms is able to capture one of the neutrons, the chances are good that the target atom will be transformed into a higher-numbered element; for example, neptunium (93) was developed by bombarding uranium (92) with neutrons. Because elements 99 through 103 are incredibly unstable, Harris chose to use californium (98) as the target for making element 104, meaning each atom of californium would have to capture six neutrons to be transformed into element 104. To this end, he acquired all of the world's supply of californium, approximately two-millionths of an ounce. He then developed a method for purifying it so that all trace elements, such as lead, were removed from the sample. He also developed the detection method for determining whether the experiment produced any atoms of element 104. The project proved to be successful when, in 1969, after hundreds of hours of bombarding the target with carbon, Harris was able to detect a few atoms of element 104 for a few seconds. When the same target was bombarded with nitrogen in 1970, Harris's detection methods indicated the brief presence of a few atoms of element 105.

A bit of a controversy ensued as to what these new elements should be named. In 1964, the Soviets had claimed to have discovered element 104, which they wanted to call kurchatovium after Igor Kurchatov, a Soviet nuclear physicist. Their work, however, could not be duplicated whereas the Rad Lab's could; so Rad Lab won the naming rights to element 104, which they named rutherfordium after Lord Rutherford, a famous British physicist. Meanwhile, element 105 was named dubnium in honor of Dubna, site of the Soviet counterpart to the Rad Lab.

Harris continued to experiment with transuranium elements until 1988, when he retired to his home in Pinole, California. Since then, he has remained active in community affairs.

See also: Chemistry

REFERENCES AND FURTHER READING

Krapp, Kristine M., ed. *Notable Black American Scientists*. Detroit, MI: Gale Research, 1999: 146–148.
Spangenburg, Ray, and Kit Moser. *African Americans in Science, Math, and Invention*. New York: Facts On File, 2003: 105–107.

Harris, Wesley L.
(1941–) Aerospace Scientist

Wesley Harris was a leading expert in the field of aeroacoustics, the noise generated by flying vehicles. His major contribution as an aerospace scientist was to discover the principles by which helicopters could be made to fly more quietly. As an administrator, he oversaw a number of research projects related to improved air and space travel.

Harris was born on October 29, 1941, in Richmond, Virginia. His parents, William and Rosa, were tobacco factory workers. As a boy, he was fascinated by flying and experimental aircraft, and when the Soviets launched *Sputnik*, the first human-made satellite, in 1957, he became interested in space travel as well. After receiving a BS in aerospace engineering from the University of Virginia (UVa) in 1964, he entered the graduate program at Princeton University and received an MA and a PhD in aerospace and mechanical sciences in 1966 and 1968, respectively. He then returned to UVa to teach engineering, leaving after four years for a position as a professor of aeronautics, astronautics, and ocean engineering at the Massachusetts Institute of Technology (MIT).

While a graduate student, Harris became interested in aeroacoustics. His first research papers, published in 1971, demonstrated the structure of normal shock waves caused by aircraft by recording the shock waves' movements through various gas mixtures; his second paper investigated nonlinear noise propagation by examining its effect on viscous solutions. In the mid-1970s, he turned his attention to the noise generated by helicopters, a subject that drew the bulk of his attention for the next 10 years. During that period, he published papers on the development of experimental techniques for studying helicopter rotor noise, an experimental study of helicopter rotor rotational noise in a wind tunnel, a simplified mach number scaling law for helicopter rotor noise [1 mach equals the speed of sound (approximately 760 miles per hour)], an experimental study of high-frequency noise from helicopter rotors, low-frequency broadband noise generated by a helicopter rotor, the acoustic power emitted by helicopter rotor blades at low tip speeds, helicopter rotor impulsive noise, and dynamic surface measurements on a model helicopter rotor during blade slap at high angles of attack. His research concerning helicopter noise permitted the Department of Defense to develop quieter military helicopters. His nonhelicopter research included noise pollution in urban ghettos and hypersonic airflow, the air currents caused by an aircraft traveling at speeds of Mach 5 or higher.

In 1985, Harris was named dean of the school of engineering at the University of Connecticut. He left five years later to become vice president and chief administrative officer of the University of Tennessee Space Institute. In this capacity, he refocused the school's research program on such topics as space propulsion, energy conversion, and laser applications. In 1993, he was recruited by the National Aeronautics and Space Administration (NASA) to become associate administrator of aeronautics. In this capacity, he oversaw the research efforts of NASA and its subcontractors on projects such as an advanced supersonic transport, the runway-to-orbit national aerospace plane, and the use of supercomputers for improving the modeling of aerodynamic forces. Two years later he returned to MIT to be the Charles Stark Draper Professor of Aeronautics and Astronautics, a position he held until the end of his career.

In addition to his duties at MIT, Harris also served as a consultant to the federal government as well as a number of defense contractors. He coauthored two books: *Defense Manufacturing in 2010 and Beyond: Meeting the Changing Needs of National Defense* (Washington, DC: National Academies Press, 1999) and *Incentive Strategies for Defense Acquisitions* (Fort Belvoir, VA.: Defense Acquisition Press, 2001). He was married twice and has seven children.

See also: National Aeronautics and Space Administration

REFERENCES AND FURTHER READING

MIT Aero | Astro. "Wesley L. Harris." [Online article or information; retrieved October 30, 2007.] http://web.mit.edu/newsoffice/2003/harris-0514.html.

Spangenburg, Ray, and Kit Moser. *African Americans in Science, Math, and Invention*. New York: Facts On File, 2003: 108–109.

Hawkins, W. Lincoln
(1911–1992) *Chemist*

Walter Lincoln Hawkins was one of the leading chemical engineers of his day. As a researcher, he not only provided a better understanding of the chemical and physical principles underlying the behavior of plastics, but he also applied those principles to the development of a number of new plastics and the processes for manufacturing them.

Hawkins was born on March 21, 1911, in Washington, D.C. His father, William, was a lawyer, and his mother, Maude, was a science teacher. After graduating from Rensselaer Polytechnic Institute in Troy, New York, in 1932, he returned to Washington, D.C., to study chemistry at Howard University, receiving an MS in 1934. Four years later he received a PhD in chemistry from McGill University in Montreal, and then went to Columbia University in New York City to conduct postgraduate research on a four-year National Research Council fellowship. In 1942, he joined the staff at the Bell Telephone Laboratories (BTL) in Murray Hill, New Jersey, where he remained for the rest of his career. In 1939, he married Lilyan Bobo, with whom he had two children.

Hawkins's early research involved alkaloid chemistry (the study of chemical compounds, such as morphine and nicotine, that have a powerful physiological effect on humans and other animals). At BTL, however, his research focused more on developing chemical compounds for use in telephone, radio, and other types of communication. While at BTL, he received almost 150 patents for his inventions and the processes by which to make them; most of these inventions and patents were related to new materials and processes for preserving and recycling plastics. Perhaps his most important development was a chemical additive used to insulate telephone wires. In the early days of telephony, lead was used to insulate wires, but by the 1950s, lead had become so expensive that researchers began looking for a cheaper alternative. A group of British researchers developed a plastic insulation that performed well under optimum conditions but became excessively brittle when exposed to extremes of heat or cold. Hawkins solved the problem by developing an additive that stabilized the plastic so that it was not altered by extreme temperatures. It is estimated that Hawkins's additive has saved telephone companies billions of dollars, thus making it economically feasible for them to provide telephone service to even the most remote customers. In addition to his duties at BTL, he taught chemistry at Polytechnic Institute in New York City.

In 1972, Hawkins was named head of BTL's department of applied research, a position he held until his retirement in 1976. He then went to work for the Plastics Institute of America in Hoboken, New Jersey, as their research director, a position he held for seven years. His many honors include the National Medal of Technology, which he received partly for his contributions to plastics science and partly because of his efforts to recruit minorities into careers as scientists. In 1983, he moved to San Marcos, California, where he died on August 20, 1992.

See also: Chemistry; Howard University

REFERENCES AND FURTHER READING

McMurray, Emily J., ed. *Notable Twentieth-Century Scientists.* Detroit, MI: Gale Research, 1995: 879–881.

Spangenburg, Ray, and Kit Moser. *African Americans in Science, Math, and Invention.* New York: Facts On File, 2003: 109–111.

Hayes, Tyrone B.
(1967–) Biologist

Tyrone Hayes demonstrated that overexposure to the herbicide atrazine disrupts the normal development of frogs. His research has led the scientific community and the federal government to rethink the policies and procedures associated with the use of atrazine.

Hayes was born on July 29, 1967, in Columbia, South Carolina. His father, Romeo, was a carpet installer, and his mother, Susie, was a homemaker. As a boy, he became interested in how amphibians such as frogs and turtles grow and develop and how changes to their habitat affect their development. He received a BA in organismic and evolutionary biology from Harvard University in 1989 and a PhD in integrative biology from the University of California at Berkeley (Cal-Berkeley) in 1993. He spent the next two years conducting postdoctoral research at Cal-Berkeley, and in 1995, he joined the Cal-Berkeley faculty as a professor of biology.

Hayes's primary research interest involves learning how changes in the external environment induce changes in the molecular structure of amphibians, how these internal changes are coordinated, what molecular mechanisms are involved, and how molecular changes affect an amphibian's ability to adapt to the changes in its external environment. In the late 1990s, he became interested in how pesticides, particularly atrazine, the active ingredient in the herbicides most widely used to kill weeds in cornfields, affect amphibians. At the time, the Environmental Protection Agency (EPA) had concluded that atrazine levels as high as 3 parts per billion (ppb) were acceptable in drinking water for humans. Hayes discovered, however, that atrazine levels as high as 1 ppb retarded the growth of vocal chords in male frogs. Further study showed that, when male frogs at a certain period in their development are exposed to atrazine levels as low as 0.1 ppb, their sex glands produce estrogen instead of testosterone, in effect prohibiting them from developing into fully functioning males. Further research showed that male frogs so affected produced eggs instead of sperm in their testes. Not coincidently, Hayes's findings came out at a time when many scientists were noting a decline in the amphibian population in the western United States, where atrazine is used extensively and where it runs off into the streams and wetlands, the habitat of amphibians. Later studies by other researchers showed that atrazine has a similar effect on fish, birds, and reptiles, and other studies linked higher incidences of breast cancer and prostate cancer in rodents and humans to exposure to atrazine. Much controversy surrounds his findings, most of it generated by the chemical company that manufactures atrazine and its business and scientific partners. Nevertheless, Hayes's work has induced the EPA to reconsider the practices and procedures it recommends for the use of atrazine as well as the acceptable level of atrazine in the water supply.

See also: Cancer

References and Further Reading

National Geographic's Strange Days on Planet Earth. "Tyrone Hayes, PhD, Biologist." [Online article or information; retrieved October 28, 2007.] http://www.pbs.org/strangedays/episodes/troubledwaters/experts/bio_ha yes_tyrone.html

Haynes, John K., Jr.
(1943–) Molecular Biologist

John Haynes's research applied the principles of biophysics to the study of sickle cell disease. His work shed important light on the nature and features of sickle-shaped cells, thus preparing the way for the eventual discovery of a cure.

Haynes was born on October 30, 1943, in Monroe, Louisiana. His father, John Sr., was a high school principal, and his mother, Grace, was a teacher. At age six, he moved with his family to Baton Rouge, where he grew up. At age 16, he entered Morehouse College in Atlanta with the intention of becoming a physician, but he soon developed an interest in embryology and opted for a career as a scientific researcher instead. After receiving a BS in biology in 1964, he entered the graduate biology program at Brown University and received a PhD in 1970. He spent the next three years conducting postgraduate research at Brown and the Massachusetts Institute of Technology, and in 1973, he was appointed to the department of genetics and molecular medicine at Meharry Medical College in Nashville. Six years later, he returned to Morehouse to teach biology, eventually rising to the position of department chair. In 1969, he married Carolyn Price.

As an undergraduate, Haynes developed an interest in embryology. His doctoral dissertation demonstrated how the enzyme that regulates energy use in the frog embryo is itself regulated by other enzymes. His postgraduate research explored the relationship between embryology and molecular biology (the study of biophysical principles as they apply to molecules) by studying phages (viruses so small that they can infect bacteria). He was particularly interested in how bacteria develop immunity to viral infection, and he looked for clues in the parts of the cell membrane that allow substances to pass into and out of a cell.

Haynes abandoned his interest in embryology in favor of molecular biology when he began studying the biophysics of sickle cell disease. This form of anemia is caused by abnormalities in the hemoglobin, the protein in the blood that carries oxygen from the lungs to the tissues, and it causes red blood cells to become rigid and take on a sickle-like shape. The shape and rigidity of the cells make it difficult for them to pass through the body's capillaries, thus causing swelling and pain. Haynes demonstrated that this rigidity is caused because the affected cell has too much calcium and not enough water, and he helped test a drug that would restore sickle-shaped cells to their original shape without also causing harmful side effects. He also performed a microscopic study of the membranes of sickle-shaped cells, which led to the development of a simple but effective screening method for quickly determining whether a person has sickle cell anemia. Later, he sought to understand how sickle-shaped cells become too rigid by studying the features of the cell membrane that are responsible for allowing compounds, such as calcium and water, to enter and leave the cell.

In addition to his teaching duties at Morehouse, Haynes served for 11 years as director of the office of health professions, and in 2000, he was named dean of the division of science and mathematics. He also served on the board of directors of the Sickle Cell Anemia Foundation of Georgia and on a number of committees for organizations such as the National Research Council, the National Institutes of Health, and the American Society for Cell Biology.

See also: American Society for Cell Biology; Biology; Meharry Medical College; National Institutes of Health; Sickle Cell Disease

REFERENCES AND FURTHER READING

Kessler, James H., J. S. Kidd, Renee A. Kidd, and Katherine A. Morin, eds. *Distinguished African American Scientists of the 20th Century.* Phoenix, AZ: Oryx Press, 1996: 157–161.

Krapp, Kristine M., ed. *Notable Black American Scientists*. Detroit, MI: Gale Research, 1999: 153–154.

Spangenburg, Ray, and Kit Moser. *African Americans in Science, Math, and Invention*. New York: Facts On File, 2003: 111–112.

Henderson, James H. M.
(1917–) Plant Physiologist

James Henderson was one of the first plant physiologists to experiment with auxins (plant growth hormones). Not only did his research in this area shed much light on the ubiquity of auxins (virtually every plant produces them), but it also provided some interesting clues for medical researchers looking for a cure for cancer in humans.

Henderson was born on August 10, 1917, in Falls Church, Virginia. His father, Edwin, was a teacher, and his mother, Mary, was a homemaker. After receiving a BS in botany from Howard University in 1939, he went off to the University of Wisconsin, where he received an MPh and a PhD in plant physiology in 1940 and 1943, respectively. He spent the next two years conducting postdoctoral research at the University of Chicago before joining the faculty at Tuskegee Institute (today Tuskegee University). He remained at Tuskegee for the rest of his career and was eventually named chair of the division of natural sciences. In 1948, he married Betty Francis, with whom he had four children.

Henderson's primary research interest involved auxins. Auxins regulate plant growth by stimulating cell elongation in stems and inhibiting it in roots, but they also influence phototropism (the growth of stems toward light) and geotropism (the growth of stems away from gravity). In 1885, the first known auxin, indole–3-acetic acid (IAA), was discovered in the by-products of plant fermentation, but it was not until 1926 that the Dutch plant physiologist Fritz Went isolated a plant growth hormone in the plant itself. By 1954, auxins remained so poorly understood that a committee of plant physiologists was set up that same year to characterize the group auxins. Hence, Henderson performed some of the earliest experiments concerning auxins. In fact, at the time he was in graduate school, the existence of auxins in every type of plant had yet to be demonstrated conclusively.

Henderson's doctoral dissertation concerned the ability of the tomato plant to control the amount of water and nutrients it intakes through its roots. In the process, he demonstrated that the tomato produces auxins that increase or decrease the rate at which its cells utilize energy. Further research with other plants showed that all the plants he studied produce some form of auxin, usually in the form of a complicated, carbon-based acidic compound such as citric acid, that they use to enhance their rate of growth.

At Tuskegee, Henderson devoted his primary research efforts to studying the sweet potato. In addition to studying the effects of auxins on sweet potato growth, he also looked for biochemical compounds contained in the sweet potato that might be beneficial to humans. He was particularly interested in finding a substance that might stop the growth of cancer cells in humans. This search led him to study the growth and development of a form of plant cancer called crown gall tumor in the sunflower. Henderson was able to demonstrate that, when crown gall tumor tissue is denied a supply of nutrients from which to obtain IAA, it can synthesize IAA from the amino acid tryptophan. Normal sunflower tissue is unable to do this because it appears to contain an inhibitor of the enzyme system involved in the conversion of tryptophan to IAA. The discovery that tumorous plant tissue can produce its own growth hormone led medical researchers studying cancer in humans to look for clues that tumorous tissue in humans possesses the same ability.

In addition to his other duties, Henderson served as director of Tuskegee's George Washington Carver Foundation, which funds scholarships for students pursuing scientific careers. He also served on committees for the American Association for the Advancement of Science, the American Society of Plant Physiologists, the Botanical Society of America, the National Institutes of Science, the American Institute of Biological Sciences, the Society for the Study of Development and Growth, and the Tissue Culture Association. He authored more than 50 scholarly articles for prestigious journals such as *American Journal of Botany* and *Plant Physiology*.

See also: American Association for the Advancement of Science; Cancer; Howard University; Tuskegee University

REFERENCES AND FURTHER READING

Kessler, James H., J. S. Kidd, Renee A. Kidd, and Katherine A. Morin, eds. *Distinguished African American Scientists of the 20th Century*. Phoenix, AZ: Oryx Press, 1996: 161–164.

Krapp, Kristine M., ed. *Notable Black American Scientists*. Detroit, MI: Gale Research, 1999: 154–156.

Spangenburg, Ray, and Kit Moser. *African Americans in Science, Math, and Invention*. New York: Facts On File, 2003: 112–113.

Henry, Warren E.
(1909–2001) Physicist

Warren Henry was one of the nation's foremost experts on low-temperature physics and magnetism. His research shed much light on the magnetic prop-

Physicist Warren Henry was a leading expert on the magnetic properties of various metals at very low temperatures. (Lawrence Berkeley National Laboratory)

erties of iron, gold, chromium, uranium, plutonium, and the rare earth elements at temperatures approaching absolute zero.

Henry was born on February 18, 1909, in Evergreen, Alabama. His parents, Nelson and Mattye, were farmers and teachers. At age 18, he entered the Tuskegee Institute (today Tuskegee University), where his parents had learned the techniques of scientific farming from George Washington Carver, and in 1931, he received a BS in mathematics. He spent the next seven years teaching mathematics, physics, and chemistry at Escambia County Training School (Alabama), Spelman College and Morehouse College in Atlanta, and Tuskegee. During that period, he coauthored *Procedures in Elementary Qualitative Chemical Analysis* (Tuskegee, AL: Tuskegee University Press, 1937) and attended Atlanta University (today Clark Atlanta University), receiving an MS in organic chemistry in 1937. In 1938, he entered the graduate program at the University of Chicago and received a PhD in physical chemistry three years later. His doctoral dissertation involved the testing of a temperature detector of his own design; placed directly in the midst of an ongoing chemical reaction, it used alternating current techniques to measure changes as small as one ten-millionth of a degree. After teaching chemistry at Tuskegee for another two years, Henry took a position as a postdoctoral researcher at the Massachusetts Institute of Technology (MIT) Radiation Laboratory, where he spent the rest of World War II. At MIT, he worked with Isidor Isaac Rabi and other eminent physicists who were adapting the techniques of the magnetic resonance method (the forerunner of the medical diagnostic technique known as magnetic resonance imaging, or MRI) for use in radar and other microwave technologies. Henry's primary contribution to the Radiation Laboratory's work was to develop a video amplifier that strengthened and clarified the signal on a portable radar screen.

After the war, Henry spent a year at the University of Chicago's Institute for the Study of Metals. He worked on a project to discover why jet aircraft, which had just been invented, were crashing at an alarming rate. The most likely reason seemed to be that metal fatigue in the alloys from which the wing spars were constructed had caused them to fail; so Henry used his temperature detector to test a number of different alloys and show how long a given alloy would last.

After a year as head of the physics department at Morehouse, in 1948, Henry became a research physicist at the Naval Research Laboratory (NRL) in Washington, D.C. For the next 12 years, he conducted research on low-temperature physics (the study of what happens to matter at temperatures just above absolute zero). He became particularly adept at achieving extremely low temperatures by employing a method known as adiabatic demagnetization, by which a system's magnetic orientation is changed so that the energy caused by the momentum of its molecules can be siphoned off. To this end, he headed the NRL team that developed a high-magnetic-field Bitter magnet, at the time one of the most powerful magnets in the nation. Named after its inventor, the American physicist Francis Bitter, a Bitter magnet uses stacked copper plates instead of coiled wires to generate magnetism; because of its design, a Bitter magnet can be cooled, which removes an important restriction on its ability to generate a powerful magnetic field.

Henry's work with low-temperature physics eventually led him to study superconductivity (the ability of certain elements to lose all resistance to electron flow in extreme low-temperature conditions) in semiconductors (substances that conduct electricity better than nonconductors such as glass but not as well as good conductors such as copper).

In 1960, Henry moved to California to work for the Lockheed Missiles and Space Company, a leading defense contractor, as a senior staff scientist. For the next nine years, he designed guidance systems for missiles and detection systems for finding enemy submarines that operated on the principles of magnetism. He also helped develop a device for measuring magnetic fields in outer space. In 1969, he returned to Howard to teach physics, having taught there during his tenure at NRL, and he remained there until his retirement in 1977.

Henry devoted much of his retirement to an organization called Minorities Access to Research Careers, which encouraged college upperclass members to become acquainted with scientists to make it easier for them to embark on scientific careers. He was married to the former Jean Pearlson. He died on October 31, 2001, in Washington, D.C.

See also: Carver, George Washington; Chemistry; Clark Atlanta University; Physics; Spelman College; Tuskegee University

REFERENCES AND FURTHER READING
Maclin, A. P., et al., *Magnetic Phenomena: The Warren E. Henry Symposium on Magnetism, in Commemoration of His 89th Birthday and His Work in Magnetism.* New York: Springer-Verlag, 1989.

Physicists of the African Diaspora. "Warren E. Henry." [Online article or information; retrieved September 26, 2005.] http://www.math.buffalo.edu/mad/physics/henry_warren.html.

Spangenburg, Ray, and Kit Moser. *African Americans in Science, Math, and Invention.* New York: Facts On File, 2003: 114–116.

Hill, Henry A.
(1915–1979) Chemist

One of the most challenging aspects of industrial chemistry is the development and management of chemical intermediates. These compounds are formed during the various steps of an extended chemical reaction that the original raw materials must go through to be made into the final product. Henry Hill was particularly adept at managing the chemical intermediates involved in making polymers (the chemical compounds from which plastics are made), and he pioneered the making of commercial dyes and flame-retardant coatings from polymers.

Hill was born on May 30, 1915, in St. Joseph, Missouri. His father, William, was a waiter, and his mother, Kate, was a homemaker. At age 16, he finished high school and went to Chicago to attend the Lewis Institute (today part of the Illinois Institute of Technology). A year later, he transferred to Johnson C. Smith College in Charlotte, North Carolina, and received a BS in mathematics and chemistry in 1936. He then studied chemistry at the University of Chicago before transferring to the Massachusetts Institute of Technology, where he received a PhD in organic chemistry in 1942. He spent the next four years as a research chemist at the North Atlantic Research Corporation in Newtonville, Massachusetts, after which he went to work in a similar capacity for the Dewey & Almy Chemical Company in Cambridge.

Hill's early research focused on learning more about the relatively new field of polymerization, the chemical process by which plastic compounds such as polyethylene and polypropylene are made. Polymerization involves the combination of small molecules consisting mostly of hydrogen and carbon into long chains, which are then molded into shapes, spun into fibers, or developed into additives or coatings. Polymerization involves many steps, each of which results in the production of a different chemical intermediate. As the steps progress, the chemical intermediates become more complex, and understanding how to get them to react to produce the next desired intermediate becomes increasingly difficult. Nevertheless, Hill developed a talent for managing chemical intermediates, and soon he was overseeing the production of a host of complicated polymers.

In 1952, Hill decided to strike out on his own by founding National Polychemicals, which specialized in the manufacture of chemical intermediates. By providing manufacturers with ready-made intermediates, he helped them save time and money in the manufacturing process. National Polychemicals gave way to Riverside Research Laboratory, which he founded in Haverhill, Massachusetts, in 1961. Riverside was set up specifically to develop chemical intermediates for use in the manufacture of synthetic fibers. Shortly after getting it started, Hill developed a method for producing dyes for synthetic fibers from polymers made from the azo compounds (organic compounds that feature a double bond between two nitrogen atoms), and by 1963 Riverside was producing two new azo compounds, azodicarbonide and barium azocarbonate. Hill then turned his attention to developing flame-retardant coatings for synthetic fibers, and by 1967, Riverside was producing one of the first flame-retardant coatings from urea-formaldehyde resin.

Hill was elected to a term as president of the American Chemical Society. He also chaired the chemistry section of the American Association for the Advancement of Science and served on the National Commission on Product Safety. In 1943, he married Adelaide Cromwell, with whom he had one child. He died on March 17, 1979, in Haverhill.

See also: American Association for the Advancement of Science; American Chemical Society; Chemistry

REFERENCES AND FURTHER READING

Carey, Charles W. Jr. *American Scientists*. New York: Facts On File, 2005: 169–170.

McMurray, Emily J., ed. *Notable Twentieth-Century Scientists*. Detroit, MI: Gale Research, 1995: 929–930.

Spangenburg, Ray, and Kit Moser. *African Americans in Science, Math, and Invention*. New York: Facts On File, 2003: 116–117.

Hinton, William A.
(1883–1959) Pathologist

Before HIV/AIDS, the deadliest sexually transmitted disease was syphilis. Untreated, syphilis causes the deterioration of virtually every organ and tissue in the body, but especially the brain and nervous system, and once it reaches a certain stage it is 100 percent fatal. Because of how it is transmitted, however, syphilis remained a poorly discussed and poorly understood disease until well into the 20th century. William Hinton contributed to a better understanding of how syphilis works in the human body, and he developed the Hinton test and the Davies-Hinton test for diagnosing syphilis so that it could be treated in a timely fashion.

Hinton was born on December 15, 1883, in Chicago. His father, Augustus, was a railroad porter, and his mother, Marie, was a homemaker. Shortly after his birth, his family moved to Kansas City, Kansas, where he grew up. After two years at the University of Kansas, he transferred to Harvard University to study science and he received a BS in 1905. He spent the next four years teaching science at Walden University in Nashville, Tennessee, and Oklahoma Agricultural and Mechanical College in Langston, Oklahoma, before entering Harvard Medical School. In 1909, he married Ada Hawes, with whom he had two children.

In 1912, Hinton received an MD, but he remained at Harvard to work as an assistant researcher at the Wassermann Laboratory, one of the world's foremost centers for the study of communicable diseases. While working at Wassermann, he also served as a pathologist at Boston's Massachusetts General Hospital. In 1915, the Wassermann Laboratory was transferred from Harvard to the Massachusetts Department of Public Health (DPH), and Hinton was named assistant director of DPH's division of biologic laboratories as well as head of the Wassermann Laboratory. Three years later he took on the additional duties of teaching preventive medicine and hygiene at Harvard Medical School, and before long he was teaching bacteriology and immunology as well.

Hinton's research was devoted to learning more about syphilis. So little was known about syphilis at the time that within two years he had become one of the world's foremost experts on how syphilis operates in the bloodstream. He then set out to develop a better test for diagnosing syphilis in humans. August von Wassermann, for whom the Wassermann Laboratory had been named, had developed a method for identifying in the bloodstream the presence of the microscopic organisms that transmit syphilis. Developed in 1906, the Wassermann test is simple and effective enough that it is still used today as a preliminary diagnostic tool. The problem with the Wassermann test, however, is that it gives a number of false positives, meaning that it sometimes indicates the presence of syphilis in the bloodstream when in fact the patient is not infected at all. These false positives always caused patients of the day to be needlessly embarrassed, and the treatment for syphilis was too long and painful to be given to people who did not really need it. Hence there was a need for a test that was more accurate than the Wassermann.

In 1915, Hinton began working to develop a test that would eliminate the number of false positives while also being quick, accurate, and simple to use. Twelve years later, he developed the Hinton test, which tests for the presence of syphilis antibodies in the blood serum. The Hinton test has an accuracy rate of 98 percent, which is a bit lower than the Wassermann, but it almost never gives a false positive. In 1931, Hinton and a colleague, John A. N. Davies, developed the Davies-Hinton test, which tests for syphilis antibodies in spinal fluid rather than in blood serum. It is as accurate as the Wassermann test, and it does not return a high rate of false positives. Unfortunately, because the drawing of spinal fluid is dangerous and expensive, the Davies-Hinton test never achieved widespread use as a tool for detecting syphilis. Despite Hinton's dissatisfaction with the Hinton test, it was widely accepted by medical personnel across the country, and in 1934, it was cited by the U.S. Public Health Service as being the best available method for detecting syphilis. That same year, Hinton began writing a textbook for physicians, public health workers, and medical students about how to diagnose and cure syphilis. Published in 1936 as *Syphilis and Its Treatment* (New York: Macmillan), it became a standard reference work in the United States and Europe.

In 1949, Hinton was named a full professor at Harvard Medical College. He retired from Harvard the following year, and in 1953, he retired from the state health department. On August 8, 1959, he died at his home in Canton, Massachusetts.

See also: HIV/AIDS

References and Further Reading
Carey, Charles W. Jr. *American Scientists*. New York: Facts On File, 2005, 170–171.
Kessler, James H., J. S. Kidd, Renee A. Kidd, and Katherine A. Morin, eds. *Distinguished African American Scientists of the 20th Century*. Phoenix, AZ: Oryx Press, 1996: 36–51.
Spangenburg, Ray, and Kit Moser. *African Americans in Science, Math and Invention*. New York: Facts On File, 2003: 118–119.

Houston, Clifford W.
(1949–) Microbiologist

As a researcher, Clifford Houston contributed to a more complete understanding of the role played by exotoxins in the development of certain diseases. As an educator and administrator, he sought to recruit and train more African Americans into careers involving scientific research.

Houston was born on December 3, 1949, in Oklahoma City, Oklahoma. His father, Edgar, was a maintenance supervisor and his mother, Mae Frances, was a homemaker. He received a BS in microbiology and chemistry and an MS in biology from Oklahoma State University in 1972 and 1974, respectively, and a PhD in microbiology and immunology from the University of Oklahoma Health Sciences Center in 1979. He spent the next two years conducting postdoctoral research at the University of Texas Medical Branch (UTMB) in Galveston, and in 1981, he joined the UTMB faculty as a professor of microbiology. He has been married and divorced and has one child.

Houston's research focused on exotoxins (substances excreted by a microorganism that are so toxic that they can damage or kill the microorganism's host). His first research endeavor studied the biochemical aspects of type A toxin, the exotoxin produced by the bacteria known as group A *streptococci*. He also demonstrated how type A toxin is synthesized in group A *streptococci* and developed a method for detecting the presence of type A toxin in humans. Next, he took up the study of the exotoxin produced by certain bacteria in the *Salmonella* genus, and again he was able to demonstrate how the exotoxin is synthesized and to develop a method for detecting it. Previously, it had been theorized that *Salmonellae* produce the exotoxin after they themselves have been infected by a type of virus known as a bacteriophage, but Houston was able to show that this is not the case.

Houston's most recent research involves Aerolysin Cytotoxic Enterotoxin (ACT), an exotoxin produced by the bacteria known as *Aeromonas hydrophila*, and the role it plays in causing disease in humans. This bacteria, which thrives in the lower intestine, has been linked to such diseases as acute bacterial diarrhea, septicemia, meningitis, endocarditis, corneal ulcers, peritonitis, and wound infections, but the exact mechanism by which it does so remains unknown. As of 2007, Houston and his collaborators had described the biochemical aspects of two forms of ACT, and they had identified and cloned the genes in *A. hydrophila* that produce ACT.

In addition to his teaching and research duties, Houston serves as the associate vice president for educational outreach at UTMB. In this capacity, he works to increase the number of African Americans and other minorities pursuing careers as scientific researchers at UTMB. He also served as deputy associate administrator for education in the National Aeronautics and Space Administration's Office of Education, and in this position he helped develop science education programs related to space for students and faculty at every level from kindergarten through undergraduate as well as for the general public. In 2006, he was elected president of the American Society for Microbiology.

See also: American Society for Microbiology; National Aeronautics and Space Administration

References and Further Reading
University of Texas Medical Branch Department of Microbiology and Immunology. "Faculty: Clifford W. Houston, Ph.D." [Online article or information; retrieved November 8, 2007.] http://microbiology.utmb.edu/faculty/houston.shtml.

Imes, Elmer S.
(1883–1941) Physicist

One of the methods physicists use to study the properties of molecules, atoms, and subatomic particles is spectroscopy, the study of the lines of electromagnetic radiation a substance emits. Elmer Imes was a pioneer in the use of infrared spectroscopy to study molecules. His work played an important role in the development of quantum mechanics (the study of subatomic particles).

Imes was born on October 12, 1883, in Memphis. His father, Benjamin, was a minister, and his mother, Elizabeth, was a homemaker. He grew up in several small towns in Ohio and Alabama, where his father was a pastor. In 1903, he received a BA in science from Fisk College (today Fisk University) in Nashville, Tennessee, and joined the faculty at Albany Normal Institute (Georgia) as an instructor of mathematics and physics. He returned to Fisk in 1910 as a graduate student and mathematics instructor, and, after receiving his MS in 1915, he entered the University of Michigan, receiving a PhD in physics three years later. He then moved to New York City, and over the next 12 years, he worked as a consulting engineer and research physicist for several companies. In 1930, he was named chair of Fisk's physics department, a position he held for the rest of his career.

Imes's research involved the use of high-resolution infrared spectroscopy (the study of the bands, or spectra, of infrared light emitted by atoms and molecules) to study the properties of atoms and molecules. Today it is known that atoms and molecules possess energy in discrete amounts known as quanta and that each type of atom and molecule emits infrared light at a specific and unique frequency. Therefore, a researcher can identify an unknown atom or molecule simply by identifying the frequency of its infrared emissions. When Imes was a graduate student, however, this was not known; in fact, the notion that quanta even existed was still a theory that Albert Einstein had advanced only a few years earlier.

Imes and Harrison M. Randall, one of Imes's physics professors at Michigan, decided to test Einstein's quantum theory by using infrared spectroscopy to study diatomic molecules, molecules that consist of only two atoms. Diatomic molecules are relatively simple; so they were the perfect subjects for the experiment. Imes and Randall studied the infrared spectra of hydrogen chloride, hydrogen bromide, and hydrogen fluoride, and in the process, they were able to make the first accurate measurement of the distance between atoms in a molecule. They also showed that chlorine exists as an isotope (a form of an element in which the nucleus has a different number of neutrons but whose physical properties are virtually identical to the normal form).

Imes and Randall's most important discovery involved the quantization of a molecule's rotational spectra. While studying the infrared spectra of hydrogen chloride, hydrogen bromide, and hydrogen fluoride, they discovered that the energy levels associated with the spectral lines that are emitted as the molecules rotate are discrete values that are integral multiples of some basic finite value; in other words, molecules emit infrared light waves in quanta as they rotate. This finding offered experimental support for quantum theory, and in 1920, the prestigious physics journal *Physical Review* announced the experimenters' discovery. Since other researchers had previously demonstrated the quantization of the vibrational spectrum, the infrared lines emitted by the atoms of a molecule as they interact with each other, Imes's and Randall's work contributed to the transformation of quantum theory into the branch of physics known as quantum mechanics.

In 1920, Imes married Nella Larsen, with whom he had no children; they divorced in 1933. He died on September 11, 1941, in New York City.

See also: Fisk University; Physics

REFERENCES AND FURTHER READING
Carey, Charles W. Jr. *American Scientists*. New York: Facts On File, 2005: 188–189.

McMurray, Emily J., ed. *Notable Twentieth-Century Scientists*. Detroit, MI: Gale Research, 1995: 993.

Spangenburg, Ray, and Kit Moser. *African Americans in Science, Math, and Invention*. New York: Facts On File, 2003: 125–126.

Jackson, Shirley A.
(1946–) Physicist

As a theoretical physicist, Shirley Jackson contributed to a better understanding of the behavior of electrons in certain unusual circumstances. As chair of the Nuclear Regulatory Commission and the International Nuclear Regulators Association, she worked to ensure the safety of nuclear power plants around the world. She was also the first African American woman to serve as president of a major research university.

Jackson was born on August 5, 1946, in Washington, D.C., to George and Beatrice Jackson. She became interested in mathematics and science at an early age, and in high school, she completed accelerated programs in each subject. After receiving a BS in physics from the Massachusetts Institute of Technology in 1968, she remained to pursue coursework in theoretical physics, the branch of physics that studies quantum mechanics (the nature and behavior of subatomic particles), receiving a PhD in elementary particle physics in 1973.

Jackson's early research involved developing and testing theories concerning the existence and behavior of subatomic particles. She was particularly interested in hadrons (particles that are bound together by the so-called strong nuclear forces within an atomic nucleus). Hadrons include highly stable particles such as protons and neutrons, but they also include some highly unstable particles such as mesons and pions, which are produced when other hadrons collide with each other. To study hadrons more closely, she conducted postgraduate research at the Fermi National Accelerator Laboratory in Batavia, Illinois, and worked as a visiting scientist at the European Center for Nuclear Research in Geneva, Switzerland, and the Stanford Linear Accelerator Center (California). All three facilities operated state-of-the-art particle accelerators (devices for accelerating subatomic particles to speeds approaching the speed of light and then causing them to collide as a means of studying the accelerated particles and the ones that result from the collision).

In 1976, Jackson took a position as a research scientist with Bell Telephone Laboratories' (BTL) theoretical physics research department in Murray Hill, New Jersey, where she spent the rest of her research career. Her research at BTL involved exploring for unknown physical phenomena that might be used to develop new or enhanced forms of telecommunications. To this end, she conducted research concerning the electronic and optical properties of semiconductors (elements that are neither good conductors of electricity like copper nor good insulators like glass) that might allow them to carry much more electrical current than was possible with the existing technology. Her most important contribution in this regard was an in-depth description of the behavior of polarons in monomolecular films. A polaron is an electron that, as it passes through a solid material, causes the electrical charges of the particles it comes in contact with to polarize; that is, positive charges move toward it while negative charges move away from it. A monomolecular film is a liquid film that is only one molecule thick; consequently, it behaves as if it has only two dimensions, length and width.

In addition to her duties at BTL, Jackson served on the advisory council of the Institute of Nuclear Power Operations. This position allowed her to gain valuable insight into how the nuclear power industry works in the United States. Thus, in 1995, President Bill Clinton named Jackson to chair the Nuclear Regulatory Commission. In this capacity, she oversaw the federal government's efforts to make sure that the peaceful use of nuclear energy did not endanger the health or safety of the general public. During her four-year tenure, she placed the nation's nuclear-powered electrical generating plants under intense scrutiny and even ordered that several of them be shut down for repeated safety violations. She also played a fundamental role in establishing the International Nuclear Regulators Association (INRA), an association made up of the most senior nuclear regulatory officials from Canada, France, Germany, Japan, Spain, Sweden, the United Kingdom, and the United States. As the first INRA chair, Dr. Jackson guided its development as a high-level forum to examine issues of nuclear safety and to offer assistance to other nations in the event of a nuclear emergency.

In 1999, Jackson was named president of Rensselaer Polytechnic Institute (RPI) in Troy, New York, thus becoming the first African American woman to serve as head of a major research institution. In this capacity, she worked to enhance RPI's ability to support cutting-edge research in science and technology. She also served as the chairperson of the Blue Ribbon Panel on Higher Education, an initiative by Building Engineering and Science Talent to include more women and African Americans in the nation's technological workforce.

Jackson is married to Morris Washington, with whom she has one child.

Her many honors include election to a term as president of the American Association for the Advancement of Science and to membership in the American Academy of Arts and Sciences.

See also: American Association for the Advancement of Science; Building Engineering and Science Talent; Physics

REFERENCES AND FURTHER READING

Hayden, Robert C. *Seven African American Scientists.* Brookfield, CT.: Twenty-First Century Books, 1992: 148–167.

Spangenburg, Ray, and Kit Moser. *African Americans in Science, Math, and Invention.* New York: Facts On File, 2003: 127–129.

Jarvis, Erich D.
(1965–) Neurobiologist

Erich D. Jarvis has shed much light on the phenomenon known as vocal learning, the ability to learn new ways to communicate vocally by imitating sounds that are not genetically innate. His most important contribution thus far is to develop the gene expression tools for locating the areas of the forebrain in parrots, hummingbirds, and songbirds that are dedicated to vocal learning.

Jarvis was born on May 6, 1965, in the Harlem section of New York City to James and Valeria Jarvis. His earliest ambition was to be a dancer, and he attended the New York High School of the Performing Arts. Upon entering

New York's Hunter College in 1983, however, he became interested in science and majored in biology and mathematics and minored in chemistry. Upon receiving a BA in 1988, he entered the graduate program at Rockefeller University, and in 1995, he received a PhD in molecular neurobiology and animal behavior. He remained at Rockefeller for three years as a postdoctoral researcher, and in 1998, he joined the faculty of the Duke University Medical Center in Durham, North Carolina, as a professor of neurobiology. In 1990, he married Miriam Rivas, with whom he has two children.

A neurobiologist studies the cells of the nervous system and how they are organized into functional circuits that process information and help govern behavior. As a neurobiologist, Jarvis's primary research interest involves vocal communication, specifically vocal learning. Only six different groups of animals possess the trait of vocal learning: parrots, hummingbirds, songbirds, bats, whales and dolphins, and humans. His first effort to learn more about the neurobiology of vocal learning involved mapping the molecular pathways that are activated during singing in the brains of the canary and the zebra finch, the two songbirds that had been studied the most by neurobiologists. His later work demonstrated the existence of seven very similar areas in the forebrain dedicated to vocal learning in songbirds, parrots, and hummingbirds, brain structures that are not found in vocal nonlearners.

As of 2007, Jarvis and his collaborators were identifying the cascade of genes that are active in these seven areas in the forebrains of songbirds when they sing their learned songs. To this end, they created a DNA microarray, also known as a gene chip, for the zebra finch as a tool for better understanding how the zebra finch's genes are expressed during vocal learning. Jarvis and his collaborators at Duke were also seeking to determine whether vocal learning evolved independently in these groups within the past 65 million years, as is generally believed, or whether all vertebrates had a common ancestor that possessed the trait of vocal learning, which was then lost via evolution to all groups but the six that possess it today.

References and Further Reading
Erich Jarvis Lab, "General Information." [Online article or information; retrieved October 26, 2007.] http://www.jarvislab.net/GenInfo.html.

Jearld, Ambrose, Jr.
(1944–) Marine Biologist

Ambrose Jearld is one of the nation's leading experts on the commercial fisheries along the Atlantic coastline. As a senior official with the National Marine Fisheries Service of the National Oceanic and Atmospheric Administration

(NOAA), he has done much to conserve and protect fish in these and other fisheries around the world.

Jearld was born on March 6, 1944, in Annapolis, Maryland. His father, Ambrose, was a naval officer, and his mother, Katherine, was a homemaker. As an infant, he was sent to live with his grandmother on a farm in Orrum, North Carolina, returning to Annapolis at age 10. After receiving a BS in biology from Maryland State College (today the University of Maryland Eastern Shore) in 1964, he went to work as an analytical chemist for Publicker Industries in Philadelphia. Two years later, he entered the biological sciences program at Oklahoma State University (Stillwater, OSU), but his studies were interrupted in 1969, when he was drafted into the U.S. Army. Discharged two years later, he returned to OSU and received an MS and a PhD in zoology in 1971 and 1975, respectively. He spent the next two years teaching biology at Lincoln University (Pennsylvania) and the following year teaching zoology at Howard University. In 1978, he went to work for NOAA's Northeast Fisheries Science Center (NFSC) at the Marine Biological Laboratory at Woods Hole in Massachusetts, where he remained for the rest of his career.

At OSU, Jearld became involved in a major research project for the U.S. Fish and Wildlife Service that sought ways to protect fish in the lakes and reservoirs along the Arkansas River and its tributaries from the effects of water pollution. As part of this project, he participated in a fish census that determined the number, general health, growth potential, feeding habits, and reproductive capacities of its subjects. His doctoral research concerned the sexual behavior of the honey gourami, a fish that can breathe air through its lungs as well as take in oxygen through its gills. While at Lincoln University, he participated in studies to determine the effects of industrial pollution on the anchovy in San Francisco Bay (California) and the grass shrimp in the wetlands of New Jersey.

Jearld's first position at NFSC was chief of the fishery biology investigation unit. In this capacity, he oversaw the transformation of the unit's research efforts from a traditional emphasis on assessing the dynamics of the cod, flounder, and shad fisheries within their area of geographic responsibility to a greater emphasis on understanding the ecosystem of the fisheries with an eye to conserving and managing it. In 1985, he was named chief of the research planning and coordination staff, and in this capacity, he was responsible for planning and evaluating NFSC's entire research program. He was later named director of academic programs of NOAA's National Marine Fisheries Service, and in this capacity, he oversaw the many scientific conferences sponsored by NFSC such as the annual flatfish biology conference (flatfish include flounder, fluke, and halibut, to name three). In addition to these duties, he chaired Expanding Opportunities in Ocean Sciences: A Conference to Strengthen the Links Between Historically Black and Minority Served

Colleges and Universities Undergraduates and Oceanic Graduate Studies, a NOAA initiative to open up more careers to blacks and minorities in marine biology and oceanography. He also oversaw NOAA's programs to assist with the development and implementation of strategic plans for the sea fisheries of South Africa, and six West African countries around the Gulf of Guinea. He and his wife, Anna, have two children.

See also: Biology; Howard University; University of Maryland Eastern Shore

REFERENCES AND FURTHER READING

Kessler, James H., J. S. Kidd, Renee A. Kidd, and Katherine A. Morin, eds. *Distinguished African American Scientists of the 20th Century*. Phoenix, AZ: Oryx Press, 1996: 185–190.

Krapp, Kristine M., ed. *Notable Black American Scientists*. Detroit, MI: Gale Research, 1999: 176–177.

Spangenburg, Ray, and Kit Moser. *African Americans in Science, Math, and Invention*. New York: Facts On File, 2003: 130–131.

Jefferson, Roland M.
(1923–) Botanist

Next to George Washington Carver, Roland Jefferson is perhaps the most famous African American botanist of all time. Jefferson is best remembered for the work he did to preserve the Japanese flowering cherry trees that grace Washington, D.C.'s Potomac Park, and serve as the focal point of that city's annual Cherry Blossom Festival.

Jefferson was born on September 3, 1923, in Washington, D.C. Little more is known about his first 33 years other than that, in 1950, he obtained a bachelor's degree in botany from Howard University. In 1956, he went to work for the U.S. National Arboretum (USNA), one of the nation's most important centers for botanical research, as a maker of plant labels. The following year, he was promoted to botanist, thus becoming the first black botanist to work at USNA. Over the next 16 years, he became an expert on the several species of the genus *Malus* that are commonly referred to as wild apple or crabapple trees.

In 1973, Jefferson started compiling historical and scientific data concerning the Japanese flowering cherry trees in Potomac Park. Some of these trees dated back to 1909, when 90 were planted at the direction of First Lady Helen Taft as a means of beautifying the park, a reclaimed mud flat on the Potomac River. These trees were joined three years later by more than 3,000 flowering trees, including 1,800 Japanese flowering cherry trees of the variety known as Yoshino. The trees were a gift from the mayor of Tokyo, Yukio Ozaki. Ozaki had befriended President William Taft when the latter had served as a member of the Portsmouth Peace Conference, which had negotiated an end to the Russo-Japanese War in 1905, and, when Ozaki heard of Mrs. Taft's plantings, he donated the trees as a token of his friendship. During the 1930s and 1940s, the trees fell on hard times; in 1936 a major flood killed almost all of the trees except for the Yoshino, and during World War II, many of the survivors were cut down and vandalized in emotional displays of anti-Japanese sentiment. After the war, however, the trees had revived to the point that new trees grown from their cuttings were planted in Tokyo to commemorate the end of the Pacific War between the United States and Japan. In 1977, Jefferson published his data concerning the Taft-Ozaki trees in "The Japanese Flowering Cherry Trees of Washington, D.C.: A Living Symbol of Friendship," a pamphlet that was later translated into Japanese.

While compiling his data, Jefferson observed that the Taft-Ozaki trees were aging—in fact, fewer than 200 of the Yoshino trees were still alive—and that, if something were not done soon, these historic trees would be gone forever. To remedy this situation, he successfully rooted three cuttings from each of the remaining Yoshinos, including the one Mrs. Taft had planted personally. By 1981, one of the rooted cuttings from the Taft tree had grown to three feet. That same year, First Lady Nancy Reagan presented it to Japanese ambassador Yoshio Ogawara as a sign of friendship between the two nations. The tree was planted in Tokyo's Toneri Park and named the President Reagan Cherry Tree.

From 1981 to 1983, Jefferson toured Japan to study, lecture, locate, evaluate, and collect germplasm from various varieties of Japanese flowering cherry trees. During the tour, he initiated a seed exchange program, whereby Japanese schoolchildren exchanged cherry tree seeds with schoolchildren in the United States for dogwood tree seeds. He also met Keiko Ishisaki, whom he married in 1983. After returning briefly to the United States, in 1986, he returned to the Far East to study cherry trees in Japan, Korea, and Taiwan. In 1987, he retired from USNA and relocated to Japan, where he continued to study and lecture on cherry trees.

See also: Carver, George Washington; Howard University

REFERENCES AND FURTHER READING

Jefferson, Roland M. "The Japanese Flowering Cherry Trees of Washington, D.C.: A Living Symbol of Friendship." *National Arboretum Contribution* 4 (1977).

National Agricultural Library. "NAL Collections: Jefferson, Roland Maurice, Collection." [Online article or information; retrieved August 10, 2007.] http://www.nal.usda.gov/speccoll/collectionsguide/collection.php?find=J.

Jemison, Mae C.
(1956–) Astronaut

Mae Jemison was probably the best-known black scientist in the United States following her return from outer space in 1992. For a number of years thereafter, she served as a role model for black girls by demonstrating that race and gender were not insurmountable obstacles to attaining a career in science.

Jemison was born on October 17, 1956, in Decatur, Alabama. Her father, Charlie, was a maintenance supervisor, and her mother, Dorothy, was a school teacher. As a young girl, she moved with her family to Chicago, where she grew up. At age 16, she enrolled in Stanford University and received a BS in chemical engineering and a BA in African and African American studies in 1977. She then entered Cornell University Medical School and received an MD in 1981. After completing her internship at the Los Angeles County/University of Southern California Medical Center the following year, she went to work as a general practitioner for a Los Angeles medical group. In 1983, she joined the Peace Corps and spent the next two years as the area medical officer for Sierra Leone and Liberia. While in Africa in this capacity, she managed the health care delivery system for U.S. Peace Corps and U.S. embassy personnel, also conducting research for the National Institutes of Health and the Center for Disease Control concerning hepatitis B, rabies, and schistosomiasis, a type of parasitic infection. In 1985, she returned to Los Angeles to work as a general practitioner for CIGNA Health Plans for the next two years.

In 1987, Jemison was accepted by the National Aeronautics and Space Administration (NASA) into the astronaut program, and for the next four years, she trained to be a mission specialist aboard a space shuttle mission. In September 1992, she became the first black woman in space when she went aloft on the shuttle *Endeavor* during STS-47, the first joint mission between NASA and the National Space Development Agency of Japan. As a mission specialist, she took part in about half of the mission's experiments; the experiments were conducted in the Spacelab-J module and were designed to investigate the effects of microgravity on various living and human-made substances. The 24 materials science experiments covered such fields as biotechnology, electronic materials, fluid dynamics and transport phenomena, glasses and ceramics, metals and alloys, and acceleration measurements; the 20 life sciences experiments included experiments on human health, cell separation and biology, developmental biology, animal and human physiology and behavior, space radiation, and biological rhythms. The experiments were conducted on the crew, Japanese koi fish (carp), cultured animal and plant cells, chicken embryos, fruit flies, fungi and plant seeds, and frogs and frog eggs.

In 1993, Jemison left NASA to become a professor of environmental studies at Dartmouth College and to head Dartmouth's Jemison Institute for

Astronaut Mae Jemison was the first African American woman to fly in space. (National Aeronautics and Space Administration)

Advancing Technology in Developing Countries. That same year, she founded the Jemison Group; based in Houston, the Jemison Group focused on researching, developing, and implementing advanced technologies that are particularly suited to the social, political, cultural, and economic conditions of the developing world. The group's many projects include the development of Alpha, a satellite-based telecommunications system for transmitting health care information to doctors in West Africa, and The Earth We Share, a international science camp designed to promote basic science literacy among youngsters ages 12 to 16. Her many honors include having the Mae C. Jemison Academy, an alternative school in Detroit, named in her honor.

See also: Biology; Biotechnology; National Aeronautics and Space Administration; National Institutes of Health

REFERENCES AND FURTHER READING

Jemison, Mae. *Find Where the Wind Goes: Moments from My Life*. New York: Scholastic Press, 2001.

Spangenburg, Ray, and Kit Moser. *African Americans in Science, Math, and Invention*. New York: Facts On File, 2003: 131–133.

Warren, Wini. *Black Women Scientists in the United States*. Bloomington: Indiana University Press, 1999: 137–140.

Julian, Percy L.
(1899–1975) Chemist

One of the most important developments in 20th-century medicine was the synthesis of pharmaceutical drugs from plants and vegetables. Percy Julian contributed to this development by finding a number of medicinal uses for the derivatives of soybean oil and the Mexican wild yam. His most important contribution was the synthesis of progesterone, most popularly used to make oral contraceptives.

Julian was born on April 11, 1899, in Montgomery, Alabama. His father, James, was a railway mail clerk, and his mother, Elizabeth, was a teacher. He became interested in becoming a chemist after reading about St. Elmo Brady, the first African American to receive a PhD in chemistry, even though the segregated schools he attended did not offer any chemistry courses. At age 17, he enrolled in DePauw University in Greencastle, Indiana, and after receiving an AB in chemistry, he taught chemistry for two years at Fisk College (today Fisk University) in Nashville, Tennessee. In 1922, he received a fellowship to attend Harvard University, and the following year he received an MA in organic chemistry. He spent the next six years teaching chemistry at West Virginia State College (today West Virginia State University) and Howard University while trying to gain admission to a PhD program in the United States. He finally decided to earn his doctorate in Europe, where the graduate schools were not concerned about skin color, and in 1931, he received a PhD in organic chemistry from Austria's University of Vienna. Upon returning to the United States, he taught at Howard for one year before returning to DePauw as a professor of chemistry. In 1935, he married Anna Johnson, with whom he had two children.

As a chemist, Julian was primarily interested in synthesis (the process by which one chemical compound is converted into another). His first project involved the synthesis of physostigmine, a pharmaceutical drug that is used to treat glaucoma and myasthenia gravis. Physostigmine is derived from d, 1-eserethole, which in turn is derived from Calabar beans, and in 1935, he published a detailed account of his findings concerning the chemical makeup of d, 1-eserethole. Julian's findings contradicted those of the eminent Oxford chemist Sir Robert Robinson, and Julian's reputation was made when it was discovered that he, not Robinson, was correct.

Julian's next research effort involved synthesizing stigmasterol from soybean oil for the purpose of synthesizing human sex hormones, which are used to treat a number of medical conditions. But before he could progress very far, word of the project reached the management of the Glidden Company in Chicago, and in 1936, Glidden recruited Julian to direct their soya products division. Glidden's primary product was paint, a major ingredient of

Chemist Percy Julian's most important contribution was to develop a method for synthesizing progesterone so that it could be used in birth control pills. (Library of Congress)

which is soybean oil, but it had decided to diversify its product line by finding new industrial and medical applications for soybean oil, which is relatively inexpensive to extract.

In addition to setting up and managing a state-of-the-art soybean oil production facility, Julian was also charged with finding new uses for soybean oil. In short order, he became the George Washington Carver of soybean oil. Julian discovered how to make soybean oil derivatives for use in the manufacture of paper products, animal feed, candy, cosmetics, food additives, ink, and textiles. Perhaps his most creative discovery is Aero Foam, more popularly known as bean soup, which is particularly effective at putting out petroleum fires.

Oddly enough, Julian's early uses for soybean oil did not include stigmasterol, which had brought him to the attention of Glidden in the first place. But in 1940, he returned to his work with stigmasterol, largely because of an accident. A large vat of soybean oil had been contaminated with water, and the result was a seemingly useless vat of oily paste. Julian realized, however, that the paste might be a good source for synthesizing stigmasterol, from which he might synthesize various pharmaceutical drugs. He quickly developed a method for doing exactly that, and before long, Glidden was producing large batches of progesterone, the female hormone that is used to prevent miscarriages and treat certain menstrual complications, and the male hormone testosterone, which is used to treat certain types of breast cancer. In 1949, he developed a way to use soybean oil as the base from which to synthesize cortisone, which was itself derived from a hormone produced by the adrenal cortex and used to treat rheumatoid arthritis.

By 1940, it had occurred to Julian that better sources than soybean oil existed for synthesizing pharmaceutical drugs, and he began looking for them. The most promising source turned out to be the Mexican wild yam known as *Dioscorea*, which is an excellent source of progesterone. In 1954, he founded Julian Laboratories so that he could focus on producing progesterone from *Dioscorea*. Serendipitously, it was discovered shortly thereafter that safe and effective oral contraceptives could be made from progesterone, and in 1960, the U.S. Food and Drug Administration approved the sale of birth control pills to the general public. Julian Laboratories was the world's foremost producer of progesterone, and Julian quickly became a millionaire.

In 1961, Julian sold his company to Smith, Kline and French, but served as its president for three more years. In 1964, he founded the Julian Research Institute and Julian Associates, both of which focused on discovering and producing synthetic pharmaceutical drugs. He died on April 19, 1975, in Waukegan, Illinois.

See also: Brady, St. Elmo; Carver, George Washington; Chemistry; Fisk University; Howard University; Virginia State University

References and Further Reading

Carey, Charles W. Jr. *American Scientists*. New York: Facts On File, 2005: 190–191.

Robinson, Louise. *The Black Millionaire*. New York: Pyramid Books, 1972.

Spangenburg, Ray, and Kit Moser. *African Americans in Science, Math, and Invention*. New York: Facts On File, 2003: 137–139.

Witkop, Bernhard. "Percy Lavon Julian." National Academy of Sciences, *Biographical Memoirs* 52 (1980): 223–266.

Just, Ernest E.
(1883–1941) Zoologist

Ernest Just's research made important contributions to a better understanding of the biochemical processes associated with the fertilization and growth of animal eggs. Although he did not originate it, he provided experimental proof to support the fertilizin theory, which explains how a sperm cell fertilizes an egg cell. He also shed light on the role played by a cell's ectoplasm (outer surface) in cellular growth and development.

Just was born on August 14, 1883, in Charleston, South Carolina. His father, Charles, was a carpenter, and his mother, Mary, was a teacher. He was raised on nearby James Island, where he and his mother moved after his father died when he was four years old. At age 16, he graduated from the Colored Normal, Industrial, Agricultural and Mechanical College (today South Carolina State University) with a teaching certificate and enrolled in Kimball Union Academy, a college preparatory school in Meriden, New Hampshire. Three years later, he entered Dartmouth College, receiving a BS in biology in 1907. He then accepted a position on the faculty at Howard University in Washington, D.C., where he taught biology for the next 23 years.

At Dartmouth, Just studied under the eminent zoologist William Patten, and he assisted him with some of the research concerning frogs that later appeared in Patten's book, *The Evolution of the Vertebrates and Their Kin* (Philadelphia, PA: P. Blakiston's Son & Co., 1912). Patten was impressed with Just, and he recommended him to Frank Lillie, director of the Marine Biological Laboratory at Woods Hole, Massachusetts. In 1909, Lillie offered to let Just conduct independent work at Woods Hole during the summer, and for the next 20 years, Just spent most of his summers at Woods Hole. It was the perfect place to study the eggs of marine animals, and before long Just was investigating the breeding habits and fertilization process in sandworms and sea urchins. In 1912, he published the first of more than 50 articles on this and related topics, most of which appeared in *The Biological Bulletin*, Woods Hole's official journal. Lillie was also chair of the department of zoology at the University of Chicago, and he allowed Just to use a number of these articles in lieu of a doctoral dissertation; so in 1916, Just received a PhD in experimental embryology from Chicago. Just also coauthored a textbook with Lillie and the Nobel laureate and geneticist Thomas Hunt Morgan (among others) covering the formation, structure, and function of cells, which appeared in 1924 under the title *General Cytology: A Textbook of Cellular Structure and Function for Students of Biology and Medicine* (Chicago: University of Chicago Press).

Just's major contribution to embryology was his work concerning the fertilizin theory. This theory had first been suggested by Lillie, who believed that the fertilization of an egg cell by a sperm cell was due to the activity of a mysterious substance he called fertilizin. Just embraced Lillie's theory and advanced it with great enthusiasm and energy. In time, he showed that fertilizin does indeed exist and that it is a gelatinous substance produced by eggs that causes sperm to stick to them. Much of his work regarding the fertilization of marine eggs in general and the fertilizin theory in particular was published in his book, *Basic Methods for Experiments on Eggs of Marine Animals* (Philadelphia, PA: P. Blakiston's Son & Co., 1939).

Meanwhile, Just had grown weary from his heavy teaching load at Howard, which encouraged its professors to be teachers first and researchers second. Longing to give up teaching and focus exclusively on research, he began seeking out grants and fellowships that would allow him to take extended leaves of absence from Howard. In 1920, he was awarded the Julius Rosenwald

Fellowship in biology by the National Research Council, a grant that afforded him the opportunity to curtail his teaching load at Howard over the next 10 years. In 1930, he resigned from Howard altogether, and he spent the next 10 years in Europe, teaching and conducting research as a visiting professor at such prestigious research centers as the Zoological Station in Naples, Italy, the Kaiser Wilhelm Institute in Berlin, and the Sorbonne in Paris. In 1939, while in Europe, he divorced his wife of 27 years, Ethel Highwarden, with whom he had three children, and married Hedwig Schnetzler.

Just's European sojourn also resulted in the publication of another book, *The Biology of the Cell Surface* (Philadelphia, PA: P. Blakiston's Son & Co., 1939). The book contained the theories and ideas that Just had experimented with throughout his career, but it also advanced his theory that, to a certain degree, a cell's ectoplasm stimulates and regulates the cell's growth and development. This theory was dismissed initially, but further investigation by other researchers produced enough evidence to have it taken more seriously. Unfortunately for Just, the acceptance of his theory did not occur until after his death.

In 1940, shortly after the outbreak of World War II, Just was captured in France by the Germans and interned as a prisoner of war. Although he was released within a year, Hitler's influence over Germany, Italy, and France made it impossible for Just to remain in any of those countries; so he reluctantly returned to Howard. Less than two years later, on October 27, 1941, he died from cancer in Washington, D.C. His many posthumous honors include the issuance in 1997 by the U.S. Postal Service of a commemorative stamp in his honor.

See also: Biology; Howard University; South Carolina State University

REFERENCES AND FURTHER READING

Carey, Charles W. Jr. *American Scientists*. New York: Facts On File, 2005: 191–193.

Manning, Kenneth R. *Black Apollo of Science: The Life of Ernest Everett Just*. New York: Oxford University Press, 1983.

Spangenburg, Ray, and Kit Moser. *African Americans in Science, Math, and Invention*. New York: Facts On File, 2003: 139–142.

King, James, Jr.
(1933–) Physical Chemist

James King was a leading expert on the behavior of natural and human-made gases. His research contributed to a better understanding of various industrial pollutants, such as chlorofluorocarbons and smog. He also played an important role in planning many of the strategic and technical aspects of the U.S. space program.

King was born on April 23, 1933, in Columbus, Georgia, to James and Lucille King. At age 16, he entered Morehouse College in Atlanta with the intention of becoming a physician, but he eventually decided to major in chemistry, receiving a BS in 1953. He spent the next five years at the California Institute of Technology (Caltech), receiving an MS in chemical physics in 1955 and a PhD in chemistry and physics in 1958. He then worked for several years in private industry, first as a research engineer for Atomics International, which made various devices for use in nuclear reactors, and then as a design engineer for a company that was attempting to develop a solar-powered automobile. When the latter venture failed, he took a position with the Jet Propulsion Laboratory (JPL) in Pasadena, California, which Caltech manages for the National Aeronautics and Space Administration (NASA). In 1966, he married Jean King, with whom he had two children.

King focused his research on gases, particularly elements that occur in nature in a gaseous state. His graduate research investigated the formation of rust via the chemical reaction between iron and oxygen. At Atomics International, he developed a thermometer for use inside a nuclear core that calculates temperature by measuring the speed of a special gas housed in a ceramic partition. His first project at JPL involved acquiring a better understanding of the physical chemistry of atomic hydrogen, a key ingredient in rocket propellant, whose ability to react with other elements depends on minute variations in its electrical charge and initial energy state. As an offshoot of this project, he demonstrated how anesthetic gases, many of which contain hydrogen, interact with the charged molecules that line the human lungs. Another JPL project demonstrated how the so-called noble, or inert, gases such as krypton and xenon can influence the outcome of a chemical reaction that takes place in their presence, even though they do not take part in the actual reaction, provided that the inert gases have been heated to extremely high temperatures. Yet another project involved the physical chemistry of chlorofluorocarbons (CFCs), a primary ingredient in aerosols and refrigerants, specifically the nature of the bond linking carbon and fluorine; CFCs have since been banned by the major industrial nations because of the role they play in depleting the Earth's ozone layer.

King began to cut back on his research in 1969, when he was named manager of JPL's physics section. From 1974 to 1976, he directed NASA's space shuttle environmental effects program, which sought to prevent shuttle flights from polluting the atmosphere, and its upper atmospheric research program. Since then, he rose steadily through the management ranks at JPL, and in 1993, he was named assistant laboratory director for technical divisions. In this capacity, he oversaw the activities of thousands of scientists, engineers, and technicians who were developing new technologies for space habitats and propulsion systems that would allow future space explorers to travel beyond the solar system.

In addition to his other duties, King helped establish a degree program in atmospheric sciences at Morehouse and served on the Los Angeles Air Pollution Control District. His honors include election to the American Association for the Advancement of Science.

See also: American Association for the Advancement of Science; Chemistry; National Aeronautics and Space Administration

REFERENCES AND FURTHER READING

Kessler, James H., J. S. Kidd, Renee A. Kidd, and Katherine A. Morin, eds. *Distinguished African American Scientists of the 20th Century.* Phoenix, AZ: Oryx Press, 1996: 204–208.

Krapp, Kristine M., ed. *Notable Black American Scientists.* Detroit, MI: Gale Research, 1999: 189.

Spangenburg, Ray, and Kit Moser. *African Americans in Science, Math, and Invention.* New York: Facts On File, 2003: 143–144.

Kittrell, Flemmie P.
(1904–1980) Nutritionist

Flemmie Kittrell focused her research attention on the importance of the early home environment to child development. She also developed programs to improve nutrition in low-income neighborhoods in the United States, as well as in several developing nations.

Kittrell was born on Christmas Day, 1904, in Henderson, North Carolina. Her parents, James and Alice, were farmers. At age 12, she enrolled in Hampton Academy, the high school associated with Hampton Institute (now University), and after finishing high school, she stayed on to major in home economics and received a BS in 1928. After teaching for a year at Bennett College's high school in Greensboro, North Carolina, she entered the graduate program at Cornell University and received an MA and a PhD in nutrition in 1930 and 1938, respectively. She spent the next two years at Bennett and then returned to Hampton Institute to serve as dean of women and head of the home economics program. In 1944, she accepted a similar position at Howard University, where she remained for the rest of her career.

Prior to Kittrell's arrival at Howard, its home economics program—indeed, virtually all college and university home economics programs—offered watered-down versions of chemistry and psychology to students. Kittrell redesigned the program to include research into the real-life problems faced by families every day, especially rural low-income families that struggled to obtain nutritious meals and sanitary living conditions. She also implemented a nursery program at Howard that gave students hands-on experience with problems related to child development and psychology; this program later served as a prototype for the federal Head Start program, and Kittrell was chosen to serve on the executive committee of the 1960 White House Conference on Children and Youth. As a result of Kittrell's direction, Howard began turning out trained home economics specialists who were capable of going into a low-income community and actually solving some of the problems the community faced.

Kittrell's revolutionary program quickly drew the attention of federal authorities, and in 1966, the U.S. State Department invited her to conduct a study of the nutritional needs of the residents of Liberia. Her research uncovered a condition that is now known as hidden hunger (malnourishment on a full stomach). Sufferers from hidden hunger ingest enough food—in the case of Liberians, plenty of rice and cassava (the tuberous root from which tapioca pudding is made)—to keep them from feeling hungry, but the food itself is of such poor nutritional quality that sufferers do not receive the proper nourishment and thus are susceptible to a number of other deleterious health conditions. Kittrell's work in this area called international attention to the problem, which resulted in some improvement in the nutritional intake of the people in developing nations, with the addition of grains, vegetables, fruits, and fish to their diets.

Following the success of her mission to Liberia, Kittrell established college-level home economics programs in India (1950) and Zaire (1962). She also conducted nutritional research throughout Africa, in the process becoming the United States' best goodwill ambassador in that region, and in 1959, she was named the official U.S. delegate to the United Nations Geneva Conference for Non-governmental Organizations. Later, she conducted similar research for the UN Food and Agricultural Organization in Southeast Asia.

Kittrell retired from Howard in 1973. For the next five years, she was a senior fellow at Cornell and at the Moton Center for Independent Studies in Philadelphia. She also continued to travel throughout the Third World, where she was highly respected as a scientist who cared about people, and she arranged for many African women to receive a scientific education at Howard. She died on October 30, 1980, at her home in Washington, D.C.

See also: Hampton University; Howard University

REFERENCES AND FURTHER READING

Spangenburg, Ray, and Kit Moser. *African Americans in Science, Math, and Invention.* New York: Facts On File, 2003: 147–148.

Warren, Wini. *Black Women Scientists in the United States.* Bloomington: Indiana University Press, 1999: 153–174.

Kornegay, Wade M.
(1934–) Physicist

Wade Kornegay was one of the chief architects of the United States' missile defense system during the Cold War. As a researcher and manager, he helped develop a number of wideband radar systems for tracking ballistic missiles and discriminating between warheads and their accompanying countermeasure devices.

Kornegay was born on January 9, 1934, in Mount Olive, North Carolina. His parents, Gilbert and Estelle, were farmers. Orphaned by age six, he grew up with his maternal grandmother. Encouraged by his teachers to go to college, he received a partial scholarship to attend North Carolina Central College (today North Carolina Central University), where he received a BS in chemistry in 1956. He spent the next year at Bonn University in Germany before entering the graduate program at the University of California at Berkeley, receiving a PhD in chemical physics in 1961. He remained at Berkeley to conduct postdoctoral research for a year, and then in 1962, he took a position as a technical staff member with the Massachusetts Institute of Technology's Lincoln Laboratory, where he remained for the rest of his career. In 1957, he married Bettie Hunter, with whom he had three children.

The Lincoln Laboratory was founded in 1951 to investigate topics crucial to national security. At first, the laboratory's efforts were geared toward defending the United States from attack by long-range bombers, but by the time Kornegay arrived, the threat of bombers had given way to the threat of missiles, particularly intercontinental ballistic missiles (ICBMs) launched from the former Soviet Union. Kornegay was assigned to the radar signature studies group, which sought ways to make radar more effective as an ICBM detection system. The major problem with tracking an ICBM is that its trajectory carries it beyond the outer limits of Earth's atmosphere, where it is extremely difficult to detect with radar. This problem was further complicated by the development of evasive tactics such as chaff, electronic countermeasures, and decoys, all of which made it more difficult to identify the actual warhead among the accompanying clutter.

Kornegay's group solved this problem by developing systems to identify radar signatures, the detailed waveform of a detected radar echo, of relatively small objects. Once an ICBM reenters the atmosphere, its launch hardware, debris, and lightweight decoys slow down and fall away from the faster-traveling warhead. Atmospheric scientists had long known from studying the radar trails of meteors that bodies entering (or reentering) the atmosphere could be identified by their bow shock (similar to the wave that appears in front of a boat as it passes through the water) and ionized wake, which combine to give an object a specific radar signature. By the late 1960s, Kornegay's group had developed a way to use wideband phased-array radars to examine small sections of ionized wakes, thus giving the United States the ability to discriminate between a warhead and its accompanying clutter. For many years thereafter, the group developed increasingly sophisticated techniques for using wideband radar as the nation's principal means of defending against an impending ballistic missile attack.

In 1971, Kornegay was named technical group leader of the radar signature studies group. By 1993, he had become head of the radar measurements division, and in 2003, he was named a division fellow. Since most of his research was classified, very little of it has been published, although several unclassified versions have appeared in *Lincoln Laboratory Journal*, which reports on the laboratory's research. His many honors include the National Society of Black Engineers' 1990 Scientist of the Year Award.

See also: Chemistry; North Carolina Central University

REFERENCES AND FURTHER READING

Kessler, James H., J. S. Kidd, Renee A. Kidd, and Katherine A. Morin, eds. *Distinguished African American Scientists of the 20th Century*. Phoenix, AZ: Oryx Press, 1996: 212–215.

Krapp, Kristine M., ed. *Notable Black American Scientists*. Detroit, MI: Gale Research, 1999: 192–193.

Spangenburg, Ray, and Kit Moser. *African Americans in Science, Math, and Invention*. New York: Facts On File, 2003: 149–150.

Kountz, Samuel L., Jr.
(1930–1981) Medical Researcher

Before 1960, almost every kidney transplant procedure in which the donor and the recipient were not twins resulted in failure because of the body's tendency to reject foreign tissue. Samuel Kountz, the foremost kidney transplant specialist of his day, developed many of the procedures and equipment that overcame this problem, so that by the 21st century, the success rate of kidney transplant procedures was acceptably high.

Kountz was born on October 20, 1930, in Lexa, Arkansas. His father, Samuel, was a minister, and his mother was a homemaker. In 1952, he received a BS from Arkansas Agricultural, Mechanical and Normal College (today the University of Arkansas at Pine Bluff) and entered the University of Arkansas, receiving an MS in chemistry in 1956 and an MD from the medical school in 1958. That same year, he married Grace Akin, with whom he had three children. He interned at the San Francisco General Hospital (California), and then, having decided to become a surgeon, he entered the

Stanford University School of Medicine. In 1966, he was named a professor of surgery at Stanford.

As a Stanford medical student, Kountz became interested in kidney transplants. At the time, these procedures were not particularly successful, but in 1961, Kountz and Roy Cohn, one of his surgery professors, performed the first successful kidney transplant between two people who were not twins. Kidney transplants were rarely successful at that time primarily because the body's immune system tends to reject a foreign kidney; so from 1961 to 1967, he experimented on dogs while looking for a way to prevent the body from rejecting a donor kidney. During this period, he discovered that the process by which the canine body rejects a donor kidney could be reversed by giving the dog large amounts of the steroid methylprednisolone immediately following surgery, but he also discovered that too much methylprednisolone was fatal to the dog. Further observations by Kountz showed why. Kidney rejection begins where the blood vessels linking the kidney to the rest of the circulatory system are joined; so the donated kidney eventually dies from lack of blood. He solved this problem by developing a method for monitoring the flow of blood to the donated kidney. When the flow of blood drops below a certain rate, more methylprednisolone is administered, but when the flow increases to its normal rate, the administration of methylprednisolone is stopped.

In 1967, Kountz left Stanford to be chief of the kidney transplant service at the University of California at San Francisco (UCSF). At UCSF, he began collaborating with Folker Belzer on ways to preserve a kidney after it had been removed from a donor's body. Together they developed what became known as the Belzer kidney perfusion machine, a device that can keep a kidney alive for up to 50 hours after it has been removed from the donor's body. Kountz also directed the UCSF team that developed tissue-typing tests to heighten the odds that a donated kidney would not be rejected by the recipient. Realizing that a patient's psychological outlook helps determine whether a kidney transplant procedure is successful, Kountz made sure that kidney recipients received intense, personalized nursing care. He also started a support group so that prospective recipients could learn more about kidney transplant procedures from kidney transplant survivors and from the medical personnel who would be performing the operation.

Under Kountz's direction, UCSF's kidney transplant research center developed into one of the best in the country. In 1972, he was recruited by the Downstate Medical Center in Brooklyn, New York, to establish a state-of-the-art kidney transplant program at that institution, and within five years, Downstate's organ transplant unit had become one of the best on the East Coast.

Kountz performed more than 1,000 kidney transplants during his career. He also traveled the world to teach his methods to other medical researchers, and on one of these trips, he performed the first successful kidney transplant in the Middle East. In 1977, he developed brain damage from an undiagnosed disease he caught while visiting South Africa, and he was never able to perform surgery again. He died from this disease on December 23, 1981, in Great Neck, New York.

See also: Chemistry; University of Arkansas at Pine Bluff

REFERENCES AND FURTHER READING

Carey, Charles W. Jr. *American Scientists*. New York: Facts On File, 2005: 207–208.

McMurray, Emily J., ed. *Notable Twentieth-Century Scientists*. Detroit, MI: Gale Research, 1995: 1130–1131.

Spangenburg, Ray, and Kit Moser. *African Americans in Science, Math, and Invention*. New York: Facts On File, 2003: 150–152.

Langford, George M.
(1944–) Cell Biologist

To a certain degree, George Langford's scientific career was shaped by his famous predecessor, Ernest Everett Just. Both were cell biologists, both were affiliated with Dartmouth College, and both conducted their most important research at the Woods Hole Marine Biological Laboratory (Massachusetts). Langford's major contribution to cell biology was to demonstrate the existence of a previously unknown network by which biochemical material is transported within the confines of a single cell.

Langford was born on August 26, 1944, in Halifax, North Carolina. His parents, Maynard and Lillie, were farmers. His curiosity about farm animals eventually grew into an interest in biology and a desire to become a science teacher. After receiving a BS in biology from Fayetteville State University (North Carolina) in 1966, he entered the Illinois Institute of Technology (Chicago), receiving an MS in zoology in 1969 and a PhD in cell biology in 1971. He spent the next two years conducting postdoctoral research at the University of Pennsylvania before joining the faculty at the University of Massachusetts in Boston. In 1977, he became a professor of biology at Howard University College of Medicine, but two years later, he left to teach cell physiology at the University of North Carolina School of Medicine. In 1991, he was named the E. E. Just Professor of Natural Sciences at Dartmouth College, a position he held for the rest of his career. In 1968, he married Sylvia Tyler, with whom he had three children.

Langford focused his graduate research on intermediary metabolism, specifically the manner in which sugar compounds are broken down within *Euglena* (the genus of single-cell green protozoans). While working on this project, however, he became more interested in intracellular motility (the movement of various biochemical compounds within a single cell) and from then on, he focused his research on this topic rather than cellular metabolism. His postdoctoral research focused on the movement of organelles (specialized parts of cells that perform specific functions); organelles are to cells what organs are to humans. While at Howard, he began focusing his efforts on understanding intracellular motility in nerve cells, and he soon became a leading expert on neuroanatomy (the structure of nerve and brain cells).

Langford conducted much of his research during the summer at Woods Hole. During the summer of 1992, he and his Woods Hole research partners at the time, the German cell biologist Dieter Weiss and the Russian cell biologist Sergei Kuznetsov, made a startling discovery. For years, cell biologists had known that a network of structures called microtubules served as the highway by which organelles travel, and it was assumed that this network accommodated all intracellular transfers. But while working with squid axoplasm (the protoplasm that comprises axons, the appendages of nerve cells that transmit impulses away from the cell), Langford and his partners discovered an alternative network for intracellular motility in the endoplasmic reticulum, a major component of the cell membrane. Although microtubules are still responsible for a great deal of organelle travel in squid axoplasm, a network of filaments composed of actin (a protein that plays an important role in muscle contraction) constitutes an additional network for intracellular motility. Further research by Langford demonstrated that the biochemical agent responsible for propelling material along the actin network is myosin-V, which is similar to the protein myosin that works in conjunction with actin to govern the motor activities of muscles. Although much work remains to be done, Langford's research also suggests that long-range intracellular movement occurs on the microtubule network, but short-range movement takes place on the actin network.

In addition to his other activities, Langford served as program director for cell biology for the National Science Foundation, chair of the Woods Hole science council, and secretary of the American Society for Cell Biology (ASCB). As holder of the E. E. Just professorship, Langford played an important role in attracting more minorities at Dartmouth to careers in science. To this end, he also served as the inaugural chair of the ASCB's minorities affairs committee, a position he held from 1985 to 1990.

See also: American Society for Cell Biology; Biology; Howard University College of Medicine; Just, Ernest E.; National Science Foundation

References and Further Reading

Kessler, James H., J. S. Kidd, Renee A. Kidd, and Katherine A. Morin, eds. *Distinguished African American Scientists of the 20th Century*. Phoenix, AZ: Oryx Press, 1996: 218–221.

Krapp, Kristine M., ed. *Notable Black American Scientists*. Detroit, MI: Gale Research, 1999: 195–196.

Spangenburg, Ray, and Kit Moser. *African Americans in Science, Math, and Invention*. New York: Facts On File, 2003: 153–154.

Lawless, Theodore K.
(1892–1971) Dermatologist

Theodore Lawless developed treatments for syphilis and other diseases that damage the skin. He also contributed generously to the financial support of a number of black students seeking to pursue careers in medicine.

Lawless was born on December 6, 1892, in Thibodaux, Louisiana. His father, Alfred, was a minister and his mother, Harriet, was a homemaker. He became interested in pursuing a medical career by working for a veterinarian as a youth. He completed his secondary education at Straight College (today Dillard University) in New Orleans, and then enrolled in Talladega College (Alabama), where he received a BA in 1914. He studied for two years at the University of Kansas Medical School and then transferred to the Northwestern University Medical School in Evanston, Illinois, where he received an MD in 1919. He remained at Northwestern for an additional year to obtain an MA in dermatology, and then he spent the next four years studying dermatology at Columbia University, Harvard University, the University of Paris, the University of Freiburg, and the University of Vienna. In 1924, he relocated to Chicago to teach dermatology at Northwestern and to open a medical practice specializing in dermatology. He also served for a while as the senior attending physician in dermatology and syphilology at Provident Hospital.

Lawless specialized in treating diseases that affected the skin, such as syphilis, leprosy, sporotrichosis (a disease caused by a fungal infection that leaves disfiguring ulcers on the skin that are painless but never heal), tinea sycosis (barber's itch, which results when bacteria infect a shaved patch of skin), and tularemia (a bacterial infection of the skin that results from coming in contact with the bodily fluids of animals). He helped develop a treatment for syphilis, called electropyrexia, that involved using electrical current to induce fever in a patient and then injecting the patient with therapeutic drugs. He also developed methods for treating the skin of syphilitic patients that had been damaged by arsenic, which was once commonly used to treat syphilis. He also developed a method for diagnosing sporotrichosis, and he worked, unsuccessfully, to find a cure for leprosy.

In 1941, Lawless left Northwestern to focus on his medical practice, which he kept open until his death. His dermatology clinic had become internationally famous, and he treated patients from all over the nation and the world, regardless of race or income. Such was his skill that he became one of the first black physicians to be admitted to the American Medical Association.

Although Lawless provided his services free of charge to those who could not afford to pay, his dermatological skills made him a moderately wealthy man. In the 1950s, he began devoting more of his time to various business interests that made him even wealthier but that also benefited Chicago's black community. For example, he served as president of a savings and loan company that financed black-owned businesses in Chicago and of a real estate corporation that built low-cost housing. By the 1960s, he had become so wealthy that *Ebony* magazine recognized him as one of the 35 richest blacks in the United States. But the more he made, the more he seemed to give away. He established and equipped a laboratory and research facility at Provident, arranged for the construction of a housing complex at Dillard University, and helped finance the construction of a dermatology clinic at the Beilinson Hospital Center in Israel. He also financed the educations of many black medical students. He died, having never married, in 1971, in Chicago.

See also: Provident Hospital and Training School

REFERENCES AND FURTHER READING

Answers.com. "Theodore K. Lawless." [Online article or information; retrieved October 26, 2007.] http://www.answers.com/topic/theodore-k-lawless

Iowa Commission on the Status of African Americans. "Scientists and Inventors." [Online article or information; retrieved October 26, 2007.] http://www.state.ia.us/dhr/saa/AA_culture/scientists_inventors.html

Lawrence, Margaret Morgan
(1914–) Pediatric Psychiatrist

Margaret Lawrence performed some of the research concerning the negative psychological effects of segregation on black children that ultimately led the Supreme Court to declare segregated schools unconstitutional. She was also one of the first psychiatrists to insist that school-age children need increased access to mental health professionals.

Lawrence was born Margaret Cornelia Morgan on August 19, 1914, in New York City. Her father, Sandy, was an Episcopal minister, and her mother, Mary Elizabeth, was a homemaker. As a young girl, she moved with her family to her father's various assignments in Virginia, North Carolina, and Mississippi, before settling in Vicksburg, Mississippi. At age 14, she returned to New York City, where her mother's family lived, to attend high school, and after graduation, she entered Cornell University, receiving a BS in biology in 1936. She then entered the Columbia University College of Physicians and Surgeons and received an

MD in 1940. She spent the next three years completing a pediatric internship and residency at Harlem Hospital and working on a master's degree in public health (MPH) at Columbia, which she received in 1943. In 1938, she married Charles Lawrence, with whom she had three children.

While working on her MPH, Lawrence came in contact with Benjamin Spock, the world famous pediatrician. Spock impressed her with his understanding of how a child's emotional development also affects his/her physical development, and she decided to pursue this line of inquiry as her specialty. After teaching pediatrics and public health at Meharry Medical College in Nashville, Tennessee, for four years, in 1947, she returned to New York City to study psychiatry at Columbia while working with emotionally disturbed children at the Babies & Children's Hospital of New York, and in 1951, she was awarded a certificate in psychoanalytic training by the Columbia Psychoanalytic Center. At that point, she returned to Harlem Hospital, eventually becoming the director of its therapeutic developmental nursery. She conducted research there and at Columbia University College of Physicians and Surgeons, where she taught and eventually became director of the child development center. Meanwhile, she and her husband maintained a private practice in pediatric psychiatry in nearby Rockland County, New York.

Around 1950, Lawrence came in contact with Mamie Phipps Clark and her husband, Kenneth, who were doing groundbreaking work on the negative effects of segregated schooling on the emotional development of black children. Over the next several years, she collaborated with the Clarks, who provided much of the expert testimony that prompted the U.S. Supreme Court's landmark decision, *Brown v. Board of Education* [347 U.S. 483 (1954)], which declared segregated public schools unconstitutional. After the Court's decision, Lawrence and the Clarks continued to impress on government officials the debilitating effects of segregation in school districts that were slow to integrate.

Throughout her career, Lawrence focused her research on the emotional well-being of children. She was one of the first to advocate that psychiatrists and psychologists should be employed by school districts as a way to help students overcome emotional problems. Much of her work in this area was published in *The Mental Health Team in the Schools* (New York: Behavioral Publications, 1971), which outlined the benefits to be accrued from having mental health professionals make regular visits to schoolchildren, partly as a way to improve their mental health and partly as a way to remove the stigma attached to having poor mental health. She also focused on the mental health of children in the lower socioeconomic echelons of urban areas, and in *Young Inner City Families: Development of Ego Strength under Stress* (New York: Human Sciences Press, 1975) she addresses the psychological aspects of poverty, particularly as it creates stress in the lives of poor children. In the

1970s, she and her husband did groundbreaking work on the similarities in terms of mental health between children in East and West Africa and children in rural Georgia and Mississippi.

In 1984, Lawrence retired from Harlem and Columbia. She continued to practice privately for a number of years thereafter.

See also: Clark, Mamie P.; Harlem Hospital; Meharry Medical College

REFERENCES AND FURTHER READING

Kessler, James H., J. S. Kidd, Renee A. Kidd, and Katherine A. Morin, eds. *Distinguished African American Scientists of the 20th Century*. Phoenix, AZ: Oryx Press, 1996: 221–224.

Lightfoot, Sarah Lawrence. *Balm in Gilead: Journey of a Healer*. Reading, MA: Addison-Wesley, 1989.

Warren, Wini. *Black Women Scientists in the United States*. Bloomington: Indiana University Press, 1999: 175–177.

Leevy, Carroll M.
(1920–) Physiologist

Carroll Leevy was one of the world's foremost experts on hepatobiliary diseases (diseases of the liver and biliary tract), which include hepatitis, gallstones, liver cirrhosis, various metabolic and genetic disorders, and hepatocellular cancer. Leevy was instrumental in developing many of the procedures and techniques for diagnosing and treating these diseases.

Leevy was born on October 13, 1920, in Columbia, South Carolina. His parents, Isaac and Mary, owned and operated a department store. As a young boy, he decided to become a physician; so after receiving a BS from Fisk College in 1941, he entered the University of Michigan Medical School (Ann Arbor) and received an MD in 1944. After completing his internship and residency in 1948 at the Jersey City Medical Center (New Jersey), today part of the University of Medicine and Dentistry of New Jersey (UMDNJ) in Newark, he joined the medical center's research staff. With the exception of a tour of duty (1954–1957) at the U.S. Naval Hospital in St. Albans, New York, he remained affiliated with UMDNJ for the rest of his career. He was eventually named chair of the department of medicine, chief physician of the university hospital, and scientific director of UMDNJ's New Jersey Medical School Liver Center, also known as the Carroll M. Leevy Center for Hepatitis Prevention and Education. In 1956, he married Ruth Barboza, with whom he had two children.

Leevy's primary research interest involved liver disease. Since many patients with liver disease also suffer from alcoholism, few medical researchers when he was a medical student were willing to devote their time and energy to studying liver disease. Moreover, few techniques existed for obtaining liver biopsies (samples of living tissue from diseased organs) or for diagnosing liver disease. Undaunted by all this, Leevy decided to take up the challenge, and by the time he finished his residency, he had devised an innovative and relatively painless method for obtaining liver biopsies and for diagnosing a host of liver ailments. By 1960, he had demonstrated that, although alcoholism caused liver cirrhosis, other liver diseases are caused by other factors, including diabetes, improper diet, and environmental pollutants. The latter part of Leevy's career was devoted to developing drug treatments for chronic hepatitis C, also known as viral hepatitis, because it is caused by the hepatitis C virus (HCV), and in this regard, he demonstrated the effectiveness of such drugs as Infergen[R] and ribavirin.

Leevy served as director of the Sammy Davis Jr., National Liver Institute and president of the International Association for the Study of the Liver, and he cofounded and served on the first board of directors of the American Liver Foundation. He authored hundreds of publications, including *Practical Diagnosis and Treatment of Liver Disease* (1957), *Evaluation of Liver Function in Clinical Practice* (Indianapolis, IN: Lilly Research Laboratories, 1965, 1974), *The Hepatic Circulation and Portal Hypertension* (New York: New York Academy of Sciences, 1970), *Liver Regeneration in Man* (Springfield, IL: Charles C. Thomas, 1973), *Guidelines for Detection of Hepatoxicity Due to Drugs and Chemicals* (Washington, DC: National Institutes of Health, 1979), and *Diseases of the Liver and Biliary Tract: Standardization of Nomenclature, Diagnosis Criteria, and Prognosis* (Washington, DC: U.S. Department of Health, Education and Welfare, 1976). His honors include the American Association for the Study of Liver Disease's 1991 Distinguished Service Award.

See also: Diabetes; Fisk University

References and Further Reading

Kessler, James H., J. S. Kidd, Renee A. Kidd, and Katherine A. Morin, eds. *Distinguished African American Scientists of the 20th Century*. Phoenix, AZ: Oryx Press, 1996: 224–228.

Krapp, Kristine M., ed. *Notable Black American Scientists*. Detroit, MI: Gale Research, 1999: 203–205.

Spangenburg, Ray, and Kit Moser. *African Americans in Science, Math, and Invention*. New York: Facts On File, 2003: 158–159.

Leffall, LaSalle D., Jr.
(1930–) Surgical Oncologist

In his day, LaSalle Leffall was one of the foremost surgical oncologists (surgeons who specialize in the removal of tumors). As president of the

American Cancer Society, he did much to heighten awareness among African Americans about the dangers of and the treatments for cancer.

Leffall was born on May 22, 1930, in Tallahassee, Florida, and grew up in nearby Quincy. His father, LaSalle, was a professor at Florida A&M College (today Florida A&M University) in Tallahassee, and his mother, Martha, was a teacher. At age 15, he entered Florida A&M and received a BS in 1948. After receiving an MD from Howard University Medical School (today Howard University College of Medicine) in 1952, he completed his internship at Homer G. Phillips Hospital in St. Louis, his residency at D.C. General Hospital and Freedmen's Hospital in Washington, D.C., and a two-year research fellowship in surgical oncology at Memorial Sloan-Kettering Cancer Center in New York City. In 1960, he entered the U.S. Army Medical Corps as a captain and served as chief of general surgery at an army hospital in Munich, Germany. In 1962, he returned to Howard to teach, and in 1970, he was named chair of the department of surgery, a position he held for the rest of his career. In 1956, he married Ruth McWilliams, with whom he had one child.

Leffall became interested in surgical oncology as a medical student, and upon his return to Howard in 1962, he took up its study in earnest. He was particularly interested in cancers of the breast, colon, rectum, head, and neck. Although he was not a laboratory researcher, he developed into a highly competent clinician, and over the course of his career, he developed a number of surgical techniques for extracting tumors without harming adjacent, nontumorous tissue.

In 1979, Leffall was elected to a term as president of the American Cancer Society. In this capacity, he organized the first National Conference on Meeting the Challenge of Cancer Among Black Americans for the purpose of raising the consciousness of the medical community and of the African American community to the dangers that cancer posed to black people. As Leffall noted at the time, the survival rate for blacks was lower than for whites for every single major cancer, not because blacks are more susceptible to cancer than whites but because medical care in general is not as accessible to blacks. As a result, blacks with cancer tended to wait longer before they saw a doctor, thus increasing their risk of dying. One result of the conference was the development of specially targeted materials and educational programs to meet the needs of cancer victims in the black community. He also served as president of the American College of Surgeons and the Society of Surgical Oncology and as a member of the National Cancer Advisory Board.

See also: Cancer; Florida A&M University; Freedmen's Hospital; Homer G. Phillips Hospital; Howard University College of Medicine

REFERENCES AND FURTHER READING
Leffall, LaSalle D. *No Boundaries: A Cancer Surgeon's Odyssey.* Washington, DC: Howard University Press, 2005.

Organ, Claude H., and Margaret Kosiba, eds. *A Century of Black Surgeons: The U.S.A. Experience.* Norman, OK: Transcript Press, 1987: 697–732.

Spangenburg, Ray, and Kit Moser. *African Americans in Science, Math, and Invention.* New York: Facts On File, 2003: 159–160.

Lewis, Julian H.
(1891–1989) Physiologist

Julian Lewis wrote *The Biology of the Negro* (Chicago: Chicago University Press, 1942), the first known textbook on comparative racial pathology (the comparison of the biological and physiological traits of two different races of humans and how those differences affect the races' ability to cope with various diseases). This work dispels the notion that white people enjoy any sort of inherent physiological superiority over black people.

Lewis was born on May 26, 1891, in Shawneetown, Illinois. His parents, John and Cordelia, were teachers. He studied biology and physiology at the University of Illinois, receiving a BS and an MA in 1911 and 1912, respectively. He then entered the University of Chicago, where he received a PhD in physiology in 1915, thus becoming the first African American to receive such a degree from an American university. Two years later, he received an MD from Chicago's Rush Medical College and joined the faculty at the University of Chicago as a professor of physiology, a position he held until 1943.

Lewis's research involved pathology (the growth and development of disease) and immunity (the ability of a living organism to resist disease). His earliest research concerned the ability of lipids (the class of fatty acid biochemical compounds that includes steroids) to inhibit anaphylaxis (an organism's increased susceptibility to a foreign protein resulting from previous exposure to that protein). But he also conducted research in other fields as well; one such study involved the suitability of beef plasma as a substitute for human blood in a transfusion, while another involved the presence of epinephrine (a hormone that plays a role in regulating blood pressure) in the human fetal adrenal glands.

Lewis is best remembered for *The Biology of the Negro.* He wrote the book as a means of exploring how his own African descent affected his immunity, but in so doing, he produced a masterful work that addresses the physiological and anatomical differences between African Americans and Americans of European ancestry. The work neither advances nor defends any particular thesis; instead, it discusses in straightforward fashion the published work of other medical researchers concerning their findings about blacks and whites. The work's chapters cover anatomy; biochemical and physiological characteristics; medical diseases; surgical diseases; obstetrics and gynecology; diseases of the skin; diseases of the eye, ear, nose, and throat; and dental diseases. Lewis presents a number of instances where blacks differ from whites; for example, he shows that blacks are much more likely to have Type B blood rather than Type A, while whites are much more likely to have Type A blood rather than Type B. However, he found no evidence to substantiate the claim, or even to suggest it, that the Negroid race is inferior to the Caucasian race. For example, he showed that many of the diseases affecting blacks do so in a way not appreciably different from the way they affect white people and that, where such differences do exist, they stem from geographical rather than physiological considerations. Although the work made little impact on whites, it greatly impressed its black audience, who took it as further proof that the myth of white supremacy is indeed nothing more than a myth.

In 1943, Lewis left the University of Chicago to become the director of the pathology department and the clinical laboratory at Our Lady of Mercy Hospital in Dyer, Indiana, a position he held for more than 40 years. He died on March 6, 1989.

See also: Biology

REFERENCES AND FURTHER READING

Salzman, Jack, David Lionel Smith, and Cornel West, eds. *Encyclopedia of African American Culture and History*. New York: MacMillan, 1996: 1609–1610.

Spangenburg, Ray, and Kit Moser. *African Americans in Science, Math, and Invention*. New York: Facts On File, 2003: 162–163.

Macklin, John W.
(1939–) Analytical Chemist

John Macklin's research contributed to a better understanding of the origins of life on Earth. He also developed techniques for identifying unknown materials as small as a billionth of a billionth of a gram.

Macklin was born on December 11, 1939, in Fort Worth, Texas. When he was very young, his father died, and he went to live on his grandmother's farm. At age seven he rejoined his mother, Vera, and his siblings in Seattle, where he grew up. As a young boy, he developed an interest in chemistry, and, after receiving a BS in chemistry from Linfield College (Oregon) in 1962, he entered the graduate program at Cornell University and received a PhD in inorganic chemistry in 1968. He then joined the faculty at the University of Washington, where he remained for the rest of his career.

Macklin's research involved analytical chemistry (the identification of the chemical components of a given sample, usually quite small, of some unknown compound). To this end, he became adept at using lasers to create a Raman effect (a slight change in the wavelength of a beam of light when it is deflected by the atoms of a molecule). Although the change in wavelength is slight, it is enough to indicate the type and arrangement of a molecule's atoms; thus, the chemical composition of an unknown compound can be identified simply by bombarding it with visible light from a laser and then observing the frequency shift of the deflected wavelength. Scientists use many other spectroscopic techniques, whereby a substance is identified by examining the various wavelengths of electromagnetic radiation, such as ultraviolet light or X-rays, it reflects. However, Raman spectroscopy is the best technique for examining extremely minute samples.

In the 1980s, Macklin was recruited by the National Aeronautics and Space Administration (NASA) to examine tiny particles of meteorites and cosmic dust. NASA researchers were looking for clues as to the origins of life on Earth, specifically the origins of the complex organic (carbon-based) compounds from which the first one-celled organisms developed in Earth's primeval oceans. Because some NASA researchers believed that complex organic compounds had been carried to Earth from outer space by meteorites, Macklin, as a leading expert in Raman spectroscopy, was invited to examine NASA's samples of space dust. After much careful examination, in 1987, Macklin demonstrated that tiny crystals of clay in the space dust are capable of magnifying and focusing light from the sun in such a way as to synthesize complex organic molecules from the carbon content of the space dust. In 1994, he offered further support for the theory that complex organic molecules reached Earth from outer space by discovering tiny traces of fullerene (a complex carbon molecule in the shape of a soccer ball), in an impact crater made by a tiny meteorite on the Long Duration Exposure Facility, a package of experiments put into orbit via space shuttle in 1984.

Macklin's later research involved developing spectroscopic methods for examining increasingly smaller samples. To this end, he created a technique that combines an enhanced form of Raman spectroscopy known as micro-Raman spectroscopy with ultraviolet/visible light spectroscopy for identifying substances in a dissolved or condensed form that are as small as one attogram (10^{-18} gram, or one billionth of a billionth of a gram). This technique has proven useful for identifying minute traces of environmental pollutants in air or water and for determining the results of certain biochemical reactions that are otherwise impossible to ascertain.

See also: Chemistry; National Aeronautics and Space Administration

REFERENCES AND FURTHER READING

Kessler, James H., J. S. Kidd, Renee A. Kidd, and Katherine A. Morin, eds. *Distinguished African American Scientists of the 20th Century*. Phoenix, AZ: Oryx Press, 1996: 234–236.

Krapp, Kristine M., ed. *Notable Black American Scientists*. Detroit, MI: Gale Research, 1999: 211.

Spangenburg, Ray, and Kit Moser. *African Americans in Science, Math, and Invention*. New York: Facts On File, 2003: 166–167.

Malcom, Shirley M.
(1946–) Science Administrator

As a high-level administrator with the National Science Foundation and the American Association for the Advancement of Science, Shirley Malcom worked to open doors to careers in science and engineering for women and minorities.

Malcom was born Shirley Mahaley on September 6, 1946, in Birmingham, Alabama. Her father, Ben, was a meatpacker, and her mother, Lillie, was a homemaker. At age 16, she completed high school and went off to the University of Washington, where she received a BS in zoology in 1967. After receiving an MS in zoology from the University of California at Los Angeles the following year, she taught high school for a few years and then enrolled in Pennsylvania State University, where she received a PhD in ecology in 1974. After teaching biology for a year at the University of North Carolina at Wilmington, she moved to Washington, D.C., to work as a research associate for the American Association for the Advancement of Science (AAAS). In 1975, she married Horace Malcom, with whom she had two children.

As a college student, Malcom had been somewhat mystified by the low number of minorities and women in her classes and on the faculties at the schools she attended. In 1977, she decided to do something about this situation by becoming the program manager for the National Science Foundation's Minority Institutions Science Improvement Program (MISIP), the predecessor of the Minority Science and Engineering Improvement Program. The purpose of MISIP was to beef up the basic sciences programs at historically black colleges and universities by providing federal funding for better equipment and facilities and higher salaries for professors, thus making careers in science more attractive to African Americans. In 1979, she returned to the AAAS, this time as head of the office of opportunities in science.

In 1989, Malcom was named head of the newly established Directorate for Education and Human Resources Programs. In this position, she was responsible for AAAS programs geared to improving the general public's understanding of science, providing technology training for students with disabilities, and creating openings for women and minorities in science and engineering, among other things. To address these concerns, she helped establish the Black Churches Project, a network of churches that were already

As a science administrator, Shirley Mal-com worked hard to attract more African Americans and other minorities to pursue careers in the sciences. (American Association for the Advancement of Science)

providing tutoring services to disadvantaged youths, as a way to improve the education African Americans receive about science, the environment, and health. She also helped establish Proyecto Futuro, a program designed to make the Hispanic community more aware of the latest developments in science and technology, and the Graduate Scholars Program, which helped finance PhD-level education for black science graduates. Other projects sponsored by her directorate include the development of Kinetic City Super Crew, an online science adventure series; Earth Explorer, a CD-ROM multimedia encyclopedia that focuses on the environment; and a network of deans at major research universities for purposes of enhancing employment and research opportunities for women and minorities.

In addition to her other duties, Malcom served as cochair of the Blue Ribbon Panel on Pre-K–12 Education for Building Engineering and Science Talent, an initiative to include more women and minorities in the nation's technological workforce. In 1994, Malcom was chosen by President Bill Clinton to serve on the President's Committee of Advisors on Science and Technology (1994–1998), and the National Science Board, the policy-making body of the National Science Foundation (1994–2001). Her many honors include election to the American Academy of Arts and Sciences and receipt of the National Academy of Sciences' 2003 Public Welfare Medal.

See also: American Association for the Advancement of Science; Biology; Building Engineering and Science Talent; Historically Black Colleges and

Universities; Minority Science and Engineering Improvement Program; National Science Foundation

References and Further Reading

AAAS Experts & Speakers Service. "Shirley M. Malcom, Ph.D." [Online article or information; retrieved December 14, 2005.] http://www.aaas.org/Science Talk/malcom.shtml.

Warren, Wini. *Black Women Scientists in the United States*. Bloomington: Indiana University Press, 1999: 185–192.

Maloney, Arnold H.
(1888–1955) Pharmacologist

Arnold Maloney was the first African American to teach pharmacology at the college level in the United States. His principal contribution to pharmacology was the discovery of a drug to treat victims of barbiturate poisoning.

Maloney was born on July 4, 1888, in Cocoye Village on the Caribbean island of Trinidad. His father, Lewis, was a building contractor, and his mother, Estelle, owned and operated several grocery stores. After receiving an AB from Trinidad's Naparima College in 1909, he briefly operated his own drugstore before immigrating to the United States to attend college. He took a few classes at Lincoln University (Pennsylvania) before relocating to New York City, where he received an MA in philosophy from Columbia University in 1910 and a bachelor's degree in theology from General Theological Seminary in 1912. That same year, he was ordained as a minister in the Protestant Episcopal Church, but he later became a bishop in the African Orthodox Church. In 1916, he married Beatrice Johnston, with whom he had two children.

In 1920, Maloney left the ministry and accepted a position as a professor of psychology at Wilberforce University (Ohio). Five years later, he enrolled in the Indiana University School of Medicine and received an MD in 1929. He began his internship at Provident Hospital in Baltimore, but before he completed it he was recruited by Howard University to teach in its medical school. The arrangement included the opportunity for Maloney to study pharmacology at the University of Wisconsin, and, after receiving a PhD in 1931, he returned to Howard to teach pharmacology. He eventually became head of Howard's pharmacology department, a position he held for the rest of his career.

Maloney's research focused on how certain biochemical compounds either stimulate or depress the breathing process in humans. At Wisconsin, he studied the effects of barbiturates, morphine, and other sedatives on that portion of the brain that controls breathing. At the time, barbiturates were particularly misunderstood, and frequently they were prescribed in dosages that depressed the patient's breathing to the point of inducing coma or even death. At the time, the preferred treatment for barbiturate poisoning was to eliminate the barbiturates by inducing an increased flow of urine and by bloodletting and then to replace the fluids withdrawn with saline solution administered intravenously. In cases involving only a slight overdose, this method worked fine, but in cases involving a heavy overdose, it seemed only to speed up the patient's demise.

In the course of his investigations, Maloney experimented with a number of biochemical compounds, including strychnine, as potential antidotes to barbiturate poisoning, but none of them worked as well as the method he hoped to replace. Eventually he experimented with picrotoxin, a natural substance derived from *Cocculus indicus*, the fruit or berry of the plant *Anamirta cocculus*, a climbing plant native to Indonesia. Picrotoxin is a peculiar substance in that it can induce narcosis (sleep) as well as stimulate, but it is also poisonous. After much experimenting, Maloney discovered that picrotoxin, when administered judiciously, is a powerful antidote for barbiturate poisoning. Most medical experts were skeptical when they first heard Maloney's claims concerning the therapeutic properties of picrotoxin, but after he published his work concerning picrotoxin in *Journal of Pharmacology and Experimental Therapuetics, Anesthesia and Analgesia*, and *American Journal of Surgery* in the mid- to late-1930s, that skepticism was laid to rest. Eventually, the administration of picrotoxin replaced the earlier method of fluid removal as the preferred treatment for barbiturate poisoning.

In addition to his other pursuits, Maloney was also intensely interested in politics, particularly as they affected African Americans and the black inhabitants of the Caribbean islands. He authored three books on these subjects, *Some Essentials of Race Leadership* (Xenia, OH: Aldine, 1924), *Pathways to Democracy* (Boston: Meador Publishing, 1945), and *After England—We; Nationhood for Caribbea* (Boston: Meador, 1949), as well as an autobiography, *Amber Gold; an Adventure in Autobiography* (Boston: Meador, 1946). He retired from Howard University in 1953, and he died on August 8, 1955, in Washington, D.C.

See also: Howard University

REFERENCES AND FURTHER READING

Maloney, Arnold H. *Amber Gold; an Adventure in Autobiography*. Boston: Meador Publishing, 1946.

McMurray, Emily J., ed. *Notable Twentieth-Century Scientists*. Detroit, MI: Gale Research, 1995: 1305–1306.

Spangenburg, Ray, and Kit Moser. *African Americans in Science, Math, and Invention*. New York: Facts On File, 2003: 167–168.

Massey, Walter E.
(1938–) Science Administrator

Walter Massey directed the affairs of several of the United States' most important scientific facilities and organizations, including Argonne National Laboratory (the first national research laboratory), the American Association for the Advancement of Science, and the National Science Foundation. He was also a highly regarded college administrator, having held a number of prominent positions at several colleges and universities.

Massey was born on April 5, 1938, in Hattiesburg, Mississippi. His father, Almar (some sources give Chester), was a steelworker, and his mother, Essie, was a teacher. At age 16, he finished high school and enrolled in Atlanta's Morehouse College, where he received a BS in physics in 1958. After teaching for a year at Howard University, he entered the graduate program at Washington University in St. Louis and in 1966, he received an MS and a PhD in physics.

Massey's graduate research involved superfluidity, the unusual properties exhibited by liquid helium when it is cooled to 2.18°K. These properties include frictionless flow, including the ability to overflow its containment vessel in defiance of the laws of viscosity, and very high heat conductivity. He was particularly intrigued by the phenomena exhibited by the isotope of helium known as helium–4, because its nucleus consists of four nucleons (two protons and two neutrons). At the time, helium–4 had demonstrated superfluidity, whereas another isotope of helium, helium–3, had not. Massey's research explored the standard explanation for this difference in behavior in terms of bosons and fermions. Bosons contain an even number of nucleons, whereas fermions contain an uneven number of nucleons; as a result, the angular momentums (spins) of the isotopes are different. Consequently, it was believed that helium–4 becomes a superfluid because it is a boson, but helium–3 cannot become a superfluid because it is a fermion.

Much of Massey's graduate research was performed at the Argonne National Laboratory, a nonprofit research and development facility operated by the University of Chicago for the U.S. Department of Energy (DOE). After completing his education, he went to work at Argonne as a staff physicist. In 1968, he became a professor of physics at the University of Illinois at Urbana, and in this capacity he began to shift the focus of his work away from scientific research and toward science administration. In addition to his teaching duties, he helped organize the Illinois Science and Mathematics Academy, a public high school for students with a strong interest in pursuing a career in science or mathematics, and he served as a trustee for the Academy for Mathematics and Science Teachers, an Illinois organization that offers public school teachers additional training in science and mathematics. In 1969, he married Shirley Streeter, with whom he had two children.

Walter Massey was the first African American director of the Argonne National Laboratory and its vice president for research before becoming director of the National Science Foundation in 1991. (Morehouse College)

In 1970, Massey exchanged his faculty position at Illinois for a similar position at Brown University in Providence, Rhode Island, and in 1975, he took on the additional duties of dean of Brown's college of arts and sciences. In 1979, he returned to the University of Chicago as a professor of physics and as laboratory director at Argonne; in this latter capacity he oversaw Argonne's various research projects. In 1984, he was named vice president of research for the university and for Argonne, a position he held until 1991. In this capacity, he was responsible for ensuring that university faculty conducting research at Argonne received the necessary support, as well as for coordinating and overseeing the work of Argonne's on-site management.

In 1987, the American Association for the Advancement of Science made Massey its president-elect. He took office the following year and became chairman of the board in 1989. During his tenure, he focused his efforts on implementing the AAAS's Project 2061, an ambitious program designed to boost the science literacy level of all Americans by rewriting the nation's middle school and high school science curricula to emphasize major scientific concepts. He also pushed the AAAS to redouble its efforts to bring more minorities and women into the sciences, and he served as cochair of the AAAS Steering Committee for the Project to Strengthen the Scientific and Engineering Infrastructure in Sub-Saharan Africa.

Shortly after taking office in 1989, President George H. W. Bush named Massey to the President's Council of Advisors on Science and Technology. In 1991, Bush named Massey director of the National Science Foundation (NSF), an independent federal agency that is the funding source for approximately 20 percent of all federally supported basic research conducted by America's colleges and universities. Massey's primary contribution to NSF was the establishment of a planning commission to develop long-range strategies for NSF so that it could continue to support first-rate research at many points on the frontiers of knowledge, as identified and defined by the best researchers, as well as to ensure the balanced allocation of resources in strategic research areas in response to scientific opportunities to meet national goals.

In 1993, Massey returned to academia, this time as provost and senior vice president of academic affairs for the University of California system. In this position, the second-most senior in the prestigious and sprawling university system, he was responsible for developing academic and research planning and policy, budget planning, and allocations. He was also responsible for programmatic oversight of the three national laboratories that the university manages for DOE. In 1995, he assumed the duties of president of his alma mater, Morehouse College. In this position, he focused on making Morehouse one of the leading undergraduate institutions in the nation by improving the quality of student and faculty recruitment and by enhancing the college's fundraising capabilities. In addition to his many other duties, Massey served a term as president of the National Society of Black Physicists and a term as vice president of the American Physical Society.

See also: American Association for the Advancement of Science; American Physical Society; Department of Energy; Howard University; National Science Foundation; National Society of Black Physicists; Physics

REFERENCES AND FURTHER READING

Physicists of the Black Diaspora. "Walter E. Massey." [Online article or information; retrieved November 24, 2005.] http://www.math.buffalo.edu/mad/physics/massey_waltere.html.

Spangenburg, Ray, and Kit Moser. *African Americans in Science, Math, and Invention.* New York: Facts On File, 2003: 168–169.

Massie, Samuel P., Jr.
(1919–2005) Organic Chemist

Samuel Massie developed pharmaceutical drugs for treating a broad range of medical conditions from anxiety to sexually transmitted diseases. He was also a noted educator and science administrator.

Massie was born on July 3, 1919, in North Little Rock, Arkansas; his father, Samuel, was a teacher, as was his mother, whose name is unknown. After finishing high school at age 13, he worked in a grocery store for a year before entering Dunbar Junior College in Little Rock. Upon completing Dunbar's program, he transferred to Arkansas Agricultural, Mechanical and Normal College (now the University of Arkansas at Pine Bluff), where he received a BS in chemistry in 1937. He then entered the graduate program at Fisk College (now Fisk University) in Nashville, Tennessee, and in 1940, he received an MS in chemistry. His doctoral studies at Iowa State University were interrupted by World War II, during which he worked on the Manhattan Project, the U.S. effort to design and construct the world's first atomic bomb. He resumed his studies at Iowa State after the war, and in 1946, he received a PhD in organic chemistry. In 1947, he married Gloria Thompkins, with whom he had three children.

Massie taught for a year at Fisk before accepting a faculty position at Langston University (Oklahoma) in 1948. Over the next five years, he became chair of the chemistry department, and in this capacity, he inaugurated a fledgling chemical research program at the university. By 1953, his reputation as a researcher and administrator had grown to the point that he was elected president of the Oklahoma Academy of Sciences.

In 1953, Massie returned to Fisk, this time as head of the chemistry department. During his seven-year tenure, he improved both the chemistry teaching and chemical research at Fisk. His most impressive achievement, however, was when he got the American Chemical Society to agree to hold its national convention at Fisk in the late 1950s, the first time a historically black college or university had hosted a major scientific meeting. Meanwhile, he had come to the attention of the National Science Foundation (NSF), an independent federal agency in Washington, D.C., that is the funding source for approximately 20 percent of all federally supported basic research conducted by America's colleges and universities, and in 1960, NSF named him associate director of special projects in science education. Upon completing that project, he joined the faculty at Howard University as a professor of pharmaceutical chemistry, and in 1963, he accepted the presidency of North Carolina College For Negroes at Durham (today North Carolina Central University).

In 1966, Massie became the first African American to be appointed to the faculty of the U.S. Naval Academy in Annapolis, Maryland. In 1977, he was named chair of the chemistry department, a position he held for the rest of his career.

In addition to being a skillful teacher and administrator, Massie was also a highly regarded researcher. His early research focused on phenothiazine (an organic compound that at the time was used chiefly as an insecticide) and vermifuge (a medical preparation that expels worms and other parasites from the intestines of cattle, horses, poultry, sheep, and swine). Phenothiazine's high toxicity makes it unsafe to administer to humans, so most chemists never considered that it might be a useful substance from which to derive pharmaceutical drugs. Massie, however, showed that certain derivatives of phenothiazine can be used safely in cancer chemotherapy, as well as to treat anxiety in humans. He published much of his work regarding phenothiazines in "The Chemistry of Phenothiazine," an article that appeared in 1954 in the prestigious journal *Chemical Reviews* (55, 6: 1179). This article was of such international interest that the journal received more than 500 requests for reprints from more than 50 countries. Two important antianxiety drugs, chlorpromazine and trifluoperazine, were later developed by medical researchers following Massie's lead. His later research focused on developing pharmaceuticals for treating a wide variety of conditions, including malaria, meningitis, gonorrhea, and herpes. He also developed a protective foam to guard against the deleterious effects of certain nerve gases.

Massie retired from the Naval Academy in 1993, but he worked for several years thereafter as vice president for education of the Bingwa Software Company. In this capacity, he oversaw the production of educational software that combines educational concepts with uplifting stories from the lives of multicultural role models. His many honors include being selected in 1998 by *Chemical and Engineering News* as one of the 75 greatest chemists of all time. He died on April 10, 2005, in Laurel, Maryland.

See also: American Chemical Society; Chemistry; Fisk University; Howard University; Langston University; National Science Foundation; North Carolina Central University; University of Arkansas at Pine Bluff

REFERENCES AND FURTHER READING

Lamb, Yvonne S. "Prof. Samuel Massie Dies; Broke Naval Academy's Race Barrier." *Washington Post*, April 15, 2005: B06.

Massie, Samuel P., with Robert C. Hayden. *Catalyst: The Autobiography of an American Chemist*. Laurel, MD: S.P. Massie, 2005.

Spangenburg, Ray, and Kit Moser. *African Americans in Science, Math, and Invention*. New York: Facts On File, 2003: 170–171.

McAfee, Walter S.
(1914–1995) Physicist

Walter McAfee was the first scientist to accurately measure the speed of the moon. The calculations he developed in the process were later used to plot the trajectories of the various spacecraft sent from Earth to the moon. He also contributed to improved methods of detecting electromagnetic radiation.

McAfee was born on September 2, 1914, in Ore City, Texas. His father, Luther, was a minister and carpenter, and his mother, Susie, was a homemaker. As an infant, he moved with his family to Marshall, Texas, where he grew up. After receiving a BS in mathematics from Marshall's Wiley College in 1934, he worked odd jobs for a year before entering the graduate program at Ohio State University (Columbus), where he received an MS in theoretical mathematical physics in 1937. For the next three years, he taught mathematics and science at a junior high school in Columbus, Ohio. In 1941, he married Viola Winston, with whom he had two children.

McAfee focused his graduate research on the various phenomena of electromagnetic radiation, which includes radio waves, infrared light, visible light, ultraviolet light, X-rays, and gamma rays. This background made him attractive to the U.S. Army Signal Corps' Electronics Research and Development Command (ERDC) in Fort Monmouth, New Jersey. In 1942, he was hired as a civilian scientist and assigned to ERDC's Theoretical Studies Unit, later known as the Radar Siting Group. At the time, the United States was involved in World War II, and this group did mathematical studies for radio propagation, radar coverage patterns, and radar antenna applications to optimize the effects of radar equipment, which was then fairly primitive. One of the group's more interesting projects was to devise a way to use radar to detect nonmagnetic mines in the Atlantic and Pacific oceans.

By 1945, McAfee had published papers on radar-echoing areas, radar cross sections, and refraction studies in the atmosphere. This experience made him a perfect fit for Project Diana, the U.S. Army effort to bounce a radio signal off the moon. The project, part of the preliminary effort to send a spacecraft to the moon, was intended to help develop a trajectory for such a craft. Earlier efforts to beam a radio signal to the moon using low- and medium-frequency radio waves had failed; so the project employed a high-frequency laser beam instead. The success of the project depended on obtaining an accurate computation of the velocity of a position on the moon relative to a position on the Earth so that a trajectory for the laser beam could be plotted that would allow it to make contact with a specific point on the moon as it traveled in its orbit. The problem was made more difficult by the fact that the moon travels at different speeds depending on its distance from Earth.

As the project mathematician, McAfee's role was to calculate the speed of the moon. Despite the various difficulties, he succeeded in arriving at an accurate calculation by computing a radar cross section of the moon, a radar coverage pattern, and the distance to the moon. Not only did he arrive at an accurate calculation of the moon's velocity, but he also calculated the size of the signal's echo so that it could be detected upon returning to Earth. Largely as a result of his efforts, in January 1946, the project recorded the radar echo of a laser beam that had been bounced off the moon.

In 1946, McAfee took a leave of absence from ERDC to attend graduate school at Cornell University. Upon receiving a PhD in physics in 1949, he returned to ERDC as head of the Theoretical (later Radiation Physics) Unit. Among other things, this group was tasked with measuring all nuclear radiation emitted during the testing of nuclear weapons. In 1953, he took over as head of the Electromagnetic Wave (Radio) Propagation Section, and in 1965, he was named head of the Passive Sensing Unit. This latter group looked for new ways to detect electromagnetic radiation, such as infrared light waves, that did not involve dispatching a signal. Over the course of his career at ERDC, he also experimented with quantum optics, laser holography, radio astronomy, and solar physics. He also directed a NATO study on surveillance and target acquisition.

In addition to his duties at ERDC, McAfee taught atomic and nuclear physics and solid state electronics at Monmouth College (New Jersey) for a number of years. In 1985, he retired to his home in South Belmar, New Jersey, where he died on February 18, 1995. In 1997, the ERDC named its newest research facility the McAfee Center in his honor; it is believed to be the first U.S. Army facility to be named after a civilian.

See also: Physics

References and Further Reading

Astronomers of the African Diaspora. "Walter Samuel McAfee." [Online article or information; retrieved November 26, 2005.] http://www.math.buffalo.edu/mad/physics/mcafee_walters.html.

Spangenburg, Ray, and Kit Moser. *African Americans in Science, Math, and Invention.* New York: Facts On File, 2003: 174–175.

McBay, Henry C.
(1914–1995) Chemist

Between 1936 and 1994, Henry McBay helped scores of African Americans gain their doctorates in chemistry and then find suitable teaching positions at historically black colleges and universities. The people McBay helped in this manner constitute the lion's share of black chemists produced in the United States during those years, thus making McBay the so-called godfather of African American chemistry. A skilled researcher, his major contribution involved the development of safe and inexpensive methods for synthesizing industrial and biomedical compounds from complicated peroxide compounds.

McBay was born on May 29, 1914, in Mexia, Texas. His father, William, owned several small businesses, and his mother, Roberta, was a seamstress. After graduating from high school at age 16, he received a BS in chemistry from Wiley College (Marshall, Texas) in 1934 and an MS in organic chemistry from Atlanta University (today Clark Atlanta University) in 1936. He spent the next four years teaching chemistry at Wiley, a junior college in Kansas, and a high school in Alabama and then the next two years conducting war-related research at Tuskegee Institute (today Tuskegee University). In 1942, he enrolled in the graduate program at the University of Chicago and received a PhD in organic chemistry in 1945. He then joined the faculty at Atlanta's Morehouse College, and in 1960, he was named chair of the chemistry department. He relinquished this post in 1982 to become a professor of chemistry at his alma mater, Atlanta University.

McBay's research covered a wide range of topics. As a graduate student at Atlanta, he analyzed the physical properties of plastics in an effort to learn how they compared and contrasted with natural rubber. His work at Tuskegee for the government involved developing a substitute for jute, whose fibers were used to make rope and sacks. World War II had interrupted the flow of jute from India; so the government was hoping to utilize in its place the fibers of the okra plant, which grows extensively across the South. At Chicago, he began working with various peroxide compounds, which tend to be unstable and therefore dangerous. In collaboration with his advisor, Morris Kharasch, he developed a method for safely handling these compounds and then for synthesizing other compounds from them. Their most important development was to synthesize from acetyl peroxide, a protein that proved to be useful in the treatment of prostate cancer. For the role he played in this discovery, McBay was awarded the university's prestigious Elizabeth Norton Prize for excellence in chemical research in 1944 and 1945.

At Morehouse, McBay's teaching load precluded him from doing much in the way of research. Instead, he focused on turning out the best African American chemists in the country. For years, he sought out talented blacks with degrees in chemistry and then helped them along their career paths, either by getting them into a doctoral program such as the one at his alma mater, the University of Chicago, or getting them a prestigious teaching position at a historically black college. By all accounts, McBay played a formative role in the training of 45 black PhDs in chemistry, many of whom went on to become important chemists and educators in their own right. Because of his reputation as an educator, in 1951, the United Nations Education, Scientific and Cultural Organization (UNESCO) invited him to help develop a chemistry education program in Liberia. In 1972, he cofounded the National Organization for the Professional Advancement of Black Chemists and Chemical Engineers (NOBCChE) as a vehicle for further assisting African American chemists to achieve their career goals.

McBay was married to the former Shirley Mathis, with whom he had two children. He retired from full-time teaching in 1986, but he continued to teach on a part-time basis until his death. His many honors include the naming of the NOBCChE's Dr. Henry C. McBay Outstanding Teacher Award in his honor. He died on June 23, 1995, in Atlanta.

See also: Cancer; Chemistry; Clark Atlanta University; Historically Black Colleges and Universities; National Organization for the Professional Advancement of Black Chemists and Chemical Engineers; Tuskegee University

REFERENCES AND FURTHER READING

Kessler, James H., J. S. Kidd, Renee A. Kidd, and Katherine A. Morin, eds. *Distinguished African American Scientists of the 20th Century*. Phoenix, AZ: Oryx Press, 1996: 245–249.

Spangenburg, Ray, and Kit Moser. *African Americans in Science, Math, and Invention*. New York: Facts On File, 2003: 175–176.

McNair, Ronald E.
(1950–1986) Astronaut

Ronald McNair was one of the first black astronauts. He was also an up-and-coming expert in the field of laser technology before his life was cut short in a tragic accident.

McNair was born on October 21, 1950, in Lake City, South Carolina. His father, Carl, was an auto mechanic, and his mother, Pearl, was a teacher. He enrolled in North Carolina A&T State University with the intention of becoming a professional saxophone player, but while in school, he decided instead to become a physicist. After receiving a BS in physics in 1971, he entered the Massachusetts Institute of Technology and received a PhD in physics in 1976. That same year, he went to work for Hughes Research Laboratories in Malibu, California, and married Cheryl Moore, with whom he had two children.

McNair's primary research interest involved the generation of laser beams (beams of visible light of only one color that have been intensified to the point that they can vaporize heat-resistant materials). Specifically, he performed some of the earliest development of chemical HF/DF (hydrogen fluorine/deuterium fluoride) and high-pressure carbon monoxide (CO) lasers, which because of their characteristics showed high potential for use in weapons systems. He also experimented with and analyzed the interaction of intense carbon dioxide (CO_2) laser radiation with molecular gases, research that provided new understandings and applications for highly excited polyatomic molecules. His assignments at Hughes included the development of lasers capable of separating isotopes (rare forms of an element that differ only in that they possess a different number of neutrons) and for use in photochemistry (the propagation of light by chemical means rather than by heat). He also conducted research concerning the use of lasers for satellite-to-satellite space communications, the construction of ultrafast infrared detectors, and ultraviolet atmospheric remote sensing.

As an astronaut, Ronald McNair conducted many scientific experiments in outer space. (National Aeronautics and Space Administration)

In 1978, McNair's application to join the astronaut program was accepted by the National Aeronautics and Space Administration (NASA), and that same year, he moved to Houston to undergo training as a space shuttle mission specialist. After six years of training, McNair was chosen to fly aboard STS 41-B, a February 1984 mission aboard the orbiter *Challenger*. This mission marked the first flight of the Manned Maneuvering Unit and the first use of the Canadian arm (operated by McNair) to position EVA (extravehicular activity, or spacewalk) crew members around *Challenger*'s payload bay. In addition to assisting with these experiments, McNair was primarily responsible for conducting experiments involving acoustic levitation and chemical separation.

McNair was chosen to return to space in 1986 aboard another flight of the *Challenger*, STS 51-L. McNair's duties on this mission included deploying a spacecraft with a telescopic camera that was to study Halley's comet; the mission also marked the first time a civilian (Christa McAuliffe, a schoolteacher) would go into space aboard a U.S. spacecraft. Unfortunately, an equipment malfunction caused the *Challenger* to explode shortly after liftoff on the morning of January 28, 1986, and all members of the crew were lost.

McNair was a member of the American Association for the Advancement of Science and the American Physical Society. He and the rest of the *Challenger* crew received innumerable posthumous honors, including the Congressional Space Medal of Honor. Lake City's Carver High School, his high school alma mater, was renamed after him, and North Carolina A&T State University, his college alma mater, established the annual Ronald E. McNair Commemorative

Celebration and Research Symposium, at which the university's undergraduates present the results of their original research in science. He was further honored by the U.S. Department of Education, which named the Ronald E. McNair Post-baccalaureate Achievement Program in his honor. This program funds undergraduate programs for preparing African Americans and other underrepresented minorities for doctoral studies via research, academic counseling, financial aid, mentoring, summer internships, and tutoring.

See also: American Association for the Advancement of Science; American Physical Society; National Aeronautics and Space Administration; North Carolina A&T State University; Physics

REFERENCES AND FURTHER READING

National Aeronautics and Space Administration. "Biographical Data: Ronald E. McNair." [Online article or information; retrieved November 26, 2005.] http://www.jsc.nasa.gov/Bios/htmlbios/mcnair.html

Spangenburg, Ray, and Kit Moser. *African Americans in Science, Math, and Invention*. New York: Facts On File, 2003: 179–180.

Nabrit, Samuel M.
(1905–2003) Marine Biologist

As a marine biologist, Samuel Nabrit conducted research that shed new light on the ability of fish to regenerate fins. As an administrator, he contributed to the advancement of science by serving as a college president and as a member of two important national science organizations.

Nabrit was born on February 21, 1905, in Macon, Georgia. His father, James, was a minister and teacher, and his mother, Augusta, was a homemaker. After receiving a BS in biology from Atlanta's Morehouse College in 1925, he remained at that school as a faculty member until 1932. Meanwhile, he also took graduate courses at Brown University in Providence, Rhode Island, where he received an MS and a PhD in biology in 1929 and 1932, respectively. In 1927, he married Constance Crocker with whom he had no children.

As a graduate student, Nabrit conducted research at the Woods Hole Marine Biological Laboratory (Massachusetts) during the summer. He was particularly interested in the ability of fish to replace their lost fins, a phenomenon he studied extensively. By 1932, he had demonstrated a correlation between the size of a fin's rays (the bony or cartilaginous rods that support the rest of the fin) and the rate at which the fin is able to regenerate. He published the results of his work in *Biological Bulletin* (56: 235–266), the prestigious journal wherein the most important results of Woods Hole research were published. "Regeneration in the Tail-Fins of Fishes" caught the attention of marine biologists around the world, and they used Nabrit's findings as a springboard for subsequent research on the regeneration of nerve and muscle tissue.

In 1932, Nabrit joined the faculty at Atlanta University (today Clark Atlanta University), eventually rising to the post of chair of the biology department. In 1947, he gave up teaching to serve as the dean of the graduate school of arts and sciences. In 1955, he left Atlanta for Houston, where he assumed the presidency of Texas Southern University (TSU). As president, he bolstered the science programs by bringing research grants to the university and more than doubling student enrollment. He also oversaw the design and construction of a modern science facility that was later renamed the S. M. Nabrit Science Center in his honor. He created a bit of controversy during the Civil Rights Movement when he invited students who had been kicked out of other historically black colleges and universities for participating in marches and sit-ins to enroll at TSU.

In 1966, Nabrit resigned as TSU president to accept an appointment from President Lyndon B. Johnson to serve on the board of directors of the U.S. Atomic Energy Commission (today the Nuclear Regulatory Commission). As a director, Nabrit helped formulate policies and develop regulations governing nuclear reactor and nuclear material safety as part of the commission's mandate to safeguard public health and protect the environment from the effects of radiation from nuclear reactors, materials, and waste facilities. He resigned the following year to become executive director of the Atlanta-based Southern Fellowship Fund, which gives grants to minority professors and graduate students to help them finance their doctoral studies.

In addition to his other activities, Nabrit served for one year (1956) as a member of the National Science Board. In this position, he advised President Dwight D. Eisenhower, who had appointed him, and the U.S. Congress on policy issues related to science and engineering. He cofounded Upward Bound, a program that provides fundamental support to high school students from low-income families or from families in which neither parent holds a bachelor's degree, to help them gain admission to college and then graduate. He was also a founding member of the National Academy of Sciences' Institute of Medicine, an independent agency that provides medical advice that is unbiased, based on evidence, and grounded in science.

In 1981, Nabrit retired to his home in Atlanta, but he continued to be active as an education activist for a number of years thereafter. He died on December 30, 2003, in Atlanta.

See also: Biology; Clark Atlanta University; Historically Black Colleges and Universities; Institute of Medicine; Texas Southern University

REFERENCES AND FURTHER READING

Baltrip, Kimetris N. "Samuel Nabrit, 98, Scientist and a Pioneer in Education, Dies." NYTimes.com. [Online article or information; retrieved October 30,

2007.] http://www.nytimes.com/2004/01/06/education/06NABR.html?ex=
1388725200&en=0e78b968bd56fde6&ei=5007&partner=USERLAND.

Spangenburg, Ray, and Kit Moser. *African Americans in Science, Math, and Invention*. New York: Facts On File, 2003: 190–191.

Norman, John C., Jr.
(1930–) Cardiothoracic Surgeon

John C. Norman was one of the leading heart surgeons of his day. He helped develop many of the techniques first used in heart transplants, and he helped perfect the artificial heart.

Norman was born on May 11, 1930, in Charleston, West Virginia. His father, John, was an architect and structural engineer, and his mother, Ruth, was a teacher. At age 15, he entered Howard University but transferred after two years to Harvard University, where he received a BA and an MD in 1950 and 1954, respectively. In 1954, he married Doris Sewell, with whom he had one child.

Norman completed his internship at Columbia-Presbyterian Medical Center in New York City. He also began his residency there, but it was interrupted by a call to serve for two years in the U.S. Navy as a lieutenant commander and ship surgeon. Upon leaving the navy in 1959, he returned to New York City to complete his residency at Bellevue Hospital and teach surgery at Columbia. At this point, he decided to become a cardiac surgeon; so when his residency was completed in 1961 he obtained a two-year National Institutes of Health (NIH) research fellowship at England's University of Birmingham. While in England, he studied artificial pacemakers (electrical devices that keep the heart beating when the body's natural pacemaker becomes dysfunctional). He then spent a year as a thoracic and cardiovascular resident at the University of Michigan Medical Center, and in 1964, he returned to Harvard to teach surgery.

Norman's research at Harvard covered a broad range of topics, from transplanting livers and lungs in animals to evaluating perfusion (the pumping of fluid through an organ or tissue) in the liver and spleen. Nevertheless, his primary interest remained cardiac surgery. He became involved in the National Heart Institute's Artificial Heart Program, whose purpose was to explore the feasibility of developing and testing mechanical devices that could be used to replace or assist the human heart. Norman's role in the project was to determine the energy and hemodynamic requirements (hemodynamics deals with the forces involved in the circulation of blood) of mechanical hearts and evaluate different fuel sources for powering them, including the first nuclear fuel source used for an artificial organ. One of the first left ventricular assist devices (LVAD), a partial artificial heart, was developed according to Norman's specifications, which he then tested on dogs and calves to establish the criteria for implantation, anesthesia, and various side effects.

In 1972, Norman left Harvard to establish and direct a cardiovascular surgical research laboratory at the Texas Heart Institute (THI) in Houston. Two years earlier, THI's Denton Cooley had performed the first implantation of an artificial heart into a human, and Norman went to THI to collaborate with Cooley in further operations of this kind. As director, Norman focused on developing an improved LVAD, and together he and Cooley implanted 22 LVADs into humans. Unfortunately, because federal and institutional guidelines prohibited LVAD implantation in patients until they reached a nearly terminal stage, none of these procedures significantly prolonged any of the recipients' lives, although the failing heart did recover in a few instances. Nevertheless, the hemodynamic studies performed by Norman for each of the 22 procedures convinced the powers that be to relax the restrictions on implanting LVADs until it was basically too late to do any good, and as a result, a number of later recipients of partial artificial hearts lived long and useful lives. Meanwhile, Norman began experimenting with the intra-aortal balloon pump, a less invasive form of circulatory assist than the LVAD, with good results.

In 1981, Norman resigned from the Texas Heart Institute. Over the next four years he served successively as director of the D.C. Heart Institute in Washington, D.C., and professor of cardiothoracic surgery at the University of Medicine and Dentistry in New Jersey. In 1986, he was named chair of the department of surgery at Marshall University in Huntington, West Virginia, a position he held for the rest of his career.

Norman's publications include *Cardiac Surgery* (New York: Appleton-Century-Crofts, 1967). He was also the founding editor of *Cardiovascular Diseases, Bulletin of the Texas Heart Institute.*

See also: Howard University; National Heart, Lung, and Blood Institute; National Institutes of Health

REFERENCES AND FURTHER READING

Organ, Claude H., and Margaret Kosiba, eds. *A Century of Black Surgeons: The U.S.A. Experience.* Norman, OK: Transcript Press, 1987: 733–774.

West Virginia Division of Culture and History. "John C. Norman Jr." [Online article or information; retrieved October 13, 2005.] http://www.wvculture.org/history/norman.html.

Olden, Kenneth
(1938–) Cell Biologist

Kenneth Olden served as director of the National Institute of Environmental Health Sciences (NIEHS). His research concerning cell biology contributed to

Dr. Kenneth Olden, director of the National Institute of Environmental Health Sciences and the National Toxicology Program of the National Institutes of Health. (National Institutes of Health)

a better understanding of glycoproteins (biomolecules composed of a protein and a carbohydrate).

Olden was born on July 22, 1938, in Newport, Tennessee, to Mack and Augusta Olden. He received a BS in biology from Knoxville College (Tennessee) in 1960, an MS from the University of Michigan in 1964, and a PhD from Temple University (Philadelphia) in 1970. After completing his education, Olden joined the faculty at Harvard Medical School as a research fellow and instructor of physiology. In 1974, he was named a senior staff fellow at the National Cancer Institute Division of Cancer Biology and Diagnosis, but he left after three years to teach biochemistry at Howard University. In 1979, he became the associate director of research at the Howard University College of Medicine Cancer Center, and he served as the center's director from 1985 to 1991.

Olden's research focused on the properties of cell surface molecules and their possible roles in cancer. He was particularly interested in glycoproteins, because these molecules help immune cells identify other biomolecules, such as antigens, that are harmful to the body. His research shed much light on how certain glycoproteins are transported within the cells that produce them and then secreted into the bloodstream. He also conducted several groundbreaking studies of the glycoprotein fibronectin. Fibronectin is an important component of the extracellular matrix, the material surrounding the cells that form a tissue without being a part of those cells, and it is bound to those cells by means of receptor proteins known as integrins. One study in particular explored the connection between fibronectin and metastasis (the process by which cancerous cells break away from a tumor, circulate through the bloodstream, and begin growing in a distant part of the body). He showed that metastasis can be prevented in certain organs by chemically blocking the interaction between the fibronectin in the extracellular matrix and the integrins binding the matrix to the tissue. This discovery led other researchers to discover that fibronectin actually seems to encourage the development of lung cancer and that it diminishes the efficacy of certain cancer chemotherapeutic drugs. Lastly, he helped develop the potential anticancer drug Swainsonine, which was still being tested as of 2007.

In 1991, Olden was named director of NIEHS, headquartered in Durham, North Carolina, and of the National Toxicology Program (NTP), which is part of the Department of Health and Human Services. As NIEHS director, he oversaw the institute's efforts to conduct and support research and research training related to how the environment influences the development and progression of human disease. As NTP director, he oversaw its efforts to evaluate the safety of the more than 80,000 chemicals registered for use in the United States in such applications as foods, personal care products, prescription drugs, household cleaners, and lawn care products.

Olden is married to the former Sandra White, with whom he has four children.

In 2004, he retired from NIEHS and NTP to his home in Durham.

See also: Biochemistry; Biology; Cancer; Howard University; Howard University College of Medicine; National Cancer Institute; National Institute of Environmental Health Sciences

References and Further Reading

Brown, Valerie J. "Kenneth Olden, Master Fencer." *American Journal of Public Health* 94, 11 (November 2004): 1905–1907.

JustGarciaHill.org. "Olden, Kenneth, Ph.D." [Online article or information; retrieved August 26, 2007.] http://justgarciahill.org/jghdocs/webbiography. asp.

Owens, Joan Murrell
(1933–) Marine Biologist

Joan Murrell Owens was one of the world's foremost experts on button corals. In addition to reclassifying these relatively unknown marine organisms, she also discovered a new genus and three new species of them.

Owens was born Joan Murrell on June 30, 1933, in Miami. Her father, William, was a dentist, and her mother, Leola, was a homemaker. As a child growing up near the ocean, she dreamed of becoming a marine biologist, and she planned to study for this career upon entering Fisk College (now Fisk

University) at age 17. Fisk had no such program, however, nor did any of the other historically black colleges and universities, because marine biology was not a career that was open to blacks at that time. Instead, she majored in fine art, and in 1954, she received a BA and entered the University of Michigan School of Architecture to pursue a master's degree in commercial art. Before graduating, however, she changed her major to guidance counseling with an emphasis on reading therapy and received an MS in 1956. She spent the next two years teaching English to emotionally disturbed children at the Children's Psychiatric Hospital in Ann Arbor, Michigan, before joining the faculty at Howard University, where she taught remedial English to college freshmen. In 1964, she went to work for the Institute for Services to Education (ISE) in Newton, Massachusetts, developing programs for teaching English to educationally disadvantaged high school students. These programs eventually served as a model for the Upward Bound Program, a U.S. Department of Education initiative to prepare potential first-generation college students for a successful college career.

Despite her success as an English teacher, Owens never lost her interest in marine biology. Moreover, by 1970 that field had changed enough that it now offered opportunities to black scientists. After transferring to ISE's offices in Washington, D.C., that same year, she entered George Washington University's geology program; by majoring in geology and minoring in zoology, she received the equivalent of an education in marine biology, even though her degrees—a BS in 1973, an MS in 1976, and a PhD in 1984—were all in geology. Meanwhile, in 1976, she returned to Howard as a professor of geology.

Owens's primary research interest involved corals (sea creatures with stony skeletons). While working on her doctorate, she was invited by the Smithsonian Institution to study a fairly sizable collection of corals that had been obtained by a British expedition in 1880. Later, she became interested in a group of deep-sea corals known as button corals, so called because of their size and shape. Unlike reef corals, button corals live below the level that sunlight penetrates, live individually rather than in colonies, and have internal as opposed to external skeletons. Other than that, little was known about button corals in the mid-1970s. Her first project regarding button corals explored evolutionary changes in their skeletons, but further study allowed her to reclassify all of the known button corals. In 1986, during the course of her reclassification, she discovered a new genus (group of related species) of button coral, which she named *Rhombopsammia*, as well as the two species that make up the genus, *R. niphada* and *R. squiresi*. She also discovered a new species in the genus known as *Letepsammia*, which she named *L. franki*, in honor of her husband, Frank Owens, whom she had married in 1973.

In 1992, Owens transferred to Howard's biology department, and for the first time in her career, she was able to teach marine biology as her primary course. She retired from Howard in 1995, but she continued to conduct research for several years thereafter.

See also: Fisk University; Historically Black Colleges and Universities; Howard University

REFERENCES AND FURTHER READING

Kessler, James H., J. S. Kidd, Renee A. Kidd, and Katherine A. Morin, eds. *Distinguished African American Scientists of the 20th Century*. Phoenix, AZ: Oryx Press, 1996: 272–275.

Spangenburg, Ray, and Kit Moser. *African Americans in Science, Math, and Invention*. New York: Facts On File, 2003: 193–194.

Warren, Wini. *Black Women Scientists in the United States*. Bloomington: Indiana University Press, 1999: 206–218.

Pierce, Chester M.
(1927–) Psychiatrist

Chester Pierce was perhaps the foremost black psychiatrist of his day. His work on the effects of extreme exotic environments on human behavior led to a better understanding of how humans are affected by such diverse environments as outer space and the ghetto.

Pierce was born in 1927, in Glen Cove, New York. His father, Samuel, was a country club attendant, and his mother, Hettie, was a homemaker. After finishing high school, he entered Harvard University, where he received a BA in 1948 and an MD in 1952. He had originally intended to become a pediatrician, but while in medical school he became interested in psychiatry. So when he went to the University of Cincinnati to complete his internship and residency at its hospital, he also began taking training in psychiatry. His studies at Cincinnati were interrupted by two years of service (1954–1956) in the U.S. Navy as a psychiatrist, and, upon completing his studies in 1957, he joined the faculty of Cincinnati's department of psychiatry. Three years later, he accepted the positions of professor of psychiatry at the University of Oklahoma and assistant chief of the department of psychiatry at the Oklahoma Veterans Administration Hospital in Oklahoma City. In 1968, he returned to Harvard, where he spent the rest of his career teaching education, psychiatry, and public health. In 1949, he married Jocelyn Blanchet, with whom he had two children.

Pierce's early research focused on sleep pathophysiology. While in the navy, he participated in a study of enuresis (bed-wetting) in recruits. During the study, it occurred to him that there might be something unique about the brain activity of a bed wetter, so he administered electroencephalograms (EEGs) to a number of subjects. By the time the study was concluded, he had demonstrated the clinical relationship of enuresis to epilepsy and somnambulism (sleepwalking). Further study demonstrated that enuresis is a form of sleep disorder, wherein dreams about urinating come after, not before, the bed wetter has wet the bed.

Although he maintained a lifelong interest in sleep pathophysiology, in 1963, Pierce began devoting more attention to the effects of extreme exotic environments on humans. That same year, he spent several months in Antarctica establishing an experimental station at the South Polar Plateau, where volunteers could be studied for their reactions to factors such as the effects of forced socialization, depression, spatial isolation, time elasticity, biological and sociological dysrhythmia, increased free time, noise extremes, loneliness, fear of abandonment, anxiety, panic, information fractionalization, boredom, and the inability to escape. Much of his work informed later studies by the National Aeronautics and Space Administration (NASA), to which he served as a consultant for a number of years, as to the effects on astronauts of being cooped up during extended voyages in space. He later adapted much of his findings to shed light on the effects of one of the most extreme exotic environments of all, the ghetto, on ethnic minorities, but especially children. He also studied and wrote about the effects of television on society and how television programs and commercials convey subtle messages of racism.

Pierce cofounded the Black Psychiatrists of America and served as its first chairperson; in this capacity, he worked to obtain greater recognition for black psychiatrists from the National Institute of Mental Health and the American Psychiatric Association, both of which began including blacks on their planning boards. He also presided over the American Board of Psychiatry and Neurology and the American Orthopsychiatric Association. His honors include election to the American Academy of Arts and Sciences and the Institute of Medicine of the National Academy of Sciences, in addition to having a mountain in Antarctica (Pierce Peak) named after him. His publications include *Basic Psychiatry* (New York: Appleton-Century-Crofts, 1971), *Capital Punishment in the United States* (New York: AMS Press, 1976), *Television and Behavior* (1978), and *The Mosaic of Contemporary Psychiatry in Perspective* (New York: Springer-Verlag, 1991).

See also: Black Psychiatrists of America; Institute of Medicine; National Aeronautics and Space Administration; National Institute of Mental Health

REFERENCES AND FURTHER READING

Griffith, Ezra E. H. *Race and Excellence: My Dialogue with Chester Pierce.* Iowa City: University of Iowa Press, 1998.

Quarterman, Lloyd A.
(1918–1982) Chemist

At the height of his career, Lloyd Quarterman knew more about the chemical reactions involving fluorine than any other chemist in the world. He used this knowledge to disprove the theory that the inert gases are incapable of reacting with other elements. One of the compounds he made from fluorine and an inert gas is used today to make chips for computers.

Little is known about the first 25 years of Quarterman's life other than that he was born on May 31, 1918, in Philadelphia, and that he received a BS in chemistry from St. Augustine's College in Raleigh, North Carolina, in 1943. At that point, he moved to Chicago to work on the Manhattan Project, the U.S. effort to build an atomic bomb during World War II. Quarterman's primary contribution to the Manhattan Project was to design and build a special distillation system for purifying large quantities of hydrogen fluoride, a highly reactive compound that was used to separate the uranium isotope known as U-235 from what was called regular uranium. The U-235 that Quarterman helped accumulate was used to make Little Boy, the uranium bomb that was exploded over Hiroshima, Japan, in 1945. After the war, the Manhattan Project's facilities in Chicago were converted into the Argonne National Laboratories (ANL), which became the federal government's primary center for conducting research concerning peaceful uses for atomic energy. Quarterman remained at ANL for the rest of his career. In 1952, he received an MS in chemistry from Chicago's Northwestern University.

Quarterman's research primarily involved the chemistry of fluorine. Of all the elements, fluorine is the most reactive, which makes it difficult to isolate from the compounds in which it naturally occurs. In fact, fluorine is so reactive that it cannot be isolated by chemical means, but only by a mechanical operation such as electrolysis, which Quarterman employed in his special distillation process. Nevertheless, Quarterman developed into one of the world's foremost experts on fluorine chemistry, largely because the remarkable purity of his hydrogen fluoride permitted him to make chemical compounds that were difficult or even impossible for other chemists to make. For example, conventional wisdom held that chemical compounds could never be made from the inert gases, because their outer rings of electrons are full, meaning they could not form covalent bonds with other elements (they could not share electrons). Quarterman proved this belief to be false by making several compounds from fluorine and the inert gas xenon. Specifically, he devised methods for combining one atom of xenon with two atoms of fluorine (xenon difluoride), with four atoms of fluorine (xenon tetrafluoride), and with six atoms of fluorine (xenon hexafluoride). While the latter two compounds are mostly just chemical curiosities, xenon difluoride (a white crystalline solid) is

MANHATTAN PROJECT

The Manhattan Project was the collective name for the United States' effort to build an atomic bomb for use during World War II. It received its name, because its earliest facilities were located at Columbia University on Manhattan Island in New York, but other important research facilities were located at the University of Chicago, Iowa State University, and in Los Alamos, New Mexico. The project's many researchers overcame innumerable difficulties en route to constructing the two bombs, called Little Boy and Fat Man, that were dropped on Hiroshima and Nagasaki, respectively, effectively ending the war against the Japanese in the Pacific.

Because of the classified nature of the Manhattan Project, it is difficult to know, even today, exactly who did what while working on the project. What is known about the involvement of African Americans with the project is that at least seven black scientists made important contributions to the project's successful completion. This article presents a brief outline of what is known about their involvement and the possible involvement of other black scientists.

For the most part, the black scientists assigned to the Manhattan Project were chemists working on the development of Little Boy, the uranium bomb (Fat Man was made from plutonium). The largest obstacle to producing such a bomb involved obtaining enough fissionable uranium to sustain a nuclear chain reaction. This meant obtaining a great deal of a particular isotope of uranium known as U-235. Most uranium is of the U-238 variety, meaning that it has 238 nucleons, or protons and neutrons combined. The Manhattan Project's scientists needed U-235 because they were trying to devise a bomb that operated on the principle of nuclear fission (the splitting apart of an atomic nucleus), and, for whatever reason, U-235 is much more fissionable than U-238, perhaps because it has three fewer nucleons than U-238.

One of the black chemists recruited to solve this problem was William J. Knox Jr. The holder of a PhD from the Massachusetts Institute of Technology, he was serving as chair of the chemistry department at Talladega College (Alabama) when he was invited to come to Columbia University to help develop Little Boy. The research team he was assigned to was charged with developing a method for separating out the U-235 from large quantities of uranium, less than 1 percent of which normally consists of U-235. Taking advantage of the fact that U-235 weighs slightly less than U-238, Knox's group developed a process known as the gaseous diffusion method, whereby uranium was vaporized and then combined with fluorine, the most reactive of all the elements, to make a gas known as uranium hexafluoride (UF_6). The UF_6 was then pumped through the microscopic holes in a barrier in such a way that the lighter U-235 rose up and the heavier U-238 drifted down.

While Knox was working on the gaseous diffusion method for isolating U-235, other black chemists were working on ways to produce more fluorine for use in the gaseous diffusion method. Chief among them was Lloyd A. Quarterman. Having received a BS in chemistry from St. Augustine's College in Raleigh, North Carolina, in 1943, he had gone to work as a chemist at the University of Chicago's Metallurgical Laboratory (Met Lab), so called because uranium and plutonium, the fuels from which atomic bombs are made, are metals. Quarterman's primary contribution to the Manhattan Project was to design and build a special distillation system for purifying large quantities of fluorine. Fluorine is more reactive than any other element, so reactive that it never occurs naturally by itself but rather in a compound with a host of other elements. No chemical reaction is sufficiently strong to separate fluorine from a compound, and so it must be done by means of electrolysis. Undaunted by this difficulty, Quarterman developed a special electrolytic distillation process whereby hydrogen fluoride, the most common source of fluorine, is separated into hydrogen and fluorine, the fluorine then being used to make UF_6.

At least three other black chemists worked with Quarterman in the Met Lab, but their contributions to the Manhattan Project are a bit hazy. Edwin R. Russell held an MS in chemistry from Howard when the war started and worked as an assistant chemist in the Met Lab. Moddie Taylor held a PhD in chemistry from the University of Chicago, and he also worked at the Met Lab during the war. Taylor's specialty was rare earth metals, the products of oxidized metals, so he probably worked on the team that developed uranium oxide for use in the Met Lab's atomic reactor, the first in the world. Ralph Gardner had just received a BS in chemistry from the University of Illinois in 1943, when he was invited to work at the Met Lab. He was involved in the development of Fat Man. The exact nature of his involvement is unknown, but he probably worked with the team that extracted plutonium from U-238. Two tons of irradiated U-238 yield approximately 2.5 grams of plutonium, and so, as with U-235, a special chemical extraction procedure had to be devised to separate such small amounts of plutonium from the mass of uranium containing it. By 1943, when Gardner joined the Met Lab, this procedure involved bombarding uranium nitrate hexahydrate (UNH) with neutrons, removing the plutonium from the UNH by introducing a solution of cerium and lanthanum, and then removing the cerium and lanthanum from the solution by mixing it with fluorine.

Samuel P. Massie Jr. was working on a PhD in chemistry at Iowa State University when the Manhattan Project was implemented. Iowa State's Frank Spedding had been designated the director of chemical research for the

(continues)

(continued)

Manhattan Project, and he established facilities at Iowa State for studying the metallurgy of uranium. Massie's mentor, Henry Gilman, was asked by Spedding to work on the project, and Gilman extended that same invitation to Massie. In time, the Iowa State group developed a method for producing enriched uranium (uranium composed almost entirely of U-235) by combining magnesium with uranium tetrafluoride, putting the mixture into a steel casing lined with calcium lime and heating it to 650°C.

Only one black physicist is known to have worked on the Manhattan Project. J. Ernest Wilkins Jr. had received a PhD in mathematics from the University of Chicago in 1942 and was teaching mathematics at Tuskegee Institute (today Tuskegee University) when he was recruited to work at the Met Lab. Inasmuch as mathematics is the language of physics, the Met Lab's theoretical physicists, Wilkins among them, explored the mechanics of nuclear fission by writing mathematical formulas.

In addition to these seven, a number of other black scientists are believed to have worked on the Manhattan Project. The ones most commonly mentioned are Harold Delaney, Benjamin Scott, and Jaspar Jefferies at the Met Lab, as well as George (sometimes given as Clarence) Turner, Cecil White, Sydney (sometimes given as Sidney) Thompson, and George Reid (sometimes given as Reed) Jr. at Columbia University. Unfortunately, nothing is known about their contributions to the project, although they most likely assisted in the chemical work done by Knox, Quarterman, Russell, Taylor, Wilkins, or Gardner. In addition, the names of Robert Omohundro, Sherman Carter, Harold Evans, and Clyde Dillard are also mentioned as having worked on the Manhattan Project, although nothing is known about where they worked or what they did.

See also: Massie, Samuel P., Jr.; Quarterman, Lloyd A.; Tuskegee University; Wilkins, J. Ernest Jr.

REFERENCES AND FURTHER READING

Brodie, James M. *Created Equal: The Lives and Ideas of Black American Innovators*. New York: William Morrow, 1993.

Carey, Charles W. Jr. *American Scientists*. New York: Facts On File, 2005.

Hoddeson, Lillian, et al., eds. *Critical Assembly: A Technical History of Los Alamos During the Oppenheimer Years, 1943–1945*. New York: Cambridge University Press, 1993.

Krapp, Kristine M., ed. *Notable Black American Scientists*. Detroit, MI: Gale Research, 1999.

Rhodes, Richard. *The Making of the Atomic Bomb*. New York: Simon & Schuster, 1986.

Spangenburg, Ray, and Kit Moser. *African Americans in Science, Math, and Invention*. New York: Facts On File, 2003.

an excellent source for introducing fluorine into organic reactions, because it is not nearly as corrosive as hydrogen fluoride, which was the preferred source of fluorine before Quarterman's discoveries. Eventually, xenon difluoride became widely used to make semiconductor material for computer chips.

In Quarterman's skilled hands, hydrogen fluoride became a very useful tool for studying the properties of a number of chemical compounds that are otherwise difficult to examine. In 1967, he built a special corrosion-resistant chamber with a tiny window made from two diamonds. In the chamber, he dissolved whatever compound he wanted to study in hydrogen fluoride, and then he shined an electromagnetic beam through the diamond window. The beam caused the dissolved compound to emit X-ray and ultraviolet light bands of specific and unique frequencies, and, by studying these frequencies with a spectroscope, he could learn much about how the compound's atoms interact.

Despite his achievements, Quarterman remains a shadowy figure in American science. Little is known about his personal life or about an ambitious project he initiated late in his career. Having become interested in biochemistry, he set out to develop synthetic blood, but he was forced to abandon the project for reasons that remain unclear. Nevertheless, his achievements as a fluorine chemist were sufficiently well known to the scientific community that he was elected to membership in the American Association for the Advancement of Science. He died in August 1982, in Chicago.

See also: American Association for the Advancement of Science; Chemistry

REFERENCES AND FURTHER READING

Carey, Charles W. Jr. *American Scientists*. New York: Facts On File, 2005: 294–295.

McMurray, Emily J., ed. *Notable Twentieth-Century Scientists*. Detroit, MI: Gale Research, 1995: 1628–1629.

Spangenburg, Ray, and Kit Moser. *African Americans in Science, Math, and Invention*. New York: Facts On File, 2003: 198–199.

Roman, Charles V.
(1864–1934) Ophthalmologist

Charles Roman was the first African American physician to receive training in both ophthalmology, which deals with the anatomy, functions, and diseases of the eye, and otolaryngology, which deals with the anatomy, functions, and diseases of the ears, nose, and throat. He was such an influential role model for the African American eyes, ears, nose, and throat specialists who followed him that they named their national organization, the Roman-Barnes Society, in his honor.

Roman was born on July 4, 1864, in Williamsport, Pennsylvania. His father, James, owned and operated a canal boat, and his mother, Anne, was a homemaker. As a boy, he moved with his family to Dundas, Ontario, Canada, where he grew up. After graduating from Hamilton Collegiate Institute (Ontario), he taught school in Trigg County, Kentucky, and Columbia, Tennessee, until 1887, when he entered Meharry Medical College in Nashville. In 1890, he received an MD from Meharry, as well as an MA in philosophy and history from Nashville's Fisk University. In 1891, he married Margaret Voorhees, with whom he had one child.

After graduating from Meharry, Roman spent the next 14 years practicing medicine in Clarksville, Tennessee, and Dallas, Texas. During this period, he obtained postgraduate medical training in ophthalmology and otolaryngology at the Post Graduate Medical School and Hospital of Chicago and the Royal Ophthalmic Hospital and Central London Nose, Throat, and Ear Hospital in England. In 1904, he joined the Meharry faculty and founded the department of ophthalmology and otolaryngology. Over the next 27 years, he taught these subjects, medical history, and ethics. In addition to these duties, he served as a special lecturer in philosophy at what is now Tennessee State University at Nashville and headed Fisk's Department of Health.

Roman cofounded the National Medical Association. He served as its president from 1904 to 1905 and as the first editor of its chief publication, *Journal of the National Medical Association,* from 1909 until 1919. He served as an associate editor of the *National Cyclopedia of the Colored Race* (1919). His books include *A Knowledge of History Is Conducive to Racial Solidarity* (Nashville, TN: Sunday School Union Print 1911), *Science and Christian Ethics* (Publisher unknown, 1913), *American Civilization and the Negro* (Philadelphia: F.A. Davis, 1916), and *Meharry Medical College: A History* (Nashville, TN: Sunday School, 1934); the latter work contains a great deal of autobiographical material.

Roman retired from teaching in 1931. He died on August 25, 1934, in Nashville.

See also: Fisk University; Meharry Medical College; National Medical Association; Roman-Barnes Society; Tennessee State University

References and Further Reading

American Academy of Otolaryngology. "Early African-Americans in Otolaryngology." [Online article or information; retrieved November 17, 2005.] http://www.entnet.org/HealthInformation/earlyAfricanAmericans.cfm.

Rouse, Carl A.
(1926–) Astrophysicist

Carl Rouse offered compelling evidence that the sun's core is composed of iron rather than helium or hydrogen. Although his theory remains unproven, it forced the astrophysical community to reconsider many of its assumptions about the nature of the sun's interior.

Rouse was born on July 14, 1926, in Youngstown, Ohio. His father owned and operated an auto repair shop, and his mother was a homemaker. After finishing high school in 1944, he was drafted into the U.S. Army and sent to engineering school at Howard University, Pennsylvania State University, and New York University. Discharged in 1946 without a degree, he worked as an engineering draftsman for a while before entering Case Institute of Technology (today Case Western Reserve University) in Cleveland, where he received a BS in physics in 1951. He then entered the California Institute of Technology (Caltech) and became a research assistant to Carl D. Anderson, who won the 1936 Nobel Prize in Physics for discovering the positron (a subatomic particle with the same mass as an electron but with a positive charge).

Anderson had made his discovery in a cloud chamber (a closed vessel filled with supersaturated steam through which charged particles leave a minute but visible trail that can be photographed). For his doctoral research, Rouse modified Anderson's cloud chamber by adding a device known as a gated proportional counter. This device permitted him to photograph particles with relatively low energy levels; consequently, he was able to offer evidence for the existence of the particle known today as the K meson.

After receiving an MS in physics in 1953 and a PhD in particle physics in 1956, Rouse went to work as a research physicist at Caltech's Lawrence Livermore National Laboratory, one of the world's foremost research facilities for the study of nuclear physics. One of his first assignments was to study the nearly instantaneous transition of a solid to a gas resulting from exposure to the extremely hot temperatures caused by the explosion of an atomic bomb. Since the sun and other stars are fueled by nuclear reactions similar to the ones that take place in an atomic explosion, Rouse soon developed an interest in the behavior of extremely hot stellar gases. He was particularly interested in pulsating variable stars such as the Cepheids, which expand and contract cyclically, causing them to pulsate rhythmically in brightness and size. He concluded that this phenomenon results from the nonlinear effects of ionization and excitation of the atoms in the atmospheres of these stars. In his spare time, he developed a computer model appropriate for highly ionized gases, and then he ran the model in a program that had been designed to model supernovas (stars whose brightness increases hundreds of millions of times when they explode violently). When his model reproduced the observed variation in star pulsations, Rouse began to construct a model for a more typical star like the sun.

Although little solar modeling had been done by the mid-1960s, there was a considerable degree of consensus in the astrophysical community concerning the nature of the sun's interior. This consensus was based on estimates of the sun's central temperature and density and on some knowledge concerning the relative abundances of hydrogen and helium in the solar atmosphere, which made it possible to guess intelligently about the internal abundances of hydrogen and helium. But when Rouse plugged these assumptions into his own computer model, the result was a star that bore no resemblance to the sun in terms of mass, brightness, or radius, values that were well known at the time. Conversely, when he modeled the sun's interior with a higher abundance of heavier elements such as iron, the model yielded a star that looks very much like the sun. Consequently, Rouse advanced the theory that the sun's core is composed of solid iron rather than a mixture of hydrogen and helium gases.

Rouse's theory was received with a great deal of skepticism by the astrophysical community for several reasons. The first concerned his total lack of formal training in astrophysics, even though his training in particle physics made him perhaps more than qualified to study stellar nuclear phenomena. The second was that Rouse's iron core theory challenged existing assumptions about the origins of the sun and the solar system. The solar system is commonly thought to have formed between 4 and 5 billion years ago from a homogeneous, well-mixed nebula composed of 71 percent hydrogen, 27 percent helium, and only 2 percent heavier elements. Rouse's theory implies that the solar system was formed, at least in part, from the remnants of one or more supernovas, because the cores of supernovas are believed to consist of iron and even heavier elements such as uranium.

Rouse's iron core theory was received with a particular lack of enthusiasm at Lawrence Livermore, whose management seems to have been embarrassed by Rouse's extracurricular research. In 1968, he left Lawrence Livermore for a small company in San Diego, known today as General Atomics, where he was granted a bit more leeway to pursue his theories. His official duties at General Atomics were to develop practical applications for nuclear energy, and in this regard, he developed several improvements in the material used to build protective shielding for nuclear power plants. Meanwhile, he continued to develop his solar model by using the computers at San Diego State College in his spare time.

Although the iron core theory has yet to be accepted by the astrophysical community, several subsequent developments have offered support for Rouse's theory. The first came in the 1990s, when Nobel Prize winner Raymond Davis demonstrated that the sun produces only about one-third of the number of solar neutrinos (subatomic particles with no charge and virtually no mass) that it was assumed to produce. A number of very interesting theories have been advanced to explain this discrepancy, but one of the most convincing explanations is Rouse's iron core theory. The second involved the development after 1970 of helioseismology (the study of sound waves on the sun's surface caused by the oscillations of solar gases). Rouse was able to incorporate helioseismology into his solar model so that the model can reproduce the observed spectrum of oscillations when a small amount of solid iron is assumed.

In 1955, Rouse married the former Lorraine Moxley. In 1992, he left General Atomics to found Rouse Research, an atomic energy consulting firm, and to devote more time to his solar models and theories.

See also: Astronomy and Astrophysics; Howard University; Physics

REFERENCES AND FURTHER READING

Kessler, James H., J. S. Kidd, Renee A. Kidd, and Katherine A. Morin, eds. *Distinguished African American Scientists of the 20th Century*. Phoenix, AZ: Oryx Press, 1996: 284–287.

Krapp, Kristine M., ed. *Notable Black American Scientists*. Detroit, MI: Gale Research, 1999: 269–270.

Spangenburg, Ray, and Kit Moser. *African Americans in Science, Math, and Invention*. New York: Facts On File, 2003: 203–204.

Satcher, David
(1941–) Science Administrator

David Satcher held a number of important positions in the federal government related to public health, including U.S. surgeon general. He also served as president of Meharry Medical College and held key managerial positions at Morehouse School of Medicine and Charles R. Drew University of Medicine and Science.

Satcher was born on March 2, 1941, in Anniston, Alabama, to Wilmer and Anna Satcher. After graduating from Morehouse College in Atlanta in 1963, he enrolled in Case Western Reserve University in Cleveland, and in 1970, he received an MD and a PhD in cytogenetics, the branch of biology dealing with the study of heredity from the point of view of cytology (the study of the formation, structure, and functions of cells). He spent the next three years completing his internship and residency at Strong Memorial Hospital in Rochester, New York, and doing postgraduate research at the University of Rochester. His research focused on the hereditary aspects of sickle cell disease (a form of anemia) caused by abnormalities in the hemoglobin (the protein in the blood that carries oxygen from the lungs to the tissues).

In 1973, Satcher joined the faculty at the University of California at Los Angeles (UCLA) School of Medicine and Public Health and the staff at the Los Angeles County-Martin Luther King, Jr. General Hospital (today the King-Drew Medical Center). Over the next six years, he developed and chaired the hospital's department of family medicine while directing the King-Drew Sickle Cell Research Center, a joint operation by King General and the Charles R. Drew Postgraduate Medical School (today the Charles R. Drew University of Medicine and Science). In 1977, he took over as interim dean of Drew Postgraduate. The school had been affiliated informally with King General since 1972, but Dean Satcher completed an agreement with the UCLA School of Medicine and the California Board of Regents that established King General as the official training hospital for interns and residents studying medical specialties at Drew.

In 1979, Satcher left King and Drew to become chair of the department of community medicine and family practice at Morehouse School of Medicine (MSM). Three years later, he was named president of Meharry Medical College in Nashville, Tennessee. In 1993, he was appointed director of the Centers for Disease Control and Prevention (CDC) and administrator of the Agency for Toxic Substances and Disease Registry (ATSDR). As CDC director, he was charged with overseeing the federal government's efforts to prevent disease, injury, and premature death. To this end, he spearheaded initiatives that increased childhood immunization rates from 55 percent to 78 percent in just four years, while expanding the CDC's comprehensive breast and cervical cancer screening program from 18 to 50 states. He also upgraded the nation's capability to respond to emerging infectious diseases and laid the groundwork for a new early warning system to detect and prevent food-borne illnesses. As ATSDR administrator, he oversaw the Department of Health and Human Services' efforts to prevent or mitigate adverse human health effects and diminished quality of life resulting from exposure to hazardous substances in the environment.

In 1998, President Bill Clinton appointed Satcher to the positions of U.S. surgeon general and assistant secretary for health in the Department of Health and Human Services. As surgeon general, he continued the battle against smoking and called for increased funding for programs to address public health issues such as youth violence, obesity, oral health, and depression. He was particularly concerned about the high rate of suicides in the United States, and as a means of lowering this rate he issued the "Call to Action to Prevent Suicide" (U.S. Department of Health and Human Services, http://www.surgeongeneral.gov/library/calltoaction/calltoaction.htm) and contributed to the National Strategy for Suicide Prevention. As an African American with a lower-class upbringing, Satcher knew firsthand about the disparities in the nation's health care system, so he championed the cause of equal access to health care for all citizens. He also issued the "Call to Action to Promote Sexual

David Satcher served as U.S. surgeon general and as president of Meharry Medical College. (National Institutes of Health)

Health and Responsible Sexual Behavior" (U.S. Department of Health and Human Services, http://www.surgeongeneral.gov/library/sexualhealth/default. htm), which promoted the distribution of condoms in public schools and called for a more enlightened outlook toward homosexuality.

Upon stepping down as surgeon general in 2002 (he had resigned as assistant secretary of health the previous year), Satcher spent six months as a senior visiting fellow with the Kaiser Family Foundation. He then returned to MSM, this time to serve as the founding director of the National Center for Primary Care. The center's activities focus on a range of health issues, particularly those affecting poor and minority populations. One of the center's initiatives was Healthy People 2010, which sought to eliminate disparities in health among different racial and ethnic groups in this country by providing these groups with improved access to primary health care.

Satcher is married to the former Nola Richardson, with whom he has four children. His many honors include election to the National Academy of Sciences' Institute of Medicine.

See also: Biology; Charles R. Drew University of Medicine and Science; Institute of Medicine; Meharry Medical College; Morehouse School of Medicine

REFERENCES AND FURTHER READING

Bigelow, Barbara C., ed. *Contemporary Black Biography*, vol. 7. Detroit, MI: Gale Research, 1994: 241–244.

U.S. Department of Health & Human Services. "David Satcher (1998–2002)." [Online article or information; retrieved December 3, 2005.] http://www.surgeongeneral.gov/library/history/biosatcher.htm.

Shaw, Earl D.
(1937–) Physicist

Earl Shaw specialized in the development of lasers (devices that produce and amplify electronic radiation in the visible light spectrum to create a beam of light so intense that it can be used to "see" into atoms and molecules). His most important contribution was the development of the spin-flip Raman tunable laser.

Shaw was born in 1937 in Clarksdale, Mississippi. At age 12, he moved with his mother to Chicago, where he grew up. He became interested in pursuing a career in physics while a student at Crane Technical High School, and after graduation, he entered the undergraduate physics program at the University of Illinois. He received a BS in physics from Illinois in 1960, an MA in physics from Dartmouth College in 1964, and a PhD in physics from the University of California at Berkeley in 1969. He then went to work for Bell Telephone Laboratories (BTL) in Murray Hill, New Jersey, as a research scientist. He and his wife, Erin, have one child.

Shaw's work at BTL mostly involved the development of new laser technologies, most importantly the spin-flip Raman tunable laser. A Raman laser makes use of the phenomenon known as Raman scattering, which was discovered in 1928 by the Nobel laureate C. V. Raman. Whenever a beam of light hits a substance, the collision causes some of the photons in the beam to gain or lose energy, thus creating a second beam of light that has a different wavelength than the first. A Raman laser captures this second beam and amplifies it into a coherent beam of laser light. Spin-flip tuning allows for the frequency of this beam to be adjusted higher or lower in infinitely small degrees, much as a dimmer switch allows for the fine-tuning of a chandelier. The ability to fine-tune a beam's frequency has proven to be highly efficacious in the study of biological systems. Cell walls are particularly vulnerable to intense light, but the spin-flip Raman tunable laser allows the researcher to dial down the intensity of the beam so that it does not harm the cell wall.

Shaw left BTL in 1988 to become a professor of physics at Rutgers University's Newark, New Jersey, campus. At Rutgers, he continued to experiment with a laser technology he had been working on at BTL, the far-infrared free electron laser. This device generates electronic radiation in the infrared spectrum by beaming electrons through a magnetic field.

In 2004, Shaw retired from Rutgers to his home in Morris County, New Jersey.

REFERENCES AND FURTHER READING

Physicists of the African Diaspora. "Earl D. Shaw." [Online article or information; retrieved October 28, 2007.] http://www.math.buffalo.edu/mad/physics/shaw-earld.html.

Stubbs, Frederick D.
(1906–1947) Surgeon

Frederick Stubbs was the first African American surgeon to specialize in thoracic surgery (surgery pertaining to the thorax, or chest), and he was one of the foremost thoracic surgeons of his day. His principal contribution to medical science was to perfect methods for removing diseased tissue from patients with pulmonary tuberculosis.

Stubbs was born on March 16, 1906, in Wilmington, Delaware. His father, Bacon, was a physician, and his mother, Florence, was a homemaker. After graduating from high school and the Cushing Academy in Massachusetts, in 1923 he entered Dartmouth College and received an AB in biology in 1927. Four years later, he received an MD from Harvard University Medical School and joined the staff at Cleveland City Hospital (Ohio). Upon completing a one-year internship, Stubbs was named a thoracic fellow, and in this capacity, he participated in Cleveland City's ongoing research project concerning thoracic surgery.

At the time, the opening and closing of the chest cavity were considered extremely difficult; thoracic surgery mostly involved surgical procedures designed to treat pulmonary tuberculosis, a bacterial infection of the lungs that, left untreated, was fatal. Such procedures usually involved either thoracoplasty (the removal of a portion of the ribs in stages to collapse diseased areas of the lungs, particularly in the case of tuberculosis) or phrenicectomy (the cutting of the phrenic, or diaphragm, nerve to immobilize a lung by inducing paralysis on one side). By the time he completed his fellowship in 1933, Stubbs had become the foremost black thoracic surgeon in the country, because he was the only one.

In 1933, Stubbs joined the staff at Douglass Memorial Hospital (formerly Frederick Douglass Memorial Hospital and Training School) in Philadelphia as a resident. The following year, he completed his residency, married Marian Turner, with whom he had one child, and joined her father's private medical practice in Philadelphia. Meanwhile, he continued to experiment with various ways to treat tuberculosis with surgery, and in 1936, he reported a technique for crushing, rather than cutting, the phrenic nerve. After spending a year as a thoracic surgery resident at New York City's Sea View Hospital, in 1938 he returned to Douglass to become chief of thoracic surgery.

At Douglass, Stubbs established a thoracic surgery research program similar to the program he had been involved in at Cleveland City. He was particularly interested in learning more about how to treat pulmonary tuberculosis, because it was one of the leading causes of death among African Americans. One of the first projects undertaken by the program involved closed intrapleural pneumolysis (the surgical separation of lesions, or patches of diseased tissue, between a tuberculous lung and the surrounding chest wall). His research described the various complications that arise from this procedure such as bronchopleural fistula (the development of abnormal tubes between the bronchi and the pleura, the membrane that enfolds the lungs) and cardiac standstill resulting from stimulation by the vagus nerve (the cranial nerve connecting the abdomen to the brain). As a result of Stubb's work in this area, closed intrapleural pneumolysis was adopted by an increasing number of thoracic surgeons as a means of treating pulmonary tuberculosis. He also continued to study new ways to interrupt the activities of the phrenic nerve and to perform thoracoplasty and resection (the closing of the chest cavity after surgery).

In addition to his duties as a thoracic surgeon, Stubbs served as Douglass's medical director after 1941. He also organized a thoracic surgery department at Philadelphia's other black hospital, Mercy Hospital, and in the early 1940s, he reorganized the medical staffs at Mercy and Douglass as part of the effort to consolidate their operations en route to a total merger of the two institutions. He almost certainly would have played a key role in the activities of Mercy-Douglass Hospital had he not died from a heart attack on February 9, 1947, in New York City.

See also: Mercy-Douglass Hospital

REFERENCES AND FURTHER READING
Organ, Claude H., and Margaret Kosiba, eds. *A Century of Black Surgeons: The U.S.A. Experience.* Norman, OK: Transcript Press, 1987: 529–558.
Salzman, Jack, David Lionel Smith, and Cornel West, eds. *Encyclopedia of African American Culture and History.* New York: MacMillan, 1996: 2583–2584.

Taylor, Welton I.
(1919–) Microbiologist

Welton Taylor developed rapid and effective methods for identifying the presence of three different types of bacteria that cause food poisoning. These methods were eventually adopted by health care officials around the world as the best means of safeguarding processed food from bacterial contamination.

Taylor was born on November 12, 1919, in Birmingham, Alabama, to Frederick and Cora Taylor. Shortly thereafter, he moved with his family to Chicago. The family moved to Peoria, Illinois, in 1929, and then back to Chicago in 1936. After receiving a BS in bacteriology from the University of Illinois in 1941, he was commissioned a second lieutenant in the U.S. Army and spent World War II in the South Pacific. He returned to the University of Illinois after the war, receiving an MA and a PhD in bacteriology in 1947 and 1948, respectively. In 1945, he married Jayne Kemp, with whom he had two children.

Taylor's early research focused on *Clostridium*, the genus of rod-shaped bacteria that occur in soil and in the intestinal tracts of humans and other animals and that grow only in the complete absence of oxygen. As a graduate student, he studied *C. botulinum*, the bacteria that cause botulism, a deadly form of food poisoning that results from eating food that has been improperly canned. His doctoral dissertation demonstrated that the growth and vigor of a colony of *C. botulinim* determines the strength of the toxins that each individual bacterium produces.

At the University of Chicago, where he taught bacteriology from 1948 to 1954, Taylor shifted the focus of his research to other poisonous strains of *Clostridium*, particularly *C. tetani*, which cause tetanus, and *C. perfringens*, *C. novyi*, and *C. septicum*, which cause certain forms of gangrene. As part of his research, he developed treatments for tetanus and gangrene that combined the use of antibiotics and pain medications with more traditional methods, such as hot soaks. He also demonstrated that boric acid, which was being touted as a germicide, actually inhibits the immune system's ability to fight bacterial infection.

In 1954, Taylor left teaching to become senior microbiologist at Swift and Company, a Chicago-based meatpacker that distributed canned meats and other processed food products nationally. The company's baby foods had recently been linked with a major outbreak of salmonellosis, a form of food poisoning caused by the bacteria *Salmonella enteritidis*. Taylor investigated the methods the company used to process its various food products and made recommendations on how to avoid contamination by *Salmonella* and other bacteria.

In 1959, Taylor left Swift to become a medical researcher at Chicago's Children's Memorial Hospital. By then, he had become a world-renowned expert on food poisoning, and he spent a considerable portion of his time conducting research for the World Health Organization and the National Institutes of Health on ways to safeguard imported foods from bacterial contamination. By 1965, he had developed new methods for detecting *Clostridium* and *Salmonella* in processed foods that were less expensive, easier to administer, and more accurate than the methods then being used. These methods were adopted quickly by a number of food processing companies, and in 1970, the U.S. Food and Drug Administration adopted them as the standard methods for proving that processed foods were free from bacterial contamination; health officials in many other countries eventually followed suit. By 1971, he had developed similar methods for detecting *Shigella dysenteriae*, the bacteria that cause a form of dysentery known as shigellosis.

In 1964, Taylor left Children's Memorial to become chief microbiologist at West Suburban Hospital in Oak Park, Illinois, and a professor of microbiology at the University of Illinois Medical Center. Thirteen years later, he gave up both positions to found his own company, Micro-Palettes Inc. Originally, the company manufactured kits for diagnosing virtually any type of biological specimen, such as blood or tissue, and marketed them for use in the home. When this product line failed economically, Taylor converted Micro-Palettes into a medical consulting firm.

Taylor authored more than 50 scholarly articles in journals such as *Applied Microbiology, Journal of Clinical Microbiology,* and *American Journal of Clinical Pathology.* Of his many honors, perhaps the most impressive came in 1985, when the U.S. Centers for Disease Control named a previously unknown form of bacteria *Enterobacter taylorae* in his honor.

See also: Microbiology; National Institutes of Health

References and Further Reading

Kessler, James H., J. S. Kidd, Renee A. Kidd, and Katherine A. Morin, eds. *Distinguished African American Scientists of the 20th Century.* Phoenix, AZ: Oryx Press, 1996: 307–311.

Krapp, Kristine M., ed. *Notable Black American Scientists.* Detroit, MI: Gale Research, 1999: 294–295.

Spangenburg, Ray, and Kit Moser. *African Americans in Science, Math, and Invention.* New York: Facts On File, 2003: 209–210.

Thomas, Vivien T.
(1910–1985) Medical Researcher

Vivien Thomas had no formal training as a surgeon, yet he made major contributions to some of the most important surgical procedures of his day. He helped train so many surgeons that, late in his career, he was named an instructor of surgery at a major medical research hospital.

Thomas was born on August 29, 1910, in Lake Province, Louisiana. His father, William, was a building contractor, and his mother, Mary, was a homemaker. As a young boy, he moved with his family to Nashville, Tennessee, where he grew up. After graduating from high school in 1929, he took a job as a laboratory assistant to Alfred Blalock, at the time a professor of surgery at the Vanderbilt University School of Medicine in Nashville. In 1933, he married Clara Flander, with whom he had two children.

As Blalock's assistant, Thomas played an active role in Blalock's research, which focused on the circulatory system. Blalock was particularly interested in how blood pressure affects the operation of the heart and arteries, as well as the role played by low blood pressure as a contributor to shock (the failure of the circulatory system to supply sufficient blood to the peripheral tissues to meet basic metabolic requirements). In the early 1930s, he transplanted an adrenal gland, in the process performing the first successful surgical joining of blood vessels. This procedure led him to seek a surgical cure for coarctation (a condition in which the aorta, the body's main artery, gets blocked and constricts the flow of blood to the lower body). He later became interested in pulmonary hypertension (high blood pressure) in the pulmonary artery (the vessel that carries blood from the heart to the lungs). Thomas's role in all of this was to perform many of the preliminary procedures on laboratory animals, usually dogs. Having received no formal training in how to cut or suture, he taught himself everything he needed to know about operating on living tissue.

During the course of his studies of the circulatory system, Blalock began experimenting with anastomosis (the surgical connection of two different arteries) in dogs. A typical experiment involved connecting the left subclavian artery, which in humans carries blood from the heart to the left arm, to the end of the right pulmonary artery. As was usual for all their experiments, Blalock developed the model for the procedure and Thomas performed the actual surgery. At the time, anastomosis was considered to be a bold and daring procedure, but Thomas's success at performing it showed the medical community that such a procedure could be performed safely after all.

In 1941, Blalock was named chair of the department of surgery at Johns Hopkins University Medical School in Baltimore and chief surgeon of the school's hospital, and he persuaded Thomas to make the move with him. At Hopkins, Thomas continued to supervise the affairs of Blalock's laboratory, which was known as the Hunterian Laboratory, and eventually he was named the Hunterian's director of personnel. In this capacity, he played a major role in directing the activities of Blalock's other assistants, residents, interns, and students. Among his other duties, he taught surgical techniques to a number of would-be surgeons, many of whom went on to become world-class surgeons. Shortly after arriving at Hopkins, Blalock figured out how to bypass the blockage caused by coarctation by connecting the subclavian artery to the aorta below the blockage. In the course of working out the procedure for carrying out this experiment, Thomas and William Longmire, one of Blalock's residents, invented a device known as Blalock's clamp for clamping an artery during surgery.

In the early 1940s, Blalock and Helen Taussig, a Hopkins colleague, developed a procedure for surgically correcting blue baby syndrome (a medical condition whereby an infant suffers from lack of oxygen to the tissues because of lack of blood to the lungs). Taussig had determined that the condition is caused by a leaking septum (the wall that separates the chambers of the heart) and a too-narrow pulmonary artery, which connects the heart to the lungs. She convinced Blalock, who by then was one of the nation's foremost experts on anastomosis, that both problems could be corrected surgically. In 1943, Thomas, Blalock, and Longmire successfully joined a dog's subclavian artery to its pulmonary artery, the type of procedure that Blalock and Taussig had determined was most likely to cure blue baby syndrome. During this procedure, Thomas took the role of lead surgeon, and Blalock and Longmire served as his assistants. The following year, the trio performed a similar operation on a 6-year-old blue baby, curing the condition completely. During this procedure, Blalock took the role of lead surgeon while Thomas stood directly behind him, and from time to time Blalock turned to Thomas to ask for advice as to how to proceed.

Taussig and Blalock published a joint account of the procedure in 1945, and in time, the procedure became known as the Blalock-Taussig procedure. In addition to curing blue baby syndrome, the Blalock-Taussig operation demonstrated to surgeons that very sick children could be operated on successfully. It also led surgeons to perform more complicated operations on adults, culminating eventually with open-heart surgery. One such procedure, performed in 1948 by Thomas, Blalock, and C. Rollins Hanlon, involved the surgical correction of a defect in the septum between the atria (the chambers in the heart that receive blood from the veins and then pump it into the ventricles, which distribute it throughout the circulatory system).

When Blalock retired from Hopkins in 1964, Thomas was invited by Blalock's replacement, George Zuidema, to remain as director of personnel of the Hunterian. In 1977, Thomas took on the additional duties of an instructor of surgery at Hopkins, a position he held until his retirement in 1979. He died on November 25, 1985, in Baltimore.

References and Further Reading
Organ, Claude H. Jr., and Margaret Kosiba, eds. *A Century of Black Surgeons: The U.S.A. Experience.* Norman, OK: Transcript Press, 1987: 559–579.

Thomas, Vivien T. *Pioneering Research in Surgical Shock and Cardiovascular Surgery.* Philadelphia: University of Pennsylvania Press, 1985.

Tolbert, Margaret Mayo
(1943–) Science Administrator

As a biochemist, Margaret Mayo Tolbert helped explain how the liver processes glucose (a form of sugar that is the primary energy source for the muscles). She is best remembered, however, as a science administrator; in addition to directing the affairs of a major nuclear research center, she worked to increase the involvement of underrepresented people in scientific research.

Tolbert was born Margaret Ellen Mayo on November 24, 1943, in Suffolk, Virginia. Her father, J. Clifton, was a landscape gardener, and her mother, Martha, was a domestic worker. Her parents had both died by the time she was 13; so she was raised by her paternal grandmother, an older sister, and a kindly neighbor family. With the latter's help, she was able to attend Tuskegee Institute (today Tuskegee University), where she received a BS in chemistry in 1967. After receiving an MS in analytical chemistry from Wayne State University in 1968, she worked as a lab technician and mathematics teacher at Tuskegee for a year before entering the doctoral program at Brown University in Providence, Rhode Island. Upon receiving a PhD in biochemistry in 1974, she returned to Tuskegee to teach chemistry until 1977, when she joined the faculty of Florida A&M University's college of pharmacy and pharmaceutical sciences as a professor of pharmaceutical chemistry. She was married and divorced twice and had one child.

A skilled biochemist, Tolbert focused her research on the biochemistry of the liver. Her work shed considerable light on how the production of glucose is regulated in liver cells. But she began to move away from research and toward science administration in 1979, when she returned to Tuskegee to be director of the Carver Research Foundation. In this capacity, she supervised the foundation's research projects and fund-raising efforts, while strengthening the research ties between Tuskegee and several universities in West Africa. In 1987, she left Tuskegee to become a senior planner with BP America, the U.S. operation of British Petroleum, a petroleum manufacturer, at its corporate research center in Warrensville Heights, Ohio. Her primary focus in this position was to help arrange better cooperation between the research departments of BP America and Shell Oil, but she also played a role in increasing BP America's commitment to science education and museums. In 1990, she went to work for the National Science Foundation (NSF), an independent federal agency in Arlington, Virginia, created by Congress to promote the progress of science in the United States. In addition to helping to coordinate the science and engineering education programs of 16 federal agencies, she also served as director of the Research Improvement in Minority Institutions Program (RIMIP), an effort to enhance the ability of historically black colleges and universities to conduct cutting-edge scientific research. In 1993, she became a consulting scientist at the Howard Hughes Medical Institute in Chevy Chase, Maryland, and in this capacity she lined up international support for medical research programs in the former Soviet bloc nations of Eastern Europe.

In 1994, Tolbert was named director of the division of educational programs at the Department of Energy's (DOE) Argonne National Laboratory in Argonne, Illinois, the largest research facility in the United States devoted to nuclear research. Her primary duty in this capacity was to coordinate the laboratory's high school and college programs in science education, but she also played an important role in making Argonne's assistance and expertise available to some of the West African universities she had worked with while at Tuskegee. In 1996, she was named director of the DOE's New Brunswick Laboratory, also in Argonne, Illinois. In this capacity, she oversaw the laboratory's activities concerning the preparation and control of nuclear materials. In 2002, she returned to the NSF as executive secretary of the Committee on Equal Opportunities in Science and Engineering. Her duties include promoting NSF's efforts to increase participation of women, underrepresented minorities, and persons with disabilities in science, technology, engineering, and mathematics. She also served as senior advisor to NSF's office of integrative activities, and in this capacity, she helped arrange grants for innovative science and technology centers that offer the research and engineering community an effective mechanism to undertake long-term scientific and technological research and education activities.

See also: Biochemistry; Carver Research Foundation; Chemistry; Department of Energy; Florida A&M University; Historically Black Colleges and Universities; National Science Foundation; Tuskegee University; Wayne State University

REFERENCES AND FURTHER READING

Kessler, James H., J. S. Kidd, Renee A. Kidd, and Katherine A. Morin, eds. *Distinguished African American Scientists of the 20th Century*. Phoenix, AZ: Oryx Press, 1996: 263–264.

Spangenburg, Ray, and Kit Moser. *African Americans in Science, Math, and Invention*. New York: Facts On File, 2003: 211–212.

Warren, Wini. *Black Women Scientists in the United States*. Bloomington: Indiana University Press, 1999: 253–254.

Turner, Charles H.
(1867–1923) Entomologist

In the early 20th century, little was known about the neurological or psychological capabilities of insects. Charles Turner contributed to the field of entomology by showing that ants, bees, and cockroaches have the ability, albeit limited, to see, hear, smell, and remember for short periods of time.

Turner was born on February 3, 1867, in Cincinnati. His father, Thomas, was a custodian, and his mother, Adeline, was a nurse. He studied science at the University of Cincinnati and received a BS in 1891 and an MS in 1892. He remained at Cincinnati for a year as an assistant in the biology laboratory before departing for Clark University (today Clark Atlanta University) in Atlanta to teach biology and chair the department of science and agriculture. During his 12 years at Clark, he published a number of research articles, mostly in the *Journal of Comparative Neurology,* on the morphology (form and structure) of various animal species.

Turner left Clark in 1905, and for the next two years, he taught biology at high schools in Tennessee and Georgia while studying zoology at the University of Chicago. After receiving his PhD in 1907, he joined the faculty at Sumner High School in St. Louis, where he taught biology for the rest of his career. While working on his doctorate, he became interested in the neurological and psychological aspects of animal behavior. He was particularly intrigued by the abilities of insects such as ants and bees to learn, and for the rest of his career he focused his research on this area.

Turner made a number of groundbreaking observations about insects. He was particularly interested in how certain ant species manage to find their way back to their nests after foraging for food, and eventually he was able to describe a pattern known today as Turner's circling. Turner discovered that when ants return to their colony, they always repeat the same cycle of steps so as not to get lost. He also discovered that ants can differentiate landscape features and that Turner's circling includes steps where they respond to these features as well as to light and scent. He discovered that when ant lions are exposed to certain external stimuli, they lie motionless for long periods of time as a result of terror paralysis, not as a survival strategy, as was previously believed. He showed that honey bees can identify certain colors, patterns, and smells and that they have a rudimentary sense of time. He discovered that wasps and burrowing bees can identify landmarks close to their nests. He demonstrated that cockroaches learn from trial and error and possess a certain amount of short-term memory. He proved that some insects hear well enough to be able to differentiate between certain high and low pitches.

Turner's findings concerning the neurological and psychological aspects of insect behavior would have been impressive enough if he had been on the faculty of a major research university. They are even more impressive, therefore, when one considers that Turner, who made most of these discoveries while teaching high school, spent his own money and experimented in his spare time to make them. Because very little work of this type had been done by zoologists or entomologists, he had to develop innovative methods and experiments for identifying the learning abilities of insects. Not surprisingly, given the groundbreaking nature of his work, he had no trouble publishing his work, and in time, prestigious journal such as *American Naturalist, Biological Bulletin, Journal of Animal Behavior*, and *Science* published more than 70 of his articles.

In 1888, Turner married Leontine Troy, with whom he had two children; she died in 1904, and he later married Lillian Porter. In 1922, he retired from teaching and moved back to Chicago, where one of his children lived. He died in Chicago on February 14, 1923.

See also: Biology; Clark Atlanta University

REFERENCES AND FURTHER READING

Abramson, Charles I., ed. *Selected Papers and Biography of Charles Henry Turner (1867–1923), Pioneer of Comparative Animal Behavior Studies.* Assisted by Latasha D. Jackson and Camille L. Fuller. Lewiston, NY: Edwin Mellen Press, 2003.

Carey, Charles W. Jr. *American Scientists.* New York: Facts On File, 2005: 372–373.

Hayden, Robert C. *Seven African American Scientists.* Brookfield, CT: Twenty-First Century Books, 1992: 34–57.

Spangenburg, Ray, and Kit Moser. *African Americans in Science, Math, and Invention.* New York: Facts On File, 2003: 212–213.

Tyson, Neil deGrasse
(1958–) Astrophysicist

Neil Tyson is one of the United States' foremost authorities on supernovas (violently exploding stars whose brightness suddenly increases to hundreds of millions of times their normal level). He also has written extensively about astronomy and astrophysics, the study of the physical properties of celestial bodies, for the general educated public.

Tyson was born on October 5, 1958, in New York City. As a young boy, he became interested in astronomy by gazing at the stars through binoculars from a rooftop, and at age 14, he bought his first telescope with money he had earned by doing odd jobs. He took special courses for young people at New York's Hayden Planetarium, a branch of the American Museum of Natural His-

Neil deGrasse Tyson is one of the few astrophysicists to have an asteroid named in his honor. (Frederick M. Brown/Getty Images)

tory, and he specialized in astrophysics at the Bronx High School of Science. He received a BS in physics from Harvard University in 1980, an MA in astronomy from the University of Texas in 1983, and a PhD in astrophysics from Columbia University in 1991. He spent the next three years conducting postdoctoral research at Princeton University, and in 1994, he returned to Hayden as a staff scientist and joined the Princeton faculty as a visiting research scientist and lecturer. In 1996, he was named Hayden's director, and in this capacity he oversaw the planetarium's efforts to explain astrophysics to the public via exhibits, books, courses, lecture series, and online resources. In 1988, he married Alice Young, with whom he has two children.

As an astrophysicist, Tyson studied various stellar phenomena by using ultraviolet photometry [the measurement of the intensity of ultraviolet (UV) light that a celestial body emits]. His first graduate research project involved determining the age and origin of blue stragglers, a handful of hot, bright, young stars that are surrounded by stars that are cooler, dimmer, and older. Next, he tried to estimate how many dwarf galaxies, so called because they contain fewer than 10 billion stars, go undetected because of problems associated with obtaining useful photometric data for dim, distant stars. In another project, he explored the possibility that the Lyman-alpha Forest, a series of lines on the UV spectrum that transcend galactic boundaries and whose meaning had been poorly understood, indicates the existence of previously undetected hydrogen-rich dwarf galaxies, and another attempted to determine the metallic content of certain so-called carbon stars in the Galactic Bulge, the vertical clumping of stars that occurs at the center of the Milky Way. As a whole, this research contributed to a better understanding of how stars and galaxies are formed.

Tyson's research at Princeton and Hayden focused primarily on super-novas. He was a major participant in the 1990–1993 Calán/Tololo Supernova Survey, a joint project by two observatories in Chile, that obtained significant photometric data emitted by 29 Type Ia supernovas, which result from the explosion of a white dwarf star in a binary star system. This data was then used to develop template light curves for the study of Type Ia supernovas in general. He copioneered the use of the expanding photosphere system to study distant Type II supernovas, which occur when the iron core of a supergiant star collapses due to gravity. In terms of nonsupernova research, his most important contribution was the codevelopment of a procedure for maximizing the number of stellar images an observer can capture in the rapidly changing surface brightness of the dusk or dawn sky.

In addition to his other duties, Tyson served on several government commissions, including a 2001 task force that made recommendations concerning the future of the aerospace industry and the 2004 Moon, Mars, and Beyond commission, which made recommendations concerning how to implement the nation's current space exploration policy. He also served as a fellow of the Committee for the Scientific Investigation of Claims of the Paranormal, an international organization devoted to the critical investigation of paranormal and fringe-science claims from a responsible, scientific point of view.

Tyson has written extensively about astrophysics and astronomy for the general public. His first book, *Merlin's Tour of the Universe* (New York: Columbia University Press, 1989), answered questions about astronomy that had been posed by the general public; it proved to be so popular that it was eventually translated into seven foreign languages. His other books include *Universe Down to Earth* (New York: Columbia University Press, 1994), *Just Visiting This Planet* (St. Charles, MO: Main Street Books, 1998), *One Universe: at Home in the Cosmos* (Washington, DC: Joseph Henry Press, 2000), and *Origins: Fourteen Billion Years of Cosmic Evolution* (New York: W. W. Norton, 2004). He has also made dozens of appearances on national television, including the nightly news programs of the major networks, to explain current developments concerning space science. His many honors include having an asteroid, 13123 Tyson, named after him by the International Astronomical Union.

See also: Astronomy and Astrophysics; Physics

REFERENCES AND FURTHER READING

American Museum of Natural History. "Neil deGrasse Tyson, Astrophysicist." [Online article or information; retrieved December 5, 2005.] http://research.amnh.org/users/tyson/.

Spangenburg, Ray, and Kit Moser. *African Americans in Science, Math, and Invention*. New York: Facts On File, 2003: 214–215.

Tyson, Neil deGrasse. *The Sky Is Not the Limit: Adventures of an Urban Astrophysicist*. New York: Doubleday, 2000.

Walker, Arthur II
(1936–2001) Astrophysicist

Arthur Walker pioneered methods for using space-borne telescopes to make high-resolution images of the sun. In addition to contributing immensely to a better understanding of the various layers of the solar atmosphere, his work made it possible to learn more about other stars as well.

Walker was born on August 24, 1936, in Cleveland. His father, Arthur, was a lawyer, and his mother, Hilda, was a social worker. At age 5, he moved with his family to New York City, where he grew up. After specializing in physics at the Bronx High School of Science, he returned to Cleveland to study at the Case Institute of Technology (today Case Western Reserve University) and received a BS in physics in 1957. He then entered the graduate program at the University of Illinois and received an MS and a PhD in physics in 1958 and 1962, respectively. He focused his graduate research on the use of radiation to produce pions (subatomic particles that are associated with the strong nuclear force, the force that binds together protons and neutrons in an atomic nucleus).

Upon completing his education, Walker was commissioned a first lieutenant in the U.S. Air Force and assigned to the Air Force Weapons Laboratory at Kirtland Air Force Base near Albuquerque, New Mexico. At this point the focus of his research shifted from nuclear physics to astrophysics, because his work for the air force involved the development of rocket-carried instruments capable of measuring radiation in the innermost of the Van Allen belts, two zones of high-energy charged particles that are trapped at high altitudes by the Earth's magnetic field. The primary purpose of the experiment was to learn how the Van Allen belts affect the operation of communications satellites, but his efforts also contributed to a better understanding of the role played by the Van Allen belts in such terrestrial phenomena as the aurora borealis (northern lights) and magnetic storms (temporary disturbances of the Earth's magnetic field that are induced by radiation and streams of charged particles from the sun).

In 1965, Walker left the air force to join the Aerospace Corporation's Space Physics Laboratory (SPL) in El Segundo, California. Over the next nine years, he developed and conducted a number of innovative experiments designed to learn more about the Earth's upper atmosphere. He also codesigned and conducted several studies of the sun's corona (upper atmosphere) via X-ray spectroscopy, which permits the identification of specific atoms and molecules by examining the electromagnetic radiation they emit in the form of X-rays. To this end, he and an SPL colleague, H. R. Rugge, developed the first space-borne X-ray spectrometer; data gathered by this device helped establish the temperature, composition, and dynamic nature of the sun's corona.

In 1974, Walker joined the faculty at Stanford University as a professor of physics and astronomy. By then, his primary research interest had shifted from the Earth's upper atmosphere to the sun, and he began looking for ways to obtain more sophisticated measurements of solar phenomena via X-ray spectroscopy. His search led him to Troy Barbee, a Stanford colleague who had developed a multilayered thin film capable of recording images produced by extremely hot solar gas. By 1987, Walker had fabricated from Barbee's film a set of synthetic mirrors, each of which selectively reflects X-rays of a specific wavelength. By mounting these mirrors on a telescope capable of detecting X-rays and then launching the telescope into space on a rocket, he obtained the first high-resolution images of the sun's corona. Later flights focused on the sun's chromosphere (the gaseous envelope surrounding the sun from which enormous masses of hydrogen and other gases erupt) and captured images of such prominent solar features as flares, bubbles, gas jets, and polar plumes. Still later flights focused on the solar upper transition region, the then-unknown region of the solar atmosphere, and they resolved one of the long-standing and most important unsolved problems of solar atmospheric physics: the role of thermal conduction from the corona and upper transition region in generating the chromosphere and lower transition region.

In 1991, Walker and his associates developed the first Multi-Spectral Solar Telescope Array for the National Aeronautics and Space Administration (NASA), consisting of 33 telescopes launched in two separate flights. He and his colleagues also played a key role in preparing for the 1998 launch of NASA's Advanced X-ray Astrophysics Facility (AXAF), today the Chandra X-ray Observatory, which studies the chromospheres and coronas of distant stars, the remnants of supernovas, and the distribution of elements throughout interstellar space.

Toward the end of his career, Walker's group established the Stanford AXAF Science Center, which provides access to AXAF observations for astronomers in the western United States. Walker also collaborated with Stanford colleague Blas Cabrera on the development of an X-ray microcalorimeter detector, the Transition Edge Sensor, which can measure the energy of individual X-rays. This method promised to make it possible to determine more precisely which of the sun's elements emit radiation, thus facilitating a more precise determination of the elements that make up the sun and other stars.

Walker's work with X-ray spectroscopy had a profound effect on astrophysics, but it had a far-ranging effect on other areas of science as well. The X-ray mirror technology he had utilized in his solar studies inspired the development of the world's first X-ray microscope. This device proved to be a powerful tool for all types of scientific research, but most especially for identifying the subatomic end products resulting from atom smashing experiments, which attempt to identify previously unknown types of subatomic particles.

Walker served on or chaired a number of important scientific committees, including the Advanced Solar Observatory Science Working Group for NASA and the Astronomy Advisory Committee of the National Science Foundation. He also served on the 1986 commission that investigated the space shuttle *Challenger* explosion. On several occasions, Walker was invited to present testimony to various science-related committees of the U.S. Congress, and in one instance, his testimony led to the establishment of the Sacramento Peak Solar Observatory (California) as the first and only national solar observatory.

Walker was married to the former Hilda Forte, with whom he had one child; they later divorced and he remarried. He taught at Stanford until his death on April 29, 2001, at his home in Stanford, California.

See also: Astronomy and Astrophysics; National Aeronautics and Space Administration; National Science Foundation; Physics

REFERENCES AND FURTHER READING

Physicists of the African Diaspora. "Arthur Bertram Cuthbert Walker, Jr." [Online article or information; retrieved December 5, 2005.] http://www.math.buffalo.edu/mad/physics/walker_arthurbc.html.

Spangenburg, Ray, and Kit Moser. *African Americans in Science, Math, and Invention.* New York: Facts On File, 2003: 216–218.

Warner, Isiah M.
(1946–) Chemist

Isiah Warner specializes in the study of complex chemical systems (systems that feature a large number of chemical reactants and reactions, such as a polluted environmental system). He has also played an important role in helping to develop more African Americans with PhDs in chemistry. Warner was born on July 30, 1946, in DeQuincy, Louisiana, to Humphrey and Irma Warner. At age 2, he moved with his parents to Bunkie, Louisiana, where he grew up. After finishing high school, he enrolled at Southern University, where he received a BS in chemistry in 1968. That same year, he married Della Blount, with whom he had three children.

After graduation, Warner went to work for Battelle Northwest in Richland, Washington, site of one of the federal government nuclear installations. In 1973, he entered the graduate program at the University of Washington, and four years later, he received a PhD in analytical chemistry. He taught chemistry at Texas A&M University for the next five years, and then he took a similar position at Emory University. In 1992, he returned to his home state to become a professor of analytical and environmental chemistry at Louisiana State University (LSU).

Warner developed and patented a process for improving the use of luminescence as a tool for measuring the amount of a specific unknown substance in a sample of material. He also developed and patented a method for removing chiral (so-called handed) species by using micelle polymers to dissolve them. In many chemical reactions, particularly those involving the production of pharmaceutical drugs, two species are produced, one of which is a mirror image of the other, in the way that the right-hand species is the mirror image of the left-hand one. In many cases, one of the hands does not behave chemically like the other; so it must be removed. A micelle polymer does this by dissolving the unwanted hand in much the same way that a detergent dissolves a stain in a piece of clothing.

In 2001, Warner took on the additional duties of vice chancellor for strategic initiatives. One of his duties in this position is to recruit more minority students into LSU's graduate programs in science, technology, engineering, and mathematics. At the time of his appointment, the LSU chemistry department was producing more African Americans with PhDs in chemistry than any other graduate program in the United States, largely as a result of his efforts to recruit and retain promising black chemists. His many awards and honors include election to fellowship in the American Association for the Advancement of Science.

See also: American Association for the Advancement of Science; Chemistry; Southern University and A&M College System

REFERENCES AND FURTHER READING

Warner Research Group, Louisiana State University, "Isiah M. Warner, Ph.D." [Online article or information; retrieved October 25, 2007.] http://www.chem.lsu.edu/imw/group/warner.htm.

Washington, Warren M.
(1936–) Meteorologist

Warren Washington was one of the first meteorologists to use computers to forecast the weather. The programs he helped write in the 1960s, although highly modified, continue to be used to forecast the weather in the early 21st century.

Washington was born on August 29, 1936, in Portland, Oregon. His father, Edwin, was a railroad porter, and his mother, Dorothy, was a homemaker. He became interested in chemistry after his high school teacher challenged him to find out on his own why egg yolks are yellow; he soon discovered that chickens consume sulfur from the grasses and grains they eat, which is stored in egg yolks, thus making them yellow. The discovery that he could "do" science led him to become interested in physics, which he majored in at Oregon State University in Corvallis. As an undergraduate, he got a job at a weather radar installation near Corvallis, which tracked storms rolling in from the Pacific Ocean, and this experience led him to become a meteorologist. After receiving a BS in physics in 1958 and an MS in meteorology in 1960, he left Oregon State for Penn State to work on a PhD.

Washington's doctoral research involved the use of computers to predict long-range changes in weather patterns. At the time, this was a highly innovative project, as was the use of computers, and in 1963, Washington was invited to work for the National Center for Atmospheric Research (NCAR) in Boulder, Colorado, during the summers. Upon receiving his PhD in meteorology in 1964, he went to work for NCAR as a research scientist, and he remained there for the rest of his career.

In the mid-1960s, Washington and an NCAR colleague, Akira Kasahara, developed the first computer model for forecasting the weather by simulating the general circulation of the atmosphere and oceans. This first program was primitive compared to today's programs for several reasons. First, computers themselves were primitive and therefore unable to process a large amount of information. Second, the few weather observatories that existed were not close to oceans, where most weather events begin; so the origins of storms could not be analyzed. Third, the instrumentation necessary to capture data pertaining to temperature, air pressure, humidity, and wind velocity was also primitive. Despite these obstacles, their program was a considerable advance over the weather forecasting methods then in use.

As equipment became more sophisticated, Washington and his NCAR colleagues wrote increasingly sophisticated programs capable of providing increasingly accurate weather forecasts. By the mid-1970s, for example, they had developed a program capable of showing how the annual monsoon in the Indian Ocean affects the jet stream (the high-speed air currents that flow eastward around the globe) over the Pacific Ocean. The groundbreaking nature of Washington's work was perhaps best recognized in 2002 by the National Academy of Engineering, which cited his pioneering development of coupled climate models, their use on parallel supercomputing architectures, and their interpretation.

In 1993, Washington was named director of NCAR's climate and global dynamics division. In this capacity, he oversees the division's efforts to develop long-range computer models for predicting the evolution of the Earth's climate and for understanding how those changes will affect the weather and the environment. Part of this work focuses on understanding the causes of variability in the current climate, including the role of humans.

Washington and his wife, Joan, had three children. He served on a number of panels and commissions, including the President's National Advisory Committee on Oceans and Atmosphere, the National Research Council, the National Science Board, and the Secretary of Energy's Biological and Environmental Research Advisory Committee. He also cofounded the Black Environmental Science Trust as a tool for increasing the number of young African Americans who choose a career in one of the environmental sciences. His publications include *An Introduction to Three-Dimensional Climate Modeling* (2nd ed., Herndon, VA: University Science Books, 2005). His honors include fellowship in the American Association for the Advancement of Science and election to a term as president of the American Meteorological Society.

See also: American Association for the Advancement of Science; Chemistry; Physics

REFERENCES AND FURTHER READING

Climate Change Research Section, National Center for Atmospheric Research. "Warren M. Washington." [Online article or information; retrieved December 8, 2005.] http://www.cgd.ucar.edu/ccr/warren/.

Kessler, James H., J. S. Kidd, Renee A. Kidd, and Katherine A. Morin, eds. *Distinguished African American Scientists of the 20th Century.* Phoenix, AZ: Oryx Press, 1996: 324–328.

Spangenburg, Ray, and Kit Moser. *African Americans in Science, Math, and Invention.* New York: Facts On File, 2003: 220.

West, Harold D.
(1904–1974) Biochemist

Harold West is best remembered as being the first African American to serve as president of Meharry Medical College. However, he was also an accomplished biochemical researcher, and his work contributed to a better understanding of the chemical composition of certain amino acids. His most important contribution in this regard was his participation in the first successful experiment to synthesize the amino acid threonine.

West was born on July 16, 1904, in Flemington, New Jersey, to George and Mary Ann West. In 1925, he received a BS in chemistry from the University of Illinois and joined the faculty at Morris Brown College in Atlanta as head of the science department. Two years later, he became a professor of physiological chemistry at Meharry Medical College in Nashville, Tennessee. Meanwhile, he continued his studies at Illinois, receiving an MS in 1930 and a PhD in 1937. After receiving his doctorate, he was named chair of Meharry's department of biochemistry, a position he held until 1952, when he became president of Meharry, the first African American to hold that post. At an unknown date, he married Jesse Penn, with whom he had two children.

While a graduate student, West began collaborating with Herbert E. Carter, one of his professors, on a study of certain amino acids, the chemical building blocks from which all proteins are constructed. They were particularly interested in synthesizing threonine (an essential amino acid that must be supplied in the diet of animals, because they cannot synthesize it) and allothreonine (a biochemical compound that is remarkably similar to threonine). The project was a success, and they published the results of their work in 1938, marking the first time that threonine had been synthesized in a laboratory. His teaching load at Meharry seriously affected his ability to devote much time to research, but after becoming president, he took up his studies of amino acids again. In 1954, he reported the successful synthesis of certain forms of amino acid cysteine. He also studied the biochemistry of bacteria and the antibiotic drugs that kill them (and that some of them produce), the various B vitamins, and the effects of aromatic hydrocarbons on the growth process of mammals.

West stepped down as Meharry's president in 1965, but he remained on the teaching faculty until he retired in 1973. His many honors included the naming of Meharry's Harold D. West Basic Sciences Center in his honor. He died on March 5, 1974, in Nashville.

See also: Chemistry

REFERENCES AND FURTHER READING

Cobb, W. Montague. "Harold Dadford West, Ph.D., LL.D.: A Good Man and True." *Journal of the National Medical Association* 68, 4 (July 1976): 269–275.

Spangenburg, Ray, and Kit Moser. *African Americans in Science, Math, and Invention.* New York: Facts On File, 2003: 220–222.

Wilkins, J. Ernest, Jr.
(1923–) Theoretical Physicist

Trained both as a physicist and as an engineer, Jesse Ernest Wilkins played a pioneering role in the development of American nuclear power for use in war and peace.

Wilkins was born on November 27, 1923, in Chicago. His father, J. Ernest Sr., was a lawyer who went on to become U.S. Assistant Secretary of Labor, and his mother, Lucille, was a teacher. After graduating from high school at age 13, he entered the University of Chicago to study mathematics, receiving a BS in 1940, an MS in 1941, and a PhD in 1942. He taught mathematics at Tuskegee Institute (today Tuskegee University) for three semesters before becoming a mathematical physicist at the University of Chicago's Metallurgical Laboratory, where he worked on the Manhattan Project, the U.S. effort to build an atomic bomb. Since most physical phenomena can be explained in terms of mathematical formulas, Wilkins's job was to develop formulas that could test theories about initiating and controlling the chain reactions that split uranium atoms, thus releasing untold amounts of energy.

In 1946, the year before he married Gloria Stevens, with whom he had two children, Wilkins went to work as a mathematician for the American Optical Company in Buffalo, New York. In this capacity, he developed the mathematical formulas needed to design and fabricate lenses for high-power telescopes capable of pinpointing a specific star in a distant galaxy. In 1950, he joined the staff at the United Nuclear Corporation in White Plains, New York, as a senior mathematician, and over the next 10 years, he directed the company's design work concerning nuclear power plants for ships and submarines. Although he was intimately knowledgeable about the physics of nuclear power, he knew little about the engineering aspects of designing power plants; so he entered the engineering program at New York University and received a BS and an MS in mechanical engineering in 1957 and 1960, respectively.

Armed with advanced degrees in physics and engineering, Wilkins was one of the most qualified people in the United States to develop new theories concerning the generation of nuclear power and then to design the systems by which those theories could be implemented. He put his skills to use at the General Atomic Company in San Diego, where from 1960 to 1970 he directed the company's computational research, as well as its defense science and engineering center. Following a six-year stint as a professor of applied mathematical physics at Howard University, where he helped to establish the first PhD program in mathematics at a historically black college, in 1976 he returned to his work with nuclear power design at the Argonne National Laboratory outside Chicago, the nation's largest laboratory devoted to developing practical applications for nuclear energy. The following year, he became a senior-level manager at the Idaho National Engineering Laboratory in Idaho Falls, whose mission was to design low-cost nuclear power plants. In 1984, he returned to Argonne; although he retired the following year, he remained as a consultant until 1990, when he accepted a professorship in applied mathematics and mathematical physics at Clark Atlanta University.

Wilkins published more than 100 technical papers during his career. The names of some of the journals and published conference proceedings in which they appeared testify to the width and breadth of his contributions to science: *Journal of Aerospace Sciences, Journal of the Optical Society of*

Physicist Ernest Wilkins helped design the world's first atomic bombs. (Bettmann/Corbis)

America, Nuclear Engineering and Design, Nuclear Science and Engineering, Physical Review, International Conference on the Peaceful Uses of Atomic Energy, and *Proceedings of the Heat Transfer and Fluid Mechanics Institute.* His most important contribution in nuclear physics is the development of radiation shielding against gamma radiation, which is emitted during electron decay of a nuclear source. He developed mathematical models by which the amount of gamma radiation absorbed by a given material can be calculated, and these models were used extensively by researchers in space-related and nuclear science projects.

In addition to his other duties, Wilkins served a term as president of the American Nuclear Society. His many honors include election into the American Association for the Advancement of Science and the National Academy of Engineering.

See also: American Association for the Advancement of Science; Clark Atlanta University; Howard University; Physics; Tuskegee University

REFERENCES AND FURTHER READING

Kessler, James H., J. S. Kidd, Renee A. Kidd, and Katherine A. Morin, eds. *Distinguished African American Scientists of the 20th Century.* Phoenix, AZ: Oryx Press, 1996: 331–334.

Mathematicians of the African Diaspora. "J. Ernest Wilkins, Jr." [Online article or information; retrieved December 9, 2005.] http://www.math.buffalo.edu/mad/PEEPS/wilkns_jearnest.

Spangenburg, Ray, and Kit Moser. *African Americans in Science, Math, and Invention*. New York: Facts On File, 2003: 222–223.

Williams, Daniel H.
(1856–1931) Surgeon

Daniel Williams performed one of the first successful surgical operations involving the human heart. He also played a leading role in founding several institutions for promoting medical education and development for black professionals and medical treatment for black patients, and he is sometimes referred to as the father of the modern black hospital.

Williams was born on January 18, 1856, in Hollidaysburg, Pennsylvania. His father, Daniel, was a barber, and his mother, Sarah, was a homemaker. At age 11, he was apprenticed to a shoemaker in Baltimore, but he left this trade shortly thereafter. After wandering the country for about five years, he settled in Janesville, Wisconsin, and went to work as a barber. One of his customers was a local physician, Henry Palmer, who took Williams on as an apprentice. In 1880, Williams completed his apprenticeship and entered Northwestern University's Chicago Medical College, receiving an MD in 1883. He interned for a year at Chicago's Mercy Hospital and then went into private practice on Chicago's South Side. By 1889, he had taken on the additional duties of attending surgeon at the South Side Dispensary, attending physician at the Protestant Orphan Asylum, instructor of anatomy at the Chicago Medical College, surgeon for the City Railroad Company, and member of the Illinois State Board of Health. He was also the driving force behind the effort to open a hospital in Chicago, where black physicians could enjoy staff privileges and where black nurses could receive better training for their profession. In 1891, this effort was rewarded by the opening of Provident Hospital and Training School. In addition to serving as Provident's founder, he also served as its first chief surgeon.

In 1893, Williams was presented with a patient who was suffering from massive internal bleeding resulting from a knife wound. At the time, most surgeons refused to even contemplate performing heart surgery, partly because opening the chest was a risky and dangerous procedure and partly because nothing was known about the various blood types, thus making it impossible to safely administer blood to a patient in need. Nevertheless, Williams determined that the procedure must be performed or the patient would surely die. He cut a small opening between the ribs through which he could observe the heart, and he discovered that the knife had ruptured a blood vessel and punctured the pericardium (the protective membrane surrounding the heart). Working quickly, he tied off the blood vessel and sutured the puncture, thus

Surgeon Daniel Hale Williams performed one of the first successful surgical operations on the human heart. (National Library of Medicine)

saving the patient's life. A Chicago newspaper reported the story immediately following the operation, and Williams quickly gained national recognition. In 1896, he published the details of the procedure in *Medical Journal*; not only did the article encourage other surgeons to begin performing heart surgery, it also provided them with a model for developing their own procedures for operating on the heart.

Williams never claimed to have performed the first successful open-heart surgery, but others argued in his favor for such an honor. It now seems clear that H. C. Dalton, a physician in St. Louis, Missouri, had performed an operation almost identical to Williams's in 1891, two years before Williams's operation, and the German physician Ludwig Rehn successfully operated in 1896 on the myocardium (the muscular substance of the heart). Nevertheless, Williams is one of the pioneers of heart surgery, and his achievement helped remove much of the mystery concerning this delicate and risky procedure.

In 1894, Williams was named chief surgeon of Freedmen's Hospital in Washington, D.C. Although Freedmen's had once been the nation's foremost institution for the medical treatment of African Americans, by the time Williams arrived it had become little more than an insane asylum for the indigent. Over the next four years, Williams worked to restore Freedmen's to its former glory, in the process setting up a department of pathology and bacteriology while reviving the existing departments. By 1898, when he returned to Provident, Freedmen's was well on its way to becoming a top-flight medical institution once again.

Williams remained at Provident until 1912, when he became attending surgeon at St. Luke's Hospital, Chicago. In addition to his duties at St. Luke's, he served as a consultant to various groups wishing to open hospitals like Provident in their communities, and in this capacity he helped to open 40 interracial hospitals in 20 states. Meanwhile, in 1895, he cofounded the National Medical Association as a professional organization for black physicians whose race barred them from admission to the American Medical Association.

In 1898, Williams married the former Alice Johnson. He retired from the practice of medicine in 1926, and he died at his home in Idlewild, Michigan, on August 4, 1931. His many honors include the issuance in 1970 of a U.S. postage stamp in his honor.

See also: American Medical Association; Freedmen's Hospital; National Medical Association; Provident Hospital and Training School

REFERENCES AND FURTHER READING

Hayden, Robert C. *Eleven African American Doctors*, rev. ed. New York: Twenty-First Century Books, 1992: 186–203.

Organ, Claude H., and Margaret M. Kosiba, eds. *A Century of Black Surgeons: The U.S.A. Experience*. Norman, OK: Transcript Press, 1987: 311–334.

Spangenburg, Ray, and Kit Moser. *African Americans in Science, Math, and Invention*. New York: Facts On File, 2003: 223–226.

Woods, Geraldine Pittman
(1921–1999) Science Administrator

Geraldine Woods gave up a promising career as a neuroembryologist to become a homemaker. She later returned to science as an administrator of government initiatives to increase the number of minorities in the basic sciences and the amount of federal funding making its way into the hands of minority researchers.

Woods was born Geraldine Pittman on January 29, 1921, in West Palm Beach, Florida. Her parents, Oscar and Susie, owned and operated a farm and a lumber mill. She attended Talladega College (Alabama) for two years before transferring to Howard University, where she received a BS in biology in 1942. She then entered Radcliffe College, the female division of Harvard University, and received an MS in biology in 1943 and a PhD in embryology from Harvard in 1945. Her doctoral research examined the process by which cells in the spinal cord of an embryo develop into nerve cells, particularly those that activate muscles.

Upon receiving her doctorate, Woods returned to Howard as an instructor of biology. She gave up her scientific career the following year, however, when she married Robert Woods and relocated to Los Angeles, where her husband had opened a medical practice. For the next 15 years, she focused her efforts on supporting her husband and raising their three children. Then, in the early 1960s, she became more involved in community affairs, particularly those designed to enhance the quality of life for minorities. A tireless worker, she was eventually named to the personnel board of the California Department of Education and to the National Advisory Council of the National Institute of General Medical Sciences (NIGMS). In 1965, she was invited by Lady Bird Johnson, the first lady, to come to Washington, D.C., to help establish Project Head Start, a federal initiative designed to provide children from low-income families with access to nursery school and kindergarten programs. Later, she was named to the Defense Advisory Commission on Women in the Service, and in this capacity, she traveled to various military bases to see how things were going for women in terms of their general treatment, their opportunities for advancement, and utilization of their skills.

While serving on NIGMS's advisory council, Woods came to realize that few of the requests for NIH grant money came from historically black colleges and universities, and that few of the requests from these colleges were approved, mostly because of how they were written. She also realized that the process by which NIH and other federal organizations award money was poorly understood in the black community. Thus, upon becoming a special consultant to NIGMS in 1969, she focused her efforts as a special consultant on establishing the Minority Biomedical Research Support (MBRS) program. As director of MBRS, she held seminars and tutorials at minority institutions so that minority scientists could learn how to write a grant application that would be approved. Eventually, officials at Xavier University of Louisiana established an annual symposium at their school for grant review committees and prospective applicants from historically black colleges all over the country so that they could better understand the procedures by which grant applications are reviewed. Largely as a result of MBRS, the percentage of NIH and other federal funding for the basic sciences earmarked for black biomedical researchers increased exponentially.

Once the success of MBRS was guaranteed, Woods turned her attention to the problem of recruiting and retaining minority students for careers in the basic sciences. To this end, she helped establish the Minority Access to Research Careers (MARC) program. This NIH-sponsored program provided scholarships and career counseling to prospective minority students while providing financial assistance to minority doctoral candidates. It also established a number of visiting professorships for minority professors at historically white colleges, where they could forge their own ties with researchers doing work similar to their own, thus elevating the quality of teaching and research at historically black colleges while making science careers at the latter even more meaningful and rewarding.

In 1991, Woods retired from NIH to her home in Aliso Viejo, California. She died on December 27, 1999, in Los Angeles.

See also: Biology; Historically Black Colleges and Universities; Howard University; Minority Access to Research Careers; Minority Biomedical Research Support; National Institute of General Medical Sciences; Xavier University of Louisiana

REFERENCES AND FURTHER READING

Kessler, James H., J. S. Kidd, Renee A. Kidd, and Katherine A. Morin, eds. *Distinguished African American Scientists of the 20th Century*. Phoenix, AZ: Oryx Press, 1996: 346–350.

Spangenburg, Ray, and Kit Moser. *African Americans in Science, Math, and Invention*. New York: Facts On File, 2003: 226–227.

Warren, Wini. *Black Women Scientists in the United States*. Bloomington: Indiana University Press, 1999: 269–277.

Wright, Jane C.
(1919–) Oncologist

When Jane Wright became an oncologist, practically nothing was known about chemotherapy as a treatment for cancer. Wright helped change this situation by testing scores of potential chemotherapy drugs on a variety of tumors in animals, tissue cultures, and humans. In addition to discovering two effective chemotherapy drugs, she helped establish many of the methods and procedures for testing potential chemotherapy drugs.

Wright was born on November 30, 1919, in New York City. Her father was the eminent medical researcher Louis T. Wright, and her mother, Corinne, was a homemaker. After receiving a BA from Smith College (Massachusetts) in 1942, she entered New York Medical College and received an MD three years later. She completed her internship at New York's Bellevue Hospital and her residency at Harlem Hospital, and in 1948, she went to work for the New York City public school system as a physician. In 1947, she married David Jones, with whom she had two children.

Shortly after Wright became a school physician, her father founded the Harlem Hospital Cancer Research Foundation. At the time, cancer chemotherapy was in its infancy; so Wright's father established his foundation to facilitate the testing of cancer chemotherapy drugs. In 1949, she returned to Harlem Hospital as a clinician with the foundation, and when her father died three years later, she took over his position as the foundation's director. One of her

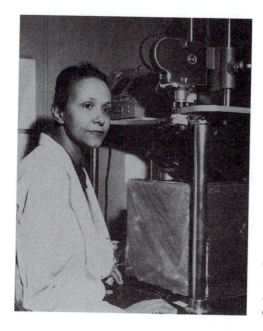

Oncologist Jane C. Wright conducted some of the earliest research concerning the use of chemotherapeutic drugs to treat cancer in humans. (Library of Congress)

first moves as director was to move the foundation to the New York University (NYU) Medical School so that it could have access to better facilities, equipment, and staffing. In 1955, she took on the additional duties of teaching surgical research at NYU and directing its cancer chemotherapy research.

When Wright began experimenting with chemotherapy, researchers had discovered only one drug that was known to work on cancer. That drug was mechlorethamine, which was effective as a treatment for certain lymphomas (tumors arising in the lymphatic system). Beginning from this slim base, Wright and her colleagues set out to learn more about how tumors respond to drugs.

Over the next 40 years, she oversaw the development of increasingly sophisticated methods for treating tumorous animals and tissue cultures with a variety of drugs, but in the early days, these methods took mostly a hit-or-miss approach, as so little was known about chemotherapy. In the process of testing potential chemotherapy drugs such as triethylene melamine, triethylene phosphoramide, puromycin, adrenocorticotropic hormone (ACTH), folic acid antagonists, actinomycin D, streptonigrin, mithramycin, and fluorouracil, they discovered that tumors do not always grow or react to treatment the same way. A tumor that spreads rapidly in one patient might spread slowly in another, a drug that is effective against one kind of tumor might not work at all against another type of tumor, and a chemotherapy drug that works against tumors in animals or under laboratory conditions might not work when administered to a human cancer patient.

Despite the difficulties facing Wright and her colleagues, they made considerable progress. First, they established many of the early protocols for testing cancer chemotherapy drugs, in the process showing other researchers which methods and procedures did and did not work. For example, Wright developed the techniques known as isolation perfusion, whereby a solid tumor is saturated with a chemotherapeutic drug, and regional perfusion, whereby the general area, usually in the head or neck, is saturated. Second, they found several drugs that were effective and safe for use in chemotherapy. These drugs include triethylene thiophosphoramide, which is an effective treatment for advanced malignant melanoma or skin cancer, and Dihydro E. 73, which they showed to be effective against a number of different tumors. Third, they taught other researchers that cancer research requires patience and fortitude but that these virtues are eventually rewarded by the discovery of a new drug or treatment.

In 1964, Wright cofounded the American Society of Clinical Oncology, a professional organization for cancer researchers, and served as its first secretary-treasurer. She also served on the President's Commission on Heart Disease, Cancer, and Stroke and the National Advisory Cancer Council. In 1967, she returned to her alma mater, New York Medical College, to serve as dean, professor of surgery, and head of the cancer research laboratory. She stepped down as dean in 1975, but she continued to teach and conduct research until her retirement in 1987.

See also: Cancer; Harlem Hospital; Wright, Louis T.

REFERENCES AND FURTHER READING

Carey, Charles W. Jr. *American Scientists*. New York: Facts On File, 2005: 400–401.

Hayden, Robert C. *Eleven African American Doctors,* rev. ed. New York: Twenty-First Century Books, 1992: 124–137.

McMurray, Emily J., ed. *Notable Twentieth-Century Scientists*. Detroit, MI: Gale Research, 1995: 2257–2258.

Warren, Wini. *Black Women Scientists in the United States*. Bloomington: Indiana University Press, 1999: 277–284.

Wright, Louis T.
(1891–1952) Medical Researcher

Louis Wright contributed to several different areas of medical research. He supervised some of the first clinical tests of antibiotic drugs, he devised and supervised the testing of some of the first cancer chemotherapy drugs, he invented two devices for handling fractured bones, and he was a world expert on certain infections of the lymph system. The first black physician to be appointed to the staff of a major U.S. hospital, he also played a leadership role in eliminating racial segregation on hospital medical staffs throughout the country.

Wright was born on July 22, 1891, in La Grange, Georgia. His father, Ceah, was a physician and minister, and his mother, Lula, was a homemaker. His father died when he was three, after which he and his mother moved to Atlanta, where he grew up. Five years later, his mother married William F. Penn, a physician who took Wright on his rounds. Watching his stepfather in action made Wright want to become a doctor too; so, after graduating from Clark University (today Clark Atlanta University) in 1911, he entered Howard University Medical School (today Howard University College of Medicine), receiving an MD four years later.

Wright interned at Freedmen's Hospital in Washington, D.C., and while he was there, he became involved in a bit of a medical controversy. At the time, diphtheria was a disease that preyed on children by making it extremely difficult for them to breathe; so in the early 1900s, the pediatrician Bela Schick developed the Schick test to identify people who were not immune to diphtheria. The test is very simple and very effective; a small amount of diphtheria toxin is injected under the skin, and if the patient lacks immunity the skin in the immediate vicinity of the injection becomes visibly inflamed. Many white physicians, however, refused to perform the test on blacks, because they believed that the pigmentation of African American skin made it impossible to detect any resulting inflammation. Wright dispelled this notion simply by administering the test to people of various skin colors and demonstrating the highly noticeable inflammation that occurred in those without immunity.

After completing his internship, Wright returned to Atlanta to join his stepfather's practice. That same year, however, the United States entered World War I and Wright volunteered for the U.S. Army; he served with distinction in France as a medical officer. In 1918, he married Corinne Cooke, with whom he had two children, and the following year, he opened a private practice in New York City, his wife's hometown. In 1919, he became a clinical visiting assistant surgeon at Harlem Hospital, where he spent the rest of his medical career. In 1943, he was named director of surgery, and five years later, he was elected president of the hospital's medical board.

As a surgeon, Wright came into regular contact with broken bones of all sorts. He quickly became an expert on treating fractures, and he even developed two devices that improved the handling of fractured bones. One was a neck brace for handling upper vertebrae that had been fractured or dislocated, and the other was a special metal plate for treating certain fractures of the femur (thighbone). In 1937, the eminent orthopedic surgeon Charles Scudder invited Wright to write the chapter on head injuries in Scudder's book,

The Treatment of Fractures (Philadelphia, PA: W. B. Saunders Co., 1938), one of the foremost medical textbooks of the day.

Wright's most important contribution to medical research involved the testing of a number of drugs, particularly for use in cancer chemotherapy. In 1948, he arranged for Harlem Hospital to conduct the first clinical tests on humans of aureomycin, one of the first antibiotic drugs, and then he personally oversaw the conduct of the tests. He also tested a number of other antibiotic drugs, and in the process developed a drug treatment for the sexually transmitted disease known as lymphogranuloma venereum or lymphogranuloma inguinale. This condition results when the lymphatic system (a system of channels and ducts that filter bacteria from the blood) becomes infected by the bacterial parasite *Chlamydia trachomatis,* and Wright discovered that *C. trachomatis* is susceptible to the antibiotic drugs chlortetracycline and chloramphenicol.

Wright's work with antibiotics led him into the study of cancer chemotherapy, and in 1948, he obtained a grant from the National Cancer Institute to establish the Cancer Research Foundation at Harlem Hospital as a vehicle for conducting some of the first clinical tests of chemotherapy drugs. So little was known about chemotherapy at the time that Wright, who was essentially an orthopedic surgeon, quickly became one of the foremost authorities on chemotherapy. One of the first groups of potential chemotherapy drugs he investigated was folic acid antagonists; because folic acid is required for cell growth, it made sense that inhibiting the action of folic acid in cancerous cells might keep those cells from reproducing. Largely as a result of his study, folic acid antagonists are widely used in cancer chemotherapy today. He helped to develop some of the earliest protocols for conducting chemotherapy research, and he wrote many of the earliest articles on chemotherapy to appear in prominent scientific and medical journals, including the *Harlem Hospital Bulletin*, which he founded and edited. He was joined in this endeavor by his daughter, Jane C. Wright, who eventually took his place as the foundation's director.

In addition to his contributions to medical research, Wright was active in the Civil Rights Movement. He was involved in the affairs of the National Association for the Advancement of Colored People (NAACP) all his adult life, and from 1935 to 1952, he chaired its board of directors. He used his influence in this position to make Harlem Hospital one of the first hospitals in the United States to integrate its medical staff. Buoyed by this success, in 1937, he helped establish an NAACP program to eliminate racial discrimination in health care throughout the country on the grounds that separate is not equal, particularly in terms of health care. He died of a heart attack on October 8, 1952, in New York City.

See also: Cancer; Clark Atlanta University; Freedmen's Hospital; Harlem Hospital; Howard University College of Medicine; Medical Research; National Cancer Institute; Wright, Jane C.

REFERENCES AND FURTHER READING

Carey, Charles W. Jr. *American Scientists.* New York: Facts On File, 2006: 401–402.

Hayden, Robert C. *Eleven African American Doctors,* rev. ed. New York: Twenty-First Century Books, 1992: 52–71.

Spangenburg, Ray, and Kit Moser. *African Americans in Science, Math, and Invention.* New York: Facts On File, 2003: 230–231.

Young, Roger Arliner
(1899–1964) Zoologist

Roger Young was the first African American woman to earn a PhD in zoology. Her research contributed to a better understanding of the inner workings of *Paramecium.* She also published several notable studies on the effects of direct and indirect radiation on sea urchin eggs.

Young was born on August 20, 1899, in Clifton Forge, Virginia. Her parents' names and occupations are unknown. As a girl she moved with her parents to Burgettstown, Pennsylvania, where she grew up. In 1916, she entered Howard University as a part-time student to study music. She took her first science course five years later from Ernest E. Just, who at the time was teaching at Howard. She immediately changed her major, and in 1923, she received a BS in zoology. That same year, she joined the Howard faculty as a zoology instructor and entered the graduate program at the University of Chicago as a part-time student, receiving an MS in zoology in 1926.

Young's early research concerned the unicellular protozoan known as *Paramecium.* Her brilliant study of *Paramecium*'s excretory apparatus was published in the prestigious journal *Science* in 1924. She later wrote an equally brilliant exposition on how *Paramecium* regulates the concentration of salt within itself. Her later work was focused on the fertilization process in the eggs of the sea urchin, and she published several papers outlining the effects of direct and indirect exposure of X-rays and ultraviolet light on the development of sea urchin eggs.

By some accounts, Young was romantically involved with Just. By all accounts, he served as her mentor. He tutored her after she received poor grades in her first science courses, he helped her get accepted into graduate school and then helped arrange for financial aid, he served as her department chair at Howard, and he invited her to conduct experiments with him during the summers at the Marine Biological Laboratory in Woods Hole, Massachusetts. In 1935, however, they had a falling-out; perhaps coincidentally, Young was fired from Howard the following year. Undaunted, she entered the graduate program at the University of Pennsylvania, receiving her PhD in zoology in 1940.

In 1940, Young joined the faculty at the North Carolina College for Negroes (today North Carolina Central University) in Durham. After a few years, she left to become head of the biology department at Shaw University in nearby Raleigh, but returned to the Durham school in 1947. Unfortunately, the strain of having to support her invalid mother, putting herself through school, and dealing with her failed relationship with Just apparently proved to be too much for her. She had suffered what was apparently a nervous breakdown in 1930, and the lingering effects of this breakdown may have contributed to her falling-out with Just and her leaving Howard. She may have had a relapse around 1947 and then again in 1953, when her mother died. Let go by North Carolina College, she taught briefly at Paul Quinn College (Texas) and Jackson State College (today Jackson State University, Mississippi) before being admitted to the Mississippi State Mental Asylum in the late 1950s. Discharged in 1962, she taught briefly at Southern University in New Orleans, before her health failed her again. She died, having never married, on November 9, 1964, in New Orleans.

See also: Howard University; Jackson State University; Just, Ernest E.; North Carolina Central University; Southern University and A&M College System

REFERENCES AND FURTHER READING

JustGarciaHill.org. "Young, Roger Arliner, Ph.D., (1899–1964)." [Online article or information; retrieved October 30, 2007.] http://justgarciahill.org/jghdocs/webbiography.asp.

Spangenburg, Ray, and Kit Moser. *African Americans in Science, Math, and Invention.* New York: Facts On File, 2003: 232–233.

Warren, Wini. *Black Women Scientists in the United States.* Bloomington: Indiana University Press, 1999: 287–295.

Issues

Even though African Americans and their institutions have made many contributions to science, a number of issues cloud their future in science. One set of issues relates to science and medical education for blacks. Despite heightened efforts by a number of public and private entities, the number of blacks who annually receive MD or PhD degrees in the sciences stubbornly refuses to increase appreciably. A number of problems have been singled out as the root cause of this situation, such as the high price of obtaining an advanced degree; indifference on the part of administrators, faculty, and fellow students regarding the educational and social needs of African American students; and a pervasive attitude among blacks themselves that scientific research is not something that black people do. A number of solutions have been suggested for each of these problems, but as of 2007, the relative absence of black science students remains an alarming problem.

Related to this problem is the issue of science and medical careers for blacks. Presumably, if African American students were assured that they could enjoy a long and successful career in science, more would be interested in pursuing careers as scientists in the first place. It has been suggested that one of the biggest reasons for the lack of science careers for blacks is the persistence of the so-called good ole boy network that pervades the nation's major research universities and institutions; because blacks do not have access to this network, they find it difficult to obtain positions at these institutions. A number of studies have been conducted in an effort to understand the true nature of the problem and to develop solutions to solve it, but as of 2007, the problem remained a real one.

Another set of issues related to African Americans and science involves health-related disparities and inequalities in the quality of health and of the health care that is available to the African American community in general. Health disparities are most disparate in terms of the diseases and medical conditions related to asthma, cardiovascular disease, cancer, diabetes, HIV/AIDS, obesity, and sickle cell disease. Again, fingers have been pointed at a number of potential root causes, such as the persistence of racial prejudice among nonminority health care providers, the inability of blacks in general to afford quality health care, the reluctance of blacks in general to seek quality health care until it is too late, and lifestyles and differences related to genetics that make blacks more susceptible to certain diseases and medical conditions. As with the other issues, much effort is being made to address health disparities, but as of 2007, the problem continued to plague the African American community and the nation.

Asthma

Asthma is one of several medical conditions that affect African Americans disproportionately, thus contributing in a major way to health disparities. Asthma is a chronic disease of the respiratory system that causes the airway to become inflamed and lined with excessive amounts of mucus. As a result, the airway narrows, causing wheezing, shortness of breath, chest tightness, coughing, and, in extreme cases, death. Asthma attacks are triggered by allergens (such as pollen and cigarette smoke), cold, warm or moist air, exercise, emotional stress, and viruses such as the ones that cause colds.

As of 1998, the death rate from asthma was three times higher for blacks than for whites, and hospitalization rates related to asthma were more than three times higher for blacks than for whites. African Americans living in big cities suffer even more disproportionately. In New York City, for example, African Americans are five times more likely to suffer from asthma than the general U.S. population, and black male New Yorkers are 11 times more likely than white male New Yorkers to die from asthma. Consequently, several historically black research institutions have taken a special interest in asthma and how to control it. The federal government also conducts and supports research designed to eliminate asthma as a health disparity under the auspices of the National Institutes of Health (NIH).

In 1991, New York City's Harlem Hospital opened the Asthma Center, one of the first clinical research centers in the country to focus on asthma. One of the center's initiatives, the Asthma Prevention Project, conducts clinical studies to identify risk factors, examine the level of care given to asthma patients who frequent emergency rooms, and determine the roles of stress, emotions, and cultural health practices on the prevalence and severity of asthma in the city's black community. The Meharry School of Graduate Studies and Research in Nashville, Tennessee, operates the NIH-affiliated Asthma Disparities Center. The center's activities focus on understanding why minorities, low-income groups, and pregnant women tend to suffer disproportionately from asthma and related conditions. At Alabama State University in Montgomery, researchers are developing a vaccine against human respiratory syncytial virus

African Americans are much more likely than European Americans to suffer or die from asthma. (U.S. Department of Health and Human Services)

(RSV), a virus that causes respiratory infections that can trigger asthma, by rearranging certain RSV genes so as to negate its ability to infect a host organism. The National Medical Association's Cobb Institute conducts a number of research projects related to understanding and controlling asthma, and Xavier University of Louisiana's College of Pharmacy in New Orleans conducts cutting-edge research concerning pharmaceutical drugs for treating asthma.

As part of its ongoing initiative to reduce and ultimately eliminate health disparities, NIH has devoted a considerable amount of attention and resources to studying asthma. The National Heart, Lung, and Blood Institute (NHLBI) conducts and supports research to identify the genes associated with asthma and to describe how they contribute to the development of mild, moderate, and severe asthma. Other NHLBI asthma-related research evaluates the efficacy of anti-inflammatory medications, as well as their long-term effects on the physical growth and development of asthmatic children, particularly the growth and development of their lungs. NHLBI has also established cooperative centers of research to study asthma disparities in relation to prevalence, emergency room use, hospitalization rates, and mortality among African Americans, other minorities, and the general population. The NHLBI National Asthma Education and Prevention Program seeks to improve asthma control in minority communities that are disproportionately affected by asthma.

The National Institute of Allergy and Infectious Diseases (NIAID) National Cooperative Inner-City Asthma Study develops innovative asthma intervention programs to reduce the severity of asthma among inner-city children in 23 urban communities nationwide. It also assists the Centers for Disease Control and Prevention in the dissemination of the Asthma Treatment Guidelines to inner-city children with asthma. The National Institute of Environmental Health Sciences (NIEHS) conducts and supports research that studies various environmental triggers of asthma. The Five Cities Study assesses the effects of ozone, acid aerosols, and particulate air pollution on the respiratory function of inner-city minority children; the Inner-City Asthma Study focuses on allergens and environmental tobacco smoke; Developing a Geographic Framework for Studying Respiratory Health in Harlem deals with diesel exhaust and smokestack emissions; the Community-Based Prevention/Intervention Research Program studies cockroaches and dust; and the National Allergen Study investigates the major allergens.

See also: Alabama State University; Harlem Hospital; Health Disparities; National Heart, Lung, and Blood Institute; National Institute of Allergy and Infectious Diseases; National Institute of Environmental Health Sciences; National Institutes of Health; National Medical Association; Xavier University of Louisiana

References and Further Reading
Kinnon, Joy Bennett. "Is Our Air Killing Us? The Asthma Attack on Black America—The Prevalence of Asthma in the African American Community." *Ebony* (July 2001). [Online article or information; retrieved August 2, 2007.] http://findarticles.com/p/articles/mi_m1077/is_9_56/ai_76285233

Cancer

Cancer is one of several medical conditions that contribute to health disparities. The disease is characterized by a group of cells in a tissue that grow and divide without limit, then invade and destroy adjacent tissues and sometimes tissues in distant parts of the body. In the developed nations of the world, cancer accounts for approximately 25 percent of all deaths. African Americans, however, tend to develop cancer at an earlier age, seek treatment for cancer at a later stage in its development, and die more frequently from cancer than the general U.S. population.

This article addresses cancer from two perspectives. The first concerns the research conducted over the years by African American medical researchers and scientists to understand more about cancer and to develop effective methods for treating it. The second concerns the scientific research efforts by public and private entities to reduce and ultimately eliminate health disparities as they relate to cancer, particularly in terms of breast cancer and prostate cancer.

Two of the earliest African American cancer researchers are Louis T. Wright and Jane C. Wright. During his early career, Louis Wright was an orthopedic

One of the first medical researchers to study how to treat cancer with chemotherapy was Louis Wright. (Library of Congress)

surgeon at New York City's Harlem Hospital, but in the 1940s, he became more interested in antibiotics (pharmaceutical drugs that can kill bacteria that are harmful to humans). With the assistance of the National Cancer Institute, he established one of the first chemotherapy testing centers, the Cancer Research Foundation of Harlem Hospital, and began testing antibiotics that could potentially be used as chemotherapeutic drugs. As the foundation's director, Wright oversaw the development of some of the earliest protocols for conducting chemotherapy research, and he wrote many of the earliest articles on chemotherapy to appear in prominent scientific and medical journals. He also experimented with folic acid, a key requirement for cell growth, and his work led to the development of folic acid antagonists, which are widely used in cancer chemotherapy today.

Wright was succeeded as director of the foundation by his daughter, Jane C. Wright. For years, Jane Wright had worked with her father and played a key role in his important discoveries. Under her direction, the foundation's research staff continued to develop new techniques for testing chemotherapeutic drugs such as isolation perfusion, whereby a solid tumor is saturated with a chemotherapeutic drug, and regional perfusion, whereby the general area in which the tumor is located, usually in the head or neck, is saturated. The father and daughter also developed two of the first chemotherapeutic drugs, triethylene thiophosphoramide, for treating skin cancer, and Dihydro E. 73, for treating a number of different tumors.

One of the researchers who worked with the Wrights is the cell biologist Jewel Plummer Cobb. Over the course of her career, she investigated the chemotherapeutic properties of a number of chemical compounds, including mustard gas, various antibiotics such as aureomycin and actinomycin, and the hormones testosterone and estradiol. In the process, she helped develop the first protocols for studying potential chemotherapeutic drugs. Cobb also pioneered methods for cultivating and experimenting with cancer cells in test tubes and petri dishes, thus making it easier for cancer researchers to study how cancer cells grow in a laboratory environment.

Three other black scientists who made contributions to the development of cancer chemotherapeutic drugs are the chemists Samuel P. Massie, Henry C. McBay, and Lloyd N. Ferguson. Massie was an organic chemist whose research on the pesticide phenothiazine eventually led to the development of an important chemotherapeutic drug for cancer. Although phenothiazine itself is too toxic to administer to humans, Massie showed that certain derivatives of phenothiazine, whose toxicity is greatly reduced, can be used to treat cancer safely and effectively. McBay was a chemist whose research interests roamed far and wide. As part of a research project to develop methods for safely handling the various peroxide compounds, which tend to be unstable, he developed a method for synthesizing various other compounds from them. The most important of these compounds was a protein that proved to be highly effective as a treatment for prostate cancer. Ferguson was a structural chemist whose research included experiments with the biochemistry of cancer chemotherapy. He sought to understand the behavior of chemotherapy drugs based on their structural arrangement, such as the angle at which a molecule's atoms bond, and in the process, he offered several insights that led to the development of more effective chemotherapy drugs.

Renty B. Franklin is a physiologist whose research focused on hormones and mineral levels, but he also did some important work concerning prostate cancer, which affects African Americans disproportionately. A normal prostate gland accumulates a large amount of zinc, and Franklin was able to demonstrate that high levels of zinc control the growth of normal prostate cells. He also demonstrated that prostate cells that have lost the ability to accumulate zinc tend to become cancerous. This finding led him and others to search for ways to control prostate cancer by restoring the ability of prostate cells to accumulate zinc.

Eugene W. Adams specialized in veterinary pathology, the study of the progression of disease in animals, but his work contributed considerably to a better understanding of how cancer progresses in humans. Adams experimented on canines, and he showed that a dog from which a tumor has been surgically removed will not develop that same type of tumor again, even if new growths of the tumor are surgically transplanted from another dog. He also showed that the blood of a dog receiving a transplanted tumor develops the same type of proteins as are produced in the blood in reaction to a viral infection. Adams's work supported the findings of a number of other cancer researchers, which led many in the medical community at large to theorize that some cancers are caused by viruses.

James H. M. Henderson is a plant physiologist who experimented with plant growth hormones known as auxins, but his work had important implications for medical researchers who study cancer in humans. While studying a form of plant cancer known as crown gall tumor in the sunflower, he discovered that the malignant tissue is able to synthesize its own growth hormone, something that normal sunflower tissue is unable to do. This discovery gave cancer researchers an important clue as to how cancerous cells are able to reproduce themselves so rapidly.

Guion S. Bluford Jr. is best remembered as one of the first black astronauts, but as a mission specialist, he conducted an important experiment related to cancer. The experiment studied the effectiveness of an advanced technology known as continuous flow electrophoresis system (CFES). CFES breaks down living molecules into their constituent chemical compounds, conducts a chemical analysis of those compounds, and then identifies the compounds that are potentially cancerous.

Patricia S. Cowings is another NASA scientist whose work is related to cancer. Her medical research focused primarily on developing a method to alleviate space sickness, a condition similar to seasickness or motion sickness. Her method, the Autogenic Feedback Training Exercise (AFTE), uses biofeedback techniques to cope with space sickness, but it was later adapted for use by cancer patients to help them cope with the nausea associated with chemotherapy treatment.

LaSalle D. Leffall is a surgical oncologist who specialized in cancers of the breast, colon, rectum, head, and neck. He developed a number of surgical techniques for extracting tumors without harming the adjacent nontumorous tissue. He also served as president of the American Cancer Society, and in this position, he did much to educate African Americans about the dangers of cancer, as well as about the necessity and availability of early diagnosis and treatment.

Because cancer poses such a serious threat to the African American community, a number of historically black colleges, universities, and organizations conduct cancer research programs. The Clark Atlanta University Center for Cancer Research and Therapeutic Development conducts a number of studies of breast and prostate cancer, and the Florida A&M University Center for Minority Prostate Cancer Training and Research focuses on prostate cancer. The Howard University College of Medicine and the Howard University

Hospital Cancer Center conduct the African-American Hereditary Prostate Cancer Study, which seeks to establish a genetic basis for prostate cancer in African American men. Other cancer research projects at Howard include investigations of how such factors as hormones, dietary fat, cooking practices, and high levels of stress lead to higher rates of breast cancer among black women. As part of its cancer research program, the Jackson State University Center of Excellence in Minority Health studies the ability of an African leafy vegetable known as ndole to inhibit the growth of breast cancer cells. The Meharry Medical College Center for Health Disparities studies how society, economics, culture, behavior, and biology contribute to disproportionately high rates of cancer among African Americans. As part of its cancer research, the Morehouse School of Medicine Clinical Research Center seeks to develop methods for reducing the incidence of colorectal cancer among middle-aged black men. The National Medical Association Cobb Institute conducts a number of research projects related to breast, prostate, and colorectal cancer. The North Carolina Central University Julius L. Chambers Biomedical/Biotechnology Research Institute studies the biochemical processes by which carcinogens cause cancer by stimulating the expression of the genes that regulate the growth and proliferation of cells. Tougaloo College has conducted research related to the epidermal growth factor receptor in human lung cancer cells and the effects of complementary and alternative medicine on patients with breast cancer. Virginia State University investigates the anticancer potential of laser-induced reagents known as indoles. The Wayne State University School of Medicine Center for Urban and African-American Health studies oxidative stress as a possible cause of the recurrence of breast cancer. Xavier University of Louisiana has conducted research concerning the ability of the chloroethoxyethane purines to fight cancer.

The federal government, working through the National Institutes of Health (NIH), has committed itself to overcoming health disparities in all areas, but it is particularly focused on cancer. To this end, a number of NIH institutes conduct and support research related to breast cancer, prostate cancer, and colorectal cancer, the types of cancer that plague African Americans the most. The National Cancer Institute Comprehensive Minority Biomedical Branch seeks to end health disparities in cancer by increasing the number of African American cancer researchers, as minority researchers have historically shown more interest in addressing health disparities than nonminority researchers. The National Institute of Complementary and Alternative Medicine studies the efficacy and safety of PC SPES, a Chinese herbal preparation, as a treatment for prostate cancer, and another project at the center investigates the impact of personal and group prayer on immune responses in African American women who have been treated for breast cancer. The National Human Genome Research Institute African American Hereditary Prostate Cancer Study

Network seeks to determine whether genetics plays a role in the development of prostate cancer in African American men. The National Institute of Dental and Craniofacial Research investigates why African Americans are twice as susceptible to oral or pharyngeal cancers as the general population. The National Institute of Environmental Health Sciences investigates the links of exposure to environmental pollutants, such as pesticides, plasticizers, and other industrial compounds to the abnormally high incidences of breast cancer in African American women.

See also: Adams, Eugene W.; Bluford, Guion S., Jr.; Clark Atlanta University; Cobb, Jewel Plummer; Cowings, Patricia S.; Ferguson, Lloyd N.; Florida A&M University; Franklin, Renty B.; Harlem Hospital; Health Disparities; Henderson, James H. M.; Howard University College of Medicine; Howard University Hospital; Jackson State University; Leffall, LaSalle D., Jr.; Massie, Samuel P., Jr.; McBay, Henry C.; Meharry Medical College; Morehouse School of Medicine; National Cancer Institute; National Human Genome Research Institute; National Institute of Dental and Craniofacial Research; National Institute of Environmental Health Sciences; National Institutes of Health; National Medical Association; North Carolina Central University; Tougaloo College; Virginia State University; Wayne State University; Wright, Jane C.; Wright, Louis T.; Xavier University of Louisiana

REFERENCES AND FURTHER READING

Blackman, Dionne J., and Christopher M. Masi. "Racial and Ethnic Disparities in Breast Cancer Mortality: Are We Doing Enough to Address the Root Causes?" *Journal of Clinical Oncology* 24, 14 (May 10, 2006): 2170–2178.

Merrill, Ray M., and Otis W. Brawley. "Prostate Cancer Incidence and Rates of Mortality among White and Black Men." *Epidemiology* 8, 2 (March 1997): 126–131.

Rebbeck, Timothy R., et al. "Genetics, Epidemiology, and Cancer Disparities: Is It Black and White?" *Journal of Clinical Oncology* 24, 14 (May 10, 2006): 2164–2169.

Cardiovascular Disease

Cardiovascular disease (CVD) is one of several medical conditions that contribute to health disparities. CVD includes all of the medical conditions and diseases that affect the heart and blood vessels, including stroke and hypertension (high blood pressure). In industrialized societies, CVD is the leading cause of death, with heart disease alone accounting for 30 percent of all deaths. CVD is even more deadly among African Americans. Black Americans suffer from the highest rates of death from CVD in the industrialized world, about 33 percent higher for black men than white men and about 38 percent higher for black women than white women. Consequently, a number of historically black scientific organizations and research institutions devote a considerable amount of attention to reducing the prevalence of CVD among African Americans. The federal government, under the purview of the National Institutes of Health (NIH), also conducts and supports research aimed at reducing the prevalence of CVD among blacks.

Two professional organizations, the Association of Black Cardiologists (ABC) and the International Society on Hypertension in Blacks (ISHIB), were founded specifically to deal with the deleterious effects of CVD on people of color. ABC conducts conferences and programs, such as the Cardiovascular Summit and Conference of the Treatment of Cardiovascular Diseases in African Americans and the Symposium on Cardiovascular Disease in Women, that are devoted to disseminating the latest information about CVD research. It also funds the Center for Epidemiology, which conducts clinical trials of pharmaceutical drugs and innovative methods for treating CVD, and the Center for Women's Health, which focuses on the connections between obesity, especially when caused by poor nutrition and lack of exercise, and CVD in black women. ISHIB sponsors annual research conferences on hypertension, stroke, and other aspects of CVD among ethnic populations around the world, and it participates in clinical trials of various pharmaceutical drugs for reducing and controlling high blood pressure. Although the National Medical Association, the nation's largest organization of black physicians and surgeons, was not established specifically to address the problem of CVD among African Americans, its Cobb Institute conducts research related to arriving at a better understanding of why African Americans are so susceptible to CVD.

A number of historically black colleges and universities conduct extensive research concerning the causes and treatment of CVD in African Americans. The Charles R. Drew University of Medicine and Science Center for Natural Medicine and Prevention investigates the efficacy of transcendental meditation in preventing and treating hypertension, arteriosclerosis (hardening of the arteries), and other forms of CVD. The Florida A&M University Center for the Study of Cardiovascular Disease works to develop pharmaceutical treatments for arteriosclerosis. Howard University College of Medicine conducts clinical tests related to evaluating and reducing the risk factors for hypertension, heart attacks, and other forms of CVD. The Jackson State University Heart Study Coordinating Center oversees the Jackson Heart Study, which examines the factors that influence the development of cardiovascular disease in African American men and women in the Jackson, Mississippi, metropolitan area. The Jackson State Center of Excellence in Minority Health and human nutrition researchers at Lincoln University of Missouri study the efficacy of fitness activities and healthy dietary practices as a vehicle for reducing obesity, a major cause of CVD. Meharry Medical College studies how society, economics, cul-

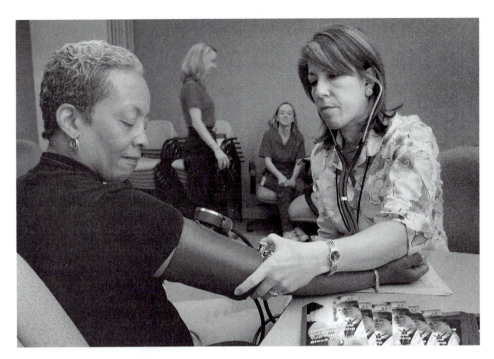

African Americans are more likely to suffer from cardiovascular disease, which includes such medical conditions as high blood pressure, than European Americans. (Centers for Disease Control and Prevention)

ture, behavior, and biology contribute to cardiovascular disease and stroke in black Americans. The Morehouse School of Medicine Clinical Research Center conducts clinical trials on CVD outpatients. The North Carolina Central University Julius L. Chambers Biomedical/Biotechnology Research Institute investigates the molecular, cellular, environmental, and genetic aspects of cardiovascular function under both healthy and diseased conditions. Undergraduate research at Tougaloo College has studied how the polymorphisms, or various physical forms, of a certain blood platelet receptor contribute to cardiovascular disease, as well as the relationship between spirituality and hypertension. The Wayne State University School of Medicine Center for Urban and African American Health studies how obesity, diet, and related lifestyle factors interact with the degree of environmental exposures, socioeconomic status, and psychosocial factors to exacerbate the development and progression of CVD in African Americans.

A number of NIH institutes, all working in cooperation with the National Center on Minority Health and Health Disparities, conduct and support research related to CVD in African Americans. The National Center for Complementary and Alternative Medicine Office of Special Populations has funded research at the Center for Natural Medicine and Prevention at Maharishi

University of Management (Iowa) concerning the use of Indian herbal formulations and meditation as a method for reducing hypertension in African Americans. The National Eye Institute studies the linkages in African Americans between glaucoma and CVD, especially hypertension. The National Heart, Lung, and Blood Institute studies the causes and development in African Americans of hypertension and ischemic heart disease, which results from restrictions in the body's blood supply. It also studies the effectiveness of reduced salt intake, increased physical activity, moderation of alcohol intake, and weight loss as means to reduce hypertension, as well as the effectiveness of diet, physical activity, and psychosocial and familial influences as ways to reduce obesity in young black Americans. The National Institute of Neurological Disorders and Stroke looks for connections in African Americans between CVD and epilepsy.

See also: Association of Black Cardiologists; Charles R. Drew University of Medicine and Science; Florida A&M University; Health Disparities; Historically Black Colleges and Universities; Howard University College of Medicine; International Society on Hypertension in Blacks; Jackson State University; Lincoln University of Missouri; Morehouse School of Medicine; National Center for Complementary and Alternative Medicine; National Center for Minority Health and Health Disparities; National Eye Institute; National Heart, Lung, and Blood Institute; National Institute of Neurological Disorders and Stroke; National Institutes of Health; National Medical Association; North Carolina Central University; Obesity; Tougaloo College; Wayne State University

REFERENCES AND FURTHER READING

American Heart Association, "Cardiovascular Disease Statistics." [Online article or information; retrieved August 3, 2007.] http://www.americanheart.org/presenter.jhtml?identifier=4478.

"The Epidemiology of Cardiovascular Disease in Black Americans." *New England Journal of Medicine* 335, 21 (November 21, 1996): 1597–1599.

Thomas, Avis J., et al. "Race/Ethnicity, Income, Major Risk Factors, and Cardiovascular Disease Mortality." *American Journal of Public Health* 95, 8 (August 2005): 1417–1423.

Diabetes

Diabetes is one of several medical conditions that contribute to health disparities. It is a metabolic disorder of carbohydrate metabolism that results from the insufficient production of insulin, a hormone that regulates the production of glucose, the source of energy in cell function. Diabetes' long-term complications include cardiovascular disease, kidney failure, blindness, nerve damage, erectile dysfunction, gangrene, amputation, and death. Diabetes is one of the most serious medical conditions in the developed world, probably as a result of the so-called Western diet, and it is estimated to account for almost one million deaths per year. African American adults are almost twice as likely to suffer from diabetes as adults in the general U.S. population, and African American children are more than four times as likely to contract diabetes as other children in the United States. African Americans with diabetes are almost three times as likely to suffer from coronary heart disease and certain other complications affecting the small blood vessels as other Americans who suffer from diabetes.

This article addresses diabetes from two perspectives. The first concerns the research conducted over the years by African American medical researchers and scientists to understand more about diabetes and to develop effective methods for treating it. The second concerns the scientific research efforts by public and private entities to reduce and ultimately eliminate health disparities related to diabetes.

The physiologist Joseph C. Dunbar is one of the nation's leading experts on diabetes. His early research investigated the possibility that diabetes is caused by a deficiency of the hormone that causes the pancreas to produce insulin. This line of inquiry led him to discover that insulin helps regulate the activities of the hypothalamus, the part of the central nervous system that regulates blood pressure and arterial flow. Dunbar also discovered that diabetes is related to a number of other medical conditions such as obesity, hypertension, and stroke, and he theorized that diabetes affects the cardiovascular system by affecting the hypothalamus, which in turn regulates the heart. He also noted that diabetes seems to increase the rate of neuronal apoptosis (the programmed cell death of nerve cells) by inducing ischemia (the reduced flow of blood through an artery). Joycelyn Elders is best remembered for serving as U.S. surgeon general, but before serving in that capacity she was a pediatric endocrinologist who specialized in diabetes. Her research focused on the connection between juvenile diabetes in young African American mothers and birth defects, such as spontaneous abortion and congenital abnormalities, in their infants. As a result, she became a promoter of sexual abstinence among young women, particularly those who suffered from juvenile diabetes. Carroll M. Leevy is a physiologist who specialized in the diseases and medical conditions that affect the liver. He demonstrated the connection between diabetes and various liver disorders.

Given the seriousness of the problem in the African American community, a number of historically black schools and organizations have devoted a considerable amount of time and energy to eliminating the health disparities associated with diabetes. The Association of Black Cardiologists Center for Women's Health conducts various research projects that explore the role played by diabetes on the high incidence of cardiovascular disease in African

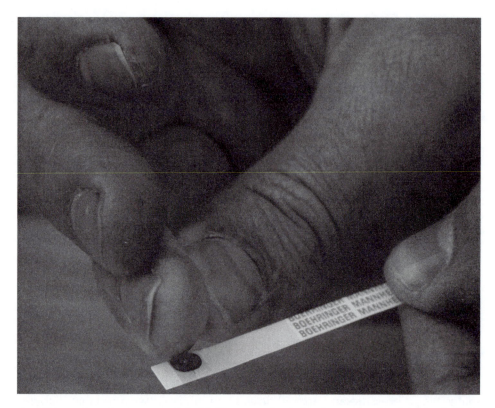

An African American man pricks his finger to check the glucose level in his blood. Tight glucose control, including frequent blood glucose monitoring, significantly reduces organ damage caused by diabetes. (National Institutes of Health)

American women. All four of the historically black medical schools—the Charles R. Drew University of Medicine and Science, Howard University College of Medicine, Meharry Medical College, and the Morehouse School of Medicine—conduct research projects that address the health disparity issues associated with diabetes, as do Jackson State University, Lincoln University of Missouri, Spelman College, Tougaloo College, Xavier University of Louisiana, the National Medical Association Cobb Institute, and the Wayne State University School of Medicine Center for Urban and African American Health. The International Society on Hypertension in Blacks sponsors research related to the role played by diabetes as a cause of hypertension.

The federal government, working through the National Institutes of Health (NIH), has made a commitment to overcome health disparities in all areas, including diabetes. To this end, a number of NIH institutes conduct and support research related to the health disparities associated with diabetes. Much of this research is conducted under the auspices of the National Center on Minority Health and Health Disparities, which funds research on diabetes and other medical conditions related to health disparities at 75 centers of excellence across the country.

The National Institute of Diabetes and Digestive and Kidney Diseases (NIDDK) studies the behavioral, socioeconomic, cultural, metabolic, and physiological reasons for disparities in the incidence of diabetes in African Americans. This research includes studies of the role played by genetics in the development of diabetes-related cardiovascular complications and the alarming rate at which diabetes has been increasing among African American children. NIDDK also works to overcome health disparities associated with diabetes by recruiting and training more minorities for careers as medical researchers in diabetes and related fields, because it has been demonstrated conclusively that minority researchers are more interested in addressing health disparities than nonminority researchers.

The National Center for Complementary and Alternative Medicine Office of Special Populations funds research on the ability of ginseng and Ginkgo biloba to regulate blood glucose levels and increase pancreatic function, respectively, as well as on the effect of chromium supplementation to reduce the need for insulin treatment among African Americans. The National Eye Institute conducts research related to diabetic retinopathy, a major cause of blindness that is caused by diabetes and that occurs more often in blacks than in whites. The National Heart, Lung, and Blood Institute evaluates the benefits of different therapies to reduce cardiovascular complications in African Americans with diabetes. The National Human Genome Research Institute conducts the African American Type–2 Diabetes Study, which investigates the potential genetic underpinnings in African Americans. The National Institute of Child Health and Human Development studies the effects of diabetes on the health of young African American mothers and the role played by diabetes in fetal programming (the early physiological interactions among a fetus, its mother, and the social and physical environment in which she lives that predispose an infant to suffer from health disparities as an adult). The National Institute of Neurological Disorders and Stroke supports research to determine whether the prevalence among minorities of lower extremity amputations resulting from diabetes is related to the development of neurological problems such as sensory motor neuropathy or to other factors.

See also: Association of Black Cardiologists; Cardiovascular Disease; Charles R. Drew University of Medicine and Science; Dunbar, Joseph C., Jr.; Elders, Joycelyn; Health Disparities; Howard University College of Medicine; International Society on Hypertension in Blacks; Jackson State University; Leevy, Carroll M.; Lincoln University of Missouri; Meharry Medical College; Morehouse School of Medicine; National Center for Complementary and Alternative Medicine; National Center for Minority Health and Health Disparities; National Eye Institute; National Heart, Lung, and Blood Institute; National Human Genome

Research Institute; National Institute of Child Health and Human Development; National Institute of Diabetes and Digestive and Kidney Diseases; National Institute of Neurological Disorders and Stroke; National Institutes of Health; National Medical Association; Spelman College; Tougaloo College; Wayne State University; Xavier University of Louisiana

References and Further Reading
Grant, R. W. "Invited Commentary: Untangling the Web of Diabetes Causality in African Americans." *American Journal of Epidemiology* 166, 4 (August 15, 2007): 388–390.
Karter, Andrew J. "Race and Ethnicity: Vital Constructs for Diabetes Research." *Diabetes Care* 26, Issue 7 (2003): 2189–2193.

Health Disparities

In the United States, minorities in general and African Americans in particular suffer from health disparities (inequalities in the quality of health and health care). Health disparities arise from cultural, socioeconomic, and environmental factors, from barriers that members of racial and ethnic groups encounter when trying to avail themselves of health care, and from the relative quality of health care that minorities actually receive. A fourth potential source of health disparities, and one that is hotly debated, is genomics (the genetic characteristics of certain racial and ethnic groups that may predispose them to contract and/or die from certain medical conditions at a disproportionately high ratio compared to the general population).

The medical conditions that contribute the most to health disparities among African Americans are asthma, cardiovascular disease, cancer, diabetes, HIV/AIDS, obesity, and sickle cell disease. As of the early 21st century, a number of private and public research institutions were conducting research to reduce and ultimately eliminate health disparities as they exist in the United States. Because each of these medical conditions is covered in a separate article, this article provides a brief overview of health disparities.

The existence of health disparities has been no secret to the African American medical community. Ever since there have been black physicians, black medical researchers have been investigating the causes of health disparities as they relate to black Americans. Much research concerning health disparities has been conducted at historically black colleges and universities, but especially at the four historically black medical colleges: Charles R. Drew University of Medicine and Science, Howard University College of Medicine, Meharry Medical College, and Morehouse School of Medicine. A great many African American medical researchers, however, have rejected the idea that African Americans are more susceptible to certain medical conditions, other than sickle cell disease, because of physiological differences having to do with race. In 1936, the physical anthropologist W. Montague Cobb demonstrated in "Race and Runners," an article that appeared in *Journal of Health and Physical Education*, that the differences in bone structures between blacks and whites are virtually indistinguishable. In 1942, Julian H. Lewis published *The Biology of the Negro* (Chicago: University of Chicago Press), in which he examined the physiological differences between black and white Americans and found the differences to be so miniscule as to be unimportant.

Nevertheless, the fact remains that African Americans, for whatever reasons, are three times as likely to suffer from asthma as European Americans, that black women are much more likely to develop breast cancer or become obese than white women, that black men are much more likely to develop prostate cancer than white men, that black Americans have the highest rate of death from cardiovascular disease in the industrialized world, that black Americans are twice as likely to develop diabetes than white Americans, and that 60 percent of the teenagers and women who suffer from HIV/AIDS are African Americans. Moreover, over the last two decades of the 20th century, statistics indicate that the health of Americans in general had improved significantly, but that the health of minorities, particularly African Americans, was not improving at the same rate and that, for some medical conditions, it was actually getting worse.

In light of these facts, the U.S. Congress passed the Minority Health and Health Disparities Research and Education Act of 2000. The act tasked the National Institutes of Health (NIH) with conducting and supporting research, under the auspices of the newly created National Center on Minority Health and Health Disparities, to find out why African Americans and other minorities suffer from health disparities. In short order, NIH had instructed each of its constituent institutes and centers to develop and implement a plan for investigating those health disparities that fall within its purview. Consequently, as of 2007, the National Heart, Lung, and Blood Institute (NHLBI) had taken the lead in investigating health disparities concerning asthma, cardiovascular disease, and sickle cell disease; the National Cancer Institute concerning cancer; the National Institute of Diabetes and Digestive and Kidney Diseases (NIDDK) concerning diabetes; and the National Institute of Allergy and Infectious Diseases concerning HIV/AIDS; NHLBI and NIDDK shared responsibility for health disparities related to obesity. Much of this research concerns the cultural, socioeconomic, and environmental aspects of life in the African American community. At the same time, other research, particularly that conducted or supported by the National Human Genome Research Institute, considers the possibility that genomics and heredity are responsible, to some degree, for certain health disparities.

See also: Asthma; Cancer; Cardiovascular Disease; Charles R. Drew University of Medicine and Science; Cobb, W. Montague; Diabetes; HIV/AIDS; Howard University College of Medicine; Lewis, Julian H.; Meharry Medical College; Morehouse School of Medicine; National Cancer Institute; National Center for Minority Health and Health Disparities; National Heart, Lung, and Blood Institute; National Institute of Allergy and Infectious Diseases; National Institute of Diabetes and Digestive and Kidney Diseases; National Institutes of Health; Obesity; Sickle Cell Disease

REFERENCES AND FURTHER READING

Health Policy Institute of Ohio, "Understanding Health Disparities." [Online article or information; retrieved October 30, 2007.] http://www.healthpolicy ohio.org/publications/healthdisparities.html.

National Center on Minority Health and Health Disparities, "National Institutes of Health Strategic Research Plan and Budget to Reduce and Ultimately Eliminate Health Disparities, Volume I." [Online article or information; retrieved July 11, 2007.] http://ncmhd.nih.gov/our_programs/strategic/pubs/VolumeI_031003EDrev.pdf.

Smedley, Brian D., et al. *Unequal Treatment: Confronting Racial and Ethnic Disparities in Health Care.* Washington, DC: National Academy Press, 2003.

HIV/AIDS

HIV/AIDS is a major contributor to health disparities in the United States. Human immunodeficiency virus (HIV) is a retrovirus that infects the body's immune system. In many cases, HIV infection results in acquired immune deficiency syndrome (AIDS), a condition whereby the body's immune system eventually fails, causing the patient to die from other life-threatening infections. Since 1981, when AIDS was first identified, it is estimated that the disease has killed more than 25 million people worldwide.

HIV/AIDS has plagued the United States as well, but by the dawn of the 21st century it was plaguing African Americans disproportionately. Since then, almost 60 percent of the teenagers diagnosed with AIDS have been African Americans, and almost 60 percent of the women who suffer from AIDS are African Americans. Of American women newly diagnosed with AIDS, more than 80 percent are African Americans. Not surprisingly, a number of African American medical scientists and research organizations, as well as the National Institutes of Health (NIH), have conducted and continue to conduct research related to HIV/AIDS and its deleterious effects on blacks in the United States.

In terms of HIV/AIDS, perhaps the two best-known African American medical researchers are Joycelyn Elders and Bernard A. Harris. Elders is best remembered for serving as U.S. surgeon general, but prior to that she conducted research related to juvenile diabetes and birth defects in infants born to young African American mothers. This work led her to promote so-called safe sex among young black women, particularly after HIV/AIDS reached epidemic proportions in the United States. As surgeon general, she advocated that public schools should teach safe sex practices such as contraception to avoid HIV infection. Harris is best remembered for being one of the first black astronauts, but as a mission specialist, he conducted research related to HIV/AIDS. As part of the joint Russian-American Space Program, he oversaw the completion of the research project known as Immune. Spaceflight tends to suppress the body's immune system; so Immune was conducted to test the efficacy of certain substances to prevent or reduce this suppression in the hopes that they might prove useful in the fight against HIV/AIDS.

A number of the nation's historically black colleges, universities, and medical research organizations conduct research related to HIV/AIDS. The Charles R. Drew University of Medicine and Science International Health Institute has implemented projects to study and prevent HIV/AIDS in Angola, and its Biomedical Research Center conducts research related to HIV/AIDS among blacks in this country. Meharry Medical College maintains the Center for Health Disparities Research in HIV, and the Morehouse School of Medicine Clinical Research Center conducts clinical trials on outpatients concerning methods for preventing and curing HIV/AIDS. The Florida A&M University College of Pharmacy and Pharmaceutical Sciences AIDS Research Center and the Xavier University of Louisiana Division of Basic Pharmaceutical Sciences seek to develop, synthesize, and test new pharmaceutical drugs for preventing and treating HIV/AIDS. The National Medical Association Cobb Institute studies ways to reduce health disparities as they relate to HIV/AIDS. The Tuskegee University Center for Computational Epidemiology and Risk Analysis uses computational science to develop computer models related to the spread and development of HIV/AIDS, while the Tuskegee School of Veterinary Medicine Center for the Study of Human-Animal Interdependent Relationships investigates how veterinary science can best be utilized to deal with the threat of HIV/AIDS to humans.

The National Institutes of Health have committed themselves to reducing and eliminating health disparities of all kinds, including HIV/AIDS. To this end, several of NIH's constituent institutes conduct research related to HIV/AIDS in the African American community. Many African Americans rely on complementary and alternative medicine to deal with HIV/AIDS; so the National Center for Complementary and Alternative Medicine seeks to identify these methods and determine their efficacy and safety. The National Center of Minority Health and Health Disparities Centers of Excellence Program supports research related to health disparities in HIV/AIDS at research institutions across the country. The National Institute of Allergy and Infectious Diseases ensures that large numbers of African Americans participate in clinical trials of potential HIV vaccines to make sure that they work for blacks as well as whites. The National Institute of Child Health and Human Development Pediatric and Maternal HIV Clinical Trials Network, the Adolescent Medicine HIV/AIDS Research Network, and the Adolescent Trials Network develop methods for preventing and treating HIV/AIDS in African American communities, and the Women's HIV Pathogenesis Program studies how HIV infection spreads among black women in minority communities and how AIDS develops differently in black women than in black men. The National Institute on Drug Abuse Epidemiological Research on Drug Abuse program studies drug abuse among African American youths as a risk factor for contracting HIV/AIDS. The National Institute of Mental Health (NIMH) studies how HIV/AIDS affects the mental health of black women who are dying from AIDS and/or caring for loved ones who are dying from AIDS, at the same time providing these women with mental health services. NIMH also seeks to develop methods that prevent HIV infection by taking into consideration the sociocultural context that induces some African Americans to engage in behaviors with a high risk of resulting in HIV infection. The National Institute of Neurological Disorders and Stroke studies NeuroAIDS (the dementia and other neurological complications that develop as AIDS progresses) in African American communities, and it supports research by the Neurological AIDS Research Consortium, which investigates the possible genetic underpinnings of NeuroAIDS.

See also: Charles R. Drew University of Medicine and Science; Elders, Joycelyn; Florida A&M University; Harris, Bernard A., Jr.; Health Disparities; Meharry Medical College; Morehouse School of Medicine; National Center for Complementary and Alternative Medicine; National Center for Minority Health and Health Disparities; National Institute of Allergy and Infectious Diseases; National Institute of Child Health and Human Development; National Institute on Drug Abuse; National Institute of Mental Health; National Institute of Neurological Disorders and Stroke; National Institutes of Health; National Medical Association; Tuskegee School of Veterinary Medicine; Tuskegee University; Xavier University of Louisiana

REFERENCES AND FURTHER READING
The Body: The Complete HIV/AIDS Resource. "HIV/AIDS Among the African American Community." June 2007. [Online article or information; retrieved August 8, 2007.] http://www.thebody.com/index/whatis/africanam.html

Medical Careers for Blacks

Unlike science careers, medical careers for African Americans have been readily available since the abolition of slavery. These careers became even more accessible as a result of the Civil Rights Movement in the 1960s and later in the 1990s. Nevertheless, black physicians, dentists, nurses, and medical researchers have always struggled to overcome a number of roadblocks, and in the early 21st century, they continued to be underrepresented in the ranks of health care professionals and medical scientists.

Very few opportunities to practice medicine presented themselves to African Americans before the Civil War. In the antebellum United States, free blacks were generally treated by white physicians, and slaves were generally tended to by their masters or overseers. The abolition of slavery, however, changed all that. Segregation prevented black physicians from achieving the same status enjoyed by white physicians, to be sure, but it also dictated that blacks physicians were permitted to minister only to African American patients. Medical education for blacks was provided by several mostly black medical schools established expressly for that purpose, the most important being Howard University College of Medicine and Meharry Medical College. After graduation, most black physicians and dentists practiced in small, black-majority communities in the South or in the black neighborhoods of the South's large cities. The Great Migration of the late 19th and early 20th centuries, in which millions of Southern blacks relocated to the industrial communities of the North and Midwest, opened up opportunities in those communities for black health care professionals.

Although black doctors and dentists never made as much money as their white counterparts, their practices seem to have thrived until the Civil Rights Movement. One result of the movement's success was that black patients could now be treated by white physicians in previously whites-only hospitals; so many blacks began leaving their black physicians. The ironic result was that many black medical and dental practitioners were forced to abandon their practices. Over time, fewer opportunities for black health care professionals meant fewer black health care professionals to serve the many small, impoverished black communities across the South, an eventuality that contributed in no small part to the health disparities of the 21st century.

Other pressures on the black doctor at the turn of the century were the growing popularity of multiphysician practices, health management organizations (HMOs), and Medicare. Many large practices are reluctant to take on a black doctor or dentist, because they fear an influx of black patients. There are two reasons for this fear: A comparatively high percentage of black patients are on Medicare, which pays considerably less than most commercial health insurance plans, and an influx of black patients might drive away their higher-paying white patients. Consequently, most black health care professionals are forced to practice by themselves or with one other black partner, which means that they struggle to afford the expensive diagnostic and treatment equipment required to practice modern medicine. HMOs, for a

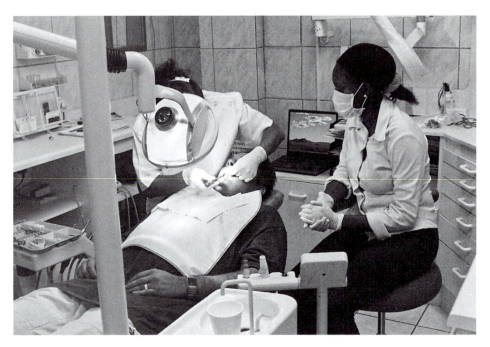

An African American dentist examines a patient. (iStockphoto)

number of financial reasons, prefer to deal with multiphysician practices, and so they do not include many individually practicing physicians on their list of approved health care providers. This situation results in a loss of patients to many black physicians and dentists, but especially of referred patients to black specialists.

Prior to the 1990s, black physicians who wished to work as medical researchers struggled to find positions in prestigious research hospitals and institutions. Part of this problem stemmed not so much from racial prejudice per se, but rather from the fact that, as in so many other fields, landing such a position depends in large part on who you know (one's network of colleagues and mentors), and most black physicians found themselves outside the good ole boy networks.

Since the 1990s, the powers that be in the health care system have realized that African Americans and other underrepresented minorities constitute a huge, relatively untapped source of the medical scientists that the system will require in the future. As a result, many organizations, chief among them the National Institutes of Health, have implemented a number of initiatives to recruit and train black physicians to conduct cutting-edge medical research. As of 2007, the growth in numbers of black medical scientists was impressive, compared to the same numbers from earlier decades, but blacks were still underrepresented in the medical professions in relation to the percentage of blacks making up the general population.

See also: Health Disparities; Howard University College of Medicine; Medical Education for Blacks; Meharry Medical College; National Institutes of Health

REFERENCES AND FURTHER READING

Bowser, Rene, "Medical Civil Rights: The Exclusion of Physicians of Color from Managed Care—Business or Bias?" (September 2005). U of St. Thomas Legal Studies Research Paper No. 05–14 [Online article or information; retrieved August 1, 2007.] http://ssrn.com/abstract=834284.

Watson, Wilbur H. *Against the Odds: Blacks in the Profession of Medicine in the United States.* New Brunswick, NJ: Transaction Publishers, 1999.

Medical Education for Blacks

Prior to the Civil War, African Americans who wished to become physicians, dentists, or nurses had few options. Although a handful of medical schools in the United States granted degrees to blacks, most prospective black doctors were forced to receive their medical training in Europe, where the color line did not exist, whereas dental training for African Americans was virtually nonexistent. Between 1868 and 1904, a number of medical schools opened that catered to black students, and these schools greatly increased the number of black physicians, surgeons, and nurses in the United States. Most of these schools fell on hard times after 1910, the year the Flexner Report on Medical Education was published, and from 1923 to the mid-1960s, African Americans experienced increased difficulty obtaining a medical education. The Civil Rights Movement, which opened the doors of many all-white medical programs to blacks, coupled with the opening of two more medical colleges for blacks and other minorities in the 1960s and 1970s, made it easier once again for blacks to go to medical school. Since 1980, however, affirmative action has come under attack, and although many groups, both public and private, advocate innovative methods for increasing the number of minority health care professionals, the number of African American doctors, dentists, and nurses remains low.

The first African American to receive an MD from an American college was David J. Peck, who graduated from Rush Medical College in Chicago, Illinois, in 1847. By 1860, two more schools, Bowdoin Medical School in Maine and Berkshire Medical School in Massachusetts, had also awarded medical degrees to blacks. Meanwhile, a number of other medical schools, most notably those at Harvard, Yale, Northwestern, the universities of Indiana, Michigan, New York, and Pennsylvania, and several smaller colleges such as Castleton Medical School in Vermont, the Eclectic Medical School of Philadelphia, and the Homeopathic College of Cleveland, had also accepted black medical students.

Emancipation made it possible for Southern blacks to consider careers in medicine, and the Jim Crow laws adopted by the former Southern slaveholding states made medical education for freedmen a necessity. Consequently, between 1868 and 1904, seven medical colleges were founded to provide medical training for Southern blacks. These schools, and the dates they were established, are (1) Howard Medical College (today Howard University College of Medicine) in Washington, D.C. (1868); (2) Meharry Medical College in Nashville, Tennessee (1876); (3) Leonard Medical School in Raleigh, North Carolina (1882); (4) New Orleans (Louisiana) University Medical College, later renamed Flint Medical College (1889); (5) Knoxville (Tennessee) College Medical Department, later renamed Knoxville Medical College (1895); (6) Chattanooga (Tennessee) National Medical College (1902); and (7) the University of West Tennessee College of Physicians and Surgeons in Memphis (1904).

Next to Howard and Meharry, Leonard was the largest and most successful of these schools. A part of Shaw University, Leonard was founded by the Baptist Mission Society for Negroes, although the state of North Carolina donated the land for the medical building, a hospital, dispensary, and dormitory. Leonard's first graduating class had six students. Like many black medical colleges, its faculty consisted primarily of white professors, in Leonard's case the leading physicians of Raleigh, the state capital.

Although African Americans could still receive medical and dental training at colleges and universities in the North, these seven schools had trained approximately 85 percent of all black doctors and dentists practicing medicine as of 1905, as well as virtually all of the black nurses. Moreover, many of the graduates of these schools opened their practices in rural black communities in the South, which were desperately in need of medical care. In 1910, however, the future of black medical schools was greatly compromised by the release of the Flexner Report, which called for standards of excellence in both teaching and biomedical research that these schools were hard pressed to satisfy. By 1923, all but two, Howard and Meharry, closed their doors. These two prestigious medical programs, which were among the best in the country, were joined in 1966 by the Charles R. Drew University of Medicine and Science and in 1978 by Morehouse School of Medicine. These four schools remained the only black-majority medical colleges for the rest of the 20th century.

The success of the Civil Rights Movement in the 1960s opened the doors of many previously all-white medical programs to African Americans, so that by 1980, blacks seeking careers as health care professionals could gain admission to any program in the country. Their quest was aided by the adoption of affirmative action admissions policies by many of the nation's leading medical

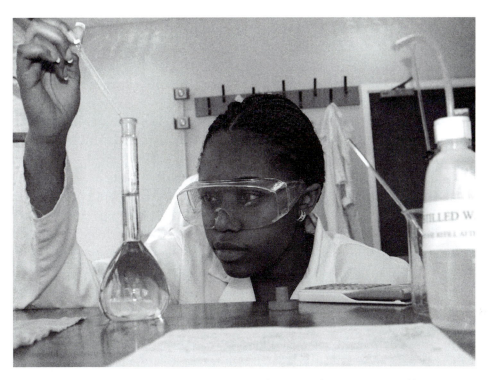

A medical student makes up a solution in a laboratory. (Laurence Gough)

schools, which wished to make their programs more culturally diverse. After 1980, however, affirmative action came under attack, as many white students who were denied admission to the medical school of their choice sued in federal court on the grounds of racial discrimination. While the battle over the constitutionality of affirmative action admissions policies continued well into the 21st century, the four historically black medical schools continued to turn out the vast majority of African American health care professionals.

In 2004, fewer than 8 percent of the first-time applicants to medical school were African Americans, and only about 40 percent of them were accepted. That same year, approximately 1,000 blacks graduated from medical schools, slightly more than one-tenth the number of whites. At the same time, only slightly more than 3 percent of the teaching faculty at medical schools were blacks, and most held the ranks of either assistant professor or instructor, rarely full professor.

After peaking in 1996, applications from blacks dropped off precipitously between 1997 and 2002. The reasons for this are unclear, but two major factors seem to have been *Hopwood v. University of Texas* (1996), the 5th Circuit Court of Appeals decision that racial preferences could not be used as part of the college admissions process, and California Proposition 209 (1996), which amended that state's constitution by prohibiting public institutions from discriminating on the basis of race, sex, or ethnicity. Conversely, the increase in blacks applying to medical school after 2002 seems to have stemmed in part from *Grutter v. Bollinger, et al.* [539 US 306 (2003)], whereby the U.S. Supreme Court upheld the affirmative action admissions policy of the University of Michigan Law School.

Efforts to increase the number of black doctors, dentists, and nurses continue to be stymied by several interlocking factors: African Americans are less likely than European Americans to graduate from high school; those who do are less likely to attend college; those who do attend college are more likely to attend two-year colleges, not four-year ones; those who do attend four-year colleges are less likely to graduate; and those who do graduate are less likely to apply to medical school. Thus, the solution to the problem begins with doing a better job of preparing minority K–12 students for careers as health care professionals, and it continues by encouraging minorities throughout their education to consider careers as health care professionals and by supporting those who pursue such careers. To this end, the Sullivan Commission on Diversity in the Healthcare Workforce, which was convened in 2003 to recommend ways to make medical education more accessible to African Americans and other underrepresented minorities, called on public and private health care education institutions to adopt innovative admissions and financial aid policies in order to increase the number of minority health care professionals in the United States.

See also: Charles R. Drew University of Medicine and Science; Howard University College of Medicine; Meharry Medical College; Morehouse School of Medicine; Sullivan Commission on Diversity in the Healthcare Workforce

References and Further Reading

Association of American Medical Colleges. "Minorities in Medical Education: Facts & Figures 2005." Spring 2005. [Online article or information; retrieved July 25, 2007.] https://services.aamc.org/Publications/index.cfm?fuseaction=Product.displayForm&prd_id=133&prv_id=154.

Watson, Wilbur H. *Against the Odds: Blacks in the Profession of Medicine in the United States.* New Brunswick, NJ: Transaction Publishers, 1999.

Obesity

Obesity is one of several medical conditions that contribute to health disparities. It is a condition in which fatty tissue, which stores the body's natural energy reserve, increases to the point that it creates an unhealthy condition. People who are obese tend to suffer disproportionately from cardiovascular disease, diabetes, and other conditions.

Obesity is a major health concern within the African American community. (Don Bayley)

As of 2007, almost half of the general population of the United States was considered overweight or obese, but the situation was even worse for African Americans. Almost two-thirds of African American women were considered to be overweight, while more than 10 percent were considered to be obese. Consequently, African Americans in general and African American women in particular suffer disproportionately from cardiovascular disease and diabetes. To eliminate health disparities connected with obesity, a number of historically black institutions and organizations, as well as the National Institutes of Health (NIH), conduct scientific research to gain a better understanding of why African Americans are more prone to becoming obese and to develop methods for reducing and preventing obesity.

Researchers at Lincoln University of Missouri and the Wayne State University School of Medicine Center for Urban and African American Health have conducted some of the most innovative research concerning obesity among African Americans. At Lincoln, nutrition researchers focus on nutrition, exercise, and the health risks associated with obesity, particularly in terms of modifying unhealthy lifestyles that contribute to obesity. Among other things, they investigate the effectiveness of nutrition education and physical exercise as ways to reduce fatty tissue levels in African American schoolchildren, and the efficacy of increasing physical activity and fruit and vegetable consumption while reducing energy and fat intake as ways to reduce fatty tissue in middle-aged black women. At Wayne State, experts in the fields of exercise physiology, sociology, psychology, internal medicine, hypertension, oncology, family medicine, nursing, epidemiology, biostatistics, bioinformatics, obstetrics and gynecology, genomics, gerontology, anthropology, and demography team up to deal with the effects of obesity, diet, and related lifestyle factors on cardiovascular disease and breast cancer. One study explores the environmental stressors, psychobehavioral attributes, and genetic factors associated with obesity, oxidative stress, and salt sensitivity, and another is focused on the connection between obesity in African American breast cancer survivors and the recurrence of breast cancer.

Other historically black institutions work to eliminate obesity as a health disparity by educating African Americans about the importance of better nutrition and daily physical activity. The Association of Black Cardiologists Center for Women's Health conducts the ABC's of Nutrition and Exercise program to educate black women about the importance of both; the Jackson State University Heart Study Coordinating Center conducts seminars and workshops to help African Americans in the Jackson metropolitan area to understand the connection between obesity and cardiovascular disease; and the International Society on Hypertension in Blacks has established a disease/lifestyle council for obesity to call attention to the connection between obesity and hypertension. Meanwhile, the National Medical Association Cobb Institute disseminates the results of its research concerning the health disparities related to obesity, and the Student National Medical Association awards Satcher Fellowships, named after former Surgeon General David Satcher who was an advocate of preventing and controlling obesity, to medical students conducting research on obesity.

NIH has made a commitment to reduce and ultimately eliminate health disparities related to obesity, and to this end, a number of NIH institutes conduct and sponsor research related to obesity in African Americans. Much of this research is conducted under the auspices of the National Center on Minority Health and Health Disparities Centers of Excellence Program, which sponsors research at 75 centers around the country. The National Heart, Lung, and Blood Institute studies the relationship between obesity and hypertension in African Americans and the importance of weight control and physical activity as factors in controlling blood pressure, particularly among young black girls at high risk for obesity. The National Institute of Arthritis and Musculoskeletal and Skin Diseases studies the connection between obesity in African Americans and the disproportionate rate at which they suffer from osteoarthritis of the hip and knee. The National Institute of Child Health and Human Development studies the degree to which obesity in the mother leads to fetal programming (the complicated physiological process that many researchers suspect is an underlying cause of health disparities) in her newborn infant.

The National Institute of Diabetes and Digestive and Kidney Diseases develops effective educational programs such as the Sisters Together: Move More, Eat Better program, an outreach program for African American women to help them reduce the health risks associated with obesity.

See also: Association of Black Cardiologists; Cardiovascular Disease; Diabetes; Health Disparities; International Society on Hypertension in Blacks; Jackson State University; Lincoln University of Missouri; National Center for Minority Health and Health Disparities; National Heart, Lung, and Blood Institute; National Institute of Arthritis and Musculoskeletal and Skin Diseases; National Institute of Child Health and Human Development; National Institute of Diabetes and Digestive and Kidney Diseases; National Institutes of Health; National Medical Association; Satcher, David; Student National Medical Association; Wayne State University

References and Further Reading

Bailey, Eric J. *Food Choice and Obesity in Black America: Creating a New Cultural Diet*. Westport, CT: Greenwood Press, 2006.

Dustan, H. P. "Obesity and Hypertension in Blacks." *Cardiovascular Drugs and Therapy* 4, 2 (March 1990): 395–402.

Science Careers for Blacks

Prior to the Civil Rights Movement, blacks were hard-pressed to qualify for and then obtain employment as scientists. Affirmative action made it much easier for blacks to obtain a scientific education and scientific jobs, but the number of African Americans who make their livings as scientific researchers remained remarkably low even into the 21st century.

Before the 1960s, most blacks were prevented from pursuing scientific careers by virtue of the fact that they could not get admitted into a prestigious college or university science program. Instead, blacks who wanted to be scientists attended a historically black college or university (HBCU), which continue to produce the majority of black scientists into the middle of the first decade of the 21st century. Most of these scientists, however, ended up working as science teachers or professors at all-black high schools or HBCUs. Those who found jobs in industry were employed mostly as industrial chemists, as in the cases of Lloyd A. Hall, Henry A. Hill, and Percy L. Julian.

Affirmative action, both in the form of public law and private initiative, opened doors for African Americans who wished to pursue careers in scientific research. By 1989, *Ebony* magazine could publish an article calling the attention of blacks to careers as biochemists, computer scientists, dentists, natural resource scientists, ophthalmologists, pharmacists, and registered nurses; these careers promised to be the hottest in the coming decade, not only for

African Americans but for the general public as well. At the same time, the leaders of the nation's scientific community had come to realize that African Americans and other underrepresented minorities constituted a vast, virtually untapped talent pool from which many of the sorely needed scientists and technologists of the future could be enticed. These leaders saw to it that public and private entities established programs to recruit more African Americans to careers as scientists by assisting them through college and by promoting the hiring of black scientists by private industry. Yet, for various reasons, the percentage of blacks working as scientists seemed never to rise above single digits, despite the fact that African Americans constitute close to 20 percent of the general population.

Several factors have been identified as contributors to this phenomenon. Many observers point out that, more often than not, black children receive their K–12 education from schools with outdated infrastructures that are under-funded and understaffed. Consequently, these children struggle throughout their educational careers to develop their skills in reading and mathematics, the two skills that are absolutely essential for a career as a scientist. In addition, the science curriculums at these schools often fail to include enrichment activities that get young students excited about science. Black children who might become scientists also suffer from the lack of role models. Most famous or successful African Americans are athletes, entertainers, or civil rights activists. Black children are taught much more about African Americans who have succeeded in these careers than they are about black scientists, and so many black youths come to believe that science is not an appropriate career for them to pursue. This impression is reinforced in college by the almost total absence of black professors in the science departments of non-HBCUs. A third problem, and perhaps the most insidious, is the sense of isolation that most black scientists must deal with throughout their careers. Often the only African American in the workplace, the black scientist often struggles to develop and maintain a network of colleagues and mentors who can help with his or her career. Consequently, few black scientists manage to advance in their fields because of their inability to make office politics work in their favor. The lack of high-profile black scientists, in turn, results in few role models and mentors to help and inspire the next generation of black scientists.

Several organizations have been created to address these issues. Since the 1980s, black scientists have been forming their own professional organizations, such as the National Institutes of Health Black Scientists Association, to provide mentors and role models for young black would-be scientists. Many of these organizations reach out to minority youth in elementary and middle schools by means of enrichment and mentoring programs. However, for blacks to achieve parity in the sciences, much more has to be done by these and other organizations, public and private.

See also: Hall, Lloyd A.; Hill, Henry A.; Historically Black Colleges and Universities; Julian, Percy L.; NIH Black Scientists Association

REFERENCES AND FURTHER READING

Chen, Adrian. "In the Shadow of Science: Blacks Scientists and Inventors Struggle for Visibility from One Generation to the Next." *The Michigan Daily* (February 22, 2005). [Online article or information; retrieved July 31, 2007.] http://media.www.michigandaily.com/media/storage/paper851/news/2005/02/22/News/In.The.Shadow.Of.Science-1429030.shtml.

"The 10 Top Careers for Blacks in the '90s." *Ebony.* February 1999. [Online article or information; retrieved July 31, 2007.] http://findarticles.com/p/articles/mi_m1077/is_n4_v44/ai_7044940/pg_1.

Science Education for Blacks

Science education has been even more difficult for African Americans to obtain than medical education. The strict segregation brought about by Jim Crow laws demanded that blacks be allowed to become doctors, dentists, and nurses, if only so that they could tend to black people. No such urgency existed, however, when it came to extending to blacks the opportunity to become scientists. By the end of the 19th century, European Americans remained convinced that African Americans lacked the minimum intelligence required to study science, and African Americans were more interested in obtaining advanced training in agriculture, the industrial arts, and education than in learning how to conduct scientific research. Consequently, very few blacks majored in science in college before World War I, and even fewer received PhDs, the badge of a full-fledged research scientist. Nevertheless, some did, including Edward A. Bouchet, the first African American to receive a PhD in physics (1876, Yale University); Alfred O. Coffin, the first African American to receive a PhD in biology (1889, Illinois Wesleyan University); and Charles H. Turner, the first African American to receive a PhD in zoology (1907, University of Chicago).

One of the most important events in early 20th-century U.S. history is the Great Migration, the relocation of millions of Southern blacks to the industrial cities of the North and Midwest. Coupled with World War I, during which a number of black troops served in the U.S. military, the Great Migration made it marginally easier for African Americans to obtain a science education, if not a science-related job. Between 1915 and the outbreak of World War II in 1939, eight African Americans became the first of their race to receive a PhD in their chosen scientific discipline: Julian H. Lewis, physiology, 1915, Chicago; St. Elmo Brady, chemistry, 1916, University of Illinois; Francis C. Sumner, psychology, 1920, Clark University; Roscoe L. McKinney, anatomy, 1931, Chicago;

Ruth E. Moore, bacteriology, 1931, Ohio State University; Robert S. Jason, pathology, 1932, Chicago; Paul B. Cornely, public health, 1934, University of Michigan; and Jessie J. Mark, botany, 1935, Iowa State University.

World War II weakened the links of Jim Crow's chains even more than the Great War had, so much so that the Civil Rights Movement followed hard on its heels. By 1970, five more African American scientific firsts in scientific education had occurred: Marguerite T. Williams received a PhD in geology in 1942 from Catholic University; Roy C. Darlington received a PhD in pharmacy in 1947 from Ohio State University; Charles E. Anderson received a PhD in meteorology in 1960 from the Massachusetts Institute of Technology; Harvey W. Banks received a PhD in astronomy in 1961 from Georgetown University; and Clarence A. Ellis received a PhD in computer science in 1969 from the University of Illinois.

Affirmative action programs, but especially race-sensitive admissions policies at the nation's leading colleges and universities, contributed immensely to the vast increase of doctorates awarded to African Americans after 1970. In 1981, for example, more than 1,000 blacks received doctorates from U.S. institutions of higher learning. However, most of these doctorates were in education and the social sciences, not the natural or life sciences, so that the number of black scientists being produced by the nation's educational system remained low. In 2004, for example, 1,971 earned doctorates were awarded to blacks, but only 455 were awarded in the natural and life sciences. Psychology doctorates accounted for 204, while 148 were awarded in the biological sciences, 46 in chemistry, 20 in the agricultural sciences, 17 in the computer sciences, 13 in physics, and 7 in the earth, atmospheric, and ocean sciences. African Americans received none of the 1,387 doctorates awarded that same year in acoustics, animal breeding and genetics, animal nutrition, astronomy, astrophysics, atmospheric dynamics, bacteriology, botany, computing theory and practice, endocrinology, engineering physics, fisheries science and management, general atmospheric science, geophysics and seismology, human and animal pathology, hydrology and water resources, marine sciences, meteorology, mineralogy and petrology, nuclear physics, optics physics, paleontology, plant physiology, polymer physics, poultry science, stratigraphy and sedimentation, topology, wildlife/range management, wood science, and zoology.

As with medical education for blacks, a number of initiatives have been advanced to increase the number of African Americans pursuing careers as research scientists. These initiatives seek to overcome the same problems involved in increasing the number of black health care professionals: African Americans are less likely than European Americans to graduate from high school; those who do are less likely to attend college; those who do attend college are more likely to attend two-year colleges, not four-year ones; those

A number of programs conducted by private and public organizations encourage and support African American students who wish to become scientists. (Virginia State University)

who do attend four-year colleges are less likely to graduate; those who do graduate are less likely to enroll in a graduate program in the natural or life sciences. Thus, the solution to the problem begins with involving minority students in more hands-on scientific research activities during the K–12 years, and continues by encouraging minorities throughout their educational careers to consider careers as research scientists and by supporting those who pursue such careers.

See also: Anderson, Charles E.; Astronomy and Astrophysics; Biology; Brady, St. Elmo; Chemistry; Computer Science; Ellis, Clarence Arthur "Skip"; Lewis, Julian H.; Physics; Turner, Charles H.

REFERENCES AND FURTHER READING

"Doctoral Degree Awards to African Americans Reach Another All-Time High." *The Journal of Blacks in Higher Education.* 2006. [Online article or information; retrieved July 30, 2007.] http://www.jbhe.com/news_views/50_black_doctoraldegrees.html.

First Science Ph.D.s Awarded to African Americans. "The Faces of Science: African Americans in the Sciences." [Online article or information; retrieved July 30, 2007.] https://webfiles.uci.edu/mcbrown/display/first_phds.html.

National Science Foundation. "Science and Engineering Doctorate Awards: 2004." [Online article or information; retrieved July 31, 2007.] http://www.nsf.gov/statistics/nsf06308/pdf/tables.pdf.

Sickle Cell Disease

Sickle cell disease, also known as sickle cell anemia, is one of several medical conditions that contribute to health disparities. It is a genetic defect that is found almost exclusively in people whose ancestors are from Africa and the islands of the Mediterranean Sea; about one out of every 500 African American infants are born with it. Although no one knows for sure, sickle cell disease may have originated as a defense mechanism against diseases such as malaria and yellow fever, which have plagued Africa and the Mediterranean for eons. Sickle cell disease creates abnormalities in the hemoglobin (the part of the blood that carries oxygen), and eventually these abnormalities cause the blood cells to assume a rigid, sickle-like shape. These cells cause pain and swelling as they pass through the body's blood vessels; over time, the cells deteriorate and cause anemia and death.

This article discusses the African American medical researchers and historically black research institutions that are best known for their work with sickle cell disease. It also discusses some of the research conducted and supported by the federal government, specifically the National Institutes of Health, regarding sickle cell disease.

Of all the African American medical researchers who have studied sickle cell disease, the three best known are Angella D. Ferguson, John K. Haynes, and David Satcher. Ferguson was one of the first medical researchers to study sickle cell disease. She began her medical career as a pediatrician, but she eventually became more interested in sickle cell disease when she discovered that many of her young patients suffered from the condition. She established a research program at Howard University College of Medicine to diagnose and treat sickle cell disease in children under the age of 12, and in the course of this project, she was able to demonstrate how the disease progresses. She also developed one of the first treatments for sickle cell disease—one glass of soda water per day—and showed that patients with sickle cell disease who undergo surgery need extra oxygen during the procedure to avoid complications. Haynes began his medical research career as an embryologist, but he switched to molecular biology when he began studying the biophysical properties of sickle cells. He demonstrated that sickle cells are rigid and sickle-shaped, because they have too much calcium and not enough water. He helped test a pharmaceutical drug to see if it would correct these imbalances in sickle cells, and he helped develop a simple method for quickly determining whether a patient has sickle cell disease. Satcher is best remembered for serv-

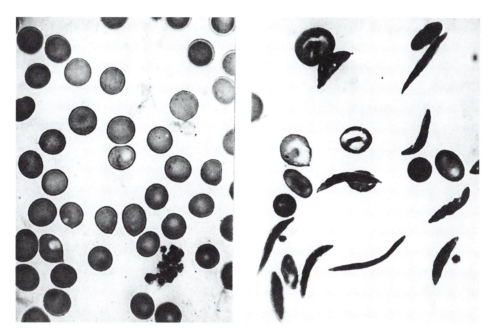

Cells in their normal elastic state (left) and those deformed by sickle cell disease. (Bettmann/Corbis)

ing as U.S. surgeon general, but in his early career, he conducted research pertaining to cytogenetics (the study of how heredity affects the structure and function of cells). He conducted several projects related to the cytogenetics of sickle cells, and later he headed the Sickle Cell Research Center at what is now the Charles R. Drew University of Medicine and Science.

A number of historically black hospitals, medical schools, and professional organizations have conducted research related to sickle cell disease. Harlem Hospital operates the Comprehensive Sickle Cell Center, one of the first centers in the United States dedicated to sickle cell research. The Howard University Hospital Center for Sickle Cell Disease, the Meharry Medical College Sickle Cell Center, and the Drew Sickle Cell Research Center provide clinical care, education, genetic counseling, and laboratory services to patients with sickle cell disease, while conducting basic research related to the condition. The Sickle Cell Disease Association of America heightens awareness about sickle cell disease and supports research related to finding a cure by offering scholarships to medical researchers studying or conducting research related to sickle cell disease.

As part of its commitment to reduce and ultimately eliminate health disparities, the National Institutes of Health conducts and supports research related to understanding sickle cell disease, improving treatments for the disease, and finding a cure. The National Heart, Lung, and Blood Institute has conducted and sponsored research that resulted in better therapies and longer lives for patients with sickle cell disease. These therapies include transfusions to prevent stroke in high-risk children, studies of pharmaceutical drugs that promise to reduce the pain and swelling associated with sickle cell disease, bone marrow transplantations, and chronic transfusions. Sadly, the institute's efforts to find a cure for sickle cell disease have thus far failed. The National Human Genome Research Institute investigates how genome science might lead to a better understanding of the biology of sickle cell disease and help develop new therapies for treating patients with the disease. The National Institute of Neurological Disorders and Stroke investigates the neurological similarities between epilepsy and sickle cell anemia as a means of effecting a cure or improved treatment.

See also: Charles R. Drew University of Medicine and Science; Ferguson, Angella D.; Harlem Hospital; Haynes, John K., Jr.; Health Disparities; Howard University College of Medicine; Howard University Hospital; Meharry Medical College; National Heart, Lung, and Blood Institute; National Human Genome Research Institute; National Institute of Neurological Disorders and Stroke; National Institutes of Health; Satcher, David; Sickle Cell Disease Association of America

REFERENCES AND FURTHER READING

Sickle Cell Disease Association of America. "What Is Sickle Cell Disease?" [Online article or information; retrieved August 9, 2007.] http://www.sicklecelldisease.org/about_scd/index.phtml.

Scientific Fields

African American scientists have made important contributions in all of the major scientific fields, including anthropology, astronomy and astrophysics, biochemistry, biology, biotechnology, chemistry, computer science, microbiology, and physics. The entries in this section highlight the contributions of notable individuals to their chosen field of scientific endeavor.

Anthropology

Anthropology is the systematic study of human behavior. It is closely related to the natural sciences in that it attempts to develop scientific methods for understanding social phenomena in terms of general principles. Such an approach allows for two different cultures to be compared to one another in more or less scientific terms.

Since its inception as an academic discipline in the 19th century, anthropology has largely focused on understanding so-called primitive peoples, including the indigenous peoples of Africa. Until the mid-20th century, most anthropologists were white people from colonizing nations, whereas most of their subjects were people of color. For a time, it was believed that people of color were unable to detach themselves sufficiently from their own cultures to the degree required of an anthropologist. Consequently, African Americans found it exceptionally difficult to pursue careers as anthropologists. One black anthropologist who managed to do so, however, was W. Montague Cobb. Cobb was a physical anthropologist who specialized in bones, and he put together the Cobb Collection, which included bones from all the races and a number of ethnic groups. Using this collection, Cobb demonstrated that the differences in bone structures among the races, specifically between blacks and whites, are virtually indistinguishable.

Zora Neale Hurston is best remembered for her works of fiction, but as an anthropologist, she did some important work concerning the secret voodoo societies of Haiti. Other important early black anthropologists include

Zora Neale Hurston studied the secret voodoo societies of Haiti before she became a well-known novelist. (Library of Congress)

W. Allison Davis, who wrote a social anthropological study of caste and class in the Deep South, and Caroline Bond Day, who studied the heredity of complexion in 350 mixed-race families in Chicago.

Although attitudes about the professionalism of black anthropologists have changed since the 19th century, the number of African Americans pursuing careers in anthropology remains low. For example, the Association of Black Anthropologists (ABA), which includes members from outside the United States, counted only 300 members in 2000. Nevertheless, black anthropologists are making original contributions to the field of anthropology. Specifically, those who belong to the ABA are practicing a new form of anthropological study that rejects the necessity of maintaining a formal distance between scientist and subject and that seeks to expose oppression in the form of racism, sexism, and economic exploitation.

See also: Association of Black Anthropologists; Cobb, W. Montague

REFERENCES AND FURTHER READING

Harrison, Ira E., and Faye V. Harrison, eds. *African-American Pioneers in Anthropology.* Urbana: University of Illinois Press, 1999.

Astronomy and Astrophysics

Astronomy is the scientific study of celestial objects and phenomena that originate outside the Earth's atmosphere, whereas astrophysics is the study of the physical properties of those objects and phenomena. Although some important differences existed between the two disciplines in years past, in the 21st century, the two are virtually indistinguishable. As of 2006, the percentage of American astronomers and astrophysicists who are African American was approximately 0.5 percent, or about 1 in 200. Nevertheless, black Americans have made important contributions to astronomy and astrophysics.

The first African American astronomer was Benjamin Banneker. Banneker had no formal education in astronomy; rather, he learned what he knew from reading books and conducting observations with a borrowed telescope. In 1789, he calculated his first ephemeris, a table giving the calculated positions of the planets and major stars on a number of future dates. The following year, he calculated ephemerides for someone else's almanac, and in 1792, he published the first of five almanacs he would produce on his own.

Little is known about black astronomers after Banneker until 1945, when Walter S. McAfee calculated the speed of the moon. The following year, he developed a method for detecting the radio echo of a laser beam bounced off the moon, thus paving the way for sending a spacecraft to land there. In 1961, Harvey W. Banks became the first African American to receive a PhD in astronomy from an American university. Banks's research focused on spectroscopy, a method for determining the elemental composition of a star by examining, through a high-powered telescope, the spectral lines emitted by its atoms and molecules. In 1962, Benjamin F. Peery became the second African American to receive a PhD in astronomy. Peery published a number of articles in the prestigious *Astrophysical Journal*, and in the 1990s, he became the first black astronomer to be featured in a television program, a Public Broadcasting System special called *The Astronomers*.

The first three prominent black astrophysicists were Carl A. Rouse, George R. Carruthers, and Arthur B. C. Walker. Ironically, none of them held a degree in astrophysics; Rouse's doctorate was in particle physics, Carruthers's was in aeronautical and astronautical engineering, and Walker's was in nuclear physics. In the 1960s, Rouse developed one of the first computer models of the sun, and he used this model to develop the theory, which remains highly controversial today, that the sun's core consists of iron rather than helium or hydrogen. In 1969, Carruthers developed the Far Ultraviolet Camera/Spectrograph, which used UV radiation to study the astrophysical properties of distant stars from its vantage point on the moon. This system allowed astrophysicists to acquire scientific data concerning stars too distant to be examined using visible light. Between the 1960s and the 1990s, Walker pioneered the development of X-ray telescopes and spectroscopes deployed in outer

Black astronomers and astrophysicists have contributed greatly to our understanding of the universe. (National Aeronautics and Space Administration)

space. He used these apparatus to obtain the first high-resolution images of the sun's outer atmosphere, as well as the atmospheres of the distant stars, the remnants of supernovas, and the distribution of elements throughout interstellar space.

Of the current generation of black astronomers and astrophysicists, the most important is Neil deGrasse Tyson. Tyson is generally considered to be the most recognized U.S. astrophysicist of the early 21st century. The director of the Hayden Planetarium, he has published numerous books and articles on astronomy. He appears regularly on television specials on astronomy and astrophysics because of his ability to "translate" scientific jargon into everyday language. Other noteworthy African American astronomers/astrophysicists of the 21st century include Ronald L. Mallett, Gibor Basri, Charles E. C. Woodward, Barbara A. Williams, Mercedes T. Richards, Reva Kay Williams, Chantale Damas, Jarita C. Holbrook, Beth A. Brown, Eric M. Wilcots, Windsor A. Morgan, Aaron S. Evans, Jason S. Best, and those working at Prairie View Solar Observatory. Mallett's work with quantum gravitational theory is being used to prove or disprove the existence of Hawking radiation, the thermal radiation that supposedly is emitted by black holes as they evaporate. Basri headed the research team that proved the existence of brown dwarfs, also known as failed stars, because they emit so little light. Woodward is best known for his work concerning the extended stellar halo of the galaxy known as NGC5907. Barbara Williams uses radio signals to observe the characteristics of compact groups of galaxies. Richards's work covers closely interacting binary stars and the magnetic activity of cool stars. Reva Williams developed a model that validates Penrose's mechanism, the gravitomagnetic effect whereby energy and momentum are extracted from a rotating black hole. Damas specializes in the physics of space plasma, a state of matter in which the atoms and molecules are so hot that they have broken down into electrons and ions. Holbrook specializes in contemporary and historical African astronomy. Brown conducts multiwavelength research on elliptical galaxies. Wilcots's research focuses on the chemical evolution of stars and galaxies. Morgan studies the X-ray–emitting nuclei of active galaxies and the early formations of hydrocarbons in our solar system. Evans specializes in galaxies that emit an inordinately high amount of X-rays, infrared rays, or radio waves, and Best analyzes galaxy clustering. Prairie View Solar Observatory, a division of Prairie View A&M University in Prairie View, Texas, is the only observatory in the country that is operated by a historically black college or university. The observatory conducts and sponsors research in solar astronomy and atmospheric plasma.

See also: Banneker, Benjamin; Basri, Gibor B.; Carruthers, George R.; McAfee, Walter S.; Prairie View A&M University; Prairie View Solar Observatory; Rouse, Carl A.; Tyson, Neil deGrasse; Walker, Arthur

REFERENCES AND FURTHER READING
Fikes, Robert Jr. "Careers of African Americans in Academic Astronomy." *Journal of Blacks in Higher Education* 29 (Autumn 2000): 132–135.

Biochemistry

Biochemistry is the study of the chemical processes that take place in living organisms. It is particularly concerned with the nature and function of biomolecules, the chemical building blocks, such as proteins, carbohydrates, and nucleic acids, from which all living matter is constructed. Although the percentage of blacks among the ranks of biochemists remains in the low single digits, African Americans have nevertheless made a number of contributions to biochemistry.

Emmett W. Chappelle specialized in bioluminescence (light produced by biochemical activity). Early in his career, he became interested in astrochemistry, the search for alien life-forms in outer space by detecting chemical activity, particularly activity involving adenosine triphosphate (ATP), the chemical compound that fuels all cellular activity. He invented a device that detects minute traces of ATP, and then, with the assistance of other scientists at the National Aeronautics and Space Administration (NASA), he began using it to look for bacteria in outer space. Later, he developed a method for detecting life in outer space by measuring laser-induced fluorescence (the optical emission from molecules that have been excited to higher-than-normal energy levels by absorbing the electromagnetic radiation generated by a laser) from sensing devices deployed on spacecraft. Over time, he and other researchers adapted these methods to study life on earth, particularly crops and aquatic plant life. He also experimented with the firefly bioluminescence reaction (the biochemical process by which fireflies produce light), and his work in this area eventually led to the development of a method for using bioluminescence to detect and count the bacteria in urine, blood, spinal fluids, drinking water, and foods.

Marie Maynard Daly was the first African American woman to earn a PhD in chemistry, but all of her research involved biochemistry. Early in her career, she studied how enzymes affect cell metabolism and gene expression. Later, she became a renowned authority on the biochemical aspects of cardiovascular conditions such as hypertension and atherosclerosis.

Lloyd N. Ferguson is a biochemist who used the techniques of structural chemistry, which studies how chemical reactions are influenced by the shape and structure of the reacting atoms and molecules. His early research focused on biomolecules that contain alicyclic compounds, which have a unique arrangement of carbon atoms. Later, he studied the biochemical process that governs the workings of gustatory chemoreceptors (specialized cells in the taste buds that indicate to the brain how a certain substance tastes). He also wrote a number of chemistry textbooks and cofounded the National Organization for the Professional Advancement of Black Chemists and Chemical Engineers.

Don N. Harris conducted a number of experiments related to biomedicine and pharmacology. His early research involved the ability of high levels of cholesterol to cause serious heart problems. Later, he studied the process by which amino acid chains are formed into complex proteins and how high levels of sex hormones can interfere with this process. His most important work involved receptors (protein molecules that receive and respond to a neurotransmitter, hormone, or other biochemical compound), radioligands (radioactive biochemical substances that are used to study receptors), and receptor antagonists (biochemical substances that inhibit the ability of receptors to do their work).

Dorothy V. McClendon used biochemistry to aid the efforts of the U.S. military. As a researcher for the U.S. Army Tank Automotive Command, she developed methods to prevent microorganisms from contaminating fuel and deteriorating military matériel in storage.

Ida Stephens Owens specializes in detoxification enzymes, by which the human body defends itself against poison. Her early research investigated how children's bodies rid themselves of dietary and environmental toxins and carcinogens such as bilirubin (the brownish-yellow pigment of bile that is produced as an end product of hemoglobin breakdown and that has no known function). Later, she discovered that detoxification enzymes must be activated

Biochemist Ida Stephens Owens, spe-cialist in detoxification enzymes. (Cour-tesy Ida S. Owens)

before they can remove noxious chemicals from the body and that, during the activation process, they remove certain therapeutic drugs before those drugs have time to take effect. This discovery has led other researchers to develop enhanced therapeutic drugs that can avoid being removed prematurely.

Several important black science administrators began their careers in science as biochemists. Joycelyn Elders is best remembered for having served as U.S. surgeon general, but before that she was an expert on pediatric endocrinology (the study of how hormones affect the growth and development of children). Margaret Mayo Tolbert served as director of the U.S. Department of Energy's New Brunswick Laboratory, which prepares and controls nuclear materials, but before that she helped explain how the production of glucose is regulated in liver cells. Kenneth Olden is director of the National Institute of Environmental Health Sciences and the National Toxicology Program, but before assuming the directorship he conducted research on how the properties of cell surface molecules might play a role in the cell's becoming cancerous. Harold D. West won high marks for his services while president of Meharry Medical College, but before that he contributed to a better understanding of the chemical composition of certain amino acids and participated in the first successful effort to synthesize the amino acid threonine.

The professional interests of all black biochemists are promoted by the National Organization for the Professional Advancement of Black Chemists and Chemical Engineers. At the organization's annual meeting, a health symposium concerning a particular topic related to biochemistry is presented as a means of encouraging more blacks to participate in clinical tests of potential pharmaceutical treatments and to encourage black chemists who have just finished their graduate work to consider careers in biochemistry.

See also: Chappelle, Emmett W.; Chemistry; Daly, Marie M.; Elders, Joycelyn; Ferguson, Lloyd N.; Meharry Medical College; National Aeronautics and Space Administration; National Institute of Environmental Health Sciences; National Organization for the Professional Advancement of Black Chemists and Chemical Engineers; Olden, Kenneth; Tolbert, Margaret Mayo; West, Harold D.

REFERENCES AND FURTHER READING

JustGarciaHill.org, "Biographies." [Online article or information; retrieved August 14, 2007.] http://justgarciahill.org/jghdocs/webbiography.asp.

Biology

Biology is the study of life. Biologists classify living organisms, describe how they function, and investigate how they interact with one another and with the natural environment. Generally speaking, there are three types of biologists: botanists, who study plants; zoologists, who study animals; and microbiologists, who study microscopic organisms. Other branches of biology that tend to blur these distinctions are cell biology and molecular biology, which are the studies of living cells and molecules, respectively. As of 2007, African Americans accounted for approximately 1 percent of the nation's scientists working in biology and related fields. Despite the paucity of their numbers, black biologists have made a number of important contributions. This article focuses on the achievements of black biologists in the fields of botany, zoology, cell biology, and molecular biology, and the accomplishments of black microbiologists are discussed in a separate article.

The most famous African American biologist of all time is George Washington Carver. Carver's specialty was botany, and as a botanist, he developed scientific methods for improving the yields of a number of crops that grow plentifully in the southern United States. His early research involved horticulture, an area he continued to experiment with throughout his career. His most important contribution in this field is Carver's Hybrid, a cotton plant that is less susceptible to being infested by the boll weevil, an insect that destroys cotton plants. Later, he became interested in improving the yields of farms in the South, which had been stripped of most of their nitrogen by cotton. Carver developed improved methods for cultivating such humble plants as the sweet potato, the black-eyed pea, the soybean, and the peanut, all of which restore nitrogen to the soil, as well as hundreds of ways to transform them into tasty yet nutritional meals and industrial products.

Another black scientist who used biology to improve agriculture was the microbiologist Carolyn Branch Brooks. Brooks discovered that, in a certain species of African groundnut, a certain type of soil bacteria forms colonies in the outer layer of the roots. These colonies cause the roots to swell and form small blisters, which absorb nitrogen from the air surrounding the blister. The bacteria then process this nitrogen into various biochemical compounds, which are absorbed by the plant, thus increasing its ability to manufacture the amino acids it needs to grow. After demonstrating her discovery to agronomists, who used it to increase the yields of other legumes besides the groundnut, she experimented with methods by which nonlegumes such as corn and wheat could attract and benefit from their own bacteria colonies. She also experimented with ways to protect a plant from insect infestations by infecting the plant with bacteria that would help it while making it unattractive to insects.

James H. M. Henderson was a plant physiologist who performed some of the first experiments related to auxins (plant growth hormones). At the time of his first experiments with auxins, biologists doubted that all plants produce substances similar to growth hormones in humans. He dispelled these doubts by showing that the tomato, the sweet potato, and every other type of plant he experimented with produce auxins that control the rate at which its cells utilize energy.

Fatimah Jackson studied the production in certain plants of repellents (chemical compounds that drive away insects and animals until its seeds are ready to be propagated) and attractants (compounds that attract insects and animals to partake of the plant's fruit and thus spread its seeds). She was particularly interested in the cassava, a tuber similar to the potato that is a staple in the diet of millions of Africans. Cassava contains deadly amounts of cyanide, but, when the tuber is properly prepared, the amount of cyanide can be reduced to levels that are nontoxic to humans. Jackson's research includes how the remaining levels of cyanide might protect humans from the worst effects of malaria, because cyanide interferes with the development of the parasite that carries malaria.

Unlike Carver, Brooks, Henderson, and Jackson, Roland M. Jefferson specialized in ornamental plants, specifically the Japanese flowering cherry tree. Jefferson played a major role in preserving the Japanese flowering cherry trees that beautify the nation's capital, and he rooted the cutting that later developed into the President Reagan Cherry Tree.

The second-most famous African American biologist is Ernest E. Just. As a zoologist, Just studied fertilization and growth in animal eggs. His work provided support for the fertilizin theory, which explains how a sperm cell fertilizes an egg cell, by demonstrating that fertilizin is in fact a gelatinous substance produced by eggs that causes sperm to stick to them. He was also the first biologist to suggest that a cell's ectoplasm (outer surface) plays a significant role in stimulating and regulating the cell's growth and development.

Just's most famous protégé was Roger Arliner Young. The first black woman to receive a PhD in zoology, she studied the structure in *Paramecium* that regulates salt concentration. She also published several notable studies on the effects of direct and indirect radiation on sea urchin eggs.

Two of the most famous black entomologists, biologists who study insects, were Margaret James Strickland Collins and Charles H. Turner. Collins was a zoologist who studied termites throughout North and South America; the specimens she collected are housed at the Smithsonian Museum of Natural History in the Collins Collection, which is named in her honor. She discovered a number of new species, including *Neotermes luykxi*, sometimes called the Florida dampwood termite, and she was the first to detect the presence of a destructive, nonnative species of termite in the Cayman Islands. Turner showed that a number of insects, including ants, bees, and cockroaches, can see, hear, and smell and that they possess limited short-term memory. He also described Turner's circling, the process ants go through when traveling away from the nest to ensure that they can find their way back.

Three noteworthy African American biologists—Ambrose Jearld, Samuel M. Nabrit, and Joan M. Owens—made names for themselves in the field of marine biology. Jearld was a leading expert on commercial fisheries, both freshwater and saltwater, in the United States. He played an instrumental role in developing many of the techniques used today for understanding and managing the ecosystems of commercially important fish. Nabrit demonstrated the process by which fish replace their lost tailfins. Owens was one of the world's foremost experts on button corals. She discovered a new genus and three new species and reclassified the rest of the known button corals.

The two most famous black cell biologists are Jewel Plummer Cobb and George M. Langford. Cobb's research focused on the growth and development of melanin in normal dark pigment cells, as well as in cancerous ones. She was the first scientist to offer evidence that melanoma (skin cancer) can be caused by overexposure to the sun's ultraviolet rays. She also served on the research team at Harlem Hospital that conducted some of the first experiments related to cancer chemotherapy drugs. Cobb contributed to the success of the project by perfecting methods for transferring cancer cells from patients to test tubes and to other laboratory media so that they could be cultivated and studied in a controlled environment. Langford's early work focused on how single-cell organisms metabolize sugar. Later, he became interested in intracellular motility (the process by which biochemical compounds are moved from one part of a cell to another). He discovered the existence of an intracellular network composed of fibers of actin (a protein that plays an important role in muscle contraction). Later research suggested that this network is used mostly to transfer biomaterial over relatively short distances.

Perhaps the most famous black molecular biologist is John K. Haynes. His early research focused on how the use of energy within an embryo is regulated and how bacteria develop immunity to phages (viruses small enough to infect bacteria). Later, he became interested in the molecular aspects of sickle cell disease, specifically the rigid, sickle shape the disease brings about in hemoglobin (the molecules that transport oxygen from the lungs to the rest of the body). He discovered that this phenomenon occurs because the cells in hemoglobin acquire too much calcium while losing a significant portion of their water. He also developed a process by which hemoglobin cell membranes can be examined microscopically to determine whether a patient has sickle cell disease.

Black biologists have also made contributions in other areas as well. Tyrone Hayes, an endocrinologist who studies the effects of pesticides on frogs, showed that atrazine, a pesticide used on corn crops, causes hermaphrodism, the possession of both male and female sex organs, in male frogs by causing them to synthesize the female hormone estrogen. Joseph L. Graves Jr., an evolutionary biologist, has contributed to a better understanding of the evolutionary genetics of postponed aging in fruit flies. Erich D. Jarvis, a neurobiologist, mapped the brain networks responsible for the ability of certain species of birds to learn new songs by imitation.

See also: Brooks, Carolyn B.; Carver, George Washington; Cobb, Jewel Plummer; Collins, Margaret S.; Graves, Joseph L., Jr.; Hayes, Tyrone B.; Haynes, John K., Jr.; Henderson, James H. M.; Jarvis, Erich D.; Jearld, Ambrose, Jr.; Jefferson, Roland M.; Just, Ernest E.; Langford, George M.; Nabrit, Samuel M.; Owens, Joan Murrell; Turner, Charles H.; Young, Roger Arliner

REFERENCES AND FURTHER READING

JustGarciaHill.org. "Biographies." [Online article or information; retrieved August 14, 2007.] http://justgarciahill.org/jghdocs/webbiography.asp.

Biotechnology

Biotechnology is technology based on biology, especially when used in agriculture, food science, and medicine. It has been used by humans since the Neolithic Revolution, when humans first cultivated crops. Although much is made of the possibilities of sophisticated biotechnological developments such as recombinant DNA and tissue-based processes to produce pharmaceutical drugs or other medical marvels, biotechnology is still most effective when it is employed to cultivate plants for food. Nevertheless, modern biotechnology utilizes the principles of genetics, molecular biology, biochemistry, embryology, and cell biology, as well as the tools of chemical engineering, information technology, and robotics, to develop all manner of useful products. Many of these developments are taking place at research institutions on the campuses of the nation's historically black colleges and universities.

Tuskegee University has conducted research related to plant biotechnology since the days of George Washington Carver, who developed hundreds of products from peanuts and sweet potatoes. Today, the university's Agricultural Experiment Station seeks to develop a genetically engineered sweet potato that is resistant to viruses and herbicides and that can be grown under hydroponic conditions. It also continues to search for new uses for the sweet potato. The Tuskegee University Center for Food and Environmental Systems for Human Exploration and Development of Space uses biotechnology to develop the systems for growing, processing, and recycling the waste by-products of peanuts and sweet potatoes during long-duration NASA missions.

Delaware State University hosts the Delaware Biotechnology Institute, a consortium of government, academic, and private industry research laboratories located across the state. Under the auspices of the institute, plant biologists use modern biotechnology methods to learn more about how plant processes occur at the molecular level so that they can enhance crop production by developing novel traits in plants. Zoologists study the genetics of poultry to develop a better understanding of the diseases to which chickens and turkeys are most susceptible so that vaccines can be developed. They also study the role played by genetics in the regulation of growth hormone in chickens to develop methods for producing healthier, meatier chickens in a shorter time period. Bacteriologists study rhizobia (soil bacteria that play an important role in fixing nitrogen in certain legumes) to develop processes for increasing the legumes' yield by increasing the amount of nitrogen it can use to produce amino acids, which are essential to plant growth. They also study the protein structures in extremeophiles (organisms that thrive under extreme conditions of temperature, pressure, and/or pH) to develop proteins that can change their conformation as the temperature or pH changes. Materials scientists seek to develop biosensors (DNA-based transistors and proteins whose surfaces either promote or prevent absorption).

The Norfolk State University Center for Biotechnology and Biomedical Sciences seeks to develop a male birth control pill. Rather than make use of hormones, as does the female birth control pill, the center's researchers investigate the efficacy and safety of using the transition-state analogues of certain amino sugars that have demonstrated themselves to be potent inhibitors of the fertilization process.

The North Carolina A&T State University Biotechnology & Bio Sciences Research Cluster supports the study of microbial, plant, and animal systems to develop new biotechnologies to enhance human health. A&T researchers

African American researchers conduct a great deal of cutting-edge research related to biotechnology, particularly as it concerns the production of better crops. (Jayson Punwani)

seek to develop biopharmaceuticals, neutriceuticals (high-tech nutrients), and biosensors. They also seek to make better use of agricultural by-products and to improve existing techniques of bioremediation (using living organisms to clean up the environment).

The Texas Southern University Research Center for Biotechnology and Environmental Health conducts the majority of its biotechnological research for the National Aeronautics and Space Administration (NASA). One project seeks to prevent the growth of microorganisms in space life support systems by embedding natural antimicrobial chemicals into materials and fabrics, including membrane and filter materials for water purification. Another project seeks to arrive at a better understanding of the microgravity environment of space microbes by using the tools and techniques of genomics and nanobiotechnology.

The Alabama A&M University Center for Forestry and Ecology focuses on how to make hardwood forests more productive through the application of science, and it conducts research related to the use of biotechnology to develop new products from hardwoods. At Fort Valley State University, animal science researchers use biotechnology to develop and produce genetically engineered plants that can serve as the sources of an edible vaccine. At Lincoln University of Missouri, animal science researchers use biotechnology to improve the reproductive abilities of livestock. Other important centers for conducting research involving biotechnology at historically black colleges and universities include the North Carolina Central University Julius L. Chambers Biomedical/Biotechnology Research Institute and the Spelman College Amgen Center for Molecular Biology. West Virginia State University conducts the Bioplex Project, which investigates the use of anaerobic digestion as a means of treating and recycling farm waste.

Historically black colleges and universities (HBCUs) work together in a number of state and regional consortiums that promote the development of biotechnology. Perhaps the most important of these arrangements is the Consortium for Plant Biotechnology Research. Headquartered in St. Simons Island, Georgia, the consortium links Alabama A&M University, Albany State University, Florida A&M University, Fort Valley State University, Hampton University, Kentucky State University, North Carolina A&T State University, Savannah State University, Tuskegee University, the University of the Virgin Islands, and West Virginia State so that they can collaborate on research projects and connect with biotechnology companies looking to finance and benefit from the consortium's research.

See also: Alabama A&M University; Biochemistry; Biology; Carver, George Washington; Delaware State University; Florida A&M University; Fort Valley State University (FVSU); Hampton University; Historically Black Colleges and Universities; Kentucky State University; Lincoln University of Missouri; National Aeronautics and Space Administration; Norfolk State University; North Carolina A&T State University; North Carolina Central University; Spelman College; Texas Southern University; Tuskegee University; University of the Virgin Islands; West Virginia State University

REFERENCES AND FURTHER READING

Consortium for Plant Biotechnology Research. "HBCU Program." [Online article or information; retrieved August 29, 2007.] http://cpbr.org/hbcu.html.

Chemistry

Chemistry is the science that studies the interactions between and among substances that result in their transformation. Generally, chemists evaluate such transformations, known as chemical reactions, in terms of the interactions between atoms and their constituent particles, protons, neutrons, and electrons. Chemistry includes a number of subspecialties, some of which are analytical chemistry, which examines materials to determine their chemical composition and structure; biochemistry, which studies the chemical reactions that take place in living organisms; nuclear chemistry, which studies how subatomic particles come together to form nuclei; and physical chemistry, which studies the principles of the physics governing chemical reactions.

As of 2007, African Americans accounted for about 3 percent of the chemists working in industry and less than 1 percent of the chemists working in academia. A study by the University of Oklahoma showed that, between 1990 and 2000, not one African American was hired to teach chemistry at a major U.S. university. Despite these low numbers, African American chemists have made a number of contributions to science. This article considers the accomplishments made by black Americans in analytical, industrial, nuclear, and physical chemistry, and those of black biochemists are discussed in a separate article.

The most chemically reactive element of all is fluorine. It is so reactive that it is never found in its pure form, but always as part of a chemical compound. The unique properties of fluorine have intrigued a number of chemists, and several black American chemists have made important discoveries regarding those properties. Lloyd A. Quarterman was the leading expert of his day regarding the chemical reactions involving fluorine. During World War II, he developed a method for making pure hydrogen fluoride for use in the Manhattan Project, the U.S. effort to build an atomic bomb. He also developed a method for dissolving a chemical compound in hydrogen fluoride and then examining its physical properties by means of an electromagnetic beam. He also disproved the theory that the inert gases are incapable of reacting chemically with other elements by making three different compounds from fluorine and the inert gas xenon.

Gloria Long Anderson experimented with fluorine–19, an isotope of fluorine, to gain a better understanding of what happens during a chemical reaction. By substituting fluorine–19 for various chemical groups in various molecules, she was able to show how certain chemicals react at the molecular level. Her most important work in this regard concerned epoxidation, whereby one atom of oxygen links two organic compounds. James King is best remembered for serving as assistant laboratory director of the National Aeronautics and Space Administration Jet Propulsion Laboratory's technical divisions, but before that he conducted experiments that contributed to a better understanding of the bond that links carbon and fluorine in chlorofluorocarbons (CFCs), a primary ingredient in aerosols and refrigerants that play a role in depleting the Earth's ozone layer. Joseph S. Francisco studied the potential replacements for chlorofluorocarbons, hydrofluorocarbons, and fluorinated ethers, to see how they would affect the ozone layer. His research demonstrated that neither hydrofluorocarbons nor fluorinated ethers posed much of a threat to the ozone layer but that fluorinated ethers absorb infrared light from the sun in such as way that produces greenhouse gases, thus

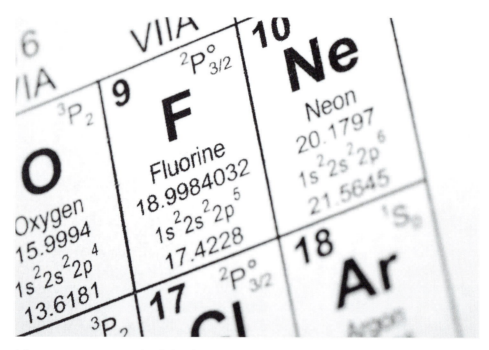

The pioneering research of Lloyd A. Quarterman and Gloria Long Anderson led to a better understanding of how fluorine reacts with other elements and compounds. (David Freund)

contributing in a major way to global warming. John R. Cooper was an expert in the field of fluoroelastomers, a unique class of synthetic rubbers used primarily in the automotive industry. He developed three processes for producing heat-resistant, fluorine-rubber compounds for making seals for jet engines.

The field of industrial chemistry has offered black chemists far more opportunities to thrive than has academic chemistry, and many African American chemists, working as research chemists for American corporations, have contributed significantly to the development of a wide range of industrial and commercial products. Lloyd M. Cooke specialized in the chemistry of cellulose (the basic structural component of plant cell walls from which such commodities as paper products, plastics, photographic film, tape, and synthetic fibers are made) and the chemistry of viscose (a cellulose-based solution used in the manufacture of rayon and synthetic films). Linneaus C. Dorman developed more than two dozen synthetic peptides (chains of proteins that do not exist in nature). He also utilized them in a number of industrial and medical applications, including a slow-release binder for chemical fertilizer that allows plants to benefit more fully from the fertilizer, a material suitably strong enough and flexible enough that it can be used as a replacement for bone, and a process for breaking down the synthetic rubber in tires so that they can be recycled.

Lloyd A. Hall specialized in the preservation of food. He developed methods for treating meats with sodium chloride and various nitrates and for sterilizing spices and other products. He also developed some of the first artificial flavors and discovered why fatty and oily foods become rancid. W. Lincoln Hawkins specialized in the chemical and physical principles underlying the behavior of plastics, and he applied these principles to the development of a number of new plastics and the processes for manufacturing them. His most important contribution was a chemical additive that insulates telephone wires without becoming brittle under conditions of extreme heat or cold, thus greatly preserving the service life of telephone lines. Henry A. Hill specialized in chemical intermediates, the by-products formed during the making of polymers (the chemical compounds from which plastics are made). He also developed methods for making some of the first commercial dyes and flame-retardant coatings made from polymers. Percy L. Julian is best remembered for developing an inexpensive and effective method for synthesizing progesterone, which is used to make birth control pills. Before that, however, he had developed dozens of industrial products, including paper products, animal feed, candy, cosmetics, food additives, ink, and textiles—all from soybean oil.

Although academia has not been very welcoming to African American chemists over the years, many have still managed to develop promising research careers at the nation's colleges and universities rather than at its industrial research laboratories. Fitzgerald B. Bramwell's research contributed to a better understanding of organotins (chemical compounds not found in nature that have at least one bond between an atom of carbon and an atom of tin). These compounds are used extensively as catalysts for chemical reactions and in glass coatings, pesticides, and fungicides. Slayton A. Evans specialized in organophosphate compounds, human-made compounds that result when hydrocarbon molecules are combined with one or more atoms of phosphorus. He developed a method for facilitating the production of the organophosphate compounds known as alpha-amino phosphonic acids, which are used to develop a wide range of pharmaceutical drugs. James A. Harris prepared the atomic samples from which the transuranium elements 104 and 105 were developed, and he developed the chemical detection methods for identifying minute samples of those elements to verify that they had been developed. John W. Macklin developed techniques for identifying unknown materials as small as a billionth of a billionth of a gram. Using his methods, he discovered the presence of fullerene (a complex carbon molecule in the shape of a soccer ball's stitched pattern) in a tiny crater made by a tiny meteorite on a space satellite, thus offering evidence to support the theory that complex organic molecules did not originate on Earth but rather came from outer space.

Samuel P. Massie's research demonstrated that phenothiazine (an organic compound used to kill insects, worms, and parasites in animals) could also

Fitzgerald B. Bramwell's research contributed to a better understanding of organotins, chemical compounds not found in nature that feature at least one bond between an atom of carbon and an atom of tin. (Courtesy Fitzgerald B. Bramwell)

be developed into safe yet effective antianxiety drugs for humans. He also contributed to the development of pharmaceutical drugs for treating malaria, meningitis, gonorrhea, and herpes. Henry C. McBay specialized in peroxide compounds, which tend to be unstable and dangerous, and he synthesized from acetyl peroxide a protein that is used to treat prostate cancer. John E. Hodge specialized in the chemical reactions involving carbohydrates. He was an expert in the chemistry of browning reactions, such as the roasting of coffee beans or the browning of the cut end of a piece of fruit that has been left exposed to the air. He also demonstrated that the reactions that take place during browning are similar to the reactions that take place in the body when food is digested. Isiah M. Warner specialized in the study of complex chemical systems. He developed a process that makes use of luminescence to measure the amount of a specific unknown substance in a sample of material. Although not much is known about their activities, at least six black chemists—Quarterman, Massie, William J. Knox, Edwin R. Russell, Moddie D. Taylor, and Ralph Gardner—participated in the Manhattan Project, the U.S. effort to construct an atomic bomb during World War II. Their work primarily involved the development of sophisticated chemical processes for separating out U-235, the isotope of uranium from which atomic bombs are made, from U-238, the more common form of uranium.

The National Organization for the Professional Advancement of Black Chemists and Chemical Engineers represents African American chemists of all subspecialties. The organization works tirelessly to help black chemists and chemical engineers develop promising careers in private industry and academia, and it recruits minority students into careers as professional chemists and provides them with financial assistance while they obtain their degrees.

See also: Anderson, Gloria L.; Bramwell, Fitzgerald B.; Cooke, Lloyd M.; Dorman, Linneaus C.; Evans, Slayton A., Jr.; Francisco, Joseph S. Jr.; Hall, Lloyd A.; Harris, James A.; Hawkins, W. Lincoln; Julian, Percy L.; King, James Jr.; Macklin, John W.; Massie, Samuel P., Jr.; McBay, Henry C.; National Aeronautics and Space Administration; National Organization for the Professional Advancement of Black Chemists and Chemical Engineers; Quarterman, Lloyd A.; Warner, Isiah M.

REFERENCES AND FURTHER READING

JustGarciaHill.org. "Biographies." [Online article or information; retrieved August 14, 2007.] http://justgarciahill.org/jghdocs/webbiography.asp

Computer Science

Computer science is the study of theories and methods for processing information and the use of computer systems to implement and apply them. As of 2007, less than 0.25 percent of all computer scientists were African Americans. Despite that low number, black Americans have made several notable achievements in computer science.

Perhaps the best known of all African American computer scientists is Philip Emeagwali. He was intrigued by the problem of parallel processing, that is, a number of computers linked together so that they can all work on the same problem at the same time. He was particularly interested in using computers to develop a global weather forecasting network, the success of which would require the rapid calculation of thousands of variables from around the globe. After studying this problem for 13 years, he wrote a program that made it possible to hook up more than 65,000 computers to work together to solve a single problem. The success of this program changed the way high-performance computers, or supercomputers, are constructed and programmed. Previously, it had been believed that a supercomputer is more powerful than any number of smaller computers working together, but the success of Emeagwali's program proved that belief to be false. As a result, computer designers began building supercomputers that used thousands of relatively small processors rather than one large processor, and in the process, made supercomputers even faster and more powerful than before. Emeagwali's network also served as the inspiration for the World Wide Web, a global network that links millions of computers.

Clarence A. "Skip" Ellis was the first African American to earn a PhD in computer science. A specialist in supercomputers, he conducted research for Bell Telephone Laboratories, IBM, Xerox, and the U.S. national laboratories at Los

Despite the contributions of African American computer scientists to the development and use of supercomputers, fewer than 1 in 400 computer scientists is African American. (National Oceanic and Atmospheric Administration)

Alamos and Argonne. His main research interest involved computer-supported cooperative work (CSCW), which studies how people work in groups and how they can best be supported by computer networks. His contributions to CSCW include the development of workflow technology (software products that improve the design of information systems) and groupware (also known as collaborative software, which helps people work together while using their own individual computers).

Roscoe C. Giles used high-performance parallel computers to solve problems in physics and materials science. He was particularly interested in problems involving micromagnetism, which studies the interactions between two or more different magnetic sources on a scale of less than one micron, and molecular dynamics, which simulates the interactions between atoms and molecules under the known laws of physics. He also cofounded and served as executive director of the Institute for African American ECulture (iAAEC). This group seeks to close the so-called digital divide, the general lack of access to computers by African Americans and other minorities. Bryant W. York specializes in supercomputing, parallel computing, and virtual reality in education. He also takes an interest in making computer programming accessible to people with disabilities. To this end, he invented and developed PBE: Programming by Ear for blind programmers.

Annie Easley was a computer scientist who spent her career with the National Aeronautics and Space Administration (NASA). She wrote computer code and developed systems for calculating the variables related to energy projects involving solar, wind, and battery power.

See also: Ellis, Clarence Arthur "Skip"; Emeagwali, Philip; National Aeronautics and Space Administration

REFERENCES AND FURTHER READING

JustGarciaHill.org. "Biographies." [Online article or information; retrieved August 14, 2007.] http://justgarciahill.org/jghdocs/webbiography.asp.

Medical Research

In all likelihood, African Americans have contributed more to the body of knowledge in medicine than to all other branches of scientific inquiry combined. Although blacks were not encouraged to become scientists until the 1960s, they were previously at least permitted to obtain a medical education and serve as physicians to their fellow blacks. In the process, many black doctors conducted self-funded medical research pertinent to the diseases and medical conditions that prevail among African Americans. In the process, several made important discoveries that apply to people of all races and ethnicities. Since the 1960s, many more blacks have embarked upon careers as medical researchers, and they too have made important contributions to the body of medical knowledge.

Many of the important surgical techniques and procedures developed in the United States resulted from research conducted by African American surgeons. W. Harry Barnes developed surgical techniques for treating conditions of the ear, nose, and throat. He was one of the first physicians to advocate removing the tonsils before they become infected. Leonidas H. Berry developed an instrument for removing diseased tissue from the stomach and another for examining the interiors of the abdominal cavity and the intestines. Benjamin S. Carson developed techniques for making the hemispherectomy (removing one hemisphere, or half, of the brain) a safe and effective procedure for treating children who suffer from severe seizures. He also served as principal surgeon during the first two successful procedures to separate Siamese twins who were joined at the head. Samuel L. Kountz helped perform the first successful kidney transplant in humans that did not involve twins. He also developed many of the procedures and apparatus used today in kidney transplants. LaSalle D. Leffall developed a number of surgical techniques for extracting cancerous tumors without harming adjacent, nontumorous tissue. John C. Norman helped develop one of the first partial artificial hearts and then successfully implanted them in humans more than a dozen times. Frederick D. Stubbs perfected methods for removing diseased tissue from patients with pulmonary tuberculosis. Vivien T. Thomas helped develop the surgical procedure known as the Blalock-Taussig procedure for treating blue baby syndrome, whereby infants suffer from a lack of oxygen to the tissues, because their lungs are not getting enough blood. Daniel Hale Williams performed one of the first successful surgical operations involving the human heart.

Not surprisingly, many African American medical researchers have focused their research on sickle cell disease, which mostly plagues people whose ancestors came from Africa. Angella D. Ferguson conducted some of the earliest research on sickle cell disease, and she developed some of the first methods for treating children with the disease. John K. Haynes demonstrated that cells with sickle cell trait become rigid because they have too much calcium and not enough water, while Herman R. Branson showed that sickle cell disease results from a genetic defect.

Black Americans have also contributed to the body of knowledge concerning nutrition, an essential aspect of human growth and development. Cecile Hoover Edwards demonstrated that a properly devised vegetarian diet can provide all the methionine and other essential amino acids the human body needs to grow and develop. Flemmie P. Kittrell discovered the medical condition known as hidden hunger (malnourishment on a full stomach), whereby the food eaten is of such poor nutritional quality that the person suffers from malnutrition without feeling the pangs of hunger.

In addition, African Americans have contributed in a number of ways to spanning the breadth and width of medical knowledge. Charles R. Drew developed the procedures for handling and preserving blood in large quantities. He also established the first large-scale blood bank program in the United States, thus making it possible for surgeons to perform operations that require large amounts of blood. Joycelyn Elders demonstrated a connection between diabetes in young mothers and a heightened risk of spontaneous abortion and congenital abnormalities in their babies. Renty B. Franklin showed that zinc plays a central role in controlling the growth of tumors in the prostate gland. A. Oveta Fuller showed how the herpes simplex virus gains access to a cell, and she developed some promising techniques for protecting cells against viral infection. Solomon C. Fuller was one of the first neuropsychiatrists, medical researchers who explore the biochemical causes of mental illness. He was one of the first medical researchers to study the physiological causes of schizophrenia, Alzheimer's disease, and manic-depressive psychosis, also known as bipolar disorder. William A. Hinton demonstrated how syphilis works in the human body. He also developed the Hinton test and the Davies-Hinton test for diagnosing syphilis. Carroll M. Leevy developed many of the procedures and techniques for diagnosing and treating the diseases of the liver and biliary tract, including hepatitis, gallstones, liver cirrhosis, various metabolic and genetic disorders, and hepatocellular cancer. Julian H. Lewis conducted research on the ability of lipids to protect an organism from repeated exposure to allergens, on the suitability of beef plasma as a substitute for human blood in a transfusion, and on the presence of epinephrine in the human fetal adrenal glands. Arnold H. Maloney discovered a drug for treating victims of barbiturate poisoning. Louis T. Wright and Jane C. Wright conducted some of the earliest research concerning cancer chemotherapy drugs, and in the process they established many of the first protocols for developing and testing such drugs.

Phillip Crews, a marine natural products chemist, extracts toxins and other biochemical compounds from various marine creatures, especially sponges, that have the potential to serve as the base for pharmaceutical drugs and other medical treatments. Monique R. Ferguson, a molecular virologist, helped design drugs that protect cells against infection from alphaviruses, flaviviruses, and arenaviruses by preventing these viruses from attaching to cellular walls. Clifford W. Houston, a microbiologist, developed a technique for detecting type A streptococcal exotoxin (the cause of scarlet fever in patients with strep throat). He also helped clarify how two toxins secreted by the bacteria *Aeromonas hydrophila*, which are often found in infected wounds, cause gastroenteritis (inflammation of the mucous membrane in the stomach and intestines) and the destruction of muscle and skin tissue. Lovell A. Jones, an endocrinologist, conducted extensive research concerning the relationships among hormones, diet, and endocrine-responsive tumors. He showed that under certain developmental conditions 17-estradiol, a form of the estrogen hormone that is present in all adult animals, can cause tumors to develop in the cervicovaginal area. Theodore K. Lawless, a dermatologist, developed a method for diagnosing sporotrichosis (a fungal disease contracted from plants). He also investigated a number of methods for treating skin damaged by drugs containing arsenic, which was often prescribed as a treatment for medical conditions caused by microbial infection. Roland A. Owens, a molecular biologist, showed that adeno-associated virus(an adenovirus that does not cause disease in humans) insinuates itself into the human genome by entering through a specific region in chromosome 19.

See also: Barnes, W. Harry; Berry, Leonidas H.; Branson, Herman R.; Cancer; Carson, Benjamin S.; Drew, Charles R.; Edwards, Cecile H.; Elders, Joycelyn; Ferguson, Angella D.; Franklin, Renty B.; Fuller, A. Oveta; Fuller, Solomon C.; Haynes, John K., Jr.; Hinton, William A.; Kittrell, Flemmie P.; Kountz, Samuel L., Jr.; Lawless, Theodore K.; Leevy, Carroll M.; Leffall, LaSalle D., Jr.; Lewis, Julian H.; Maloney, Arnold H.; Norman, John C., Jr.; Sickle Cell Disease;

Stubbs, Frederick D.; Thomas, Vivien T.; Williams, Daniel H.; Wright, Jane C.; Wright, Louis T.

REFERENCES AND FURTHER READING

JustGarciaHill.org. "Biographies." [Online article or information; retrieved August 14, 2007.] http://justgarciahill.org/jghdocs/webbiography.asp.

Microbiology

Microbiology is the branch of biology that studies microscopic organisms such as bacteria, viruses, and parasites. Microbiologists classify the various living microorganisms, describe how they function, and investigate how they interact with one another and with their environment, which often consists of a plant or animal. As of 2007, African Americans accounted for approximately 1 percent of the nation's microbiologists. Nevertheless, black microbiologists have made a number of important contributions.

Four of the most important black bacteriologists were Carolyn Branch Brooks, Charles W. Buggs, Welton I. Taylor, and Dale Brown Emeagwali. Brooks studied soil bacteria that form colonies in the roots of legumes. She discovered that these colonies cause small blisters to form on the roots; the blisters absorb nitrogen from the air in the soil around them. The bacteria then process the nitrogen into biochemical compounds, thus serving as an additional source of nitrogen for the legumes, which need nitrogen to produce the amino acids necessary for their growth and development. Later, she experimented with developing soil bacteria colonies that could increase the nitrogen yield for crops such as corn and wheat. She also experimented with nonharmful bacterial infections that would protect plants from insect infestations by making the plants unattractive to insects.

While Brooks studied potentially beneficial bacteria, Buggs, Taylor, and Emeagwali focused on the ones that are capable of harming humans. Buggs focused on developing methods of killing such bacteria, and his early research tested the efficacy of electrophoresis as a means of killing *E. coli* and *Staphylococcus*. Later, he demonstrated that certain bacteria are able to build up an immunity to streptomycin, one of the earliest antibiotic drugs. Taylor developed tests to identify three different types of bacteria that cause food poisoning. His early research investigated the strength of the toxins produced by a colony of *Clostridium botulinum*, the bacteria that cause botulism (a deadly form of food poisoning that results from eating food that has been improperly canned). Later, he broadened the scope of his research to include *C. tetani*, which cause tetanus; *C. perfringens*, *C. novyi*, and *C. septicum*, which cause certain forms of gangrene; *Salmonella enteritidis*, which causes salmonellosis, a deadly form of food poisoning; and *Shigella dysenteria,* which causes a form

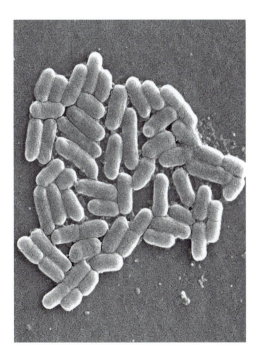

African American microbiologists study all forms of microbiological life, including the bacteria known as E. coli *(pictured).* (Janice Carr/Centers for Disease Control and Prevention)

of dysentery known as shigellosis. He eventually developed safe and effective methods for detecting the presence of each of these types of bacteria in processed food. The bacterium known as *Enterobacter taylorae* was named in his honor. Emeagwali discovered the presence of isozymes of kynurenine formamidase in a strain of *Streptomyces*; previously, it was believed that such biochemical compounds were found only in higher-level organisms.

One of the most noteworthy black virologists was A. Oveta Fuller. She was one of the world's foremost experts on herpes viruses, which cause a number of diseases such as cold sores, genital herpes, mononucleosis, shingles, and chicken pox. Her work concerning the herpes simplex virus, which causes certain sexually transmitted diseases, as well as a fatal form of viral encephalitis, identified the process by which the virus is able to enter a cell. Her research showed how herpes simplex virus enters a cell, information that gave medical researchers important clues about how to develop pharmaceutical drugs to prevent all sorts of viral infections.

One of the most noteworthy black parasitologists was Herman Eure. Eure specialized in parasites that infest reptiles and fish. His work shed much light on seasonal abundances, the phenomenon whereby parasites increase and decrease their populations during certain seasons of the year.

See also: Brooks, Carolyn B.; Buggs, Charles W.; Emeagwali, Dale Brown; Eure, Herman E.; Fuller, A. Oveta; Taylor, Welton I.

REFERENCES AND FURTHER READING
JustGarciaHill.org. "Biographies." [Online article or information; retrieved August 14, 2007.] http://justgarciahill.org/jghdocs/webbiography.asp.

Physics

Physics is the branch of science concerned with discovering and characterizing universal laws that govern matter, energy, space, and time. Physicists are particularly interested in understanding the four forces of nature: electromagnetism, gravity, the strong nuclear force (which governs the behavior of quarks and gluons, the basic building blocks of all matter), and the weak nuclear force (which governs certain forms of radioactive decay). Generally speaking, modern physics can be broken down into two main areas of approach, theoretical physics and experimental physics. Theoretical physicists develop mathematical formulas and theoretical models as a means of understanding fundamental physical principles, whereas experimental physicists observe the behavior of physical phenomena to understand the universe. Additionally, most modern physicists, regardless of how they approach the study of physics, concentrate their efforts in one of five main areas. (1) Condensed matter physics deals with the properties of solids, liquids, and gases. (2) Atomic, molecular, and optical physics involves the interaction between light and matter and between single atoms or molecules. (3) High-energy physics entails the study of the behavior of subatomic particles, such as protons, neutrons, electrons, mesons, pions, quarks, and gluons. (4) Astrophysics studies the physical forces that govern the behavior of stars and other phenomena of the universe. (5) Applied physics applies the physical knowledge gathered by the other areas to problems of engineering and technology.

As of 2007, fewer than 2 percent of all the physicists working in the United States were African Americans. Nevertheless, black physicists have made a number of important contributions to physics. This article discusses the contributions of all of them except for astrophysicists, who are discussed in a separate article.

Two of the most important black theoretical physicists have been Sylvester J. Gates and J. Ernest Wilkins. Gates specialized in quarks and leptons (the most elementary particles from which all matter is made) and in the processes by which subatomic particles interact with one another. His major contribution to theoretical physics involved the graviton, the elusive particle that supposedly serves as the carrier of the gravitational force in much the same way that the electron carries the electromagnetic force. Gates suggested that the graviton might not be a particle but rather a string, and he described the qualities of this string in considerable detail. Although the graviton remains undiscovered, Gates's theory is now accepted by many theoretical physicists as the best explanation to date as to how gravity is transmitted. Wilkins is a theoretical physicist who worked on the Manhattan Project, the U.S. project during World War II to build an atomic bomb. Wilkins helped develop mathematical formulas for testing theories about initiating and controlling the chain reactions that split apart uranium atoms, thus releasing untold amounts of energy. After the war, he developed many of the mathematical formulas used to develop nuclear power for peaceful purposes, and he helped design some of the first nuclear power plants. His most important contribution in this regard is a shielding system to protect workers against gamma radiation, which is emitted during electron decay of a nuclear source.

Several important black applied physicists have been Randolph W. Bromery, Meredith C. Gourdine, and Wade M. Kornegay. Bromery pioneered the use of magnetic detection and radiometrics (the measurement of radioactive material) to identify the potential locations of major deposits of crude oil, copper, and other valuable minerals. Gourdine's research provided a better understanding of how force is generated by electrogasdynamics (the flow of electrically charged particles suspended in a gas through an electric field) and magnetohydrodynamics (which substitutes a magnetic field for the electric field). He also developed methods for using electrogasdynamics and magnetohydrodynamics to generate huge amounts of high-voltage electricity at a relatively low cost. Kornegay helped to develop a number of wideband radar systems for tracking intercontinental ballistic missiles. He also assisted in developing systems that were so sophisticated they could distinguish between the radar signature given off by a warhead and the radar signatures of various countermeasure devices.

Several black physicists have gone on to enjoy careers as administrators of scientific or educational organizations. George E. Alcorn is best remembered as a top-level administrator for the National Aeronautics and Space Administration (NASA), but before that he developed a process to use plasma (the extremely hot, soupy mixture of ions and electrons that is neither a solid, liquid, nor gas) in the manufacture of semiconductor material. He also developed an imaging X-ray spectrometer for studying heavenly bodies and a chemical ionization mass spectrometer that is so sensitive that it can detect the presence of amino acids on a distant planet, thus making it useful in the search for extraterrestrial life. Shirley A. Jackson is best remembered for serving as chair of the Nuclear Regulatory Commission and being the first African American woman to serve as president of a major research university, but before that she conducted research on the behavior of highly unstable subatomic particles. Her most important contribution was an in-depth description of the behavior of polarons (electrons that polarize the charges of the particles they come in contact with) in a monomolecular film (a liquid film so thin that it behaves as if it has only two dimensions). Walter E. Massey is best remembered for serving as president of the American Association for the Advancement of Science and director of the National Science Foundation, but before that he conducted important research concerning superfluidity (the unusual properties exhibited by liquid helium when it is cooled to 2.18°K, such as the ability to overflow its containment vessel in defiance of the laws of viscosity and very high heat conductivity).

Other noteworthy African American physicists include Herman R. Branson, Warren E. Henry, Elmer S. Imes, Katherine G. Johnson, Roscoe Koontz, and Earl D. Shaw. Branson helped discover that polypeptides (the molecules from which proteins are built) are arranged in helical form, thus contributing indirectly to the later discovery that DNA takes the shape of a double helix. He also contributed to the discovery that sickle cell disease is caused by a genetic deformity that causes the red corpuscles in hemoglobin to become misshapen. Henry was one of the nation's foremost experts on low-temperature physics and magnetism. His research shed much light on the magnetic properties of iron, gold, chromium, uranium, plutonium, and the rare earth elements at temperatures approaching absolute zero. It also contributed to a better understanding of superconductivity (the phenomenon whereby certain elements lose all resistance to electron flow at temperatures approaching absolute zero). Imes pioneered the use of high-resolution infrared spectroscopy (the study of the infrared light emitted by atoms and molecules) to study the properties of the various elements and compounds. Using this technique, he made the first accurate measurement of the distance between atoms in a molecule and discovered an isotope of chlorine. Most important, he provided evidence to support Albert Einstein's quantum theory, which stated that atoms and molecules emit light in discrete packets that Einstein called quanta.

As an aerospace technologist for the National Aeronautics and Space Administration (NASA), Johnson developed many of the mathematical formulas for calculating interplanetary trajectories, space navigation, and the orbits of spacecraft. She also studied new navigation procedures to determine more practical ways to track manned and unmanned space missions. Koontz was one of the nation's first formally trained health physicists. He helped develop many of the early practices, instruments, and techniques for protecting people from the hazards of ionizing radiation. His most important contribution in this area was the design and fabrication of automatic air and water sampling equipment and radiation activity measuring devices. Shaw was the coinventor of the spin-flip Raman tunable laser, which has proven to be highly efficacious in the study of biological systems. Spin-flip tuning allows the beam frequencies of the laser to be adjusted higher or lower in infinitely small degrees, much as a dimmer switch allows for the fine-tuning of a chandelier. Thus, a frequency that could destroy the surface of a cell wall can be adjusted to a lower frequency to avoid damage.

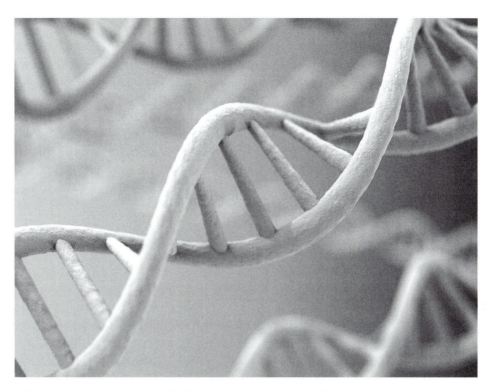

The development of the double-helix theory concerning the nature of DNA was influenced by the work of African American biophysicist Herman R. Branson. (Mark Evans)

As of 2007, the professional interests of black physicists were represented by two organizations. The National Society of Black Physicists offers membership to African American physicists regardless of their subspecialty. The organization seeks to increase the number of black physicists in the United States, support their efforts to conduct physical research, and increase the nation's appreciation for their contributions to physics. The National Association of Black Geologists and Geophysicists represents black geologists and geophysicists, most of whom work in private industry rather than academia. It seeks to help its members establish professional relationships with each other and with the various companies they work for, as well as to develop professional standards and practices for members as employees and as entrepreneurs.

See also: Alcorn, George E., Jr.; American Association for the Advancement of Science; Astronomy and Astrophysics; Branson, Herman R.; Bromery, Randolph W.; Gates, Sylvester J., Jr.; Gourdine, Meredith C.; Henry, Warren E.; Imes, Elmer S.; Jackson, Shirley A.; Kornegay, Wade M.; Massey, Walter E.; National Aeronautics and Space Administration; National Association of Black Physicists; Shaw, Earl D.; Wilkins, J. Ernest Jr.

REFERENCES AND FURTHER READING

Physicists of the African Diaspora. "Who Are the Black Physicists?" [Online article or information; retrieved August 17, 2007.] http://www.math.buffalo.edu/mad/physics/physics-peeps.html.

Bibliography

AAAS Experts & Speakers Service. "Shirley M. Malcom, Ph.D." 2008.
  http://www.aaas.org/ScienceTalk/malcom.shtml.

Abramson, Charles I., ed. *Selected Papers and Biography of Charles Henry Turner
  (1867–1923), Pioneer of Comparative Animal Behavior Studies.* Assisted by
  Latasha D. Jackson and Camille L. Fuller. Lewiston, NY: Edwin Mellen Press, 2003.

Alabama A&M University, School of Agricultural and Environmental Sciences.
  "Agricultural Research Centers." n.d. http://saes.aamu.edu/Research/
  AgResearchProgram.html.

Alabama A&M University. "Welcome to Alabama A&M University." 2006.
  http://www.aamu.edu/.

Alabama State University. "Research Infrastructure in Minority Institutions at
  Alabama State University." 2008. http://www.alasu.edu/RIMI.

Alabama State University. "Welcome to Alabama State University." 2008.
  http://www.alasu.edu/.

Alfred P. Sloan Foundation. "Programs: Education and Careers in Science and
  Technology." n.d. http://www.sloan.org/programs/pg_education.shtml.

Alfred P. Sloan Foundation. "Welcome." n.d. http://www.sloan.org/main.shtml.

American Academy of Otolaryngology. "Early African Americans in
  Otolaryngology." n.d. http://www.entnet.org/HealthInformation/
  earlyAfricanAmericans.cfm

American Association for the Advancement of Science. "AAAS: Advancing Science,
  Serving Society." 2008. http://www.aaas.org.

American Association for Cancer Research. "American Association for Cancer
  Research." 2001–2008. http://www.aacr.org/default.aspx.

American Association for Cancer Research. "Minorities in Cancer Research." n.d.
  http://www.aacr.org/home/membership-/association-groups/minorities-in-cancer-
  research.aspx.

American Chemical Society. "ACS Department of Diversity Programs." n.d.
  http://portal.acs.org/portal/acs/corg/content?_nfpb=true&_pageLabel=PP_TRANS
  ITIONMAIN&node_id=1166&use_sec=false&sec_url_var=region1.

American Chemical Society. "American Chemical Society." 2008.
  https://portal.acs.org/portal/acs/corg/memberapp.

American College of Veterinary Pathologists. "American College of Veterinary Pathologists." 2007. http://www.acvp.org/.

American College of Veterinary Pathologists. "Minority Fellowship." 2007. http://www.acvp.org/training/pfizer.php.

American Dental Education Association. "American Dental Education Association." 2007. http://www.adea.org/.

American Dental Education Association. "Center for Equity and Diversity." n.d. http://www.adea.org/ced/default.htm.

American Dental Education Association. *Opportunities for Minority Students in U.S. Dental Schools,* 5th ed., 2006–2008. Washington, DC: American Dental Education Association.

American Geological Institute. "American Geological Institute." 2008. http://www.agiweb.org/index.html.

American Heart Association, "Cardiovascular Disease Statistics." March 25, 2008. http://www.americanheart.org/presenter.jhtml?identifier=4478.

American Institute of Biological Sciences. "American Institute of Biological Sciences." April 5, 2008. http://www.aibs.org/core/index.html.

American Institute of Biological Sciences. "Diversity Programs and Resources." 2008. http://www.aibs.org/diversity.

American Medical Association. "AMA—Helping Doctors Help Patients." 1995–2008. http://www.ama-assn.org/.

American Medical Association. "Minority Affairs Consortium." 1995–2008. http://www.ama-assn.org/ama/pub/category/20.html.

American Medical Student Association. "Achieving Diversity in Dentistry and Medicine." 2008. http://www.amsa.org/addm/index.cfm.

American Medical Student Association. "American Medical Student Association." 2008. http://www.amsa.org/.

American Museum of Natural History. "Neil deGrasse Tyson, Astrophysicist." 2006–2007. http://research.amnh.org/users/tyson/.

American Physical Society. "Committee on Minorities in Physics Annual Report for January 2006—December 2006." January 2006. http://www.aps.org/about/governance/committees/commin/upload/COM_AnnualReport_2006.pdf.

American Physical Society. "APS Physics." 2008. http://www.aps.org/.

American Psychological Association. "American Psychological Association." 2008. http://www.apa.org/.

American Society for Cell Biology. "The American Society for Cell Biology." 2008. http://www.ascb.org/.

American Society for Cell Biology. "The Minority Affairs Committee." 2008. http://www.ascb.org/index.cfm?navid=90.

American Society for Microbiology. "American Society for Microbiology." 2008. http://www.asm.org/.

American Society for Microbiology. "Underrepresented Minority Groups in the Life Sciences." n.d. http://www.asm.org/general.asp?bid=16715.

Answers.com. "Theodore K. Lawless." 2006. http://www.answers.com/topic/theodore-k-lawless.

APA Online. "Ethnic Minority Affairs Office." 2008. http://www.apa.org/pi/oema/aboutus.html.

Association of American Medical Colleges. "Diversity." 1995–2008. http://www.aamc.org/diversity/start.htm.

Association of American Medical Colleges. "Minorities in Medical Education: Facts & Figures 2005." Spring 2005. https://services.aamc.org/Publications/index.cfm?fuseaction=Product.displayForm&prd_id=133&prv_id=154.

Association of American Medical Colleges. *Minority Student Opportunities in United States Medical Schools.* Washington, DC: AAMC, 2005.

Association of Black Anthropologists. "Association of Black Anthropologists." May 1999. http://www.indiana.edu/~wanthro/candice1.htm.

Association of Black Cardiologists. "Association of Black Cardiologists, Inc." n.d. http://www.abcardio.org/.

Association of Black Psychologists. "The Association of Black Psychologists." n.d. http://www.abpsi.org/index.htm.

Astronomers of the African Diaspora. May 27, 1997. http://www.math.buffalo.edu/mad/physics/index.html.

Astronomy Department, the University of California at Berkeley. "Gibor Basri, Professor of Astronomy." July 22, 2007. http://astro.berkeley.edu/~basri/.

Bailey, Eric J. *Food Choice and Obesity in Black America: Creating a New Cultural Diet.* Westport, CT: Greenwood Publishing, 2006.

Baltrip, Kimetris N. "Samuel Nabrit, 98, Scientist and a Pioneer in Education, Dies." NYTimes.com. January 6, 2004. http://www.nytimes.com/2004/01/06/education/06NABR.html?ex=1388725200&en=0e78b968bd56fde6&ei=5007&partner=USERLAND.

Bedini, Silvio A. *The Life of Benjamin Banneker: The First African-American Man of Science,* 2nd ed. Baltimore: Maryland Historical Society, 1999.

Berry, Leonidas H. *Gastrointestinal Pan-Endoscopy.* Springfield, IL: Charles C. Thomas, 1974.

Berry, Leonidas H. *The Clinical Significance of Gastrointestinal Endoscopy.* Nutley, NJ: Roche Laboratories, 1976.

Berry, Leonidas H. *I Wouldn't Take Nothin' for My Journey: Two Centuries of an Afro-American Minister's Family.* Chicago: Johnson Publishing, 1981.

BEST: Building Engineering and Science Talent. "The BEST Initiative." 2007. http://www.bestworkforce.org.

Beta Kappa Chi. "Beta Kappa Chi (BKX) National Scientific Honor Society." n.d. http://www.betakappachi.org.

Bigelow, Barbara C., ed. *Contemporary Black Biography,* vol. 7. Detroit, MI: Gale Research, 1994.

Biophysical Society. "Biophysical Society." n.d. http://www.biophysics.org/.

Biophysical Society. "Minority Resource Center." n.d. http://www.biophysics.org/minority/.

The Bioplex Project at West Virginia State University. "Welcome to the Bioplex Project." 2005. http://bioplexproject.wvstateu.edu.

Black Entomologists. "Black Entomologists." n.d. http://www.blackentomologists.org/.

Blackman, Dionne J., and Christopher M. Masi. "Racial and Ethnic Disparities in Breast Cancer Mortality: Are We Doing Enough to Address the Root Causes?" *Journal of Clinical Oncology* 24, 14 (May 10, 2006): 2170–2178.

The Body: The Complete HIV/AIDS Resource. "HIV/AIDS Among the African American Community." June 2007. http://www.thebody.com/index/whatis/africanam.html.

Bowser, Rene. "Medical Civil Rights: The Exclusion of Physicians of Color from Managed Care—Business or Bias?" (September 2005). U of St. Thomas Legal Studies Research Paper No. 05–14. http://ssrn.com/abstract=834284.

Brown, Valerie J. "Kenneth Olden, Master Fencer." *American Journal of Public Health* 94, 11 (November 2004): 1905–1907.

Burns, Khephra, and William Miles. *Black Stars in Orbit: NASA's African American Astronauts.* New York: Harcourt Brace, 1995.

Camille and Henry Dreyfus Foundation. "The Camille & Henry Dreyfus Foundation, Inc." n.d. http://www.dreyfus.org/.

Carey, Charles W. Jr. *American Scientists.* New York: Facts On File, 2005.

Carson, Ben, and Cecil B. Murphey. *Gifted Hands: The Ben Carson Story.* Grand Rapids, MI: Zondervan, 1990.

Carson, Ben. "Mini-Biography." n.d. http://www.drbencarson.com/snapshot.html.

Central State University. "Central State University." n.d. http://www.centralstate.edu/.

Central State University. "Water Resources Management." n.d. http://www.centralstate.edu/academics/bus_ind/water_res/wrm/index.html.

Cerami, Charles A. *Benjamin Banneker: Surveyor, Astronomer, Publisher, Patriot.* New York: Wiley, 2002.

Charles R. Drew University of Medicine and Science. "Welcome to Drew." n.d. http://www.cdrewu.edu/_022/_html/.

Chen, Adrian. "In the Shadow of Science: Blacks Scientists and Inventors Struggle for Visibility from One Generation to the Next." *The Michigan Daily* (February 22, 2005). http://media.www.michigandaily.com/media/storage/paper851/news/2005/02/22/News/In.The.Shadow.Of.Science-1429030.shtml.

CIRTL Diversity Institute. "Mission, Goals & Strategy." 2004. http://cirtl.wceruw.org/DiversityResources/about/mission/.

Clark Atlanta University. "Clark Atlanta University." n.d. http://www.cau.edu/.

Clark Atlanta University. "Research Programs: Research Centers." n.d. http://www.cau.edu/acad_prog/default.html.

Climate Change Research Section, National Center for Atmospheric Research. "Warren M. Washington." January 3, 2008. http://www.cgd.ucar.edu/ccr/warren/.

Cobb, W. Montague. "Race and Runners." *Journal of Health and Physical Education* 3, 56 (1936).

Cobb, W. Montague. "The First Hundred Years of the Howard University College of Medicine." *Journal of the National Medical Association* 57 (1967): 408–420.

Cobb, W. Montague. "Harold Dadford West, Ph.D., LL.D.: A Good Man and True." *Journal of the National Medical Association* 68, 4 (July 1976): 269–275.

Collins, Daniel. *Your Teeth: A Handbook of Dental Care for the Whole Family.* Garden City, NY: Doubleday, 1968.

Computer Scientists of the African Diaspora. May 25, 1997. http://www.math. buffalo.edu/mad/computer-science/.

Consortium for Plant Biotechnology Research. "HBCU Program." n.d. http://cpbr.org/hbcu.html.

Contemporary Black Biography. (Multivolume series) Detroit, MI: Gale Cengage.

Cooke, Lloyd M. *Cleaning Our Environment—The Chemical Basis for Action.* Washington, DC: American Chemical Society, 1969.

Council for Chemical Research. "CCR Diversity Award." n.d. http://www.ccrhq.org/ about/Diversityaward.htm.

Council for Chemical Research. "The Council for Chemical Research." n.d. http:// www.ccrhq.org/.

Cowings, Patricia S., and William Toscano. "Motion and Space Sickness." In *Motion and Space Sickness,* edited by George H. Crampton. Boca Raton, FL: CRC Publishing, 1990: 354–372.

Daniel Hale Williams Preparatory School of Medicine. "Welcome to Our School!" 2002. http://www.wpsm.cps.k12.il.us/.

Delaware State University. "Delaware State University." 2008. http://www.desu. edu/.

Delaware State University, Office of the Associate Provost for Research. "Research Administration and Centers." 2008. http://www.desu.edu/research.

Delta Sigma Theta. "Delta Sigma Theta Sorority, Inc." 2005–2007. http://www. deltasigmatheta.org/cms/.

Dental Pipeline, "About Us." 2006. http://www.dentalpipeline.org/au_aboutus. html.

Development Fund for Black Students in Science and Technology. "Development Fund for Black Students in Science and Technology." April 2, 2007. http://dfbsst.dlhjr.com/.

"Doctoral Degree Awards to African Americans Reach Another All-Time High." *The Journal of Blacks in Higher Education.* 2006. http://www.jbhe.com/news_ views/50_black_doctoraldegrees.html.

Dummett, Clifton O., and Lois D. *NDA II: The Story of America's Second National Dental Association.* Washington, DC: National Dental Association Foundation, 2000.

Dustan, H. P. "Obesity and Hypertension in Blacks." *Cardiovascular Drugs and Therapy* 4, 2 (March 1990): 395–402.

The Education Coalition. "Reflections on the Star Schools Program After Eight Years." n.d. http://www.tecweb.org/vault/stars/reflect.html.

Edwards, Cecile Hoover, et al. *Human Ecology: Interactions of Man with His Environment; an Introduction to the Academic Discipline of Human Ecology.* Dubuque, IA: Kendall/Hunt, 1991.

Elders, Joycelyn, and David Charnoff. *Joycelyn Elders, M.D.: From Sharecropper's Daughter to Surgeon General of the United States of America.* Waterville, ME: Thorndike Press, 1997.

Embree, Edwin R., and Julia Waxman, *Investment in People: The Story of the Julius Rosenwald Fund.* New York: Harper, 1949.

Endocrine Society. "The Endocrine Society." n.d. http://www.endo-society.org/

Endocrine Society. "Minority Activities." n.d. http://www.endo-society.org/minorityactivities/.

Environmental Careers Organization. *Beyond the Green: Redefining and Diversifying the Environmental Movement.* Boston: Environmental Careers Organization, 1992.

Environmental Careers Organization. "Diversity Initiative." n.d. http://www.eco.org/site/c.dnJLKPNnFkG/b.942795/k.122B/Diversity_Initiative.htm.

Environmental Careers Organization. "Welcome to ECO!" n.d. http://www.eco.org/site/c.dnJLKPNnFkG/b.795025/k.AA86/The_Environmental_Careers_Organization.htm.

"The Epidemiology of Cardiovascular Disease in Black Americans." *New England Journal of Medicine* 335, 21 (November 21, 1996): 1597–1599.

Erich Jarvis Lab. "General Information." n.d. http://www.jarvislab.net/GenInfo.html.

The Faces of Science: African Americans in the Sciences. "St. Elmo Brady." n.d. https://webfiles.uci.edu/mcbrown/display/brady.html.

FAMU College of Pharmacy and Pharmaceutical Sciences. "Research Centers and Programs." 2003. http://pharmacy.famu.edu/Research.asp.

Federation of American Societies for Experimental Biology. "Federation of American Societies for Experimental Biology." n.d. http://www.faseb.org/.

Federation of American Societies for Experimental Biology. "Minority Access to Research Careers." n.d. http://marc.faseb.org/.

Ferguson, Lloyd. *Electron Structures of Organic Molecules.* Upper Saddle River, NJ: Prentice Hall, 1952.

Ferguson, Lloyd. *The Modern Structural Theory of Organic Chemistry.* Upper Saddle River, NJ: Prentice Hall, 1963.

Ferguson, Lloyd. *Textbook of Organic Chemistry*, 2nd ed. New York: Van Nostrand, 1965.

Ferguson, Lloyd. *Organic Chemistry: A Science and an Art.* Bel Air, CA: Willard Grant Press, 1972.

Ferguson, Lloyd. *Highlights of Alicyclic Chemistry.* Danbury, CT: Franklin Books, 1973.

Ferguson, Lloyd. *Organic Molecular Structure: A Gateway to Advanced Organic Chemistry.* Bel Air, CA: Willard Grant Press, 1975.

Ferguson, Lloyd N., with Gabrielle S. Morris. *Increasing Opportunities in Chemistry, 1936–1986.* Berkeley, CA: Regional Oral History Office, The Bancroft Library, University of California, 1992.

Fikes, Robert Jr. "Careers of African Americans in Academic Astronomy." *Journal of Blacks in Higher Education* 29 (Autumn 2000): 132–134.

First Science Ph.D.s Awarded to African Americans. "The Faces of Science: African Americans in the Sciences." November 25, 2007. https://webfiles.uci.edu/mcbrown/display/first_phds.html.

Fisk University. "Fisk University." 2007. http://www.fisk.edu/.

Fisk University. "Natural Sciences and Mathematics." 2007. http://www.fisk.edu/page.asp?id=185.

Florida A&M University. "Florida A&M University." 2008. http://www.famu. edu/.

Fort Valley State University. "College of Agriculture, Home Economics and Allied Programs." 2007. http://www.ag.fvsu.edu/.

Fort Valley State University. "Fort Valley State University." 2008. http://www.fvsu. edu/.

Gates, Henry L., and Cornel West. *The African-American Century: How Black Americans Have Shaped Our Country.* New York: Free Press, 2000.

The Gates Millennium Scholars. "About GMS." n.d. http://www.gmsp.org/ publicweb/aboutus.aspx.

Gates, Sylvester. *Superspace or 1001 Lessons in Supersymmetry.* San Francisco: Benjamin/Cummings Publishing, 1983.

Gates, Sylvester. "Taking the Particle Out of Particle Physics." *Quotient* 12, 4 (1986).

GEM: The National GEM Consortium. "About GEM." 2008. http://www. gemfellowship.org/.

Gordon Research Conferences. "Gordon Research Conferences." 2008. http://www.grc.org/.

Gordon Research Conferences. "The GRC Underrepresented Minority (URM) Diversity Initiative." 2008. http://www.grc.org/diversity.aspx.

Granat, Diane. "America's 'Give While You Live' Philanthropist." *APF Reporter*, 21, 1 (2003). http://www.aliciapatterson.org/APF2101/Granat/Granat.html.

Grant, R. W. "Invited Commentary: Untangling the Web of Diabetes Causality in African Americans." *American Journal of Epidemiology* 166, 4 (August 15, 2007): 388–390.

Grants.gov. "Research Infrastructure in Minority Institutions (RIMI)[P20]." February 16, 2007. http://www.grants.gov/search/search.do?oppId=12637&mode=VIEW.

Graves, Joseph. *The Emperor's New Clothes: Biological Theories of Race at the Millennium.* New Brunswick, NJ: Rutgers University Press, 2001.

Graves, Joseph. *The Race Myth: Why We Pretend Race Exists in America.* New York: Plume Books, 2005.

Griffith, Ezra E. H. *Race and Excellence: My Dialogue with Chester Pierce.* Iowa City: University of Iowa Press, 1998.

Haas Center for Public Service. "Mickey Leland Energy Fellowship: A Summer Internship Program Providing Energy Opportunities for Minority Students." n.d. http://haas.stanford.edu/external_fellowships/fellowship.php?ef_id=142&.

Hall, W. Dallas, Neil B. Shulman, and Elijah Saunders. *Hypertension in Blacks: Epidemiology, Pathophysiology and Treatment.* Chicago: Year Book Medical Publishers, 1985.

Handbook of Texas Online. "Roman, Charles Victor." n.d. http://www.tsha.utexas. edu/handbook/online/articles/RR/frost.html.

Harris, Wesley L., *Defense Manufacturing in 2010 and Beyond: Meeting the Changing Needs of National Defense.* Washington, DC: National Academies Press, 1999.

Harris, Wesley L. *Incentive Strategies for Defense Acquisitions.* 2001. Fort Belvoir, Va.: Defense Acquisition University Press.

Harrison, Ira E., and Faye V. Harrison, eds. *African-American Pioneers in Anthropology*. Urbana: University of Illinois Press, 1999.

Hayden, Robert C. *Eleven African American Doctors*, rev. ed. New York: Twenty-First Century Books, 1992.

Hayden, Robert C. *Seven African American Scientists*. New York: Twenty-First Century Books, 1992.

The HBCU Network, "The History of HBCUs." 2008. http://www.hbcunetwork.com/The_History_Of_HBCUs_Timeline.cfm.

Health Policy Institute of Ohio. "Understanding Health Disparities." November 2004. http://www.healthpolicyohio.org/publications/healthdisparities.html.

Health Professionals for Diversity Coalition. "About Health Professionals for Diversity." 2007. http://www.hpd-coalition.org/about.htm.

Henry, Warren E. *Elementary Qualitative Chemical Analysis*. Tuskegee, AL: Tuskegee University Press, 1937.

HHC-Harlem Hospital Center. "Harlem Hospital Center." 2008. http://www.ci.nyc.ny.us/html/hhc/html/facilities/harlem.shtml.

Howard University. "Howard University." n.d. http://www.howard.edu/.

Howard University College of Medicine. "Howard University College of Medicine." n.d. http://www.med.howard.edu.

Howard University Office of Research Administration. "Research Centers and Institutes." 2003. http://ora.howard.edu/centers/int.htm\#top.

Institute of Medicine. *The Right Thing to Do, the Smart Thing to Do: Enhancing Diversity in Health Professions: Summary of the Symposium on Diversity in Health Professions in Honor of Herbert W. Nickens, MD*. Washington, DC: National Academies Press, 2001.

Institute of Medicine. *In the Nation's Compelling Interest: Ensuring Diversity in the Health Care Workforce*. Washington, DC: National Academies Press, 2004.

Institute of Medicine of the National Academies. "About." February 15, 2008. http://www.iom.edu/CMS/AboutIOM.aspx.

International Society on Hypertension in Blacks. "About ISHIB." 2005. http://www.ishib.org/AI_index.asp.

Iowa Commission on the Status of African Americans. "Scientists and Inventors." n.d. http://www.state.ia.us/dhr/saa/AA_culture/scientists_inventors.html.

Jackson State University. "Jackson State University." 2007. http://www.jsums.edu/.

Jackson State University, Office of Vice President for Research Development & Federal Relations. "Centers & Institutes." 2005. http://www.jsums.edu/~ordsfr/centers.htm.

Jefferson, Roland M. "The Japanese Flowering Cherry Trees of Washington, D.C.: A Living Symbol of Friendship." *National Arboretum Contribution* 4 (1977).

Jemison, Mae. *Find Where the Wind Goes: Moments from My Life*. New York: Scholastic Press, 2001.

Johns Hopkins Medicine "Hopkins Neurosurgeon Separates Zambian Siamese Twins, Practiced with 3-D 'Workbench.'" January 15, 1998. http://www.hopkinsmedicine.org/press/1998/JANUARY/980115.HTM

Just, Ernest E., Robert Chambers, Warren H. Lewis, Edwin G. Conklin, Frank R. Lillie, Merle H. Jacobs, Clarence E. McClung, Albert P. Mathews, Margaret R. Lewis, Thomas H. Morgan, Edmund B. Wilson, Edmund V. Cowdry, and Ralph S. Lillie. *General Cytology: A Textbook of Cellular Structure and Function for Students of Biology and Medicine.* Chicago: University of Chicago Press, 1924.

Just, Ernest E. *Biology of the Cell Surface.* Philadelphia, PA: P. Blakiston's Son & Co., 1939.

Just, Ernest E. *Basic Methods for Experiments on Eggs of Marine Animals.* Philadelphia, PA: P. Blakiston's Son & Co., 1939.

JustGarciaHill.org, "Biographies." 2007. http://justgarciahill.org/jghdocs/webbiography.asp.

Karter, Andrew J. "Race and Ethnicity: Vital Constructs for Diabetes Research." *Diabetes Care* 26, 7 (2003): 2189–2193.

Kentucky State University. "Kentucky State University." 2004. n.d. http://www.kysu.edu/.

Kentucky State University Aquaculture. "KSU's Program of Distinction." http://www.ksuaquaculture.org/.

Kessler, James H., J. S. Kidd, Renee A. Kidd, and Katherine A. Morin, eds. *Distinguished African American Scientists of the 20th Century.* Phoenix, AZ: Oryx Press, 1996.

Kinnon, Joy Bennett. "Is Our Air Killing Us? The Asthma Attack on Black America— The Prevalence of Asthma in the African American Community." *Ebony* (July 2001). http://findarticles.com/p/articles/mi_m1077/is_9_56/ai_76285233.

Krapp, Kristine, ed. *Notable Black American Scientists.* Detroit, MI: Gale Research, 1999.

Lamb, Yvonne S. "Prof. Samuel Massie Dies; Broke Naval Academy's Race Barrier." *Washington Post*, April 15, 2005: B06.

Langston University. "Research & Extension." 2000. http://www.luresext.edu/index.htm.

Langston University. "Langston University." 2007. http://www.lunet.edu/.

Lawrence, Margaret Morgan. *The Mental Health Team in the Schools.* New York: Behavioral Publications, 1971.

Lawrence, Margaret Morgan. *Young Inner City Families: Development of Ego Strength under Stress.* New York: Human Sciences Press, 1975.

Leadership Alliance. "The Leadership Alliance." 2008. http://www.theleadershipalliance.org/matriarch/default.asp.

Leevy, Carroll M. *Practical Diagnosis and Treatment of Liver Disease.* New York: Medical Book Department of Harper & Brothers, 1957.

Leevy, Carroll M. *Evaluation of Liver Function in Clinical Practice.* Indianapolis, IN: Lilly Research Laboratories, 1965, 1974.

Leevy, Carroll M. *The Hepatic Circulation and Portal Hypertension.* New York: New York Academy of Sciences, 1970.

Leevy, Carroll M. *Liver Regeneration in Man.* Springfield, IL: Charles C. Thomas, 1973.

Leevy, Carroll M. *Diseases of the Liver and Biliary Tract: Standardization of Nomenclature, Diagnosis Criteria, and Prognosis*. Washington, DC: U.S. Department of Health, Education and Welfare, 1976.

Leevy, Carroll M. *Guidelines for Detection of Hepatoxicity Due to Drugs and Chemicals*. Washington, DC: National Institutes of Health, 1979.

Leffall, LaSalle D. *No Boundaries: A Cancer Surgeon's Odyssey*. Washington, DC: Howard University Press, 2005.

Lewis, Julian H. *The Biology of the Negro*. Chicago: University of Chicago Press, 1942.

Lightfoot, Sarah Lawrence. *Balm in Gilead: Journey of a Healer*. Reading, MA: Addison-Wesley, 1989.

Lincoln University of Missouri. "Cooperative Research." 2008. http://www.lincolnu.edu/pages/375.asp

Lincoln University of Missouri. "Lincoln University of Missouri." 2008. http://www.lincolnu.edu/pages/1.asp.

Love, Spencie. *One Blood: The Death and Resurrection of Charles R. Drew*. Chapel Hill: University of North Carolina Press, 1996.

Maclin, A. P., et al., eds. *Magnetic Phenomena: The Warren E. Henry Symposium on Magnetism, in Commemoration of His 89th Birthday and His Work in Magnetism*. New York: Springer-Verlag, 1989.

Maloney, Arnold H. *Some Essentials of Race Leadership*. Xenia, OH: Aldine Publishing, 1924.

Maloney, Arnold H. *Pathways to Democracy*. Boston: Meador Publishing, 1945.

Maloney, Arnold H. *Amber Gold; an Adventure in Autobiography*. Boston: Meador Publishing, 1946.

Maloney, Arnold H. *After England—We; Nationhood for Caribbea*. Boston: Meador, 1949.

Manning, Kenneth R. *Black Apollo of Science: The Life of Ernest Everett Just*. New York: Oxford University Press, 1983.

Massie, Samuel P. "The Chemistry of Phenothiazine." Chemical Reviews, 54, 697 (1954).

Massie, Samuel P., with Robert C. Hayden. *Catalyst: The Autobiography of an American Chemist*. Laurel, MD: S.P. Massie, 2005.

Mathematicians of the African Diaspora. "J. Ernest Wilkins, Jr." 2005. http://www.math.buffalo.edu/mad/PEEPS/.

Mayberry, B. D. *The History of the Carver Research Foundation of Tuskegee University, 1940–1990*. Tuskegee, AL: Tuskegee University Press, 2003.

McMurray, Emily, ed. *Notable Twentieth-Century Scientists*. Detroit, MI: Gale Research, 1995.

McMurry, Linda O. *George Washington Carver: Scientist and Symbol*. Norwalk, CT: Easton Press, 1994.

Medical Makers. "Dr. Daniel Collins." n.d. http://www.thehistorymakers.com/biography/biography.asp?bioindex=1080&category=medicalMakers.

Meharry Medical College. "Meharry Medical College." n.d. http://www.mmc.edu/.

Merrill, Ray M., and Otis W. Brawley. "Prostate Cancer Incidence and Rates of Mortality Among White and Black Men." *Epidemiology* 8, 2 (March 1997): 126–131.

Minority Environmental Leadership Development Initiative. "Minority Environmental Leadership Development Initiative." January 30, 2003. http://www.umich.edu/~meldi/index.html.

Minority Environmental Leadership Development Initiative. *The Paths We Tread: Profiles of the Careers of Minority Environmental Professionals, MELDI Career Resource Guide to Environmental Jobs,* and *MELDI Guide to Negotiating the Job Market.* Ann Arbor: University of Michigan, School of Natural Resources and Environment, 2005. http://www.umich.edu/~meldi/PDF/ProfilesBook_0605.pdf.

Minton, R. F. "The History of Mercy-Douglass Hospital." *Journal of the National Medical Association* 43, 3 (May 1951): 153–159.

MIT Aero│Astro. "Wesley L. Harris." n.d. http://web.mit.edu/aeroastro/people/harris/.

Morehouse School of Medicine. "About MSM." 2007. http://www.msm.edu/aboutmsm/index.htm.

Morgan State University Estuarine Research Center. "Research Programs." n.d. http://www.morgan.edu/erc/research.html.

Morgan State University. "Morgan State University." n.d. http://www.morgan.edu/.

Nabrit, Samuel N. "Regeneration in the Tail-Fins of Fishes." *Biological Bulletin* 56: 235–266.

NASA Astrobiology Institute. "About the NAI-MIRS Program in Astrobiology." n.d. http://www.nai-mirs.org/about.php.

NASA Astrobiology Institute. "NASA Astrobiology Institute." April 8, 2008. http://nai.arc.nasa.gov/.

The National Academies. "Welcome to the Ford Foundation Diversity Fellowships Home Page." 2008. http://www7.nationalacademies.org/fordfellowships/.

National Aeronautics and Space Administration. "Biographical Data: Bernard A. Harris, Jr. (M.D.)." January 1999. http://www.jsc.nasa.gov/Bios/htmlbios/harris.html.

National Aeronautics and Space Administration. "Biographical Data: Ronald E. McNair." December 2003. http://www.jsc.nasa.gov/Bios/htmlbios/mcnair.html.

National Aeronautics and Space Administration. "Astronaut Bio: Michael P. Anderson." May 2004. http://www.jsc.nasa.gov/Bios/htmlbios/anderson.html pp. 132–135.

National Aeronautics and Space Administration. "Astronaut Bio: Guion S. Bluford, Jr." February 2007. http://www.jsc.nasa.gov/Bios/htmlbios/bluford-gs.html.

National Aeronautics and Space Administration. "National Aeronautics and Space Administration." April 18, 2008. http://www.nasa.gov/.

National Aeronautics and Space Administration, Goddard Space Flight Center. "Minority University—Space Interdisciplinary Network." October 17, 2006. http://muspin.gsfc.nasa.gov/.

National Agricultural Library. "NAL Collections: Jefferson, Roland Maurice, Collection." June 13, 2007. http://www.nal.usda.gov/speccoll/collectionsguide/collection.php?find=J.

National Association of Black Geologists and Geophysicists. "NABGG: Home of National Association of Black Geologists and Geophysicists." n.d. http://www.nabgg.com.

National Association for Equal Opportunity in Higher Education. "HBCU/MI Environmental Technology Consortium." 2005. http://www.nafeo.org/etc/index.html.

National Association for Equal Opportunity in Higher Education. "National Association for Equal Opportunity in Higher Education." 2007. http://www.nafeo.org/home

National Association of Minority Medical Educators. "National Association of Minority Medical Educators, Inc." 2008. http://www.nammenational.org/.

National Cancer Institute. "National Cancer Institute." n.d. http://www.cancer.gov/.

National Cancer Institute, Comprehensive Minority Biomedical Branch. "Opportunities for Minorities in Cancer." n.d. http://minorityopportunities.nci.nih.gov/index.html.

National Center for Complementary and Alternative Medicine. "National Center for Complementary and Alternative Medicine." n.d. http://nccam.nih.gov/.

National Center for Complementary and Alternative Medicine. "Office of Special Populations Strategic Plan to Address Racial and Ethnic Health Disparities." October 24, 2007. http://nccam.nih.gov/about/plans/healthdisparities/index.htm.

National Center on Minority Health and Health Disparities. "About NCMHD." n.d. http://ncmhd.nih.gov/about_ncmhd/mission.asp.

National Center on Minority Health and Health Disparities. "National Institutes of Health Strategic Research Plan and Budget to Reduce and Ultimately Eliminate Health Disparities, Volume I." 2002. http://ncmhd.nih.gov/our_programs/strategic/pubs/VolumeI_031003EDrev.pdf.

National Center on Minority Health and Health Disparities. "NIH Comprehensive Strategic Plan and Budget to Reduce and Ultimately Eliminate Heath Disparities." n.d. http://www.ncmhd.nih.gov/strategicmock/our_programs/strategic/pubs/NEI-rev.pdf.

National Coalition of Underrepresented Racial and Ethnic Groups in Engineering and Science. "National Coalition of Underrepresented Racial and Ethnic Groups in Engineering and Science." n.d. http://www.ncourages.org/.

National Dental Association. "National Dental Association." 2004. http://www.ndaonline.org.

National Energy Technology Laboratory. "Advanced Research: Historically Black Colleges and Universities and Other Minority Institutions (HBCU/OMI) Program." n.d. http://www.netl.doe.gov/technologies/coalpower/advresearch/hbcu.html.

National Eye Institute. "National Eye Institute." n.d. http://www.nei.nih.gov/.

National Geographic's Strange Days on Planet Earth, "Tyrone Hayes, PhD, Biologist." 2008. http://www.pbs.org/strangedays/episodes/troubledwaters/experts/bio_hayes_tyrone.html.

National Heart, Lung, and Blood Institute. "National Heart, Lung, and Blood Institute." n.d. http://www.nhlbi.nih.gov/.

National Heart, Lung, and Blood Institute. "National Heart, Lung, and Blood Institute Strategy for Addressing Health Disparities, FY 2002–2006." http://www.nhlbi.nih.gov/resources/docs/plandisp.htm.

National Human Genome Research Institute. "Initiatives and Resources for Minority and Special Populations." September 10, 2007. http://www.genome.gov/10001192.

National Human Genome Research Institute. "National Human Genome Research Institute." n.d. http://www.genome.gov/.

National Institute on Aging. "National Institute on Aging." n.d. http://www.nia.nih.gov/.

National Institute on Aging. "Review of Minority Aging Research at the NIA." February 16, 2008. http://www.nia.nih.gov/AboutNIA/MinorityAgingResearch.htm.

National Institute on Alcohol Abuse and Alcoholism. "National Institute on Alcohol Abuse and Alcoholism." n.d. http://www.niaaa.nih.gov/.

National Institute on Alcohol Abuse and Alcoholism. "NIAAA's Strategic Plan to Address Health Disparities." n.d. http://pubs.niaaa.nih.gov/publications/HealthDisparities/Strategic.html.

National Institute of Allergy and Infectious Diseases. "Office of Special Populations and Research Training." March 10, 2008. http://www3.niaid.nih.gov/about/organization/dea/osprtpage.htm.

National Institute of Allergy and Infectious Diseases. "National Institute of Allergy and Infectious Diseases." March 25, 2008. http://www3.niaid.nih.gov/.

National Institute of Arthritis and Musculoskeletal and Skin Diseases. "National Institute of Arthritis and Musculoskeletal and Skin Diseases." n.d. http://www.niams.nih.gov/.

National Institute of Arthritis and Musculoskeletal and Skin Diseases. "Strategic Plan for Reducing Health Disparities." n.d. http://www.niams.nih.gov/About_Us/Mission_and_Purpose/strat_plan_hd.asp.

National Institute of Child Health and Human Development. "Health Disparities: Bridging the Gap." n.d. http://www.nichd.nih.gov/publications/pubs/upload/health_disparities.pdf.

National Institute of Child Health and Human Development. "National Institute of Child Health and Human Development." April 9, 2008. http://www.nichd.nih.gov/.

National Institute on Deafness and Other Communication Disorders. "National Institute on Deafness and Other Communication Disorders." April 1, 2008. http://www.nidcd.nih.gov./

National Institute on Deafness and Other Communication Disorders. "National Institute on Deafness and Other Communication Disorders Health Disparities Strategic Plan Fiscal Years 2004–2008." April 1, 2008. http://www.nidcd.nih.gov/about/plans/strategic/health_disp.asp.

National Institute of Dental and Craniofacial Research, "Health Disparities Program." January 28, 2008. http://www.nidcr.nih.gov/Research/Extramural/ClinicalResearch/HealthDisparitiesProgram.htm.

National Institute of Dental and Craniofacial Research. "National Institute of Dental and Craniofacial Research." n.d. http://www.nidcr.nih.gov/.

National Institute of Diabetes and Digestive and Kidney Diseases. "Strategic Plan on Minority Health Disparities." November 1, 2007. http://www.niddk.nih.gov/federal/planning/mstrathealthplan.htm.

National Institute of Diabetes and Digestive and Kidney Diseases. "National Institute of Diabetes and Digestive and Kidney Diseases." April 9, 2008. http://www2.niddk.nih.gov/.

National Institute on Drug Abuse. *Preventing Drug Abuse Among Children and Adolescents: A Research-Based Guide*, 2nd ed. Washington, DC: National Institute on Drug Abuse, 2003.

National Institute on Drug Abuse. *Principles of Drug Addiction Treatment: A Research-Based Guide*. Washington, DC: National Institute on Drug Abuse, 2000.

National Institute on Drug Abuse. "Strategic Plan on Reducing Health Disparities." June 6, 2007. http://www.drugabuse.gov/StrategicPlan/HealthStratPlan.html.

National Institute on Drug Abuse. "National Institute on Drug Abuse." April 4, 2008. http://www.nida.nih.gov/.

National Institute of Environmental Health Sciences. "Environmental Health Topics." n.d. http://www.niehs.nih.gov/health/topics/index.cfm.

National Institute of Environmental Health Sciences. "National Institute of Environmental Health Sciences." n.d. http://www.niehs.nih.gov/.

National Institute of General Medical Sciences. "Minority Biomedical Research Support." December 17, 2007. http://www.nigms.nih.gov/minority/mbrs.html.

National Institute of General Medical Sciences. "Minority Access to Research Careers." January 2, 2008. http://www.nigms.nih.gov/minority/marc.html.

National Institute of General Medical Sciences. "Minority Programs." April 9, 2008. http://www.nigms.nih.gov/minority.

National Institute of General Medical Sciences. "National Institute of General Medical Sciences." April 9, 2008. http://www.nigms.nih.gov/.

National Institute of Mental Health. "Five-Year Strategic Plan for Reducing Health Disparities." n.d. http://www.nimh.nih.gov/about/strategic-planning-reports/nimh-five-year-strategic-plan-for-reducing-health-disparities.pdf.

National Institute of Mental Health. "National Institute of Mental Health." April 9, 2008. http://www.nimh.nih.gov/.

National Institute of Neurological Disorders and Stroke. "Five-Year Strategic Plan on Health Disparities." July 11, 2007. http://www.ninds.nih.gov/about_ninds/plans/disparities.htm.

National Institute of Neurological Disorders and Stroke. "National Institute of Neurological Disorders and Stroke." n.d. http://www.ninds.nih.gov/.

National Institutes of Health. "National Institutes of Health." n.d. http://www.nih.gov/.

National Library of Medicine. "Finding Aid to the Leonidas H. Berry Papers, 1907–1982." November 1, 2006. http://www.nlm.nih.gov/hmd/manuscripts/ead/berry.html.

National Medical Association. "The National Medical Association: The Conscience of American Medicine." 2006. http://www.nmanet.org.

National Organization for the Professional Advancement of Black Chemists and Chemical Engineers. "NOBCChE: National Organization for the Professional Advancement of Black Chemists and Chemical Engineers." 2008. http://www.nobcche.org/.

National Science Foundation. "Science and Engineering Doctorate Awards: 2004." http://www.nsf.gov/statistics/nsf06308/pdf/tables.pdf.

National Science Foundation. "Commission on the Advancement of Women and Minorities in Science, Engineering and Technology Development (CAWMSET)." August 24, 2005. http://www.nsf.gov/od/cawmset.

National Science Foundation. "Sampling of Active Programs by Target Audience or Activity." June 26, 2006. http://www.nsf.gov/od/sampling_activeprograms/sampling.jsp.

National Science Foundation. "National Science Foundation." February 8, 2008. http://www.nsf.gov/.

National Society of Black Physicists. "National Society of Black Physicists." n.d. http://nsbp.org/.

Network of Minority Research Investigators. "Network of Minority Research Investigators (NMRI)." n.d. http://nmri.niddk.nih.gov/.

The NIDA Clinical Toolbox: Science-Based Materials for Drug Abuse Treatment Providers. n.d. http://www.nida.nih.gov/tb/clinical/clinicaltoolbox.html.

NIH Black Scientists Association. "NIH Black Scientists Association." n.d. http://www1.od.nih.gov/oir/sourcebook/comm-adv/black-sci.htm.

Norfolk State University. "Norfolk State University." n.d. http://www.nsu.edu/.

Norfolk State University. "Research@NSU." n.d. http://www.nsu.edu/researchatnsu/index.html.

Norman, John C. *Cardiac Surgery.* New York: Appleton-Century-Crofts, 1967.

North Carolina A&T State University, Division of Research and Economic Development. "Centers & Institutes." 2006. http://www.ncat.edu/~divofres/centers.

North Carolina A&T State University. "North Carolina A&T State University." n.d. http://www.ncat.edu/.

North Carolina Central University. "North Carolina Central University." 2007. http://www.nccu.edu/.

North Carolina Central University. "Research at NCCU." 2007. http://www.nccu.edu/research/.

Oak Ridge Associated Universities. "About ORAU: Diversity in Action." n.d. http://www.orau.org/diversity/.

Oak Ridge Associated Universities. "Oak Ridge Associated Universities." n.d. http://www.orau.org/.

Oak Ridge Institute for Nuclear Studies. "Our Commitment to Diversity." n.d. http://see.orau.org/Diversity.aspx.

Organ, Claude H., and Margaret Kosiba, eds. *A Century of Black Surgeons: The U.S.A. Experience.* Norman, OK: Transcript Press, 1987.

Partnership for Minority Advancement in the Biomolecular Sciences. "Who We Are." n.d. http://www.unc.edu/pmabs/whoweare.html.

Patten, William. *The Evolution of the Vertebrates and Their Kin.* Philadelphia, PA: P. Blakiston's Son & Co., 1912.

Physicists of the African Diaspora. "Who Are the Black Physicists?" May 27, 1997. http://www.math.buffalo.edu/mad/physics/physics-peeps.html.

Pierce, Chester M. *Basic Psychiatry.* New York: Appleton-Century-Crofts, 1971.

Pierce, Chester M. "The Formation of the Black Psychiatrists of America." In *Racism and Mental Health; Essays,* edited by Charles V. Willie, Bernard M. Kramer, and Patricia P. Rieker. Pittsburgh, PA: University of Pittsburgh Press, 1973.

Pierce, Chester M. *Capital Punishment in the United States.* New York: AMS Press, 1976.

Pierce, Chester M. *Television and Behavior.* Beverly Hills, CA: Sage Publications, 1978.

Pierce, Chester M. *The Mosaic of Contemporary Psychiatry in Perspective.* New York: Springer-Verlag, 1991.

PositiveProfiles.com., "About PMHI." n.d. http://www.positiveprofiles.com/content/about/tier_2/about_landing.asp\#mission.

Prairie View A&M University. "Prairie View A&M University." 2003. http://www.pvamu.edu/pages/1.asp.

Prairie View A&M University. "Research Centers." 2003. http://www.pvamu.edu/pages/634.asp.

Prairie View Solar Observatory. "Prairie View Solar Observatory." n.d. http://www.pvamu.edu/cps/.

The Provident Foundation. "History: Provident Hospital." 2000–2008. http://www.providentfoundation.org/history.

Quality Education for Minorities Network. "Quality Education for Minorities." April 2008. http://qemnetwork.qem.org/.

Rebbeck, Timothy R., Chanita Hughes Halbert, and Pamela Sankar. "Genetics, Epidemiology, and Cancer Disparities: Is It Black and White?" *Journal of Clinical Oncology* 24, 14 (May 10, 2006): 2164–2169.

Robinson, Louise. *The Black Millionaire.* New York: Pyramid Books, 1972.

Salzman, Jack, David Lionel Smith, and Cornel West, eds. *Encyclopedia of African-American Culture and History.* New York: MacMillan, 1996.

Sammons, Vivian Ovelton. *Blacks in Science and Medicine.* New York: Hemisphere Publishing, 1990.

Satcher, David. *Oral Health in America: A Report of the Surgeon General.* 2000. http://profiles.nlm.nih.gov/NN/B/B/J/T/segments.html.

Satcher, David. "Call to Action to Prevent Suicide." U.S. Department of Health and Human Services. January 4, 2007. http://www.surgeongeneral.gov/library/calltoaction/calltoaction.htm.

Satcher, David. "Call to Action to Promote Sexual Health and Responsible Sexual Behavior." U.S. Department of Health and Human Services. January 5, 2007. http://www.surgeongeneral.gov/library/sexualhealth/default.htm.

SEE Science and Everyday Experiences. "Delta Sigma Theta and DREF Implement SEE." 2004. http://www.deltasee.com.

Sellers, Sherill L., Jean Roberts, Levi Giovanetto, Katherine Friedrich, and Caroline Hammargren. *Reaching All Students: A Resource Book for Teaching in Science, Technology, Engineering and Mathematics (STEM)*. n.d. http://www.cirtl.net/DiversityResources/resources/resource-book/contents.html

Sickle Cell Disease Association of America. "About SCDAA." 2005. http://www.sicklecelldisease.org/info/index.phtml.

Sickle Cell Disease Association of America. "What Is Sickle Cell Disease?" 2005. http://www.sicklecelldisease.org/about_scd/index.phtml.

Significant Opportunities in Atmospheric Research and Science. "About SOARS." April 8, 2008. http://www.soars.ucar.edu/.

Smedley, Brian D., Adrienne Y. Stith, and Alan R. Nelson, eds. *Unequal Treatment: Confronting Racial and Ethnic Disparities in Health Care*. Washington, DC: National Academies Press, 2003.

Society of Black Academic Surgeons. "Welcome to the Society of Black Academic Surgeons." 2005. http://www.sbas.net.

Society for Neuroscience. "Diversity in Neuroscience." 2008. http://www.sfn.org/index.cfm?pagename=DiversityInNeuroscience.

Society for Neuroscience. "Society for Neuroscience." 2008. http://www.sfn.org/.

South Carolina State University. "Research & Outreach." n.d. http://www.scsu.edu/researchoutreach.aspx.

South Carolina State University. "Savannah River Environmental Sciences Field Station." n.d. http://www.cnrt.scsu.edu/fieldstation/.

South Carolina State University. "South Carolina State University." 2008. http://www.scsu.edu/.

Southern Regional Education Board Doctoral Scholars Program. "About the Program." 1999–2005. http://www.sreb.org/programs/dsp/process/about_the_program.asp.

Southern Regional Education Board. "Southern Regional Education Board." 1999–2008. http://www.sreb.org/.

Southern University and A&M College System. "Agricultural Research and Extension Center." 2003. http://www.suagcenter.com.

Southern University and A&M College System. "Southern University and A&M College." 2006. http://web.subr.edu/.

Spangenburg, Ray, and Kit Moser. *African Americans in Science, Math, and Invention*. New York: Facts On File, 2003.

Spelman College. "Center for Biomedical and Behavioral Research (RIMI)." 2004. http://www.spelman.edu/academics/research/rimi/.

Spelman College. "Spelman College." 2004. http://www.spelman.edu/.

Spurlock, Jeanne, ed. *Black Psychiatrists and American Psychiatry*. Washington, DC: American Psychiatric Association, 1999.

Student National Medical Association. "Welcome to SNMA." 2006–2007. http://www.snma.org/.

Sullivan Commission. "Missing Persons: Minorities in the Healthcare Workforce: A Report of the Sullivan Commission on Diversity in the Healthcare Workforce." September 20, 2004. http://www.jointcenter.org/healthpolicy/docs/ SullivanExecutiveSummary.pdf.

"The 10 Top Careers for Blacks in the '90s." *Ebony*. February 1999. http://findarticles.com/p/articles/mi_m1077/is_n4_v44/ai_7044940/pg_1.

Tennessee State University Digital Library. "Meharry Medical College (1876–)." n.d. http://www.tnstate.edu/library/digital/meharry.htm.

Tennessee State University. "Research at TSU." n.d. http://www.tnstate.edu/ interior.asp?mid=77.

Tennessee State University. "Tennessee State University." n.d. http://www.tnstate. edu/

Texas Southern University. "Research Center for Biotechnology and Environmental Health." 2002. http://www.tsu.edu/academics/science/research/nasa.asp.

Texas Southern University. "Welcome to Texas Southern University." January 8, 2008. http://www.tsu.edu/.

Thomas, Avis J., Lynn E. Eberly, George Davey Smith, James D. Neaton, and Jeremiah Stamler. "Race/Ethnicity, Income, Major Risk Factors, and Cardio-vascular Disease Mortality." *American Journal of Public Health* 95, 8 (August 2005): 1417–1423.

Thomas, Vivien T. *Pioneering Research in Surgical Shock and Cardiovascular Surgery*. Philadelphia: University of Pennsylvania Press, 1985.

Thurgood Marshall College Fund. "Philip Morris USA/Thurgood Marshall Scholarship Fund." 2004. http://www.thurgoodmarshallfund.org/ scholarships/pm.htm.

Tiner, John H. *100 Scientists Who Shaped World History*. San Mateo, CA: Bluewood Books, 2000.

Tougaloo College. "The Tougaloo Center for Undergraduate Research." 2006. http://www.tougaloo.edu/content/academics/programs/undresearch.htm.

Tougaloo College. "Tougaloo College." 2006. http://www.tougaloo.edu/.

Tuskegee University. "Research." 2003–2008. http://www.tuskegee.edu/Global/category.asp?C=34615&nav=menu200_15.

Tuskegee University. "School of Veterinary Medicine." 2003–2008. http://www.tuskegee.edu/Global/category.asp?C=41703.

Tuskegee University. "Tuskegee University." 2003–2008. http://www.tuskegee. edu/.

Tyson, Neil de Grasse. *Merlin's Tour of the Universe*. New York: Columbia University Press, 1989.

Tyson, Neil de Grasse. *Universe Down to Earth*. New York: Columbia University Press, 1994.

Tyson, Neil de Grasse. *Just Visiting This Planet*. St. Charles, MO: Main Street Books, 1998.

Tyson, Neil de Grasse. *One Universe: At Home in the Cosmos*. Washington, DC: Joseph Henry Press, 2000.

Tyson, Neil de Grasse. *The Sky Is Not the Limit: Adventures of an Urban Astrophysicist*. New York: Doubleday, 2000.

Tyson, Neil de Grasse. *Origins: Fourteen Billion Years of Cosmic Evolution*. New York: W. W. Norton, 2004.

United Negro College Fund Special Programs Corporation. "United Negro College Fund Special Programs Corporation." 2005–2008. http://www.uncfsp.org/spknowledge/default.aspx?page=home.default.

University of Arkansas at Pine Bluff, Aquaculture and Fisheries. "Aquaculture/Fisheries—Center of Excellence." August 5, 2004. http://www.uaex.edu/aqfi/.

University of Arkansas at Pine Bluff. "University of Arkansas at Pine Bluff." 2008. http://www.uapb.edu/.

University of California Office of the President. "MESA USA." 2008. http://mesa.ucop.edu/about/mesausa.html.

University of Colorado at Boulder Department of Computer Science. "Clarence (Skip) Ellis, Professor." n.d. http://www.cs.colorado.edu/~skip/Home.html.

University of the District of Columbia. "Center of Excellence for Renewable Energy." n.d. http://www.udc.edu/cere/index.htm.

University of the District of Columbia. "University of the District of Columbia." 2007. http://www.udc.edu/.

University of Maryland Baltimore County. "The Meyerhoff Scholarship Program." 2005. http://www.umbc.edu/meyerhoff/.

University of Maryland, Department of Physics. "Sylvester J. Gates Jr." 2003. http://www.physics.umd.edu/people/faculty/gates.html.

University of Maryland Eastern Shore. "Academics and Research." August 31, 2007. http://www.umes.edu/Academic/index.aspx.

University of Maryland Eastern Shore. "University of Maryland Eastern Shore." August 31, 2007. http://www.umes.edu/.

University of Maryland Eastern Shore. "Association of Research Directors, Inc." November 2007. http://www.umes.edu/ard/Default.aspx?id=11342.

University of Texas Medical Branch Department of Microbiology and Immunology. "Faculty: Clifford W. Houston, Ph.D." 2004–2005. http://microbiology.utmb.edu/faculty/houston.shtml.

University of the Virgin Islands. "Research and Public Service." n.d. http://www.uvi.edu/pub-relations/uvi/home.html.

University of the Virgin Islands. "University of the Virgin Islands." n.d. http://www.uvi.edu/.

University Studies at North Carolina A&T University. "Joseph L. Graves, Jr., Ph.D." September 2007. http://www.ncat.edu/~univstud/faculty.html.

U.S. Department of Agriculture, Cooperative State Research, Education and Extension Service, "Evans-Allen Program Formula Grant." February 19, 2008. http://www.csrees.usda.gov/business/awards/formula/evansallen.html.

U.S. Department of Education. "Minority Science and Engineering Improvement Program." January 25, 2008. http://www.ed.gov/programs/iduesmsi/index.html.

U.S. Department of Education. "Star Schools Program." May 1, 2007. http://www.ed.gov/programs/starschools/index.html.

U.S. Department of Energy. "Minority Educational Institution Student Partnership Program." http://www.doeminorityinternships.org/.

U.S. Department of Energy. "U.S. Department of Energy." http://www.energy.gov/.

U.S. Department of Health & Human Services. "David Satcher (1998–2002)." January 4, 2007. http://www.surgeongeneral.gov/library/history/biosatcher.htm.

U.S. Department of Veterans Affairs. "Central Alabama Veterans Health Care System, East Campus." October 2, 2007. http://www1.va.gov/directory/guide/facility.asp?ID=141&dnum=ALL.

Ventures Scholars Program. "Welcome to the Ventures Scholars Program." 2006. http://www.venturescholar.org/.

Virginia State University. "Research." 2008. http://www.vsu.edu/pages/152.asp.

Virginia State University. "Virginia State University." 2008. http://www.vsu.edu/pages/1.asp.

Warner Research Group, Louisiana State University. "Isiah M. Warner, Ph.D." 1998–2004. http://www.chem.lsu.edu/imw/group/warner.htm.

Warren, Wini. *Black Women Scientists in the United States*. Bloomington: Indiana University Press, 1999.

Watson, Wilbur H. *Against the Odds: Blacks in the Profession of Medicine in the United States*. New Brunswick, NJ: Transaction Publishers, 1999.

Wayne State University, "Center for Urban and African American Health." 2008. http://www.med.wayne.edu/intmed/CUAAH/cuaah.htm.

Wayne State University. "Wayne State University." 2008. http://www.wayne.edu/.

West Virginia Division of Culture and History. "John C. Norman Jr." 2008. http://www.wvculture.org/history/norman.html.

West Virginia State University. "West Virginia State University." 2008. http://www.wvstateu.edu/.

Winston-Salem State University. "Biomedical Research Infrastructure Center." 2005. http://www.wssu.edu/WSSU/UndergraduateStudies/College+of+Arts+and+Sciences/Biomedical+Research+Infrastructure+Center.

Winston-Salem State University. "Winston-Salem State University." 2008. http://www.wssu.edu/wssu.

Witkop, Bernhard. "Percy Lavon Julian." National Academy of Sciences, *Biographical Memoirs* 52 (1980): 223–266.

Wright, Charles H. *The National Medical Association Demands Equal Opportunity: Nothing More, Nothing Less*. Southfield, MI: Charro Book Co., 1995.

Wright, Louis T. *The Treatment of Fractures*. Philadelphia, PA: W. B. Saunders Co., 1938.

Wynes, Charles E. *Charles Richard Drew: The Man and the Myth*. Urbana: University of Illinois Press, 1988.

Xavier University of Louisiana. "Center for Undergraduate Research." n.d. http://www.xula.edu/CUR/.

Xavier University of Louisiana. "Division of Clinical and Administrative Sciences: About the Clinical Trials Unit." n.d. http://newsite.xula.edu/cop/clinicaltrials.php.

Xavier University of Louisiana. "Xavier University of Louisiana." n.d. http://www.xula.edu/

General Index

acetyl peroxide, 161

actin, 140

actinomycetes, 70

actinomycin, 46

Adams, Eugene W. (Veterinary Pathologist), **4–5,** 222–223

adenosine triphosphate (ATP), 257

Adolescent Medicine HIV/AIDS Research Network, 236

Adolescent Trials Network, 236

Advanced Research Projects Agency Network (ARPANET), 72

aeroacoustics, 103, 104

Aerolysin Cytotoxic Enterotoxin (ACT), 117

Aeromonas hydrophila, 117, 275

African Americans

  and autoimmune diseases, 482

  disproportionate incidence of trauma and illness among, 490–491

  hospitals of, 370–371, **371** (photo)

  and organ transplantation, 482

  reproductive health care of, 488–489

  scientific contributions of, 1–3

  See also Asthma; Cancer; Diabetes; HIV/AIDS; Medical Careers for Blacks; Medical Education for Blacks; Obesity; Science Careers for Blacks; Science Education for Blacks; sexually transmitted diseases (STDs); Sickle Cell Disease

aging, biology of, 95, 96

Airborne LIDAR Topographic Mapping System (ALTMS), 6

alcoholism, 144–145

Alcorn, George E., Jr. (Physicist), **5–7,** 279, 438

alicyclic compounds, 79–80

Alzheimer, Alois, 88

American Cancer Society, 146

American Red Cross (ARC), 61–62

A-methopterin, **46**

amino acids, 57, 65, 110

  threonine, 201, 202

amino sugars, 530

analytical chemistry, 148

anastomosis, 189

Anderson, Charles E. (Meteorologist), **7–9,** 248

Anderson, Gloria L. (Physical Chemist), **9–10,** 267

Anderson, Michael P. (Astronaut), **10–13, 12** (photo), 438, 444

Andrew, John A., 404

antibiotics, 31, 46, 214

antioxidants, 98

Apollo 13 mission, 34

Argonne National Library, 154, 173, 192, 204

aromatic hydrocarbons, 24–25, 203

artificial hearts, implantation of, 167

asthma, **218–220, 219** (photo), 233, 471, 482–483

  studies related to development of, 503–504

astronauts, 172, 437–438

  and biofeedback training, 54–55

  See also National Aeronautics and Space Administration (NASA), Astronaut Program

Selected Topical Index